Psychology and Religion

Selected Readings

Edited by L. B. Brown

Penguin Education

Penguin Education,
A Division of Penguin Books Ltd,
Harmondsworth, Middlesex, England
Penguin Books Inc, 7110 Ambassador Road,
Baltimore, Md 21207, USA
Penguin Books Australia Ltd,
Ringwood, Victoria, Australia

First published 1973
This selection copyright © L. B. Brown, 1973
Introduction and notes copyright © L. B. Brown, 1973
Copyright acknowledgement for items in this volume
will be found on page 390

Printed in Great Britain by
Hazell Watson & Viney Ltd,
Aylesbury, Bucks
Set in Monotype Times

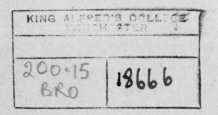

Contents

Part Seven
Pathological and Possibly Related States 343

Introduction

In the latter part of the nineteenth century, religion was an important concern for the developing social sciences, and its study became an established field within psychology. Many textbooks were written about religion, and numerous theories have been advanced to interpret it. These psychological theories range between those that have emphasized religion as an internal, personality-based process (Freud, 1971, pp. 624–39) and those that emphasize the social and communal effects involved and neglect some of the individual variability (Wundt, 1915). Religious behaviour is now recognized to be an amalgam of personal and socially derived responses, and different orientations and emphases have been identified.

Opinion polls show the considerable support there is for religious institutions and the wide acceptance of religious beliefs (Marty, Rosenberg and Greeley, 1968). But common answers to the specific question, 'Why accept or reject religion?' are often complex and elaborated, while psychological answers include reference to social learning and conjectures about some adjustive mechanism or coping process. Religion has also been studied by anthropologists and sociologists. Psychological theories overlap with the sociological theories (Durkheim, 1961; Weber, 1930), which entail psychological concepts because any analysis in terms of social norms or institutional pressure implies some response from those who are involved or influenced.

One task for systematic research in religion is to test different theories and explanations against sound evidence. This requires a conceptual analysis of the processes involved and appropriate behavioural data from controlled samples. Some theories have not stood up well to these empirical tests, and while a theory may be intuitively attractive and can give intriguing interpretations, it is of limited use if it only describes differences between institutions or between religious positions, or redefines religious phenomena in psychological terms and does not allow predictions to be tested.

Basic to any psychological interpretation of religion may be the fact that religions are used to explain and guide experience, and to tame the environment, and that they also refer to a particular set of values or orientations to life. There are developmentally-based changes in religious functioning and a person's religion interacts with other psychological effects and adapts to the contexts in which it occurs. Ambiguities and some believed reality are both important in religious response. Taking a child for baptism may for example involve unexpressed beliefs and expectations about what effects might be involved. Some of these expectations can be elicited by careful questioning, but more detailed inquiry would be needed to establish how much was 'half-belief' or magical, and whether seeking baptism was largely in conformity with social expectations. Beliefs about sin, salvation and the future life are other religious concepts in which idiosyncratic distortions can be expressed. Perhaps because of this, religion has been construed as a negative, controlling activity rather than as one that can have positive effects on behaviour.

It is widely assumed that people express needs and other psychological characteristics in their religion. Whether this is so, and if so whether it is primarily a matter of motivation, cognition or conformity is still to be settled by observation and experiment rather than by further theorizing and argument. Whatever psychological characteristics religious people may be found to have, a religious orientation involves a recognition and acceptance of some other-wordly, transcendental processes that can penetrate or extend to the natural world. A religious stance is psychologically interesting to psychologists because many of the beliefs a person comes to hold are in principle untestable and yet may influence other aspects of behaviour. Religious beliefs have also invited interpretation because of their relationships with experience on the one hand and with traditions on the other. They have been described as derived or secondary because they are not 'taken-for-granted, uncontroversial beliefs supported by a unanimous consensus among those in a position to know' (Rokeach, 1967). In general there is greater certainty about these secondary religious beliefs than about other beliefs (Thouless, 1935). This certainty is reached through many paths, including argument, authority, habit or some religious experience.

There are many definitions of religion (Leuba, 1912, refers to forty-eight). Rather than reiterate them, it is better to consider the variables through which religion has been operationally defined and investigated, and which will reflect the assumptions beneath any particular study. The main religious variables that will be considered relate to:

1. The *behaviour* or practices that express a religious stance, assessed commonly through the frequency of church-going, Bible reading and so on.

2. Religious thinking and *belief*. Religious beliefs are usually defined with reference to the general or particular doctrines of a recognized tradition, but they can be uniquely categorized and integrated by any believer. Second-order beliefs about the ways in which religious beliefs are to be derived and tested may be a further important aspect of them as are religious attitudes.

3. Religious feelings or *experience*, and an awareness of the transcendent that can validate and personally express a religious position.

4. *Involvement* with a religiously defined group or institution sanctions an identity and forms attitudes and values, as well as beliefs. A direct method of assessing these effects is through sociometric ratings, but social attachments and reference group functions can also be observed, or reported about by those involved.

5. A religious orientation may have *consequential effects* on non-religious behaviours, beliefs and attitudes, and on moral behaviour.

This is not a complete list of the components that have been studied: religious devotion, faith, doctrines and a knowledge of the scriptures and religious conversion or change have all been examined, as have customs and myths, theologians and clergymen. There has also been recent interest in the developing para-religious forms and in the effects of different techniques of meditation. Although separate facets have been advanced as a key to understanding the whole of religion, beliefs and attitudes can be taken as especially significant unless it can be shown that people regularly engage in religious behaviour without making any assent to the associated beliefs. Beliefs and attitudes can also be readily assessed.

Cultural and denominational traditions differ in what they emphasize: while there may be uniformities of *belief* among Christians there are stronger pressures to uniform *behavioural* observance among Moslems. Individuals acquire a religion from their environment, and responses to it can be examined either for their consistencies across defined samples, or for their uniqueness. The ways in which a religion is presented will influence the kinds of response to it, but many religious responses are covert and, like religious motivations, can only be studied indirectly. Despite this, most studies have been based on self-report methods, whether by questionnaire or attitude inventory, and less commonly from the observed or reported behaviour that reflects involvement or conviction.

Early work on religion was largely introspective and anecdotal, but there have been many systematic studies since about 1930 when the modern methods were developed. These now extend from self-report techniques and indirect projective measures using verbal or pictorial material as a stimulus, to the use of semantic differential scales. Indirect measures disguise the purpose of the inquiry and so aim to avoid or reduce the possibility of deliberate distortion in the replies. But the use of any method raises questions about validity, with argument about how subjects might 'really respond', and whether the most critical elements have been tapped. Consistency across independent measures increases confidence in any results, and a continuing aim is to refine and improve the methods of measurement and study.

Just as the truth of religion cannot be established with psychological data, a reductionistic analysis can't destroy the features of religion to which people respond and which influence them. But the *believed* reality of religion is important, especially when it influences people's lives. The results of empirical studies may themselves have an influence on evaluations of the truth of religion, and may bear on questions about its mature and immature forms. Religious materials also interact with other predispositions, and may focus maladjustment or influence non-religious responses like the need for achievement (McClelland, 1961). Psychological skills and some empirical findings have been applied by religious groups, especially in counselling, group training, religious education and staff selection, and in the use of survey data to fix plans or policies.

The worth of any study rests largely on its use of agreed and accepted methods and on the proper sampling of subjects for study. The common methods for measuring a person's 'religion' have been derived from those used in studies of social attitudes, and in the study of personality. Despite the variety of tasks that has been used to derive information, they all involve responses that relate to a latent variable or dimension. Other methods have used the careful observation of behaviour in an actual situation or during the performance of an experimental task, like learning religiously relevant material, to assess functional differences between identified groups. But whatever the data, they can be analysed to identify the *content* that has been elicited and to give information about the *numbers* who hold certain beliefs, or to identify *patterns* in the relationships between religious and other variables.

Although committed religious people will sometimes protest the privacy of their religion and its inaccessibility to systematic study, a person's religion may have recognizable effects on his public behaviour, even if this is rather stereotyped. Others will object to studies of religion because of their 'scientific priggishness', or because positivism has undervalued religion (Allport, 1966, pp. vii, ix). Still others will argue that only a close personal involvement with religion can give any relevant information about it, or that the effects of social desirability are strong and will bias any responses. But under the appropriate conditions most people can report on their beliefs and on their religious experiences. Such information forms a basis for studies of religion and although the data may be coarse, good progress has been made towards understanding the psychological factors that are involved in religious responsiveness.

Many studies have simply described the characteristics of selected groups. The problems of experimental design are less easily satisfied in religious studies than are the problems surrounding data collection. Numerous psychological experiments can serve as models for experimental studies, and an ideal study might arbitrarily allocate subjects to a religious position or 'treatment' and then measure its effects on dependent variables. But the nature of religious commitment, its recognized importance and the ways in which it develops all prohibit studies in which religious variables can be independently manipulated. One technique has instructed subjects to adopt a specified religious position and to respond *as if* the religious variable were being manipulated. But religion is an organismic and not a treatment variable and the most common design has compared differences between subjects from criterion groups that are already known to differ. Any correlations are difficult to interpret, especially if a causal explanation is to be tested, and religious denomination defines criterion groups rather weakly because of our inadequate information about the shaping that has produced any observed differences.

The methods used in psychology have changed since the beginning of this century, and so have the questions that psychologists address to religion. Questions that have not proved readily amenable to research include the psychological origins of (especially primitive) religion, the symbolism and the hidden meanings of religious myths, and perhaps the patterns of emotional response to religion. Current analyses concentrate on functional interpretations of the responses to stimuli, and the results are interpreted with more emphasis on institutional, or at least on social, controls than on unconscious and personality-based processes, for which the results have been rather equivocal. Detailed case studies must be used to explore those influences. Religious institutions give a context that forms a consensus and tends to suppress idiosyncratic forms. Religious behaviour can be construed as role-related and related to social expectations. This interpretation invites many questions about the forms of response both to religious beliefs and to religious institutions.

Although religion has been well studied by psychologists we cannot yet specify what makes a religious man (or a scientist or artist). There are not only unresolved questions about religious development, but about the ways in which people align themselves with a religious system so that innovation and adaptation are possible. Despite common assumptions about the stability and the conservatism of established religion, there have been some recent changes towards openness and greater responsiveness in the Churches. Some church members are responding slowly to these changes, and others believe that the Churches are not changing quickly enough. Conservative reactions suggest further questions about the ways in which religious orientations are held, and about the nature of belief change; people do not integrate with institutional patterns in one way only, and it is a characteristic of religious beliefs (and of other beliefs and attitudes) that they can be modified by those who adhere to them. People are taught about a set of beliefs, and they emphasize or abstract from the available repertory those aspects which have a particular relevance for them. But the explanatory power and applicability of religious beliefs change with a person's developing insight and as explanations that involve supernatural processes are pushed back by increasing knowledge. These changes may require a resolution of the belief dilemmas that are produced (Abelson, 1959).

Answers to the question 'Why accept or reject religion?' are therefore complex, but any answer in psychological terms should be tested against data, with reproducible results. Thus an explanation in terms of adjustment might imply that those holding similar beliefs will share similar personality characteristics, or at least that there will be some consistent relationships between personality and belief. An alternative cognitive explanation might show age-related developmental changes in belief, and an absence of consistent relationships with personality.

The Readings included here set out to show some of the empirical and research based approaches, perspectives and formulations that psychology has brought to religion, and to its nature and functions. Only a small proportion of the total literature on psychology and religion uses systematically collected data (estimates are usually around 12 per cent) and that very few studies have extended beyond Judeo–Christian traditions. The one most common source for these readings has been the *Journal for the Scientific Study of Religion*. This journal was established in 1961 and marks a turning of interest towards systematic studies of religion.

Some will regard these Readings as too behaviourist, and will complain that they do not deal with religious experience, with what the inside of a religion might be like, or with its phenomenology. That kind of information can be found among the contemporary approaches to religion, and has its greatest psychological relevance when questions and issues are being formulated and prepared for detailed study. If this collection of papers had emphasized theories, therapies and phenomenology, it would have shown little of what psychology has been doing with (and to) religion over the last twenty or so years. Although the humanistic and the behaviourally oriented approaches to psychology have been contrasted by setting meaning against methods, subjective experience against actions, and the individual, exceptional and unpredicted against the regular, the universal and the conforming (Bugental, 1967, p. 9), that dividing line may be blurring. The study of religion is contributing to a synthesis of approaches and although objective approaches to religion may discount some of its subjective qualities. whether these are an essence of religion is a definitional question that we have left on one side. There are many other gaps in the material that is here. A glaring example is the absence of any study of the clergy as a group professionally involved with religion, and there is little about denominational differences, but the papers show what the research-based approaches have been, and can accomplish. Because one aim of this collection is to stimulate discussion and stimulation, it will be found that the papers vary a little in their quality.

References

ABELSON, R. P. (1959), 'Modes of resolution of belief dilemmas', *J. Conflict Resolution*, vol. 3, pp. 219–29.

ALLPORT, G. W. (1966), in N. L. Farberow (ed.), *Taboo Topics*, Atherton.

BUGENTAL, J. F. T. (1967), *Challenges of Humanistic Psychology*, McGraw-Hill.

DURKHEIM, E. (1961), *The Elementary Forms of the Religious Life*, Collier.

FREUD, S. (1971), *The Complete Introductory Lectures on Psychoanalysis*, Allen & Unwin.

LEUBA, J. H. (1912), *A Psychological Study of Religion*, Macmillan Co.

MCCLELLAND, D. C. (1961), *The Achieving Society*, Van Nostrand.

MARTY, M. E., ROSENBERG, S. E., and GREELEY, A. M. (1968), *What Do We Believe? The Stance of Religion in America*, Meredith.

ROKEACH, M. (1967), 'The organization and modification of beliefs', in E. P. Hollander and R. G. Hunt (eds.), *Current Perspectives in Social Psychology*, Oxford University Press, pp. 374–83.

THOULESS, R. H. (1935), 'The tendency to certainty in religious belief', *Brit. J. Psychol.*, vol. 26, pp. 16–31.

WEBER, M. (1930), *The Protestant Ethic and the Spirit of Capitalism*, Scribner.

WUNDT, W. (1915), *Elements of Folk Psychology*, Allen & Unwin.

Part One
History

Two historically relevant accounts are presented to show how religion has been analysed, and to give a context in which more recent studies can be assessed. The constructs and categories that have been used derive from religious systems themselves, with concepts like conversion, guilt, orthodoxy and fundamentalism, or from psychological theories, and especially from the study of attitudes and attitude change, from developmental psychology and personality study, and from the study of learning. The religious response was once taken to be unique and was even described as an instinct, although with a meaning better expressed as 'religious intuition'. It is now treated like any other aspect of psychological functioning. Of the better known people there is nothing here by Starbuck or by James (except later for his answers to Pratt's questionnaire), and nothing by Pratt or Leuba, by Thouless or Flower, nothing by Freud or Jung, and no interpretation of the history. Yet there are passing references to the early work in some papers that are included, and there is a select bibliography at the end.

1 L. S. Hearnshaw

The Psychology of Religion

Excerpt from L. S. Hearnshaw, *A Short History of British Psychology,*
1840–1940, Methuen, 1964, pp. 292–5.

The flood of books on religious psychology and the growth of
popular psychology which followed the return of peace in 1919
was primarily the result of the Freudian impact on minds un-
settled by war and social change. The foundations, however, had
been laid much carlier. As far back as 1857, Frederick Temple,
later Archbishop of Canterbury, wrote 'our theology has been
cast in a scholastic mould, i.e. all based on logic. We are in need
of, and we are being gradually forced into, a theology based on
psychology. The transition, I fear, will not be without much pain;
but nothing can prevent it.' In this development four contributory
streams can be traced back into the last decades of the nineteenth century. First, Galton initiated an experimental attack on
the manifestations of religion with his famous 'Statistical inquiries into the efficacy of prayer', first published in the *Fort-*
nightly Review (1873), and included in the first edition of *Inquiries*
into Human Faculty (1883), though tactfully omitted from later
editions. Secondly, the anthropologists, Robertson, Smith, Frazer,
and others, had collected much data relating to the comparative
study and the origins of religions. Thirdly, the theologians themselves turned to the neglected fields of mysticism and religious experiences. Dr W. R. Inge, later Dean of St Paul's, heralded the
new era with his Bampton Lectures on *Christian Mysticism* (1899).
Two lay theologians followed in his wake. Baron F. von Hugel, a
Catholic of Germanic origin who lived from an early age in this
country and wrote extensively on religious questions, produced a
particularly important study of *The Mystical Element in Religion*
(1908); and Evelyn Underhill wrote her well-known book
Mysticism shortly after, in 1911. Finally, the Americans, beginning with Starbuck's *Psychology of Religion* (1899), systematized
the psychological study of religion. The most famous of all works
of this kind, William James's *Varieties of Religious Experience*
(1902), was delivered as Gifford Lectures in Edinburgh. The

ground was therefore ready, with the advent of the 1920s, for the burgeoning of religious psychology.

The development was a two-sided one, from psychology and from religion. Thouless in his *Introduction to the Psychology of Religion* (1923) broadly followed James's approach. He considered the various factors involved in religious belief, the part played by both conscious and unconscious processes, the role of instincts and the phenomena of prayer, conversion and mystical experience. The emphasis of the book, as Thouless has pointed out in the preface to a paperback reissue (1961), was on religious consciousness rather than on religious behaviour, and more attention was paid to case history material than to statistical and experimental inquiries. But its general conclusions and its 'faith in the ultimate mysteries' Thouless was prepared to uphold forty years later. In the meantime Thouless had conducted some empirical investigations into 'The tendency to certainty in religious belief' (1935), and had come to believe that 'psychical research does provide impressive empirical evidence for the continuance of existence after bodily death'.

Crichton Miller's *The New Psychology and the Preacher* which appeared a year after Thouless's book (1924) was a slighter, more immediately topical work. It applied psychoanalytic findings to religion, discussed the influences of conflict, compensation, projection, fantasy, autosuggestion, sex, the 'mother complex', and symbolism generally on religious experience and practice. Miller held that religion could be purged and purified by means of psychoanalytic concepts, and at the same time that the materialistic bias of psychoanalysis could be counteracted by religion. In a rather similar vein J. A. Hadfield, who turned to medicine and psychotherapy after a theological training at Oxford, stressed in *Psychology and Morals* (1923) the essentially moral and spiritual nature of many psychoneurotic problems.

The theologians, partly no doubt because they were thicker on the ground, wrote even more profusely on the psychology of religion. Only a few of the key works can be referred to here. They came from most of the main sects: from the Anglicans, F. R. Barry and L. W. Grensted; from the Methodists, E. S. Waterhouse and L. D. Weatherhead; from the Congregationalists W. B. Selbie and T. H. Hughes; and later from the Catholics, R. Hostie and V. White. There was, not unnaturally, much doubt, hesitation and ambivalence in the first tentative theological flirtations with the new psychology. Psychology, stated Barry, 'is an ally, but a dangerous ally, to the Christian thinker' (1923). Psychology in many Christian minds aroused 'a feeling of prejudice amounting to repugnance', noted W. F. Halliday of Selly Oak College (1929). Indeed J. C. M. Conn, a Presbyterian minister who had studied psychology under Watt and Thouless in Glasgow, later wrote a book on *The Menace of the New Psychology* (1939); while A. C. Headlam, the formidable Bishop of Gloucester warned against psychology's 'extravagant claims' and lack of 'sound scientific principles' (Selbie, 1924). In spite of this opposition, however, there was a growing number of enlightened Christians who held with Barry that basically psychology, so far from being antagonistic to Christianity, was a 'republication from the scientific standpoint of essential religious truths' (1923). And indeed so august and authoritative a body as the Lambeth Conference of 1920 urged that ordinands 'should be equipped by training in psychology, and be given some acquaintance with methods and principles of healing'.

There were, in fact, as the Lambeth resolution suggests, two sides to the theological interest in psychology. There was an interest in the light which psychology could throw on the nature of religious experience, and there was an alliance between psychology and religion in the practical tasks of healing.

The most scholarly works of a theoretical stamp were those of W. B. Selbie, Principal of Mansfield College, Oxford, *The Psychology of Religion* (1924) delivered as Wilde Lectures in Oxford, and of Canon L. W. Grensted, Professor of the Philosophy of the Christian Religion at Oxford, *Psychology and God* (1930) delivered as Bampton Lectures in Oxford. Canon Grensted was sufficiently knowledgeable in psychology to be elected a Fellow of the British Psychological Society. Both were somewhat critical of the psychoanalytic emphasis on the unconscious mind, and preferred as a basis for the psychology of religion the systems of Ward and Shand. Thus Selbie maintained that religion is not an instinct, but a sentiment; not something that can be relegated to the unconscious, but something essentially normal and reasonable. Grensted also took Ward as a basis for a psychology of religion which knew its own limitations and did not destroy 'those values which have meant so much to man'. Oddly enough it was Jung rather than Freud who came in for Grensted's heaviest objurgations. We must remember however that Jung, whose 'perversity' in interpreting Christianity in terms of solar mythology Grensted objected to, did not write his *Psychology and*

Religion until 1938, and it was only during the 1930s that he rediscovered the psychological value of the numinous and the sacred.

The alliance between psychology and religion in the work of therapy was preceded by a revived interest in spiritual healing in the Christian Churches towards the close of the nineteenth century. An extreme manifestation of this revival was, of course, Christian Science, which from its Boston home began to colonize Britain about the turn of the century. By 1910 there were fifty-eight Christian Science churches in Great Britain, by 1925 there were 148, and in 1960 over 300. Within the Anglican communion there were movements, less radical in their beliefs, with partly similar aims: the Guild of Health to promote spiritual healing, and to study the interaction of the spiritual, mental and physical factors in well-being, was founded in 1904; and the Guild of St Raphael, with rather more exclusive emphasis on the spiritual, in 1915. Clearly psychotherapy had a close connection with these movements; on the one hand spiritual healing was a-form of psychotherapy; on the other religion might well prove to be in itself a psychotherapeutic force. It seemed not unreasonable, therefore, to suggest that psychiatrist and pastor should work together, that the pastor should receive some psychological training, and that he might even undertake certain forms of psychotherapy. To promote this cooperation further the Guild of Pastoral Psychology, Jungian in its predominant outlook, was established in 1936. Even before this, however, individual ministers had been practising pastoral psychology: J. G. McKenzie (1881–1963), a Nottingham Congregationalist, for example, and most conspicuously, Leslie Weatherhead, a Leeds Methodist who after his translation to the City Temple in London in 1936 established a City Temple Psychological Clinic with medical collaboration. The general interest in psychology of other faiths was shown by the starting of a Catholic Psychological Society in 1936, with E. B. Strauss the psychiatrist as their first president, and of a Church of Scotland Committee on Psychology in 1937.

References

BARRY, F. R. (1923), *Christianity and Psychology.*
HALLIDAY, W. F. (1929), *Psychology and Religious Experience.*
SELBIE, W. B. (1924), *The Psychology of Religion.*
THOULESS, R. H. (1935), 'The tendency to certainty in religious belief', *Brit. J. Psychol.,* vol. 26, pp. 16–31.

2 M. Argyle

Seven Psychological Roots of Religion

M. Argyle, 'Seven psychological roots of religion', *Theology*, 1964,
vol. 67, no. 530, pp. 1–7.

The Bishop of Woolwich says that we should abandon psychologically motivated forms of religion, such as regarding God as a
father-figure (1963). H. A. Williams says that there is too much
emphasis on guilt in Anglican worship (1962). These are examples
of two of the psychological roots of religion, and there are
probably five more such processes at the minimum. It would be
expected on general psychological grounds that if all psycho-
logically-motivated elements were eliminated from religion, people
would simply cease to be religious.

It does not follow, however, that because a belief has psychological roots it is therefore false. Consider the belief, held by
some psychologists, that personality is primarily inherited. The
psychological origins of this belief may be studied, but this
would throw no light at all on the truth of the belief. To investigate its truth quite different studies, of identical and fraternal
twins, must be pursued. It is not therefore necessary to purge our
beliefs of their psychological components; in this paper we shall
review recent research into what the main psychological roots of
religion are.

A major factor behind all attitudes and beliefs, religious or
otherwise, is the social influence of parents, friends and mass
communications. From knowledge of the influences to which a
person has been exposed it is possible to make a reasonably good
prediction of his beliefs. In a study of young people converted at a
revival, it was found that 42 per cent said they had been converted
mainly through social pressure (Argyle, 1958). However, there
are individual differences in response to such influences, and a set
of beliefs would not persist unless it met deeper needs, or was
related to basic mechanisms in the personality: to these we now
turn.

Direct need-reduction

There is extensive evidence that people are more likely to accept patterns of behaviour which they think will satisfy states of need or motivation. Children pray for the gratification of childish desires; Africans who are ill attend churches that have services of healing, as do some that are incurably ill in our own country. It has been maintained by many writers that religion is a response to frustration – that it offers gratification in fantasy to people who are deprived in reality. From this it would follow that working-class people, who are deprived both of worldly goods and social status, should be more religious. In the two countries for which the best statistics are available (UK and USA) there is no doubt that working-class people are *less* interested in religion and less likely to hold religious beliefs (Argyle, 1958, p. 129) – the opposite of what this theory predicts. However, if we look at one particular type of religious activity, the minor Protestant sects are found to flourish very largely among the socially and economically underprivileged. Furthermore, the beliefs entertained by these bodies are of a wish-fulfilling character – that this world is shortly going to end, and that when it does so the members will be superior to those who are now better off. These sects are extremely numerous in the USA and in Western Canada. A very similar phenomenon exists in Africa, where it is reported that there are at least 700 such sects in the Union alone (Sundkler, 1961). The practices of these African churches in particular draw attention to another respect in which religion can be directly instrumental. The ecstatic services consist of dancing, clapping and singing, sometimes for twelve hours on end. This is capable of reducing tension in people in an acute state of anxiety as a result of social stresses.

Another type of belief found in underdeveloped areas is the 'cargo cult' – the belief that a ship full of goods is shortly going to arrive, so that there is no need to do any more fishing or farming. Worsley, in a study of these movements in South-East Asia, concludes that they take place among people oppressed by colonial powers and who are longing for deliverance and a happier life (Worsley, 1962). Both the beliefs in the end of the world and in ships full of cargo are instrumental in that they make people feel happier, but they are really maladaptive in that they prevent people from doing anything more constructive about their social and economic difficulties. It is perhaps for this reason that this is a type of belief which appeals only to un-educated or primitive people.

Anxiety-reduction

Situations that are a source of stress and anxiety can be rendered harmless by the adoption of certain beliefs about them. For people who are worried about death, belief in an after-life is a highly satisfactory adjustment. Several lines of evidence suggest that this is an important basis of religious belief. As people get older, after thirty or thirty-five, more are religious and believe in the after-life; 100 per cent of subjects over the age of one hundred held this belief in one survey! The proportion of people who said they went to church for reassurance about immortality similarly increased. Old people who hold this belief are somewhat better adjusted than those who do not – showing that this belief really is successful in relieving anxiety. About 75 per cent of soldiers who have been in action report that they were helped by prayer, and this was particularly true of those who experienced the most anxiety and had been exposed to most stress. Though other students at British universities show a decline of religious beliefs while at college, medical students have been found to show an increase (Poppleton and Pilkington, 1963); this may be due to contact with dying people creating concern about death.

One of Freud's ideas about religion was that it resembled an obsessional neurosis. Malinowski had the same theory about primitive ritualistic practices. In each case the principle is the same – the performance of a ritual is able to reduce anxiety. There are various possible psychological explanations for this, but we need go no further than saying that under some conditions ritualistic observances can have this effect. In a cross-cultural study of primitive societies there was a close connection between the use of ritual and certain patterns of child-rearing (Spiro and d'Andrade, 1958). Pfister produced historical evidence to show that whenever the Jewish and Christian churches have been under external stress there has been a shift of emphasis to greater ritualism (Pfister, 1948).

Internal conflict

Religion can be a product of inner conflict in two ways. First guilt feelings can be aroused and relieved by Protestant doctrines and practices. The arousal of a sense of sin was a standard technique of nineteenth-century revivalism; it has been found that adolescents converted at revivals have often experienced a period of guilt feelings beforehand; Protestant mental patients are more likely than others to be preoccupied with feelings of guilt and unworthiness (Argyle, 1958, p. 134); Protestant doctrine places considerable emphasis on sin and salvation. This theory has been further investigated by the writer in a study of 700 young people aged eleven to twenty-one. It was found that there was a correlation between guilt feelings and frequency of church attendance – those with the strongest guilt went to church most often. Closer analysis revealed that this relationship did not hold for all subjects: it held specifically for females rather than males, especially those over fifteen, who were Protestants. It was previously predicted that this mechanism would apply particularly to female Protestants (Argyle, 1958); this theory gives an explanation of the greater appeal of religion to women, and of the fact that this sex ratio is greater for Protestants than Roman Catholics. Baptist ordinands in the study were much 'guiltier' than Catholic ordinands, but there was no difference for lay*men*. This theory has also been confirmed by Dr L. B. Brown, working at the University of Adelaide. He found that Protestants had more inwardly directed aggression than Catholics: this is expected since people with strong consciences are likely to direct aggression towards themselves rather than to others (1965).

A second theory about religious reaction to conflict is that some people when faced with a conflict between the self and the demands of conscience will 'project' the latter, so that moral demands are experienced as coming from an externalized deity. There are grounds for thinking that this mechanism is more likely to occur among Catholics. Earlier studies show that Roman Catholics make more use of 'projection' as a defence mechanism; their greater dependence on a social hierarchy is probably due to similar psychological processes. Projection is likely to occur if there is a great divergence of wishes between self and conscience. In the same study mentioned above we found clear evidence that Catholics have greater conflict of this kind than Protestants or non-religious people. A key to the explanation of this failure of internalization in Catholics is provided by our finding that there is a less close relation between Roman Catholic parents and children; this in turn is probably due to their comparatively harsher child-rearing methods, which have been reported in several studies.

To conclude, there seems to be considerable evidence that the relief-of-guilt process functions for Protestants, especially for females. The projected-conscience mechanism applies mainly to Roman Catholics.

Gods as fantasy parent-figures

The theory just discussed is one type of theory linking gods and parents. On that theory, God is a re-projection of a parent-figure previously internalized as a super-ego. On Freud's theory people reconstruct a fantasy father-figure when later in need of care and protection. In either case God should be perceived as similar to the real parent. There has been some interesting recent confirmation of this principle. It was found, in a cross-cultural study of sixty-two primitive societies, that where child-rearing was nurturant, the gods were regarded as benevolent, but that when child-rearing was punitive, the gods were seen as malevolent (Lambert, Triandis and Wolf, 1959). In the other cross-cultural study mentioned above it was found that primitive beliefs were associated with parental patterns of child-rearing in other ways too. Initial satisfaction of dependence, together with anxiety about dependence, produced a belief in supernatural rewards which are conditional upon obedience; low anxiety about dependency produced a belief in supernatural rewards regardless of obedience. High socialization anxiety was associated with belief in punitive gods.

This process clearly applies to certain kinds of primitive religion, and it may also be relevant to Christianity, with its father- and mother-figures. An American survey has in fact found that people with punitive parents tended to believe in a sterner, more punitive, God (Adorno et al., 1950).

Ego-identity

Here we have a recently discovered psychological process, little understood, but essential for the explanation of some religious phenomena. It is important for people to have a conception of themselves, which is clear and distinct from their conception of others, and at the same time fairly favourable. Erikson has shown how in late adolescence in particular there is often an 'identity crisis', when young people suddenly alter or crystallize their ego-identity (Erikson, 1956, p. 378). As well as adolescents, the socially uprooted and the socially mobile are greatly affected by this process. We have discussed the wish-fulfilment functions of sect beliefs. and the release of tension provided by their services.

Sects also provide an ego-identity to people who have been socially uprooted and do not belong anywhere in the community. In the USA the sects flourish on the outskirts of big cities among people who have migrated from a stable country environment. In Canadian sects people were attracted by the large number of offices, involving up to 15 per cent of the members, which gave a position in the community (Mann, 1955). In Africa the separatist churches appeal to people who have left the closely knit kinship structure of the village and moved into the anomic new African city – a shambles of tin sheds and mud huts (Sundkler, 1961). In the Middle Ages the millennial movements began under essentially similar conditions.

People will also join groups because these enhance their self images (as when working-class voters support the Conservative party). There is a close parallel for American church members, who are often influenced in their choice of a church by its social standing, since there are considerable differences in the class composition of churches. Whereas 56·8 per cent of Episcopalians are white collar or above, only 26·3 per cent of Baptists are. In a given area, more extreme differences are found: in part of California 84 per cent of Pentecostalists are unskilled while only 1 per cent of Congregationalists are (Argyle, 1958, p. 132). Socially mobile people often change their religious denomination on their path upwards.

Cognitive clarity, the need for understanding

People may adopt beliefs primarily because they provide some solution to a puzzling cognitive situation. A good example of this is rumour: rumours arise and spread when there have been unusual happenings and an absence of satisfactory explanation. Primitive religion provides the most obvious illustration of beliefs meeting a cognitive need. Primitive people are puzzled by natural phenomena like thunder, and explain it by postulating a thunder god. While education and science have removed the need for the explanation of these phenomena, present-day primitives are still inclined to seek a supernatural explanation of why a particular child should die of one disease rather than another.

In modern society it is older adolescents who are most interested in religion for cognitive reasons. The problems which they are most concerned about are general issues of motivation, 'What is the purpose of life?', 'What ought we to do?', etc.

There is no scientific answer to such questions: they can only be resolved by the acceptance of a general philosophy of life, such as religion provides. It is hard to withhold making a decision about such important matters; Thouless found that subjects were far more prone to hold definite views about whether there are 'angels in Heaven' than whether there are 'tigers in India' (Thouless, 1935). Developmental studies show how, between twelve and twenty, young people gradually come to polarize their cognitive world round a religious or non-religious point of view, so that by their early twenties they are no longer puzzled or concerned about these questions (Argyle, 1958, p. 59).

These needs are most successfully met by dogmatic systems of belief. It has been found that Roman Catholics have the most dogmatic and rigid beliefs, and that anxious people are the most dogmatic about their beliefs (Rokeach, 1960).

Biochemical factors

While the previous process discussed is the most acceptable to theologians, this one is the least. Nevertheless there is clear evidence that religious emotional and mystical experiences can be brought on by alterations in the body chemistry. Experiments with mescaline and LSD produce visual hallucinations, intensified brilliance of perception, experiences of timelessness, depersonalization and euphoria. In some subjects the experience is regarded as a religious one, especially in people with a religious background. Mexican tribes commonly chew peyote for religious purposes; the ensuing experiences vary with the religion practised – in Roman Catholic tribes they include visions of the Virgin (Argyle, 1958, p. 170). It has been objected that 'mystical' experiences induced by drugs are inferior and different from those of the classical masters of the spiritual life. They are probably not inferior to the 'milder form of mystical experience' which occurs among many young people (Pratt, 1924). In either case the experience may be the product of a certain physiological condition which is interpreted as religious through possession of a past background of religious training: the more intensive this training, the more complex the experience.

It is likely too that the cosmic experiences reported by about one psychotic mental patient in seven have similar origins, in view of the known biochemical disturbances of these patients, and the similarity of these states to those induced by drugs.

These psychological factors must however be kept within their proper perspective. There needs to be no relation between the psychological basis for a belief, and the truth of that belief. Furthermore the spheres of activity and relevance of psychology and religion may be separated in a more fundamental sense. Sciences deal with the publicly observable; psychology is primarily concerned with the outward behaviour of other people, it does not do justice to the inner point of view, which, predictable or not, has a validity of its own. A horticulturalist can grow roses, but it takes an artist or poet to convey and interpret the appearance of a rose. A psychologist could organize an evangelical campaign, but is not competent to deal with the inner truth with which religion is concerned.

References

ADORNO, T. W. et al. (1950), *The Authoritarian Personality*, Harper & Row.

ARGYLE, M. (1958), *Religious Behaviour*, Routledge & Kegan Paul.

BROWN, L. B. (1965), 'Aggression and denominational membership', *Brit. J. soc. clin. Psychol.*, vol. 4, pp. 175–8.

ERIKSON, E. H. (1956), 'The problem of ego identity', *J. Amer. Psychoanal. Assoc.*, vol. 4, pp. 58–121.

LAMBERT, W. W., TRIANDIS, L. M., and WOLF, M. (1959), 'Some correlates of beliefs in the malevolence and benevolence of supernatural beings: a cross societal study', *J. abnorm. soc. Psychol.*, vol. 58, pp. 162–9.

MANN, W. E. (1955), *Sect, Cult and Church in Alberta*, University of Toronto Press.

PFISTER, O. (1948), *Christianity and Fear*, Allen & Unwin.

POPPLETON, P. K., and PILKINGTON, G. W. (1963), 'The measurement of religious attitudes in a university population', *Brit. J. soc. clin. Psychol.*, vol. 2, pp. 20–36.

PRATT, J. B. (1924), *The Religious Consciousness*, Macmillan Co.

ROBINSON, J. A. T. (1963), *Honest to God*, SCM.

ROKEACH, M. (1960), *The Open and Closed Mind*, Basic Books.

SPIRO, M. E., and D'ANDRADE, R. G. (1958), 'A cross cultural study of some supernatural beliefs', *Amer. Anthropol.*, vol. 60, pp. 456–66.

SUNDKLER, B. G. M. (1961), *Bantu Prophets in South Africa*, Lutterworth.

THOULESS, R. H. (1935), 'The tendency to certainty in religious belief', *Brit. J. Psychol.*, vol. 26, pp. 16–31.

WILLIAMS, H. A. (1962), 'Theology and self-awareness', in A. R. Vidler (ed.), *Soundings*, Cambridge University Press, 1962.

WORSLEY, P. (1962), *The Trumpet Shall Sound*, MacGibbon & Kee.

Part Two
Dimensionality and Orientation to Religion

An important question recently has concerned the dimensionality of different measures or indices of religion. This question derived from the theory that religion is based in personality functioning, but it also reflects the fact that people differ in their involvement with religion. Two solutions have been advanced: one finds a single religious factor and the other has found that religion divides to several independent factors. These solutions usually rely on the use of factor analysis to break down the intercorrelations between the scores of samples of subjects, but a few have simply outlined the factors that should emerge, or have used content analysis to distinguish them. Studies that examine a multitude of factors include King (1967) and King and Hunt (1969), and Faulkner and de Jong (1966). The statistical techniques, the actual content of the measures (which usually relate to different religious beliefs), and the samples selected all contribute to the differing solutions. Much more work is needed to resolve or integrate these results.

Another approach to questions about the dimensionality of religion has been through an examination of the specific ways in which religious responding shows its effects, especially in non-religious variables. The best of this work derives from Allport's observation that for some believers religion can focus prejudice while for others it leads to an increased tolerance. There are now several variants of the distinction that Allport made between extrinsic and intrinsic religious orientations, which Dittes has summarized in terms of religion as explicit, public and social against religion as internal, intrinsic, subjective, committed and spiritual (1971). Basic to any of these distinctions is the ambiguity of religious responding, which has itself led to the suggestion that religious ideation can be used diagnostically, particularly for those who show defensive or pathological reactions. This is a difficult area in which to find good evidence It has been common simply to assume that unconscious needs, wishes and tendencies are expressed through religion, and that religion focuses delusions, or regressive and immature responses. Yet for some, religion fosters growth and a constructive integration and for others it may be simply a social conformity.

References

DITTES, J. E. (1971), 'Two issues in measuring religion', in M. P. Strommen (ed.), *Research on Religious Development*, Hawthorn, pp. 78–106.

FAULKNER, J. E., and DE JONG, G. F. (1966), 'Religiosity in 5-D: an empirical analysis', *Social Forces*, vol. 45, pp. 246–54.

KING, M. B. (1967), 'Measuring the religious variable: nine proposed dimensions', *J. sci. Study Relig.*, vol. 6, no. 2, pp. 173–90.

KING, M. B., and HUNT, R. A. (1969), 'Measuring the religious variable: amended findings', *J. sci. Study Relig.*, vol. 8, no. 2, pp. 321–3.

3 L. B. Brown

A Study of Religious Belief

L. B. Brown, 'A study of religious belief', *British Journal of Psychology*, 1962, vol. 53, no. 3, pp. 259–72.

Introduction

Common observation suggests that individuals differ in both the direction and intensity of their religious beliefs, and that these primary beliefs often influence other functions and characteristics. Differences occur not only grossly between believers and non-believers, but among believers, for example, between Methodists and Roman Catholics. It is not clear, however, which are crucial differences, and whether they depend on the performance of characteristic activities, on personality variables, on values or on social support. Alternatively, the differences may depend on an individual's psychological development leading to the establishment of a religious belief–disbelief system, with implications for beliefs about non-religious matters. Obviously, a knowledge of the functional relationships between religious belief and other psychological characteristics is a prerequisite for any adequate psychology of religion.

Accepting that the strength of belief is a central determinant of religious behaviour, Thouless's (1935) questionnaire seems a suitable technique for its assessment. Thouless in his original report showed that religious belief statements are assented to more strongly than are statements of fact, and the present work was begun as a repetition of that study.

The strength of religious belief is therefore defined operationally through the Thouless questionnaire, which implies that religious belief is a cognitive function with varying degrees of subjective certainty, and relationships with other psychological characteristics. Relationships have been hypothesized between the strength of belief and personality variables, general social attitudes, institutionalization and individualism as well as denominational membership. With the Thouless questionnaire it is also possible to study the influence of religious belief on other belief and opinion systems.

The measures

The variables in the study were defined by measures incorporated in two questionnaires, administered during two testing sessions separated by six weeks. The questionnaires had the following components.

Intensity of belief

This was assessed by the use of Thouless's questionnaire, to which eight additional items were added. The items were broken down to areas defined, following Thouless's procedure, in terms of item content. Thouless's classification of the items has been used when making direct comparisons with his material, but because that classification was thought to have deficiencies it was replaced in the later handling of the data by an empirical one. For this purpose the assessments of ten judges were used, and a criterion of at least 80 per cent agreement in the allocation of each item was obtained. The areas arrived at in this way were beliefs about Christ and God, other orthodox Christian beliefs, general religious belief (e.g. 'There are such spiritual beings as angels'), opinion (e.g. 'Sex is evil'), fact (e.g. 'Moses was the author of the first five books of the Bible' and 'Tigers are found in parts of China') and a group of miscellaneous items including, for example, 'The spirits of persons who have died can sometimes communicate with the living.'

Each subject was asked to 'show the degree of certainty with which you believe or disbelieve' each of the statements, on a scale from $+3$, 'a complete certainty that the belief is true', to -3, 'a complete certainty that the belief is false'. This scale was later converted to a score for each item by a simple arithmetical weighting in which -3 was scored 1 and $+3$ scored 8, and the score for each area was the mean of the weighted scale values for that area.

Thouless had only one sort of uncertainty, namely, 'the statement is as likely to be true as false', but suggested that another could be included. A second kind of uncertainty, 'uncertainty of conviction as a result of lack of information or interest', was therefore allowed. The first of these was scored 4, and the second 5.

Personality measures

These assessments were made by the use of the shortened six-item forms of Eysenck's questionnaires for neuroticism (N) and extraversion (E) (Eysenck, 1958), as well as by the Taylor Manifest Anxiety Scale (M.A.S.) (Taylor, 1953) and the items of the M.M.P.I. Lie Scale (L) embedded in the masculinity–femininity items of the same Inventory, although the M–F scale was not itself scored. The measures used were chosen for their general relevance.

Attitude measures

A ten-item form of the California F scale (Adorno *et al.*, 1950) had been constructed for this population, so that and Lovibond's modification of previous humanitarianism scales were used to assess some general attitudes.

Institutionalization and individualism

From a collection of attitude items previously used by Jeeves (1959), two sets of four which had high face validity were included. The institutionalization items entail a high evaluation of the Church; a person strongly agreeing with them all accepts the Church as a primary point of reference in religious matters. Such people may show 'religious conservatism' as Argyle (1958) uses the expression. These items included, 'The Church is necessary to establish and preserve concepts of right and wrong.' Individualism is probably similar to the 'personalism' referred to by Thouless (1959) and the items included, 'A man ought to be guided by what his own experience tells him is right rather than by what any institution such as the Church tells him to do.' They emphasize an individual's own judgements made independently of an external authority, rather than internalized acceptance of a point of view. For the attitude measures and for institutionalization and individualism, the attitude items were in a single questionnaire, with an instruction to show 'how much you agree or disagree with each one'. Strong agreement was then given a weight of 7, strong disagreement a weight of 1, and the scores for each measure obtained by summing weights from the component items.

In addition to these measures, information on age, sex and denominational affiliation was obtained. This last information was derived in a deliberately off-hand way, the question being put orally in the form, 'If you call yourself a Christian, indicate the denomination to which you belong.' This form was used in the hope of counteracting any habitual tendency to mention a denomination in order to conform.

Table 1 Classification of, and weightings for, denomination, compared with scale positions adopted by Rokeach

Denomination	Assigned score	Rokeach scale	Sample size
Roman Catholic	1	0	19
Church of England	3	4	56
Methodist	4	15	40
Other Non-Conformists	5		45
including Lutheran		10	
Presbyterians		14	
Baptist		17	
Miscellaneous	6		18
Atheist and 'nothing'	9		25
Total			203

To enable denomination to be a variable in the analysis, the denomination given by each subject was assigned a score. In the scoring it was assumed that Roman Catholics stand at one end of a continuum, with those not mentioning a denomination at the other. The scores allocated to the denominations, placed along this continuum, are shown in Table 1 with Rokeach's (1960) results (available after this work had been done) for comparison. To determine his values Rokeach 'applied an "unfolding method" technique similar to that developed by Coombs (1950)' (Rokeach, 1960, p. 297). There are other methods of classification; Argyle (1958), for example, groups denominations as conservative religion, protestantism, sects and liberalism, but a direct weighting of denominations was considered to be more suitable for this study.

The subjects

In work of this kind there are problems of definition, not only of what 'religious behaviour' is, but also of who is 'religious' and consequently who should be studied. At one extreme would be 'religiosity', studied by selecting subjects from 'Pentecostal' and

'Disciples of Christ' sects as did Broen (1957), and at the other there would be no special definition, and so the sample would not be selected for religious bias. The latter course seems to be appropriate when the nature of Christian belief as a cognitive system is being investigated. It was therefore thought defensible to use students for this inquiry. They constitute a reasonably homogeneous group, and in this sample they all shared a similar Judeo–Christian background, with only a minority (four people) drawn from unorthodox groups, such as Seventh Day Adventists. Table 1 shows the numbers in each denominational group for the main sample.

The Thouless questionnaire was given in 1959, and repeated in 1960, together with the personality and attitude questionnaires. This is the main sample, in which there were 203 first-year psychology students in the University of Adelaide, with a mean age of twenty-two years.

Results

The data were analysed first for comparison with previous work, particularly Thouless's findings. A factor analysis was then carried out.

Reliability of the measures

Reliability of the Thouless questionnaire and of the institutionalization and individualism measures was assessed by a retest after eight months of forty subjects from the original group, who went on to the second-year psychology course. Although this method of assessing reliability has disadvantages, it is the only one appropriate in this situation. The test–retest correlations were:

Orthodox beliefs	0·85
General religious beliefs	0·92
Opinion	0·35
Fact	0·30
Miscellaneous	0·50
Institutionalization	0·53
Individualism	0·60

The low reliability coefficients for the opinion and fact scores are probably spurious, although they are not without interest in themselves; they may be due in part to the instability of beliefs about these questions, and to homogeneity in the scores. There are no significant differences between men and women.

The correlation between the extraversion and neuroticism scores is -0.09, which conforms to the correlation of -0.05 for these questionnaires reported by Eysenck (1958). These measures were also found to be independent for the males and females separately. The correlation between neuroticism and manifest anxiety is $+0.511$. The attitude measures of authoritarianism and humanitarianism were independent of the personality measures.

Jeeves (1959) found his institutionalized type correlating with anti-semitism more than the other types, and a similar result was obtained here with a correlation of $+0.466$ between institutionalization and authoritarianism, and $+0.022$ between individualism and authoritarianism. Humanitarianism has low correlations with both of these variables (-0.169 and $+0.095$ respectively).

Intensity of belief

Thouless in his first table shows the 'mean certainty of different test statements' and concludes that 'the tendency to certainty is less strong amongst non-religious (statements) than amongst those of a religious order'. Identical results were obtained here, with samples taken in each of two succeeding years. In the main sample the mean certainty for religious statements was 2·10 (Thouless 2·13) and for the non-religious statements it was 1·56 (Thouless 1·575). The detailed results are shown in Table 2.

When the degree of certainty for each item is considered, the results are again essentially the same as those obtained by Thouless. The correlation of mean certainty for each item between Thouless's order and the present one is $+0.65$ (s.e. $= 0.16$). The small differences that occur can be explained from the item content in terms of a shift of interest after thirty years and a different culture. The differences are not in the religious belief items, but in items like 'The total national debt of Great Britain is more than a thousand million pounds' (40), which showed the greatest difference, 'Members of the leisured class are supported by the surplus value created by the workers' (37) and 'Tariffs improve trade' (38), although none of these differences reaches the 0·05 level of significance.

It is of some interest that the essential similarity of results occurs despite the addition of a second kind of zero category. Thouless commented that a difficulty with his results was the ambiguity of the zero response, and as has been already stated two kinds of uncertainty were allowed in this study. A further point of interest because of the close similarity are the responses to the item, 'Green is a primary colour' for which Thouless was unable to 'explain the high certainty'. He found a mean certainty of 2·33 for this item, and in the present study the mean certainty was 2·32.

Denominational differences in belief

Thouless used an internal criterion to distinguish between believers and non-believers, but the results set out in Table 2 with the percentages in each of the denominational groups showing 'complete certainty' about the items make the nature of differences between believers and non-believers clearer. As the primary interest is in the extremes of certainty it seems preferable to examine the proportions who strongly assent to each item rather than to use an overall mean of certainty.

Looking first at the Group D items, Thouless's 'affectively indifferent non-religious beliefs', it is seen that there are no significant differences between the denominational groups. On the other hand, when the Methodists and Roman Catholics as the most homogeneous religious groups in the sample are compared, the following items in Group A (the religious beliefs) show differences with significance better than the 0·05 level: 'There is a Hell in which the wicked will be everlastingly punished' (23), 'There are such spiritual beings as angels' (9), 'There is a personal Devil' (5), 'Attendance at church is a better way of spending Sunday than taking a walk in the country' (18) and 'There are spiritual realities of some kind' (3). When Methodists and atheists ('nothing') are compared, it is only in the items 3, 9 and 18 that they differ significantly from each other. However, the mean percentages with complete certainty on items in Group A are: 'nothing' 15·3, Methodists 50·8 and Roman Catholics 73·1. The differences between these means are significant beyond the 0·05 level.

It is clear from these results that although Thouless's findings about differences between religious and non-religious statements are substantiated, when the results are seen in greater detail, a more complex pattern of responses emerges. If the beliefs belong to a formally prescribed religious or theological system, they are strongly adhered to by people who accept other parts of the system, and regard themselves as belonging to the institution that sanctions the beliefs. The differences between Methodists and

Table 2 Showing mean certainty of different test statements (after Thouless), and percentages in the denominational groups having 'a complete certainty that the belief is true', or for statements followed by − 3, false

Group*	Item	Mean certainty		Complete certainty				
		Thouless	Brown	Nothing	Others	Methodist	C of E	RC
A	1 God	2·25	2·44	26	76	84	45	83
	2 Christ	2·27	2·43	15	76	87	52	96
	3 Spirit real	2·40	2·22	30	59	55	50	79
	4 Created world	2·19	2·33	11	76	76	45	92
	5 Devil	2·19	1·98	11	47	24	17	50
	7 God power	2·32	2·44	21	76	84	52	96
	8 God good	2·38	2·42	23	79	84	52	96
	9 Angels	1·67	1·86	2	38	20	10	79
	10 Jonah	2·01	1·74	2	32	13	10	25
	14 Spirit after death	2·07	2·24	13	59	67	40	88
	18 Sunday Church	1·82	1·74	0	24	33	2	58
	20 Christianity > Buddhism	1·80	1·70	6	50	44	19	63
	21 Bible literal	2·44	2·25	0	24	2	2	17
	22 Man responsible	2·62	2·63	64	65	73	62	83
	23 Hell	2·35	2·10	6	47	16	10	92
B	6 Matter (− 3)	2·25	2·06	23	44	62	50	83
	16 God (− 3)	2·34	2·55	34	79	95	74	92

C	11 Evolved	2·23	2·11	30	29	44	52	8
	12 God impersonal(−3)	1·89	1·91	21	56	60	29	58
	13 Evil reality	2·32	2·21	19	65	62	50	75
	19 Moses(−3)	1·30	1·24	17	12	31	19	13
	24 Spirits commune(−3)	1·66	1·61	15	38	13	13	25
	26 Evolution	2·17	2·11	26	41	62	50	50
D	28 Mary, Queen of Scots	1·22	0·67	6	3	7	10	4
	30 Tigers	1·23	1·20	5	3	16	2	4
	31 Hornets(−3)	1·21	1·60	19	26	35	33	21
	33 Light speed(−3)	2·01	1·94	47	29	38	33	29
	35 Green	2·33	2·32	21	35	27	31	29
E	40 National debt	1·82	0·51	5	6	5	5	4
	17 Expand universe(−3)	0·95	1·14	11	12	15	19	17
	34 Bacon(−3)	1·83	1·84	25	32	42	40	25
	37 Leisured class(−3)	1·99	1·23	9	9	11	5	21
	38 Tariffs(−3)	1·72	0·98	4	3	4	7	4
	39 India	1·78	1·34	12	12	20	7	4
F	15 Religion opium(−3)	2·07	1·81	13	32	49	12	54
	25 Right triumphs	2·01	1·80	13	50	60	24	79
G	27 Hardship	1·77	1·55	6	18	18	14	0
	29 Relative	1·87	1·39	21	6	13	10	25
	32 Sex evil(−3)	2·48	2·68	74	82	87	71	88
	36 Sunlight	2·83	2·59	68	76	76	67	54

*The grouping is that made by Thouless (1935). He called the groups: A and B, Religious beliefs; C, Unorthodox religious beliefs; D, Affectively indifferent non-religious beliefs; E, Political beliefs; F, Religious 'tabloids'; G, non-religious 'tabloids'.

Roman Catholics that have already been noted are reflexions of the eschatological theology of these two Churches.

Table 3 shows the responses for 'complete certainty' and 'strong conviction' for the item, 'There is a God who is all-powerful' (7), which is central to any religious position, and also for the item 'Mary, Queen of Scots, was beheaded between 1580 and 1590' (28). The pattern of answers for the first of these is a common one for the religious items, and differs from the pattern in other types of question. Members of the Church of England (see Table 3) do not maintain such a strong degree of certainty about religious items, more of them than of other groups tending to accept 'strong conviction' rather than 'complete certainty'.

Table 3 Showing the two highest degrees of conviction for item 7, 'There is a God who is all-powerful', and for item 28, 'Mary, Queen of Scots, was beheaded between 1580 and 1590', by percentages

	'Nothing'	Others	Methodists	C of E	R C	Mean
Item 7						
+3	21	76	84	52	96	65·8
+2	13	12	9	24	4	12·4
Sum	34	88	93	76	100	78·2
Item 28						
+3	6	3	7	10	4	6
+2	9	9	5	14	13	10
Sum	15	12	12	24	17	16

In questions of fact which Christians might be expected to know about, such as 'Moses was the author of the first five books of the Bible' (19), there are few significant differences between non-Christians and Christians. For example, 31 per cent of the Methodists were certain that this statement was false, while 15 per cent of all other denominations and 17 per cent of non-Christians gave this reply. There is a similar pattern in the item, 'Man has evolved from lower forms of life' (11), except that the miscellaneous Christian group and the Roman Catholics are closer together with 32 per cent and 21 per cent respectively showing complete certainty compared with only 5 per cent of all other groups.

Table 4 Showing mean scores of the denominational groups on the personality and attitudinal variables

		Manifest anxiety	Lie	Neuroticism score	Extraversion	Authoritarianism	Humanitarianism
N							
25	Nothing	18·0	2·7	8·45	7·0	34·0	58·3
63	Others	15·6	3·7	7·0	6·3	42·5	55·1
40	Methodists	15·5	3·1	7·1	8·2	40·2	56·2
56	C of E	14·1	3·2	7·7	7·0	45·1	53·7
19	RC	15·9	3·5	8·1	6·8	43·6	47·7
	Over all mean	15·40	3·21	7·45	6·83	42·00	53·66
	S.D.	6·87	2·02	3·75	3·23	11·04	10·21

Table 5 Matrix of correlations (being output of SILLIAC programme K2), corrected to two places and with the decimal points omitted

	M.A.S.	L	N	E	F	H	Christ	God	O.B.	G.B.	Opin.	Fact.	Misc.	Instit.	Indiv.	Denom.	Sex
M.A.S.	−06																
L	−04	−23															
N	−18	+51	−22														
E	−13	−12	+04	−09													
F	−12	+02	+19	+04	+06												
H	+13	+16	+04	−01	+02	−18											
Christ	−34	−01	+22	+02	+12	+43	−19										
God	−22	+02	+15	−01	−02	+41	−10	+76									
O.B.	−28	+01	+15	−05	+03	+44	−14	+82	+86								
G.B.	−22	−01	+16	−07	+01	+41	−11	+73	+68	+76							
Opin.	−15	+18	−03	+07	+04	+24	−02	−04	−01	−02	+01						
Fact.	+01	+05	−03	+08	+03	+08	−03	−07	−11	−11	−01	+30					
Misc.	+06	+10	−05	+06	+04	−05	+04	−09	−17	−11	−07	+09	+23				
Instit.	−13	−12	+14	−04	+08	+47	−17	+47	+47	+49	+45	+11	+09	−01			
Indiv.	+02	+17	−11	+13	+01	+02	+10	−16	−20	−19	−26	+11	+11	−07	+18		
Denom.	+10	+14	−02	−00	−02	−34	+27	−47	−37	−42	−38	+03	+03	+02	+05	−36	
Sex	−35	+03	+17	+09	+14	+21	−16	+27	+26	+24	+13	+06	+04	+06	+04	+19	+02	−15

O.B.: Orthodox Belief; G.B.: General Belief; Opin.: Opinion strength; Fact.: Factual certainty; Misc.: Miscellaneous items; Instit.: Institutionalization; Indiv.: Individualism; Denom.: Denomination.

Other denominational comparisons

The assertion that denominational groups differ from one another in personality characteristics and in attitudinal variables has been commonly made, some of the material being summarized by Argyle (1958) in his chapters 8 and 9. The results from the present study are summarized in Table 4. the only significant findings being a higher anxiety score (M.A.S.) and lower authoritarianism (F) score for those not belonging to any denomination. Argyle's summary statement that 'for people between the ages of sixteen and thirty the religious individuals are somewhat more neurotic' (Argyle, 1958, p. 106) is not supported. The finding relating to authoritarianism is not a clear one because of the significant difference between the non-denominational males (mean 27·7) and females (mean 40·3) that is concealed here, and the fact that the mean for these females is close to the mean of the denominational groups. Rokeach reports an equivalent mean on ten authoritarianism items of 37·8 for Catholics and 31·6 for non-believers (1960, p. 110).

The factor analysis

All of the component scores were inter-correlated (using the SILLIAC programme K2); the resulting matrix is given in Table 5. A factor analysis was then carried out with programme M7, and six iterations were made to obtain stable communalities (using programme K7). Because the factors obtained from this refactored material were readily interpreted, there seemed no advantage to be gained by a quartimax rotation. [Sanai (1950) adopts a similar procedure.] Thus the factor analysis presented is a principal axis solution with the factors having latent roots greater than 1·00 after six iterations interpreted directly.

The latent root of the first factor is 4·63, and on refactoring after six iterations the latent root is 4·30. The principal loadings are:

Orthodox Christian belief	+0·894
General religious belief	+0·812
Institutionalization	+0·656
Authoritarianism	+0·598
Individualism	−0·278
Age	−0·365
Denomination	−0·581

The loadings of the personality variables on this factor are:

Manifest anxiety	+0·072
Neuroticism	+0·033
Extraversion	+0·074

The loadings of the factual and opinionative scores are:

Opinion strength	−0·032
Certainty of facts	+0·061
Miscellaneous items	+0·144

This factor accounts for 43 per cent of the total variance.

The first is clearly a religious belief factor, which shows religious belief to be a system isolated from the opinionative and factual systems, without a relationship with the personality measures and yet strongly associated with both an orientation to the Church (institutionalization) and to denominational membership. The loading on authoritarianism confirms previous findings, and as might be expected individualism has a negative loading.

The second factor has a latent root of 1·93 and on refactoring the latent root is 1·41. The principal loadings are:

Manifest anxiety	+0·725
Neuroticism	+0·704
Opinion strength	+0·500
Factual certainty	+0·339
Miscellaneous items	+0·285
Individualism	+0·376
Lie score	−0·312
Age	−0·337

This factor accounts for 15 per cent of the variance and is obviously a personality factor of neuroticism or anxiety. Extraversion has a loading of −0·019 on this factor, orthodox religious belief a loading of −0·009 and general religious belief one of −0·015. Authoritarianism has a loading of +0·216.

The second factor is similar to one identified by Rokeach (1960, chapter 19), who found dogmatism and anxiety to be part of a single psychological factor, in which authoritarianism is not included. However, Rokeach goes on to report differences in dogmatism and anxiety between groups of Catholics, Protestants and non-believers.

It is of considerable importance theoretically that the opinion and factual scores, rather than the religious belief measures, have high loadings on this personality factor. This is a finding that is contrary to expectations from other studies; for example Funk (1956) found a correlation of $+0.29$ between manifest anxiety and orthodoxy of belief in students.

In summary it appears that the strength of religious belief is associated with acceptance and membership of a Church, while certainty about opinionative and factual matters is associated with personality variables, and specifically with measures of anxiety.

The remaining factors all have latent roots less than unity after refactoring, and their content in no case adds to the interpretation. The third factor has a latent root of 1.47 on the first factorization and 0.95 after six iterations. It is a bi-polar factor, again showing the relationship between opinion strength and personality. while the fouth factor with latent roots of 1.28 and 0.67 after iteration is an age factor on which factual certainty has a loading of $+0.405$ and orthodox religious belief a loading of $+0.053$.

Discussion

The results of the study point towards religious belief being a relatively isolated cognitive system, in which intensity of belief is independent of the strength of opinions about other matters. The relationships between belief and Church membership, attitudinal acceptance of the Church (institutionalization) and authoritarianism suggest that strong social support is required for the maintenance of a system of religious belief.

Denominational adherence also varies systematically with the strength of religious belief Historically the Church has maintained its doctrines in ways that differ from one denomination to another. and each church has usually handled heresies vigorously. This study shows that such a system of external controls is paralleled in the internal structure of individuals There is clearly no outside agency to enforce or test positive religious beliefs apart from some form of the Church, and with this analysis it is difficult to see how a highly 'individualized' person can have strong conventional religious beliefs. which are necessarily institutionalized. In another study by the present writer an open-ended question about attitude to the Church revealed lack of social support as a reason for developing an unfavourable attitude to the Church. This social basis of religious beliefs is confirmed by the absence of correlations with personality factors and the small but negative correlations (−0·34 to −0·21) between belief and age in this sample, which is however both homogeneous and young. It is therefore church membership and attitudinal acceptance of the Church, rather than personality variables, that are related to the strength of belief here. The relationship in older groups remains to be established.

The acquisition of religious beliefs may be explained by the operation of social learning and it might be possible to identify some critical social experiences among believers, as Witkin suggests in another context (quoted by Murphy, 1958). As religious beliefs are learned under conditions of inter-denominational rivalry with varying authorities quoted to support beliefs, and differing uses made of biblical authority, institutionalized religion frequently is inconsistent with liberal attitudes. It is a well-documented fact that more religious people tend to be less tolerant (Prothero and Jensen, 1950; Wilson, 1960) and the present analysis shows the same relationship. Argyle's (1958, p. 84) suggestion that it is not the genuinely devout, but the conventionally religious who are prejudiced is consistent with the present interpretation.

Religious certainty is unrelated to certainty about factual and opinionative matters in this study, while the relationship between anxiety and certainty about matters of opinion is similar to that reported by Rokeach, and also to Brengelmann's (1960) finding from very different material. Rokeach reports scores on dogmatism and anxiety correlating from 0·36 to 0·44 in various groups (1960, p. 364), and although the correlation between manifest anxiety and opinion strength in this study is +0·18, the factorial relationship is clearer than the correlation suggests. There is thus confirmation of a relationship between dogmatism and anxiety.

Ordinarily it would be expected that statements which cannot in principle be tested directly, such as the existence of 'such spiritual beings as angels' might be held less strongly than are statements which can be settled by reference to common-sense experience. However, the results show that these religious statements are held more strongly than the factual ones, perhaps to avoid the uncertainty which would necessarily follow from a weaker acceptance. The results also show that it is easier to be uncertain about a factual matter which can be settled, than to be uncertain about something which is literally a matter of belief; certainty about religious matters is possible because of the social support that can be evoked to sustain these beliefs. Anxiety plays a role in holding matters of opinion strongly, but not in matters of belief.

A cognitive theory of religious behaviour is suggested by this study, but as Argyle shows, there are other theories. The present cognitive interpretation can be extended to include affective components by drawing attention to the attachments to and arousal value of signs, symbols, objects and verbal formulations in any religious system. The function of these things is to maintain appropriate responses and so, for example, it is common for preachers to repeat well-known formulations, and particularly texts, for their arousal value, and not for their cognitive significance.

Appendix

The items of the attitude measures, measures of institutionalization and individualism and the enlarged Thouless questionnaire are grouped together in areas. The numbers in brackets refer to the order of items in the Thouless questionnaire set out in Table 2.

Authoritarianism

1. Obedience and respect for authority are the most important virtues children should learn.
2. No weakness or difficulty can hold us back if we have enough will power.
3. Every person should have complete faith in some supernatural power whose decisions he obeys without question.
4. What the youth needs most is strict discipline, rugged determination, and the will to work and fight for family and country.
5. Young people sometimes get rebellious ideas, but as they grow up they ought to get over them and settle down.
6. Sex crimes, such as rape and attacks on children, deserve more than mere imprisonment; such criminals ought to be publicly whipped, or worse.
7. People can be divided into two distinct classes: the weak and the strong.
8. There is hardly anything lower than a person who does not feel a great love, gratitude and respect for his parents.
9. If people would talk less and work more, everybody would be better off.
10. No sane, normal, decent person could ever think of hurting a close friend or relative.

Humanitarianism

1. The death penalty is barbaric and should be abolished.
2. The dropping of the first atomic bomb on a Japanese city, killing thousands of innocent women and children. was morally wrong and incompatible with the standards of a civilized community.
3. Women have a moral right to complete equality with men in every sphere of life.
4. The Australian aborigines should immediately be granted full citizenship rights and complete social equality, including equal opportunities for education and employment, equal wages, etc.
5. Bodily punishment should not be applied to prison inmates, regardless of their behaviour.
6. Regardless of provocation we should indulge in no brutality against enemy prisoners during time of war.
7. Under no circumstances whatever could a decision to make the first use of any nuclear or biological weapons be morally justified.
8. At the very least a quota of Asian migrants should be admitted to this country to demonstrate our goodwill towards our neighbours to the North.
9. Prostitutes should be regarded as victims of social circumstances who require assistance to become socially useful citizens.
10. Blood sports, such as fox hunting, greyhound racing with live hares, etc., are vicious and cruel and should be forbidden.

Institutionalization

1. The Church is necessary to establish and preserve concepts of right and wrong.
2. Every person needs to have the feeling of security given by a Church.
3. For the vast majority of people, in order to live a truly religious life, the Church or some such other organized religious body is an essential.
4. The aim of missionaries should be to establish church buildings where religious services and ceremonies can be conducted.

Individualism

1. A man ought to be guided by what his own experience tells him is right rather than by what any institution, such as the Church, tells him to do.

2. It is more important for an individual to understand the principles of his personal faith than to have a detailed knowledge of his own denomination.

3. Private devotions are more important in the religious life of a person than is attendance at public church services.

4. True Christianity is seen in the lives of individual men and women rather than in the activities of the Church.

Beliefs about Christ

1. (2) Jesus Christ was God the Son.
2. Jesus changed water into wine.
3. Jesus Christ was born of a Virgin.
4. Jesus walked upon the water while his disciples waited for him in their boat.

Beliefs about God

1. (1) There is a personal God.
2. (4) The world was created by God.
3. (7) There is a God who is all-powerful.
4. (8) There is a God who is altogether good.
5. God made man out of dust and breathed life into him.
6. (16) There is no God (personal or impersonal) (with scoring reversed).

Other orthodox Christian beliefs

1. (3) There are spiritual realities of some kind.
2. (5) There is a personal Devil.
3. (13) Evil is a reality.
4. (14) The spirits of human beings continue to exist after the death of their bodies.
5. (18) Attendance at church is a better way of spending Sunday than taking a walk in the country.

General religious belief

1. (6) Matter is the sole reality (with scoring reversed).
2. (9) There are such spiritual beings as angels.
3. (10) Jonah was swallowed by a great fish and afterwards emerged alive.
4. (20) Christianity is a better religion than Buddhism.
5. (21) The Bible is literally true in all its parts.

6. (23) There is a Hell in which the wicked will be everlastingly punished.
7. (25) Right will triumph.
8. There is no life after death (with scoring reversed).

Opinion

1. (15) Religion is the opium of the people.
2. (22) Man is, in some degree, responsible for his actions.
3. (27) Hardship strengthens character.
4. (32) Sex is evil.
5. (37) Members of the leisured class are supported by the 'surplus value' created by the workers.
6. (39) India has, on the whole, benefited from British rule.

Fact

1. (11) Man has been evolved from lower forms of life.
2. (17) The universe is expanding.
3. (19) Moses was the author of the first five books of the Bible.
4. (28) Mary, Queen of Scots, was beheaded between 1580 and 1590.
5. (30) Tigers are found in parts of China.
6. (31) Hornets live in nests under the ground.
7. (33) Light travels to us from the sun in less than one minute.
8. (34) Bacon was the author of the plays attributed to Shakespeare.
9. (35) Green is a primary colour.
10. (36) Sunlight is good for human health.
11. (38) Tariffs improve trade.
12. (40) The total national debt of Great Britain is more than a thousand million pounds.

Miscellaneous

1. (24) The spirits of persons who have died can sometimes communicate with the living.
2. (26) Belief in evolution is compatible with belief in a Creator.
3. (29) Everything is relative.
4. It makes no difference whether one is a Christian or not, so long as one has good will for others.
5. Salvation is only for Christian believers.
6. (12) There is an impersonal God.

References

ADORNO, T. W. *et al.* (1950), *The Authoritarian Personality*, Harper & Row.

ARGYLE, M. (1958), *Religious Behaviour*, Routledge & Kegan Paul.

BRENGELMANN, J. C. (1960), 'Learning and personality: IV. Certainty and output motivation', *Acta Psychol.*, vol. 17, pp. 326–56.

BROEN, W. E. (1957), 'A factor analytic study of religious attitudes', *J. abnorm. soc. Psychol.*, vol. 54, pp. 176–9.

COOMBS, C. H. (1950), 'Psychological scaling without a unit of measurement', *Psychol. Rev.*, vol. 57, pp. 145–8.

EYSENCK, H. J. (1958), 'A short questionnaire for the measurement of two dimensions of personality', *J. appl. Psychol.*, vol. 42, pp. 14–17.

FUNK, R. A. (1956), 'Religious attitudes and manifest anxiety in a college population' (abstract), *Amer. Psychol.*, vol. 11, p. 375.

JEEVES, M. A. (1959), 'Contributions on prejudice and religion', in Symposium on problems of religious psychology, *Proceedings of the 15th International Congress of Psychology, Brussels*, pp. 508–9, North Holland.

MURPHY, G. (1958), *Human Potentialities*, Basic Books.

PROTHERO, E. T., and JENSEN, J. A. (1950), 'Interrelations of religious and ethnic attitudes in selected southern populations', *J. soc. Psychol.*, vol. 32, pp. 45–9.

ROKEACH, M. (1960), *The Open and Closed Mind*, Basic Books.

SANAI, M. (1950), 'A factorial study of social attitudes', *J. soc. Psychol.*, vol. 31, pp. 167–82.

TAYLOR, J. A. (1953), 'A personality scale of manifest anxiety', *J. abnorm. soc. Psychol.*, vol. 48, pp. 285–90.

THOULESS, R. H. (1935), 'The tendency to certainty in religious belief', *Brit. J. Psychol.*, vol. 26, pp. 16–31.

THOULESS, R. H. (1959), 'Discussion of symposium: problems of religious psychology', *Proceedings of the 15th International Congress of Psychology*, 1957, North Holland.

WILSON, W. C. (1960), 'Extrinsic religious values and prejudice' *J. abnorm. soc. Psychol.*, vol. 60, pp. 286–8.

4 G. W. Allport

Traits Revisited

Excerpts from G. W. Allport, 'Traits revisited', *American Psychologist*, 1966, vol. 21, no. 1, pp. 5–7.

Many investigations show conclusively that on the broad average church attenders harbor more ethnic prejudice than nonattenders. (Some of the relevant studies are listed by Argyle, 1958, and by Wilson, 1960.) At the same time many ardent workers for civil rights are religiously motivated. From Christ to Gandhi and to Martin Luther King we note that equimindedness has been associated with religious devoutness. Here then is a paradox: religion makes prejudice; it also unmakes prejudice.

First we tackle the problem rationally and form a hypothesis to account for what seems to be a curvilinear relation. A hint for the needed hypothesis comes from Adorno *et al.* (1950) which suggests that acceptance of institutional religion is not as important as the *way* in which it is accepted. Argyle (1958) sharpens the hypothesis. He says, 'It is not the genuinely devout who are prejudiced but the conventionally religious (p. 84).'

In our own studies we have tentatively assumed that two contrasting but measurable forms of religious orientation exist. The first form we call the *extrinsic* orientation, meaning that for the churchgoer religious devotion is not a value in its own right, but is an instrumental value serving the motives of personal comfort, security, or social status. (One man said he went to church because it was the best place to sell insurance.) Elsewhere I have defined this utilitarian orientation toward religion more fully (Allport, 1960, 1963). Here I shall simply mention two items from our scale, agreement with which we assume indicates the extrinsic attitude: 'What religion offers me most is comfort when sorrows and misfortune strike'; 'One reason for my being a church member is that such membership helps to establish a person in the community.'

By contrast the *intrinsic* orientation regards faith as a supreme value in its own right Such faith strives to transcend self-centered needs, takes seriously the commandment of brotherhood that is found in all religions, and seeks a unification of being. Agreement with the following items indicates an intrinsic orientation: 'My religious beliefs are what really lie behind my whole approach to life'; 'If not prevented by unavoidable circumstances, I attend church, on the average (more than once a week) (once a week) (two or three times a month) (less than once a month).'

Table 1 **Correlations between measures of religious orientation among churchgoers and various prejudice scales**

Denominational sample	N	r
Unitarian	50	
Extrinsic – anti-Catholicism		0·56
Intrinsic – anti-Catholicism		−0·36
Extrinsic – anti-Mexican		0·54
Intrinsic – anti-Mexican		−0·42
Catholic	66	
Extrinsic – anti-Negro		0·36
Intrinsic – anti-Negro		−0·49
Nazarene	39	
Extrinsic – anti-Negro		0·41
Intrinsic – anti-Negro		−0·44
Mixed*	207	
Extrinsic – anti-semitic		0·65

*From Wilson (1960).

This second item is of considerable interest, for many studies have found that it is the irregular attenders who are by far the most prejudiced (e.g., Holtzmann, 1956; Williams, 1964). They take their religion in convenient doses and do not let it regulate their lives.

Now for a few illustrative results in Table 1. If we correlate the extrinsicness of orientation with various prejudice scales we find the hypothesis confirmed. Likewise, as predicted, intrinsicness of orientation is negatively correlated with prejudice.

In view of the difficulty of tapping the two complex traits in question, it is clear from these studies that our rationally derived hypothesis gains strong support. We note that the trend is the same when different denominations are studied in relation to differing targets for prejudice.

Previously I have said that empirical testing has the ability to correct or extend our rational analysis of patterns. In this particular research the following unexpected fact emerges. While those who approach the intrinsic pole of our continuum are on the average less prejudiced than those who approach the extrinsic pole, a number of subjects show themselves to be disconcertingly illogical. They accept both intrinsically worded items and extrinsically worded items, even when these are contradictory, such as: 'My religious beliefs are what really lie behind my whole approach to life'; 'Though I believe in my religion, I feel there are many more important things in my life.' It is necessary, therefore, to inspect this sizable group of muddleheads who refuse to conform to our neat religious logic. We call them 'inconsistently pro-religious'. They simply like religion; for them it has 'social desirability' (cf. Edwards, 1957).

The importance of recognizing this third mode of religious orientation is seen by comparing the prejudice scores for the groups presented in Table 2. In the instruments employed the lowest possible prejudice score is twelve, the highest possible, forty-eight. We note that the mean prejudice score rises steadily and significantly from the intrinsically consistent to the inconsistently pro-religious. Thus subjects with an undiscriminated pro-religious response set are on the average most prejudiced of all.

Having discovered the covariation of prejudice with both the extrinsic orientation and the 'pro' response set, we are faced with the task of rational explanation. One may, I think, properly argue that these particular religious attitudes are instrumental in nature;

Table 2 **Types of religious orientation and mean prejudice scores**

	Mean prejudice scores			
	Consistently intrinsic	Consistently extrinsic	Moderately inconsistent (pro-religion)	Extremely inconsistent (pro-religion)
Anti-Negro	28·7	33·0	35·4	37·9
Anti-semitic	22·6	24·6	28·0	30·1

Note: $N = 309$, mixed denominations. All differences significant at 0·01 level.

they provide safety, security, and status – all within a self-serving frame. Prejudice, we know, performs much the same function within some personalities. The needs for status, security, comfort and a feeling of self-rightness are served by both ethnic hostility and by tailoring one's religious orientation to one's convenience. The economy of other lives is precisely the reverse it is their religion that centers their existence, and the only ethnic attitude compatible with this intrinsic orientation is one of brotherhood, not of bigotry.

This work, along with the related investigations of Lenski (1963), Williams (1964), and others, signifies that we gain important insights when we refine our conception of the nature of the religious sentiment and its functions. Its patterning properties in the economy of a life are diverse. It can fuse with bigotry or with brotherhood according to its nature.

As unfinished business I must leave the problem of nonattenders. From data available it seems that the unchurched are less prejudiced on the average than either the extrinsic or the inconsistent churchgoers, although apparently more prejudiced on the average than those whose religious orientation is intrinsic. Why this should be so must form the topic of future research.

References

ADORNO, T. W., FRENKEL-BRUNSWIK, E., LEVINSON, D. J., and SANFORD, R. N. (1950), *The Authoritarian Personality*, Harper & Row.

ALLPORT, G. W. (1960), 'Religion and prejudice', in *Personality and Social Encounter*, Beacon Press, ch. 16.

ALLPORT, G. W. (1963), 'Behavioral science, religion and mental health', *J. Relig. Health*, vol. 2, pp. 187–97.

ARGYLE, M. (1958), *Religious Behaviour*, Routledge & Kegan Paul.

EDWARDS, A. L. (1957), *The Social Desirability Variable in Personality Assessment and Research*, Dryden Press.

HOLTZMAN, W. H. (1956), 'Attitudes of college men toward non-segregation in Texas schools', *Public Opinion Q.*, vol. 20, pp. 559–69.

LENSKI, G. (1963), *The Religious Factor*, Doubleday.

WILLIAMS, R. M., JR (1964), *Strangers Next Door*, Prentice-Hall.

WILSON, W. C. (1960), 'Extrinsic religious values and prejudice', *J. abnorm. soc. Psychol.*, vol. 60, pp. 286–8.

5 R. O. Allen and B. Spilka

Committed and Consensual Religion:
A Specification of Religious Prejudice Relationships

R. O. Allen and B. Spilka, 'Committed and consensual religion:
a specification of religious-prejudice relationships', *Journal for the
Scientific Study of Religion*, 1967, vol. 6, pp. 191–206.

Inspired by various motives, religious spokesmen have repeatedly
espoused noble and humanitarian ideals, wherein they extol the
virtues of brotherhood, proclaim the importance of the Golden
Rule and love to all mankind, and maintain that every person has
a dignity and an integrity which must be respected and safe-
guarded. However, the historical record shows that the gulf between ideals and practices has been wide. We have had human
slavery, pogroms, religious persecution, witch hunts, and discrimination based on different customs, beliefs, skin colors, and
national origins. Religion, which has been the repository of
man's highest ideals and which should be a deterrent to social
prejudice in reality seems to be a correlate to it. This is the
apparent paradox of religious belief. 'It is not confined to history. In milder but more personal form it exists in our daily lives'
(Rokeach, 1965, p. 9).

The cumulative evidence from empirical research regarding the
relation of religion and prejudice also attests to the discrepancy
between ideals and practices. although the results are not unequivocal.

Most of the studies have found a positive relationship; others
have reported that no correlation was present; while still others
have concluded that the findings were inconclusive or ambiguous.
For example, Adorno, Frenkel-Brunswik, Levinson and Sanford (1950), Allport and Kramer (1946), Frenkel-Brunswik and
Sanford (1945), Gough (1951), Jones (1958), Levinson and Sanford (1944), and Rosenblith (1949) have reported that people
who acknowledge church membership tend to be less tolerant
than those who do not, but other investigators like Evans (1952),
Harlan (1942), Martin and Nichols (1962), Parry (1949), Siegman
(1962), Tumin (1958), and Turbeville and Hyde (1946) found no
relationship among these variables or reported ambiguous and
inconclusive findings.

This syndrome appears to be exceedingly common, for many investigators show that, on the average, church goers and professedly religious people have considerably more prejudice than do non-church goers and non-believers. . . . Still there are many cases where [church influence] is precisely in the reverse direction. . . . The role of religion is paradoxical. It makes prejudice and it unmakes prejudice (Allport, 1959, p. 8; 1954, pp. 444, 420).

Argyle (1959) provides a similar summary.

Some of the empirical studies have indicated that prejudiced and unprejudiced religious persons may be distinguished by distinct *types* of religious beliefs, attitudes and behaviors. Martin and Nichols (1962) found that religious subjects 'low' on religious information were more prejudiced than those 'high' on the same scale. Bettelheim and Janowitz (1949) reported that veterans with stable religious convictions, which they define as internalization of the central teachings, tended to be more tolerant. In his volume on prejudice, Allport (1954) reported a study in which 'those who were considered the most devout, more personally absorbed in their religion; were far less prejudiced than the others' (p. 421). He then distinguished an institutionalized and an interiorized religious outlook, postulated to be differentially associated with prejudice. Spilka (1958) found partial support for this theory. Later Allport (1959) revised this conception to what he termed intrinsic and extrinsic religious orientations. Assessing the extrinsic orientation with a specially devised scale, Wilson (1960) reported substantial correlations with the E-scale. Friedrichs (1959) found that members of religious study groups were more tolerant than members of governing boards or Sunday-school teachers and that persons attending more than sixty services in a year exhibited greater tolerance than those who attended less than ten times. Those whose church activity beyond worship was limited to church societies were the least tolerant.

Contradictions – such as the independence of religion and humanitarianism (Kirkpatrick, 1949), of religiousness and stand on social issues (Ferguson, 1939), of religion as man's relation to deity and as church ritual and practices (Allen and Hites, 1961) and of religion and morals (Sanai, 1952) – also suggest that prejudice is associated with different kinds of religious belief and behavior.

Difficulties in previous research
Crude measures

A major source of confusion and possible overgeneralization in some of the previous research may be the use of rather limited religious categories. Studies which define religiosity simply in terms of religious affiliation, membership or denominational preference reveal little regarding the way religion and prejudice may be coordinated within the individual. Some of the equivocality evidenced in relating the research literature may well be due principally to the use of such gross, single indices of religiousness. So long as research concern is focused on whether people accept or reject religion, whether or not they are affiliated with or prefer respective denominations, whether or not they 'believe in God' or even subscribe to particular theological doctrines, then the way in which the various elements of the belief system are organized is not of major concern. But, to understand individual expression and orientation, it is important to specify ways by which private, individual beliefs are focused and organized. If we are to understand how an individual is both religious and prejudiced, or religious and not prejudiced, it would seem necessary to index religion more comprehensively.

Whether or not an individual prays daily or only at times of stress, possesses more or less religious information, joins different kinds of clubs or societies, attends church regularly or irregularly are assuredly important observations. But they do not reveal the functional role these observable differences have for the individual. nor do they indicate the reason for the differential relation to prejudiced attitudes and discriminatory practices. Conclusions from some of the early work in this area tend to corroborate this criticism. Sanford and Levinson (1948) related E-scale scores to religious and denominational preferences, frequency of church attendance. and responses to open-end questions regarding the importance of religion and the church. They concluded that such gross objective factors were less significant than certain psychological trends reflected in the individual's religious ideology. Adorno *et al.* (1950) also suggested that acceptance or rejection of religion is not as important as the way in which it is accepted or rejected and the particular meanings it has for the individual. It would seem that insight into the religious-prejudice syndrome would necessitate something more than simply a cataloging of stereotyped beliefs and a listing of socially acceptable affiliations, memberships, and attendances.

Contradicting dichotomies

Another difficulty with some of the previous research lies in possible contradictions as to the content of the religious belief systems postulated to be differentially associated with prejudice. Several bi-polar religious orientations have been proposed. For example, Fromm (1941) has discussed authoritarian and humanistic religious frameworks, while a recent factor analytic study (Broen, 1957) reported evidence for a fundamentalism–humanitarianism factor. While Bettelheim and Janowitz (1949) present evidence for 'stable' and 'unstable' religious convictions, Woodruff (1945) distinguished a 'higher' and a 'lower' value system. Lenski (1961), in his careful study of religion in a Mid-West city, differentiated a conventional and a devotional orientation to religion, and Allen and Hites (1961) categorized religion as a personal relation to deity versus an emphasis on religious rites and practices, while Adorno *et al.* (1950) earlier distinguished between a religion which is conventional, externalized and neutralized and one that is more personal and internalized. Allport's distinctions have been mentioned above. It may be that the differences and contradictions in the manifest content of the previous bi-polar distinctions can be amalgamated through a conceptual scheme which emphasizes the way the individual focuses and organizes his belief system. Stylistic variations, rather than distinctions in belief content or religious behaviors, may reveal distinctive functions.

Undue emphasis on pathology

A more subtle difficulty is seen in some of the previous research is the implicit tie to pathological considerations. It is tempting to explain prejudicial attitudes and a kind of religion associated with such attitudes by reference to pathological dynamics and expressions and related value judgements. Reference to the distinctions between intrinsic and extrinsic orientations would appear to illustrate this temptation.

Extrinsic religion is a self-serving, utilitarian, self-protective form of religious outlook, which provides the believer with comfort and salvation at the expense of outgroups. *Intrinsic* religion marks the life that has interiorized the total creed of his faith without reservation, including the commandment to love one's neighbour. A person of this sort is more interested in serving his religion than in making it serve him. In many lives, both strands are found; the result is inner conflict, with prejudice and tolerance competing for the upper hand (Allport, 1960, p. 257).

An understanding of religious-prejudice attitudes admittedly must consider possible pathological correlates and utilitarian–altruistic contrasts, but to anchor the religious-prejudice syndrome in such attributes or to overemphasize pathological sympto-matology seems unduly restrictive. Research has demonstrated that most prejudicial attitudes tend to be adopted and continued according to the prevailing social climate. 'No pathology or aggression or repression (or conflict) is involved. These beliefs of racial prejudice, however, direct much of our comings and goings and may be found among the gentlest . . . and best adapted people' (Krech and Crutchfield, 1948, p. 427). It would seem reasonable that a bi-polar focus perhaps could be more com-pletely realized by recognizing that religious beliefs and practices, as well as prejudicial attitudes and practices, are socially condi-tioned and supported. Thus they may be articulated in normal terms and need not rely exclusively on pathological variables.

Confounding intensity and types

One final difficulty in coordinating the previous research litera-ture concerns possible confounding of differences in the degree of 'religiousness' with the dichotomization of religious belief and behavior. We may be simply sorting between more and less religious persons rather than isolating kinds of religiosity among equally religious persons. This distinction is not clear in most of the previous research, where such possible confounding has led to the apparent ambiguities. It would seem important that future research provide a reasonable assurance that the subjects classi-fied dichotomously are, within certain practical limits, 'equally religious'.

Implications for this research

While it is not possible to articulate definitively many of the dimensional relationships between religion and prejudice, it seemed reasonable, on the basis of the reported literature on both religion and prejudice to specify some of the pertinent social psychological variables which appear to be involved in the appar-ent religious-prejudice paradox. At the current stage of the development of research in this area it appears possible to postulate those aspects of personal religion which might be susceptible to stylistic variation.

Where previous research has employed group affiliation, preference and interest indices, belief content, particular religious practices, pathological components, or personality characteristics, our research has taken a somewhat different approach. We have focused on the expressive aspects of beliefs by emphasizing the way the individual himself formulates and structures his religious beliefs. To understand individual expression and orientation, it is important to specify ways by which private, individual beliefs are focused and organized. To probe behind the facade of relatively stereotyped belief to the individual mode of expression seemed a promising, though intricate. approach to a substantive rationale regarding differential religious orientations. It does seem important to capture for research scrutiny the way the individual himself formulates or structures his religious beliefs. Continuing research must also attempt to consider both individual and social factors. For this reason, the writers placed an emphasis on the 'texture' of a person's expectations and beliefs, which can be assumed to have developed through the normal socialization process and which may well reflect socially sanctioned behavior tendencies and expressions.

Consequently, this study was directed toward determining the particular styles of religious belief and behavior which might differentiate between religious persons high in social prejudice and religious persons low in prejudice. Dichotomous cognitive orientations were postulated and then characterized as reflecting a 'committed' and a 'consensual' style of religiosity. Since the primary concern here was with selected differences in the cognitive components of religion, these orientations led us to focus on the way the individual formulates, structures and organizes his religious beliefs, thus emphasizing aspects of personal religion which might be susceptible to stylistic variation.

It was hypothesized that religious-prejudiced subjects would express a consensual orientation and that religious-unprejudiced subjects would evidence a committed orientation to religion as well as reveal a differentiable pattern of religious and social outlooks. The procedure for testing these hypotheses involved coded responses from a standardized interview and a number of specific expectations with reference to several quantitative measures of religious attitudes and social opinion.

Procedure

The materials for this study included a personal data sheet, eight measures of religion, six measures of social opinion, a semi-structured interview, and a set of interview coding categories to distinguish the committed and consensual religious orientations.

The personal data sheet included such standard information as age, sex, year in school, academic major, religious affiliation, denominational preference, and certain other ad hoc questions concerning church attendance and religious belief.

Measures of religiosity

Frequency of church attendance (FCA). Subjects reported the typical frequency of attending church and church affiliated activities. The seven categories were: never; one or two times a year; five or six times a year (bi-monthly); one or two times a month; once a week; two or three times a week; four or more times a week.

Rated importance of religion (RIR). Subjects were requested to 'estimate the extent to which you feel religion is important in your life today' along an eight-point continuum where one was anchored as 'extremely important' and eight as 'not at all important'.

Importance of religion (IR). This Likert-type scale is one of three constructed to measure an ideological dimension of religious belief (Putney and Middleton, 1961). The authors state that the scale reflects 'the degree of which convictions about religion are felt to be a central and essential element of the self' (p. 286).

Religious identity (RI). This was an ad hoc scale on which the Ss checked whether 'I consider myself to be: very religious, quite religious, moderately religious, not very religious, not at all religious.' It scored one to five, respectively.

Attitude toward the church scale (ATC). This forty-five-item equal-appearing-interval scale devised by Thurstone and Chave (1929) has had wide acceptance as a measure of religiosity. For purposes of this study, the lower the score, the more favorable the attitude toward religion (Chave, 1935).

Religious individualism (RID). The four items on this scale 'emphasize an individual's own judgements made independently of an external authority, rather than internalized acceptance of a point of view' (Brown, 1962, p. 261). The scale correlates inversely with orthodoxy belief scales and not at all with humanitarianism or authoritarianism (Brown, 1962).

Religious institutionalization (RIS). The four items composing this scale entail a high evaluation of the Church as a formal organization. A person strongly agreeing with them all accepts the Church as a primary point of reference in religious matters (Brown, 1962). This instrument correlates significantly with anti-semitism (Jeeves, 1959) and with authoritarianism, but not with humanitarianism (Brown, 1962).

Extrinsic religious values scale (ERV). This instrument was designed to reflect the ideas of Allport (1959) regarding an extrinsic religious orientation and has provided significant correlations with anti-semitism. The scale is composed of fifteen dichotomous forced choice items reflecting an allegiance to, and dependence upon, the external or institutional structure of the Church as well as a utilitarian orientation toward religion (Wilson, 1960).

Measures of social opinion

Prejudice scale (P). This is a ten-item scale measuring prejudicial attitudes toward ethnic, national and racial groups in general. It was designed to eliminate some of the criticism directed toward the California E-scale, namely, the stress on specific ethnic groups. The P-scale was factorially constructed and each item assigned a weight in proportion to its loading on the general factor I from Struening's (1963) study. 'Work with this scale has shown that ... [the] weights and items demonstrate good factorial invariance' (Spilka and Reynolds, 1965). Since it is not widely known and since it provides the operational definition of prejudice for this study, sample items may be helpful: 'Pupils of all races and nationalities should attend school together everywhere in this country.' 'There are people of some races and nationalities who are by nature less capable of advancement.' 'People of different races and nationalities should be allowed to live in the same neighborhoods.'

World-mindedness scale (W). This instrument was devised to assess 'a frame of reference, or value orientation, favoring a world view of the problems of humanity, with mankind, rather than the nationals of a particular country, as the primary reference group' (Sampson and Smith, 1957, p. 105). Research with the instrument has indicated inverse relationships with authoritarianism and ethnocentrism. The use of this scale in the present study provides a validity check on the P-scale, which was used as a criterion measure of prejudicial attitudes.

Alienation scales. A recrudescence of interest in the concept of alienation and the reported correlations with apathy, authoritarianism, conformity, and prejudice led to the selection of the twenty-four-item bi-polar scale developed by Dean (1950). This instrument measures three sub-types of alienation. The first represents *Powerlessness* (Po), which is characterized as a feeling of helplessness or a loss of a feeling of effective control over one's destiny, or of being used for purposes other than one's own. The second is presented as *Normlessness* (Nr), which may be either a lack of clear norms and values that might give purpose or direction to life or it may also reflect conflict among norms such as the standards of Christianity and the success imperative of our culture. The third sub-dimension, *Social Isolation* (SI), is conceptualized as the perception of losing effective contact with significant and supporting groups.

Social desirability scale (S D S). The Crowne and Marlow (1960) instrument was selected to assess the influence of social desirability response sets, and to provide an indication of possible differential 'social approval' motivations.

Interview schedule

A standardized interviewing procedure was selected as the main means for collecting data to test the proposed committed and consensual analytic schema. The lack of available instruments by which an assessment of cognitive components could be made necessitated the use of an exploratory interview technique. A number of writers (Bettelheim and Janowitz, 1950; Selltiz, Jahoda, Deutsch and Cook, 1963; Smith, Bruner and White, 1956) have attested to the fruitfulness of such techniques even though they lack the precision and many of the quantitative advantages of more widely employed, objective research techniques.

The interview used here followed a semi-structured or open-end question form with the questions centering around typical belief-content areas such as God, prayer, Bible, church, faith, etc. Considerable attention was given to question phrasing, incorporating specific suggestions of those whose major research efforts have utilized interviewing procedures.[1] The questions were pretested for clarity, meaningfulness, and subject comprehension with a group of volunteer college students prior to the initiation of data collection for this study.

Selection of subjects

The personal data sheet and the various quantitative measures were assembled into a single questionnaire and administered to a total sample of 497 college students enrolled in introductory psychology courses at Colorado State University. To assure a more homogeneous ideological focus and to provide a reasonably consistent theological framework, a sample of 335 Protestant subjects was first determined by including those who had checked the Protestant identification (preference) item of the personal data sheet and had also completed all the questionnaire scales.

Equal degree of religiosity. Since the central hypothesis of this study implies differential religious belief structures, it was important that the Ss to be classified as holding a committed or consensual religiosity were within certain practical limits, 'equally religious'. At least some assurance that we were in fact dealing with 'religious' subjects seemed necessary. Even though individual differences in degrees of commitment to religion may remain, the restriction in the range of religiousness may ameliorate possible confounding with kinds of religiosity. A set of criteria was devised by which the subjects could be operationally defined as 'religious'. These were: (1) the rated importance of religion; (2) frequency of church attendance; (3) religious identity; and (4) the Attitude towards the church scale. A multiple cut-off

1. The specific suggestions regarding question phraseology summarized by Maccoby and Maccoby (1954) proved helpful. For example, they suggest asking questions in terms of the respondent's own immediate experience, rather than in terms of generalities (such as, 'Think back to the last time ... etc.'), and phrasing questions so as to minimize ego defences (such as, 'Some feel that.... Others feel that.... How do you feel about ... etc.?'). Smith, Bruner and White (1956) utilized what they term 'apperception questions' with apparent success, e.g. they gave a conventional or popular phrase or statement and then asked what the subject made of it or what it meant to him. Another technique adopted was suggested by Kinsey, Pomeroy and Martin (1948), wherein by assuming a 'low value' attitude on the part of the respondent, the burden of denial or the framework for response is placed on the subject; for example, 'What do you feel is the main difference between Christians and other people?'

procedure was followed.[2] This yielded a 'Religious Group' of 210 subjects.

High and low prejudiced Ss. Using an array of the Prejudice scale scores for the 210 Religious Group Ss extreme high and low scoring individuals were selected by counting from each end of the P-scale distribution. Seventy-three subjects were thus selected. All but two of these individuals were subsequently interviewed individually following the standard interview schedule. Ten of these seventy-one subjects were randomly selected to provide empirical anchorage and refinement of the coding category system but were not used in the analysis of the data.

The remaining sixty-one Ss composed a religious-prejudiced group ($N=29$) and a religious-unprejudiced group ($N=32$). Note that these subjects were selected first because they scored above critical values on the religious criterion measures (thus operationally defined as religious) and then because they were high and low scorers on the Prejudice measure (thus considered prejudiced or unprejudiced).

Interviews. All seventy-one interviews were tape recorded. The interviews demonstrated what was regarded as excellent rapport, and extremely personal, straightforward responses were secured. The interviews varied in length from thirty minutes to an hour, with most being completed in approximately forty-five minutes. Precautions were taken to insure that neither the interviewer nor the raters would know the prejudice scores or the religious scale responses. All interviewing was completed during a four-week period of time by the principal investigator.

Classifying subjects as to committed or consensual religiosity

Five cognitive components of the hypothesized 'committed' and 'consensual' orientations were specified: content, clarity, complexity, flexibility and importance. The taxonomy for the defini-

2. Those individuals who reported they attended less than five or six times a year were first eliminated from the sample. The cut-off on the eight-point scale reflecting the rated importance of religion was set to eliminate those who checked positions six, seven or eight. On the Religious identity measure, those individuals who considered themselves to be very, quite or moderately religious were included in the Religious Group. The cut-off score on the Attitude toward the church scale was set one standard deviation above the mean (low scores reflect more favorable attitudes). All individuals whose score on the ATC scale was equal to or less than 12·5 were therefore included in the Religious Group.

tion of committed and consensual religion is presented in Table 1.

The tape-recorded response protocol of each subject was judged by tallying each response indicative of the defining category. These tabulations were then summarized and the individuals classified as 'committed' or 'consensual' on the basis of total tabulations across all components and for each component (content, clarity, complexity, flexibility. and importance). The interviewer served as rater on all the recorded interview protocols.

Reliability. Four other members of the psychology faculty served as raters to determine the reliability of the classification procedure. A four-hour training session was conducted by the principal investigator to explain and illustrate the consensual and committed orientations. Each item of the category system was discussed. and excerpts from the ten practice interview tapes were used to illustrate the categories and to provide practice in coding responses.

Seven interviews were then randomly selected from the combined R-P, R-UP groups and independently coded by the raters. Neither the interviewer-rater nor the four raters were aware of the prejudicial scores, the religiosity scale responses, or the R-P, R-UP group membership of any of the Ss, thus lessening the possibility of systematic bias of the rating procedure.

Inter-rater reliabilities were determined for the five variables (content, complexity, clarity, flexibility, importance) and for the total following the procedure outlined by Smith and Rosen (1960). A classification of either committed or consensual by each of the five raters for all seven subjects provides seventy possible comparisons for each cognitive component and for the summarized total, a total of 420 possible comparisons. There was agreement on 362, or 86 per cent of these. There was 88 per cent agreement for the complexity, importance and total components, 83 per cent for clarity, and 77 per cent agreement for the content and flexibility components. Utilizing an analysis of variance technique the estimated reliability coefficient across categories was 0·93.

Table 1 **Interview coding categories**

Cognitive Specification of the Committed and the Consensual Religious Orientations

Committed	Consensual

Content

Refers to the way the individual conceptualizes the topic area.

Abstract-Relational: Religiosity seems to be largely anchored in abstract principles, intangible ideas, and relational expressions. There is use of general categories, philosophical notions or formulated theology.	*Concrete-Literal:* Religiosity seems to be rooted in concrete, tangible, specific or literal statements and judgements. Practical, observable referents and concrete, graspable images used in preference to more philosophical ideas.

Clarity

Refers to the precision and coherent structure of the beliefs of the individual. The relative ability to perceive meaning and implications clearly.

Discerning: Tends to order religious concepts and to express ideas in a discerning manner, using non-ambiguous referents and relatively clear word choices. Answers to questions or discussion of topics are clear and exact in meaning and reference.	*Vague:* Tends to give non-referential or routine answers, apparently preferring to make vague generalizations and allusions about specific religious topics. Discussion of topics is vague, obscure, unclear, or indistinct in meaning and reference. Makes use of amorphous, subjective impressions.

Committed	Consensual

Complexity

Refers to the number of categories, elements, or aspects of religiosity which the individual uses. The degree to which there is a differentiation among and between various aspects of religion.

Differentiated: Religiosity tends to be composed of a relatively large number of categories or elements. Distinguishes and delineates a number of different parts, attributes, characteristics and functions. Ideas tend to be multiple rather than simple, global or overgeneralized. Religious categories may form a number of differentiated clusters.	*Monopolistic-Dichotomous*: Religiosity is composed of a relatively small number of categories or elements. Ideas tend to be typologized and global. *Monopolistic*: Religiosity tends to be composed primarily of a single category. May make repeated reference to a single concept. *Dichotomous*: Discussion reflects a tendency to use bifurcated categories and to think in terms of diametrical opposites. Language seems to be based on bi-polar ideas and 'two-valued' judgements.

Flexibility

Refers to the adaptable or accommodating quality of ideas, beliefs or attitudes when the individual compares his beliefs with others' or his own belief–disbelief components.

Candid-Open: A relatively greater tolerance for diversity. *Candid*: A frank, straightforward approach to the evaluation of similar or different ideas and practices. Discussion may evidence a 'testing' or conformance of expressed ideas both with deeper and more general values and with available information. *Open*: A tendency to examine or thoughtfully consider different opinions, beliefs or feelings. Relatively accessible or open to differing ideas and beliefs.	*Restrictive*: Relatively inaccessible or closed to differing ideas. *Non-accessible*: Tends to restrict admissability of different beliefs or practices. Apparently tries to narrow or encapsulate religiosity by rejection, distortion, or a 'screening out' of different ideas and practices. *Constrictive*: Refers to an apparent attempt to restrict or constrict diversity within their own beliefs. Discussion may evidence an 'insistence' on appropriate ideas, proper behavior, 'right' beliefs or esoteric feelings.

Table 1 – continued

Committed	Consensual

Importance

Refers to the strength, importance or value of religious beliefs in the everyday functioning of the individual. The extent to which religiosity is central in, or relative to, the everyday concerns of the individual.

Relevant: Religiosity is a matter of personal concern and central attention. There is an emotional commitment to religious ideas, ideals, and values. Ideals and values incorporated in the religious beliefs seem to account for or be relevant to daily activities.

Detached-Neutralized: *Detached Ideological Form;* Religion is considered thoroughly important, but is mainly severed from substantial individual experience or emotional commitment. Ideals remain abstracted from specific behavior and rarely realistically influence daily activities. *Detached Affect*: Religion is primarily an emotional 'clinging' or over-dependency. A magical or encapsulated feeling tone which is not meaningfully related to daily activities. *Neutralized*: The importance of religion is neutralized, reduced or rendered ineffectual by other concerns or by lack of positive affect and identification. There may be an unrestrained admiration for religious ideals or ideas which are selectively neutralized or attenuated by use of exceptions or diffusions.

The information from the personal data sheet showed that the college in which students are enrolled, the year in school, age and sex were not notably different for the two groups. Nor does there appear to be a significant difference between the two groups in denominational preference or in whether or not the students are members of a religious club. This would suggest that campus religious clubs and various Protestant denominations do not provide differential influences or associational attraction with respect to the dichotomous religious orientations as here defined.

Table 2 Committed and consensual religious orientations and
Religious-Prejudiced and Religious-Unprejudiced classification

Component	Religious-Prejudiced $N = 29$	Religious-Unprejudiced $N = 32$	χ^2	Contingency Coefficient[a]
Total:				
Committed	2	18		
Consensual	27	14	14·65**	0·44
Content:				
Committed	5	18		
Consensual	24	14	8·26**	0·35
Clarity:				
Committed	3	12		
Consensual	26	20	4·67*	0·27
Complexity:				
Committed	4	14		
Consensual	25	18	5·20*	0·28
Flexibility:				
Committed	4	17		
Consensual	25	15	8·76**	0·35
Importance:				
Committed	3	16		
Consensual	26	16	9·38**	0·36

[a]Upper limit of contingency coefficient $= 0·71$.
*$p < 0·05$.
**$p < 0·01$.

Table 3 presents the means of the questionnaire scales for the
Ss classified as Committed (Cm) or Consensual (Cs). The Cm
attend church more frequently. Comparing those who attend
once a week with those who attend one or two times a month, we
noted that the Cm are significantly more apt to attend at least
once a week ($\chi^2 = 15·01$, $p > 0·01$). Another item from the personal data sheet asked the subjects to say whether they considered
themselves to be faithful, regular, fairly regular or casual attenders; the Cm are more likely ($\chi^2 = 7·43$; $p > 0·01$) to consider
themselves faithful or regular attenders

Since the Committed–Consensual classification evidences differential association with prejudice, it would seem that these differences with respect to church attendance support the conclusions
from previous research that the 'regular and devout church
attenders tend to be less prejudiced' (Argyle, 1959, p. 85). How-

Table 3 Comparison of committed and consensual groups on the major religious variables and social opinion measures

Variable[a]	Committed Mean	SD	Consensual Mean	SD	t
FCA	5·0	0·56	4·3	0·78	4·01**
RIR	2·2	1·16	2·7	1·40	1·41
RI	2·4	0·61	2·8	0·50	2·69**
ATC	6·0	1·87	7·5	1·98	2·83**
RID	21·7	4·22	21·2	3·29	0·50
RIS	18·1	2·75	17·0	4·95	1·11
IR	36·8	4·47	32·7	6·06	2·95**
ERV	5·8	1·80	5·6	2·23	0·39
P	7·7	13·09	35·9	27·61	5·41**
W	121·6	17·82	94·3	22·79	4·89**
Po	20·3	3·59	21·2	3·77	0·86
Nr	13·8	4·88	14·9	4·33	0·80
SI	20·2	5·69	21·5	5·38	0·83
SDS	13·7	5·23	13·1	5·74	0·41

**$p < 0.01$.
[a]See abbreviations given in procedure section.

ever, results from some other analyses made but not reported in detail here, indicated that the Religious-Prejudiced and Religious-Unprejudiced groups are not significantly different with respect to church attendance. It would seem that church attendance *per se* is not as important as the meanings of attendance to the individuals involved. To the extent that the committed orientation reflects an attitude that religion is a 'matter of personal concern and central attention' and the consensual orientation reflects an attitude where religious practices are 'neutralized and attenuated by other concerns' (see importance component), church attendance, both in terms of reported attendance and self-perception of attendance, will be differentially associated with prejudice.

As also seen in Table 3, the Committed group consider themselves to be more religious than the Consensual ($t = 2·69$) according to the Religious identity scale. When these responses are viewed in terms of the actual categories, ten of the Cm consider themselves very or quite religious and ten consider themselves moderately religious, whereas only five of the Cs consider themselves very or quite religious and thirty-six consider themselves moderately religious ($\chi^2 = 8·42, p > 0·01$). These data tend to validate the Committed–Consensual classification. The committed report that religion as a 'way of life' is more important than do those subjects presenting a consensual orientation to religion.

Similarly validating is the significant difference for the six-item importance of religion scale, which asked about religion in terms of 'self-concept and way of life'. When the subjects merely rated the importance of 'religion', providing their own meaning to the term, as with the one-item Rated importance of religion scale, no differences were evidenced.

Our data do not suport the findings of Wilson (1960). The extrinsic religious values scale does not differentiate between individuals holding a committed or consensual orientation. where the consensual orientation would appear to parallel the extrinsic religious orientation proposed by Allport (1959) and measured by Wilson. This further suggests either that the consensual and extrinsic orientations differ or, more likely, that the E R V scale does not adequately distinguish religious individuals who admit to prejudicial attitudes from those who do not. This latter interpretation gains support from the practical failure of this instrument to distinguish significantly between the upper and lower 27 per cent of the total Protestant sample on the P-scale or between the Religious-Prejudiced and Religious-Unprejudiced groups.

The Religious individualism and the Religious institutionalization scales failed to separate the Committed and Consensual groups, as was expected from the previous research and theorizing of Brown (1962). The precise nature of the R I scale, although purportedly emphasizing independence of religious judgement, seems ambiguous. Since the R I S scale purportedly involves 'a high evaluation of the Church as a formal organization' (Brown, 1962, p. 261), the possibility exists that individuals could hold such an opinion of the Church for different reasons. Examination of the items tentatively suggests 'external anchorage or social identity' for the Consensual and 'social-contribution and shared activity' for the Committed, although it should be noted that this is largely speculative. It does seem clear, however, that there are real differences in the attitude toward the Church as revealed by the A T C and F C A scales and by the self-view of church attendance. The ambiguity with the R I S scale highlights the need for additional research on 'perception of the Church'.

Turning now to the social opinion variables, the Consensual subjects scored significantly higher on the Prejudice scale, and lower on the World-mindedness scale, again supporting the hypothesis that a consensual orientation to religion will accommodate ethnocentrism while those holding a committed orientation will tend to be unprejudiced and to present 'a frame of reference, or value orientation, favoring a world view of the problems of humanity, with mankind, rather than the nationals of a particular country, as the primary reference group' (Sampson and Smith, 1957, p.105).

Factor analysis of items

In the larger study, of which this report is a part, a factor analysis of selected tests was conducted with the 335 Protestant subjects to provide additional data and help clarify some of the ambiguous findings. The failure of the measure of extrinsic religion to distinguish among subjects holding prejudicial attitudes, the lack of conceptual and empirical clarity with the alienation scale responses, and the apparent differences in importance of the two religion measures suggested the potential utility of examining the items from these instruments in greater detail. The correlations among the items from the Extrinsic religious values scale, the three alienation scales, the two Importance of religion scales, and the Prejudice scale resulted in a 62×62 intercorrelation matrix which was factored by the principal components method. Rotation of ten theoretically meaningful factors, which accounted for 70 per cent of the total variance. was accomplished by means of the varimax procedure. Factor loadings above 0·30 were used in interpreting the obtained factors which were named and described from an examination of the manifest content. Questionnaires for the Committed and Consensual subjects were rescored and compared with respect to five of these factor-derived scales. Table 4 presents these data.

Table 4 Comparison of the Committed and Consensual groups with the factorially developed scales

| | Committed | | Consensual | | |
Variable	Mean	SD	Mean	SD	t
Religious certitude	47·1	6·45	41·7	7·60	2·87**
Meaninglessness	16·5	3·44	19·0	4·45	2·41*
Extrinsic Religiosity	1·4	0·86	1·8	1·07	1·30
Religious Dependency	10·9	3·21	10·7	2·89	0·26
Trust-Mistrust	12·5	1·60	16·0	5·32	3·84**

*$p < 0.05$.   **$p < 0.01$.

The statistically significant difference between Committed and Consensual groups with Factor 1, *religious certitude*, indicates that those holding a committed religious orientation evidence a certainty about a religion which is more individually authentic, personalized and salient to daily activities and religious practices. By comparison, those holding a consensual religious orientation tend to lack assurance regarding the importance and authentic nature of an interiorized, integrative religious outlook which has ultimate importance in their life and daily activities.

Differences in *meaninglessness* would imply that those holding a consensual orientation to religion have a greater tendency to express ideas reflecting a lack of personal worth or meaningfulness, and a loss of self-determination or adequacy. In other words, by agreeing with these items they may feel that their ideas, values or abilities are not meaningful to others or the social world. The *trust–mistrust* scale differences suggest that the Consensual group agrees with statements reflecting a view that the world is not a safe and dependable place and that standards of behavior and other people are not to be trusted, with consequent feelings of confusion and doubt regarding what is to be believed or trusted. By contrast the Committed Ss tend to reject items reflecting these perceptions of the self and the world. There do not appear to be any important differences between the mean scores for *extrinsic religiosity* or *religious dependency*.

Conclusion

The attempt to specify empirically selected cognitive dimensions of the relationship between religion and prejudice has provided evidence for at least two kinds of personal religion which are differentially associated with prejudice. We have seen that consensual religiosity is tied to prejudicial attitudes, and a typologized, concretistic, restrictive outlook on religion. While verbally conforming to 'traditional' values and ideals, these are vague, non-differentiated, bifurcated and neutralized or selectively adopted. In contrast, Committed Religiosity utilizes an abstract, philosophical perspective; multiplex religious ideas are relatively clear in meaning and an open and flexible framework of commitment meaningfully relates religion to daily activities. Thus tentatively it has been demonstrated that the institutional domain of religion as individually structured can be meaningfully and consistently interrelated to other social frameworks. It may be recommended that the conceptions of committed and consensual religious orientations be included among the theoretical constructs which attempt to tie the individual, his social behavior and the institutional complex of religion together.

References

ADORNO, T. W., FRENKEL-BRUNSWIK, LEVINSON, D. J., and SANFORD, R. N. (1950), *The Authoritarian Personality*, Harper & Row.

ALLEN, E. E., and HITES, R. W. (1961), 'Factors in religious attitudes of older adolescents', *J. soc. Psychol.*, vol. 55, pp. 265–73.

ALLPORT G. W. (1954), *The Nature of Prejudice*, Doubleday.

ALLPORT, G. W. (1959), 'Religion and prejudice', *Crane Rev.*, vol. 2, pp. 1–10.

ALLPORT, G. W. (1960), *Personality and Social Encounter*, Beacon Press.

ALLPORT, G. W., and KRAMER, B. M. (1946), 'Some roots of prejudice', *J. Psychol.*, vol. 22, pp. 9–39.

ARGYLE, M. (1959), *Religious Behavior*, Free Press.

BETTELHEIM, B., and JANOWITZ, M. (1949), 'Ethnic tolerance: a function of social and personal control', *Amer. J. Soc.*, vol. 55, pp. 137–45.

BETTELHEIM, B., and JANOWITZ, M. (1950), *Dynamics of Prejudice*, Harper & Row.

BROEN, W. E., Jr (1957), 'A factor-analytic study of religious attitudes', *J. abnorm. soc. Psychol.*, vol. 54, pp. 176–9.

BROWN, L. B. (1962), 'A study of religious belief', *Brit. J. Psychol.*, vol. 53, pp. 259–72.

CHAVE, E. J. (1935), *Measure Religion*, University of Chicago Press.

CROWNE, D. P., and MARLOWE, D. (1960), 'A new scale of social desirability independent of psychopathology', *J. consult. Psychol.*, vol. 24, pp. 349–54.

DEAN, D. G. (1960), 'Alienation and political apathy', *Soc. Forces*, vol. 38, pp. 185–9.

DEAN, D. G. (1961), 'Alienation: its meaning and measurement', *Amer. sociol. Rev.*, vol. 26, pp. 753–8.

EVANS, R. I. (1952), 'Personal values as factors in anti-Semitism', *J. abnorm. soc. Psychol.*, vol. 47, pp. 749–56.

FERGUSON, L. W., (1939), 'Primary social attitudes', *J. Psychol.*, vol. 8, pp. 217–23.

FRENKEL-BRUNSWIK, E., and SANFORD, R. N. (1945), 'Some factors in anti-Semitism', *J. Psychol.*, vol. 20, pp. 271–91.

FRIEDRICHS, R. W. (1959), 'Christians and residential exclusion: an empirical study of a northern dilemma', *J. soc. Issues*, vol. 15, pp. 14–23.

FROMM, E. (1941), *Escape from Freedom*, Holt, Rinehart & Winston.

GOUGH, H. G. (1951), 'Studies of social intolerance: IV. Related social attitudes', *J. soc. Psychol.*, vol. 33, pp. 263–9.

HARLAN, H. H. (1942), 'Some factors affecting attitude toward Jews', *Amer. sociol. Rev.*, vol 7, pp 816–27.

JEEVES, M. A. (1959), 'Contribution on prejudice and religion in symposium on problems of religious psychology', *Acta Psychologia*, vol. 15, pp. 508–10.

JONES, M. B. (1958), 'Religious values and authoritarian tendency', *J. soc. Psychol.*, vol. 48, pp. 83–9.

KINSEY, A. C., POMEROY, W. P., and MARTIN, C. E. (1948), *Sexual Behavior in the Human Male*, Saunders.

KIRKPATRICK, C. (1949), 'Religion and humanitarianism', *Psychol. Monogr.*, vol. 63, pp. 1–23.

KRECH, D., and CRUTCHFIELD, R. S. (1948), *Theory and Problems of Social Psychology*, McGraw-Hill.

LENSKI, G. (1961), *The Religious Factor*, Doubleday.

LEVINSON, D. J., and SANFORD, R. N. (1944), 'A scale for the measurement of anti-Semitism', *J. Psychol.*, vol. 17, pp. 339–70.

LIPSET, S. (1959), 'Religion in America: what religious revival?', *Rev. rel. Res.*, vol. 1, pp. 17–24.

MACCOBY, E. E., and MACCOBY, N. (1954), 'The interview: a tool of social science', in G. Lindzey (ed.), *Handbook of Social Psychology*. Addison-Wesley (1962).

MARTIN, C., and NICHOLS, R. C. (1962), 'Personality and religious belief', *J. soc. Psychol.*, vol. 56, pp. 3–8.

MIDDLETON, R., and PUTNEY, S. (1962), 'Religion, normative standards and behavior', *Sociometry*, vol. 25, pp. 141–52.

PARRY, H. J. (1949), 'Protestants, Catholics and prejudice', *Int. J. opin. attit. Res.*, vol. 3, pp. 205–13.

PUTNEY, S., and MIDDLETON, R. (1961), 'Dimensions and correlates of religious ideologies', *Soc. Forces*, vol. 39, pp. 285–90.

ROKEACH, M. (1965), 'Paradoxes of religious belief', *Trans-Action*, vol. 2, pp. 9–12.

ROSENBLITH, J. (1949), 'A replication of "some roots of prejudice"', *J. abnorm. soc. Psychol.*, vol. 44, pp. 470–89.

ROSS, M. G. (1950), *Religious Beliefs of Youth*, New York Association.

SAMPSON, D. L., and SMITH, H. P. (1957), 'A scale to measure worldminded attitudes', *J. soc. Psychol.*, vol. 45, pp. 99–106.

SANAI, M. (1952), 'An empirical study of political, religious and social attitudes', *Brit. J. Psychol., Stat. Sec.*, vol. 5, pp. 81–91.

SANFORD, R. N., and LEVINSON, D. J. (1948), 'Ethnocentrism in relation to some religious attitudes and practices', *Amer. Psychologist*, vol. 3, pp. 350–52.

SELLTIZ, C., JAHODA, M., DEUTSCH, M., and COOK, S. W. (1963), *Research Methods in Social Relations*, Holt, Rinehart & Winston.

SIEGMAN, A. W. (1962), 'A cross-cultural investigation of the relationship between religiosity, ethnic prejudice and authoritarianism', *Psychol. Rep.*, vol. 11, pp. 419–24.

SMITH, H. P., and ROSEN, E. W. (1960), 'Some psychological correlates of worldmindedness and authoritarianism', *J. Pers.*, vol. 26, pp. 170–83.

SMITH, M. B., BRUNER, J. S., and WHITE, R. W. (1956), *Opinion and Personality*, Wiley.

SPILKA, B. (1958), 'Some personality correlates of interiorized and institutionalized religious beliefs', *Psychol. Newsltr*, vol. 9, pp. 103–7.

SPILKA, B., and REYNOLDS, J. F. (1965), 'Religion and prejudice: a factor analytic study', *Rev. rel. Res.*, vol. 6, pp. 163–8.

STRUENING, E. L. (1963), 'Anti-democratic attitudes in midwest university', in H. H. Remmers (ed.), *Anti-Democratic Attitudes in American Schools*, Northwestern University Press.

THURSTONE, L. L., and CHAVE, E. J. (1929), *The Measurement of Attitude*, University of Chicago Press.

TUMIN, M. (1958), *Desegregation: Resistance and Readiness*, Princeton University Press.

TURBEVILLE, G., and HYDE, R. E. (1946), 'A selected sample of attitudes of Louisiana State University students toward the Negro: a study in public opinion', *Soc. Forces*, vol. 24, pp. 447–50.

WILSON, C. W. (1960), 'Extrinsic religious values and prejudice', *J. abnorm. soc. Psychol.*, vol. 60, pp. 286–8.

WOODRUFF, A. D. (1945), 'Personal values and religious background', *J. soc. Psychol.*, vol. 22, pp. 141–7.

6 G. Stanley

Personality and Attitude Characteristics of Fundamentalist University Students

G. Stanley, 'Personality and attitude characteristics of fundamentalist university students', *Australian Journal of Psychology*, 1963, vol. 15, no. 3, pp. 199–200.

In a previous report (Stanley, 1963) fundamentalist theological students were found to be more conservative, more certain and more dogmatic than non-fundamentalists. They did not differ on MPI measures of extraversion and neuroticism, but had significantly higher lie scale scores. The present study uses university students and a wider range of personality measures.

Method

Sample

Seventy-two university students of both sexes attending vacation camps sponsored by the Evangelical Union (EU, $N=39$) and the Student Christian Movement (SCM, $N=33$).

Measures

The Neuroticism Scale Questionnaire (Cattell and Scheier, 1961), the short-form MPI, nineteen of the best discriminating items from Rokeach's (1956) Dogmatism Scale, the five-item version of the F Scale to measure authoritarianism (cf. Srole, 1956), Srole's (1956) five-item measure of *anomie*, Bronfenbrenner's (1960) three-item Mistrust Scale, Barron's (1953) Independence-of-Judgement Scale and Brown's (1962) measures of religious institutionalization and individualism. Conversion was measured by the Ss' response to simple questions about whether or not they ever had made a definite decision in favour of religion. Ss were categorized as fundamentalist if they affirmed that all of the Bible is divinely inspired and literally true (Stanley, 1963).

Results and discussion

Twenty-nine Ss checked the fundamentalist item. Table 1 lists biserial correlations computed between fundamentalism and the personality and attitude variables.

As in the previous study with theological students, the present

Table 1 Correlations between fundamentalism and personality and attitude measures

Neuroticism scale questionnaire	0·18
Extraversion (MPI)	−0·05
Neuroticism (MPI)	−0·10
Dogmatism	0·44**
Authoritarianism	0·27*
Anomie	0·14
Mistrust	−0·13
Independence	−0·06
Institutionalization	0·31**
Individualism	−0·04
Conversion	0·27*
EU/SCM	−0·73**

$*p < 0.05$.
$**p < 0.01$.

result indicates a definite association of fundamentalism with measures of dogmatism and authoritarianism. Religious institutionalization, conversion and membership in the EU are also significantly related to fundamentalism. This study also confirms the previous finding that there is no relationship between fundamentalism and questionnaire measures of neurosis, and thus supports Brown's (1962) general finding of the independence of religious belief from personality measures.

References

BARRON, F. (1953), 'Personality style and perceptual choice', *J. Pers.*, vol. 21, pp. 287–97.

BROFENBRENNER, U. (1960), 'Personality and participation: the case of vanishing variables', *J. soc. Issues*, vol. 16, pp. 54–60.

BROWN, L. B. (1962), 'A study of religious belief', *Brit. J. Psychol.*, vol. 53, pp. 259–72.

CATTELL, R. B., and SCHEIER, I. H. (1961), *The Neuroticism Scale Questionnaire*. I.P.A.T.

ROKEACH, M. (1956), 'Political and religious dogmatism: an alternative to the authoritarian personality', *Psychol. Monogr.*, vol. 70, no. 18.

SROLE, L. (1956), 'Social integration and certain corollaries: an exploratory study', *Amer. soc. Rev.*, vol. 21, pp. 709–16.

STANLEY, G. (1963), 'Personality and attitude characteristics of fundamentalist theological students', *Aust. J. Psychol.*, vol. 15, pp. 121–3.

7 Glenn M. Vernon

The Religious 'Nones': A Neglected Category

Glenn M. Vernon, 'The religious "nones": a neglected category',
Journal for the Scientific Study of Religon, 1968, vol. 7, pp. 219–29.

The language which any group uses inevitably betrays evaluation, even when only description is intended, and much more than referent identification may be implied by a particular label. This appears to be the case with the 'none' label, as when it designates the last category, following 'Catholic, Jew . . ', in a list headed by 'Religion'.[1] It provides a negative definition, specifying what a phenomenon is not, rather than what it is. Intentionally or not, such a use implies that only those affiliated with a formal group are religious. In fact, the label 'no religion' is used in the 1957 US Census and by some researchers (e.g. Svalastoga, 1965), to identify those who do not belong to a formal church.

By way of contrast, the social scientist classifies as '*independent*' those who do not report affiliation with a particular political party. The use of the 'independent' label suggests that the lack of political-party affiliation does not mean that one is apolitical or has no political convictions. He is still viewed as a political person. Perhaps this is because the act of voting serves as the primary validation of political participation. There is no comparable religious phenomenon, no clearly recognized religious behavior other than membership, attendance, or other identification with a formal religious group. Thus, 'none' is used in religious research, designating no religious affiliation, but also adding the gratuitous implication of a non-religious person.[2]

Like the 'nones', the political independents have no visible

1. Frequently included under this label are atheists, agnostics, those with 'no preference', those with no affiliation, and also members of small groups and others who, for one reason or another, do not fall within the classification scheme being used and who more properly belong in a residual or 'other' category. The discussion in this article concentrates on those who have no affiliation.

2. At times other terms such as 'free thinker' and 'non-affiliated' have been used. Norman Thomas used the label 'Independent Christian' in a classification of conscientious objectors (1923, p. 48).

organization; however, political independents do not suffer as greatly from non-visibility as do the religious independents. In fact, they are assiduously polled, heeded and courted. But there is no recognized voice or spokesman or ready audience for the religious independent. The 'nones' are less likely to be heard on social issues, and public awareness of the position of such individuals is low. As Nathanson (1955, pp. 166–72) has indicated, whenever moral or religious questions are being considered, opinions of Catholics, Protestants and Jews are sought, while the unchurched are almost never consulted. Lipman and Vorspan (1962, p. 315) suggest that the atheist agnostic, and non-believer to some degree have become second-class citizens. The public media are less likely to take the 'non-affiliated' into account in stories designed for public consumption. Visibility of the group is reduced accordingly; the public image is blurred and indistinct.

Scientific neglect

Much attention has been given to research which explores the differential characteristics of various religious groups and the correlates of religious affiliation. Considerable attention has also been given to differences which are related to various types or degrees of religiosity. Non-affiliates may be included among those studied, but they are rarely singled out for specific analysis. A somewhat extensive, though certainly not exhaustive, search of the literature has identified approximately eighty cases where they are essentially ignored in the analysis of the data. In this respect, 'nones' are a neglected category, included in research designs so that percentages might total one hundred, rather than because it is a category worthy of analysis.

For any particular research the 'nones' may be a small group, and primarily for this reason considered a residual category. However, there are a large number of independents available for and worthy of research. The fruitfulness of testing hypotheses about the functions or consequences of religion by comparing religious and non-religious is suggested by Magill and Campbell (1967) in their study of religious and intellectual values. In their pretest they checked the validity of their questions by the 'method of known groups'. Religious individuals were represented by Sisters in a religious order and non-religious individuals were represented by self-defined atheistic university students. The two groups had 'completely different response patterns' on the questions, and their scores on the composite index were on different ends of the scoring continuum. However, very little research of this nature has been done. Even in the Magill–Campbell report, the differences were reported in a footnote, and apparently once the research instrument had been pretested the atheists were forgotten. The only research effort of which this author is aware in which the 'nones' were the major focus of attention was the Vetter and Green study of atheists in 1932.

O'Dea (1966) and others who endorse the premise that religion is functional for society might also have considered the function of 'nones' for society, a question which is usually ignored, implying a negative answer. There is little research upon which to base any conclusions or even to suggest that such a question be entertained. Herberg (1956) and others who speak of the 'American Religion' (or societal religion) might have considered whether the non-affiliated are stronger or weaker than the affiliated religionist on such measures. The strong endorsement of the democratic way of life by a humanist such as Sidney Hook (1964, pp. 138–51) suggests that at least some of the 'nones' would score high on an 'American-Religion-Orthodoxy Scale'. Although Herberg essentially ignores the 'nones', he does suggest that

Through the nineteenth century and well into the twentieth, America knew the militant secularist, the atheist or 'free-thinker' as a familiar figure in cultural life, along with considerably larger number of 'agnostics' who would have nothing to do with churches and refused to identity themselves religiously. These still exist, of course, but their ranks are dwindling and they are becoming more and more inconspicuous, taking the American people as a whole (1956, pp. 59–60).

He also suggests that many second generation Americans tend to draw away from the religion of their fathers and become 'religionless' (p. 32). Here he seems to equate 'religion' with organized religion, but nothing more is done with the category.

Relationship between non-affiliation and other religious factors

If, as we have suggested, the scientific study of religious 'nones' has been neglected, it follows that definitive answers are not available for whether the 'nones' are as characteristically 'nonreligious' as the name implies. But we turn now to some limited research providing information about some of the characteristics of independents. The material presented is only suggestive – selected because the findings *suggest* relationships quite contrary to many assumptions, rather than because its findings are conclusive or even representative of all available research.

Religious behavior

Religious beliefs. Studies concerning 'belief in God' usually include atheists and agnostics in the 'none' category.[3] Evidence from a study by the author[4] (Table 1) questions the premise that all 'nones' do not believe in God, and conversely that all agnostics and atheists should be classified in the 'none' category if this implies an absence of religious belief. The 'none' category in Table 1 includes anyone who did not provide a label for himself, even the broad label of 'Protestant'. (Groups which had less than thirty-five members were not included in the tabulation.)

The percentage of 'nones' in the two categories most strongly endorsing a belief in God was lower than that for any of the 'religious' groups. Conversely, the per cent of 'nones' in the two categories most strongly rejecting or questioning such belief was higher than for any other group. At the same time, there were 17·7 per cent of the 'nones' in the two most positive categories, and there were some from every formal group endorsing the agnostic position, and even, in most cases, the 'I don't believe in God' alternative.

Other research suggests a similar pattern with respect to other religious beliefs. Cuber (1940), for instance, in his study of four Metropolitan churches in Detroit, emphasized that non-members who were non-attenders manifested many traditional moral and doctrinal views and favored churches as institutions. In another study, De Jong and Ford (1965) found that religious fundamentalism was negatively correlated with class level among the 9·3 per cent of Southern Appalachian respondents classified as 'no religion or religion not reported', like the pattern which obtained for affiliated religionists. Also, those in the 'no religion or religion not reported' category were more liberal than the total

3. Vetter and Green (1932) found it meaningful to subdivide atheists into 'certain atheists' and 'uncertain atheists' depending on how committed respondents were to an atheistic position. Moberg (1962, p. 66) suggests using the concept 'marginal non-membership'. Putney and Middleton (1961), combined atheists, agnostics and deists under a label of 'sceptic'.

4. A study of attitudes toward death. Analysis of the data is currently underway. The respondents involved in the data presented here include mainly students from several colleges and universities in the U S. The questions analysed here are taken from Stark (1965). See also Glock and Stark (1965).

Table 1 Per cent selecting specific answer to question:
'Which of the following statements comes closest to what you believe about God?'

Religious affiliation	N	No[1] doubt	Some[2] doubt	Some[3] times	No[4] personal God	Agnostic[5]	Atheistic[6]	No answer
None	85	7·1	10·6	8·2	18·8	27·1	23·5	4·7
Roman Catholic	466	53·2	30·7	5·4	5·8	3·6	0·6	0·6
Methodist	269	34·6	40·9	8·6	7·1	5·9	1·5	1·1
Presbyterian	35	28·6	40·0	2·9	11·4	14·3	2·9	
Episcopal	73	26·0	42·5	15·1	6·8	6·8		
Congregational	208	24·5	35·6	13·0	13·5	8·2	2·9	2·4
Lutheran	58	46·6	36·2	8·6	5·2	3·4		
Baptist	181	50·8	35·9	5·5	2·8	2·8	0·6	1·7
Mormon	275	81·5	13·1	1·5	0·7	2·5	0·4	0·4
Protestant	43	44·2	27·9	2·3	7·0	4·7	9·3	4·7
Jew	84	53·6	21·4	8·3	7·1	3·6	5·0	4·8

1. I know God really exists and have no doubts about it.
2. While I have doubts, I feel that I do believe in God.
3. I find myself believing in God some of the time, but not at other times.
4. I don't believe in a personal God, but I do believe in a higher power of some kind.
5. I don't know whether there is a God and I don't believe there is any way to find out.
6. I don't believe in God.

sample. These findings seem to add support to the premise that there are similarities between the religious beliefs of 'nones' and those of affiliated religionists which need to be explored.

Participation in formal religious activities. Cuber (1940) also found that from 18 to 37 per cent of those attending church were non-members. He also indicated that almost every clergyman interviewed stated that he received numerous requests from non-members for religious ceremonies at weddings and funerals. Likewise, a 1949 census of Madison, Wisconsin (Bultena, 1949), found that about 10 per cent of the 'no church' group were regular church attenders.

Religious experiences. The findings presented in Tables 2 and 3 suggest that some individuals classified as 'nones' have had religious experiences. Compared with members of religious groups, these figures are low – as would be expected. Yet using this one question as our criterion of religiousness, certain of the 'nones' are more religious than certain of the members of formal groups.

Summary. The 'non-religion' implication of the 'none' label does not seem to find complete validation from the material which we have analysed. Some of those categorized as 'none' may, in fact, at least on certain religious measures, be more 'religious' than some of those categorized as affiliated. On certain types of analyses, those usually classified as 'nones' clearly fall

Table 2 Answers to question: 'Have you ever had a feeling that you were somehow in the presence of God?'

Religious affiliation	N	'Yes, I'm sure I have' (per cent)	'Yes, I think I have' (per cent)	'No' (per cent)	No answer
None	85	5·9	20·0	70·6	3·5
Roman Catholic	466	40·8	39·7	17·4	1·9
Methodist	269	31·6	46·5	20·8	0·7
Presbyterian	35	28·6	42·9	28·6	
Episcopal	73	27·4	53·4	17·8	1·4
Congregational	208	27·4	44·2	26·9	1·4
Lutheran	58	41·4	39·7	19·0	
Baptist	181	37·6	45·9	15·5	1·1
Mormon	275	47·3	28·4	22·9	1·5
Protestant	43	41·9	23·3	32·6	2·3
Jew	84	36·9	42·9	15·5	3·6

within a 'religious' category. That there is a difference between the 'nones' as a group and affiliated religionists is certainly documented here; however, it seems as inaccurate to consider all 'nones' to be 'of one piece' as it is to consider all Methodists to be alike in all religious matters.

Table 3 **Have you ever had a feeling that you were being punished by God for something you had done?**

Religious affiliation	N	' Yes, I'm sure I have' (per cent)	' Yes, I think I have' (per cent)	'No' (per cent)	No answer
None	85	7·1	16·5	72·9	3·5
Roman Catholic	466	30·7	42·1	26·0	0·9
Methodist	269	18·6	43·5	36·1	1·5
Presbyterian	35	22·9	40·0	37·1	
Episcopal	73	11·0	42·5	45·2	1·4
Congregational	208	15·9	42·8	40·4	1·0
Lutheran	58	29·3	46·6	24·1	
Baptist	181	33·7	39·8	26·0	0·6
Mormon	275	31·3	30·5	37·8	0·4
Protestant	43	30·2	20·9	46·5	2·3
Jew	84	39·3	36·9	20·2	1·2

Relation between non-affiliation and other behavior

If religious beliefs and practices contribute to socially approved behavior, we would not expect, on the basis of the evidence presented here, to find such behavior the monopoly of either group. We turn, therefore, to consider whether related social behavior of 'nones' is different from that of affiliated individuals.

Social behavior. Functional analyses of religion frequently suggest that religion contributes to societal integration and sanctifies or validates society's value definitions. Are affiliates, then, more law-abiding than 'nones'? Lunden (1964, p. 154) presents the following answer from a survey of available research.

In spite of the general opinion that religion creates 'good' conduct and irreligion causes delinquency the statistical data available tend to prove the contrary almost to the point of paradox. Accepting the Bonger hypothesis in a 1916 study, 'as irreligion increases, crime tends to decrease', the advocates of this position can now declare after almost fifty years 'hypothesis proven'.

Independents, then, appear to contribute as much as affiliates to socially approved behavior.

Prejudice. Do affiliates evidence less socially disruptive racial and ethnic prejudice than independents? Many studies have indicated a higher frequency of expressed prejudice toward racial or ethnic outgroups among members of organized religious bodies than among non-members and similarly greater prevalence of such prejudice among persons who frequently attend religious services than among those who do not. On the other hand, there are studies that present data suggesting a curvilinear association – both the completely inactive and the highly active being less prejudiced.[5] Independents, then, apparently are as free from racial-ethnic prejudice as affiliated religionists.

Security and anxiety. If as Sapir (Mandelbaum, 1951, pp. 346–56) suggests, 'religion is omnipresent fear ... paradoxically turned into bedrock security', are independents less secure or more anxious than affiliates? Death is one area with high fear potential. The author's research posed the question, 'Do you feel that you could currently adequately face the death of a loved one?' While 46·4 per cent of the total group answered 'yes', 50·6 of those in the 'none' category did. The Mormons (62·2 per cent) were the only group exceeding the 'nones'. Independents apparently evidence as much 'bedrock security' as affiliates.

Marital adjustment. If religion serves an integrating function, not only for society, but for subgroups within society as well, does the marital adjustment of affiliates exceed that of 'nones'? Peterson (1965, ch. 18), in a study of 420 persons in the Los Angeles area, worked out an overall marital adjustment score which he found to be related to his religious classifications as seen in Table 4.

According to these data, being a religious independent does not seem to depress the adjustment score of the males, who in fact evidence a higher adjustment level than either the sect-conservative or the institutional-authoritarian categories. Lack of church affiliation does depress the female adjustment score, but these scores are not very different from those in the institutional-authoritarian category. The female pattern may be related to the

5. See for instance Williams (1964, p. 21) and Simpson and Yinger (1965, pp. 397–403). Allport has suggested that it is those with an 'extrinsic' orientation toward religion as contrasted with those with an 'intrinsic' orientation, who tend to be most prejudiced. It would be worth checking to see if the Independents tend to have an 'intrinsic' orientation (1960, p. 33).

Table 4

Religious classification	Adjustment scores	
	Men	Women
Liberal	78	82
Jewish	77	85
No-Church Agnostic	77	65
Sect-Conservative	72	77
Institutional-Authoritarian	55	68

tendency for the female to exceed the male on most measures of religiosity.

Analysis of other research related to the family suggests that the following relationships may obtain. When compared with affiliated individuals, independents attach less importance to religious endogamy as a contributor to marital happiness, but are still more likely before marriage to express doubts about the future success of their subsequent marriage. When married, they are less likely to experience certain types of sexual problems. They are more likely to experience divorce, although there is a high likelihood of the marriage enduring. In contrast to an affiliated–affiliated marriage, an independent–independent marriage. is more likely to have children low on ritualistic and consequential dimensions of religion, and an independent (female) affiliated marriage to have children high on the consequential dimension and low on the ritualistic dimension of religion (Vernon, 1968).

The question of positive correlation between social behavior and religious beliefs and practices as a characteristic distinguishing the affiliates from the independents appears to warrant further investigation. The consequences of a lack of affiliation may not be what some have assumed. Independents do not seem disproportionately to evidence socially disapproved behavior. Theory about the functions of religion, then. may involve unwarranted interpretations if 'religion' is interpreted to mean 'organized religion'.

Some methodological and theoretical considerations

Variation within the 'none' group

Affiliation: membership or preference? In order to increase our understanding of religious phenomena, there is a need to refine both the affiliated and the independent categories.

The categories most consistently used to classify religious affiliates have been Protestant, Catholic and Jew. In recent years, extensive subdivisions of each of these categories have been made, particularly in the Protestant category. Accordingly, research has been directed to within-group variation as well as to between-group variation, finding that on many variables the within-group variation is the greater of the two. As a result, alternate methods of classification have been suggested (see, for instance, Glock and Stark, 1965, ch. 5; Lipset, 1964, pp. 60–89; Peterson, 1965; Vernon, 1962, ch. 13.

This within-group variation obtains for independents as well as for affiliates and without doubt the 'none' category needs considerable refinement also. One meaningful distinction is that between those who have 'no affiliation' according to the official records of the churches and those who do not themselves report any identification with or a preference for any particular group. The percentage of those who will provide an affiliation identification when asked is much higher than the percentage who are carried on the official records. Comparison of official church membership statistics with population figures for the U S indicate that around one-third of the population is not considered to be an official member of an established religious group (Vernon, 1962, ch. 12). It is apparently to this group that the *Lutheran Witness Reporter* referred when it reported that the unchurched outnumbered the churched in twenty-nine states, with the highest percentage of the unchurched to be found in Oregon, Washington and West Virginia, and the lowest percentage of the unchurched in Rhode Island, Utah and Massachussetts (4 December 1960). This contrasts sharply with the 95 to 97 per cent who provide an identification or a preference when asked by researchers. The difference between these two labels needs to be explored. Having a preference for a formal grouping is not the same as belonging to it.

Other distinctions calling for further research include atheist, agnostic, non-affiliated participant, non-affiliated believer, 'no-preference', committed and non-committed independents, converted and lifelong independents, as well as, independents with various social characteristics such as prejudiced or non-prejudiced, secure or insecure, deviant or conforming, etc.

Some of this has been done within studies, such as the analysis of poll data relating to religious affiliation and social class shown in Table 5. Schneider (1952, p. 228) found a difference between those classified as 'no preference' and those classified as 'atheist, agnostic'. Although the number in the second category is small, the data do suggest that meaningful differences would be found between various types of independents.

Table 5 **Social class profile of American religious groups as percentages**

	Upper	Middle	Lower	N
No preference	13·3	26·0	60·7	466
Atheist, agnostic	33·3	46·7	20·0	15

Affiliated–independent interrelationships

Discussion of affiliation usually assumes that non-affiliation is the reciprocal of affiliation. We have tended to dichotomize the two terms, or to conceive of an affiliation–non-affiliation continuum. Are these two types of phenomena in fact the obverse of each other, or do measures of affiliation and of independence really get at two somewhat different phenomena?

Analogous research in Industrial Sociology may clarify this issue. Research by Herzberg, Mausner and Snyderman (1960) indicates that factors that lead to job satisfaction are not the same as those that lead to job dissatisfaction. Studying employees of nine organizations in the Pittsburgh area, they concluded that the most satisfying aspects of the work experience were those associated directly with the actual doing of the job – achievement, recognition, responsibility, advancement and the work itself. The absence of these factors, however, did not cause dissatisfaction. On the other hand, the factors which contributed to job dissatisfaction were peripheral – company policy and administration, supervision, interpersonal relations and working conditions. In this case the improvement of these conditions did not necessarily cause satisfaction. Friedlander and Walton (1964) arrived at similar conclusions from their interviews with engineers and scientists.

A similar hypothesis might be entertained with reference to religious phenomena: the reasons one remains with a formal religious organization are different from and not merely the opposite of the reasons one leaves or does not affiliate with such an organization.

If the 'content' of religion is beliefs about God, for instance, then there are those who accept such beliefs while staying outside the formal structure. Perhaps the context in which the affiliated religionist is expected to display or make public such beliefs is not the context in which the non-affiliate desires to do so. Likewise, individuals may stay within a religious organization for 'context' reasons – 'good business' or family pressures, for example – even though the 'content' (beliefs) may diminish in importance.

The research generated by the Herzberg–Friedlander hypothesis has not all been confirmatory.[6] Further, the pretest research involving atheists by Magill and Campbell seems to contradict this hypothesis. However so little evidence is available that the relationship between affiliation and nonaffiliation warrants further consideration.

Functional analysis

Discussions about the functions of religion in society imply that everything labeled 'religious' has the same consequences in a given system at any given time, and conversely, that everything that is 'non-religious' lacks these consequences or functions. This paper challenges these assumptions. The 'nones' may serve some societal functions similar to those served by the affiliated religionist.

Herberg (1964), Luckmann (1967), and others suggest a distinction between societal religion and formal religion. *Societal religion* incorporates the high-intensity value definitions which hold society together and thus fulfill a societal integrative function. *Formal religion* maintains a set of beliefs and rituals which may or may not serve to integrate the society, even though they may integrate the church group. The 'nones', who may 'belong' to the societal religion, even though they do not 'belong' to a formal church group, may contribute to the integration of a society as well as the affiliates.

The more intriguing question for sociology, however, is whether those in the 'none' category serve a unique and distinctive function for society. For instance does the presence of non-affiliated individuals in a society reduce the intergroup conflict between established religious groups? What are the consequences of having 'nones' as an appropriate other toward whom missionary or proselytizing efforts of the church may be directed?

6. Research by students of B. S. Bolaria at the University of Maine has provided both support and non-support for aspects of the Herzberg–Friedlander hypotheses.

Or, when non-affiliated are considered to be intransigents who have repeatedly resisted evangelistic approaches or to be immoral, unreliable, irresponsible and 'without self respect', as Vidich and Bensman (1958, pp. 251–2) suggest is the case in small communities, and are therefore neglected in church recruiting and evangelism, what are the results? Does religious-group identification take on increased meaning to those who do belong as a result of the presence of a negative reference group with which to compare themselves? Or, does the presence, or opposition, of a negative reference group facilitate the achievement of certain goals? It may be suggestive that the 'ideal society' envisioned by most religious groups is a stratified society in which distinct differences are recognized and taken into account.

When religious affiliation is a norm, the 'nones' are deviant individuals. To what extent do the conclusions about the functions of deviant behavior apply to the religiously deviant 'nones'? Durkheim, for instance, says of crime:

To classify crime among the phenomena of normal sociology is not to say merely that it is an inevitable, although regrettable phenomenon, due to the incorrigible wickedness of men; it is to affirm that it is a factor in public health, an integral part of all healthy societies (1938, p. 67).

And Mead suggests:

The criminal does not seriously endanger the structure of society by his destructive activities, and on the other hand he is responsible for a sense of solidarity, aroused among those whose attention would be otherwise centred upon interest quite divergent from those of each other (1918).

Does the conclusion of Mead, Durkheim and other sociologists that crime as a universal phenomenon never could and *never should* be eliminated apply also to the religious 'nones'? Does the existence and presence of 'nones' in a society contribute to the 'health' of existing religions? To what extent does the existence of 'nones' facilitate the accommodation of religious groups to society and society to the religious groups? Does the existence of 'nones' encourage religious groups to attempt to relate their 'eternal' truths to the existing conditions in which their members are living and dying?

Conclusions

The 'none' label carries negative evaluative implications, unwarranted by the limited research and unproductive of further research. The 'independent' label carries neutral implications, with research suggesting that such individuals have the following characteristics:

1. Independents reject membership in formal religious groups, but a limited percentage do attend formal services. These are non-affiliated participants.

2. Independents may have experiences defined as involving the supernatural, but they tend to de-emphasize the relationship to the supernatural, apparently with a concomitant humanistic emphasis.

3. Independents are ethical and moral, but they relate their morality less than affiliates to supernatural or church-related variables.

4. Independents should be classified as religious along with those affiliated with church groups. Differences between various types of religious people should, of course, be studied.

5. There are different types of independents. Subcategories need to be developed.

6. Independents are more oriented toward and influenced by societal religion than by formal religion.

7. The reasons for being an independent may not simply be the obverse of the reasons of the affiliate for belonging to a formal group. The influence of societal religion on the behavior of affiliates may, accordingly, be inaccurately and unknowingly attributed exclusively to church or affiliation variables.

8. Independents in a pluralistic society may have latent functions for church groups and society *per se*.

Functional interpretations of religious behavior are inadequate to the extent that 'religion' is equated with formal religion. Furthermore, functional theory would better facilitate the investigation and understanding of both independents and affiliates if the basic premise were presented as, 'There are certain functional requisites *of society* which formal religion *may* fulfill', rather than, 'There are certain functions *of religion* which contribute to societal integration.'

References

ALLPORT, G. W. (1960), *Religion in the Developing Personality*, New York University Press.

BULTENA, L. (1949), 'Church membership and church attendance in Madison, Wisconsin', *Amer. soc. Rev.*, vol. 14, pp. 384–9.

CUBER, J. F. (1940), 'Marginal church participants', *Sociol. soc. Res.*, pp. 57–62.

DE JONG, G., and FORD, T. R. (1965), 'Religious fundamentalism and denominational preference in the Southern Appalachian region', *J. sci. Stud. Relig.*, vol. 5, no. 1, pp. 24–33.

DURKHEIM, E. (1938), *Rules of Sociological Method*, Free Press.

FRIEDLANDER, F., and WALTON, E. (1964), 'Positive and negative motivations toward work', *Admin. Sci. Q.*, vol. 8, pp. 143–207.

GLOCK, C. Y. and STARK, R. (1965), *Religion and Society in Tension*, Rand McNally.

HERBERG, W. (1956), *Protestant–Catholic–Jew*, Doubleday.

HERZBERG, F., MAUSNER, B., and SNYDERMAN P. (1960), *The Motivation to Work*, Wiley.

HOOK, S. (1964), 'Religious liberty from the viewpoint of a secularist humanist', in E. Raab (ed.), *Religious Conflict in America*, Doubleday.

LIPMAN, E. J., and VORSPAN, A. (eds.) (1962), *A Tale of Ten Cities*, Union of American Hebrew Congregations.

LIPSET, S. M. (1964), 'Religion and politics in American history', in E. Raab (ed.), *Religious Conflict in America*, Doubleday.

LUCKMANN, T. (1967), *The Invisible Religion*, Macmillan Co.

LUNDEN, W. A. (1964), *Statistics on Delinquents and Delinquency*, C. C. Thomas.

MAGILL, D. W., and CAMPBELL, D. F. (1967), 'Commitment to religious values among university students', Canadian Sociology and Anthropology Association Mimeograph.

MANDELBAUM, D. G. (ed.) (1951), 'Selected writings of Edward Sapir', in *Language, Culture and Personality*, University of California Press.

MEAD, G. H. (1918), 'The psychology of primitive justice', *Amer. J. Sociol.*, vol. 3, no. 5, p. 591.

MOBERG, D. O. (1962), *The Church as a Social Institution*, Prentice-Hall.

NATHANSON, J. (1955) 'Sixty-four million Americans do not go to church: what do they believe?' in L. Rosen (ed.), *A Guide to the Religion of America*, Simon & Schuster.

O'DEA, T. F. (1966), *The Sociology of Religion*, Prentice-Hall.

PETERSON, J. A. (1965), *Education for Marriage*, Scribner.

PUTNEY, S., and MIDDLETON, R. (1961), 'Rebellion, conformity and parental religious ideologies', *Sociometry*, vol. 24, pp. 125–36.

SCHNEIDER, H. (1952), *Religion in Twentieth-Century America*, Harvard University Press.

SIMPSON, G. E., and YINGER, J. M. (1965), *Racial and Cultural Minorities*, 3rd edn, Harper & Row.

STARK, R. (1965), 'Social context and religious experience', *Rev. relig. Res.*, vol. 7, no. 1, pp. 17–28.

SVALASTOGA, K. (1965), *Social Differentiation*, McKay.

THOMAS, N. (1923), *The Conscientious Objector in America*, Huebsh.

VERNON, G. M. (1962), *The Sociology of Religion*, McGraw-Hill.

VERNON, G. M. (1968), 'Mental characteristics of religious independents', *Rev. relig. Res.*, vol. 9, no. 3, pp. 162–70.

VETTER, G. B., and GREEN, M. (1932), 'Personality and group factors in the making of atheists', *J. abnorm. soc. Psychol.*, vol. 27, pp. 154–79.

VIDICH, A. J., and BENSMAN, J. (1958), *Small Town in Mass Society*, Princeton University Press.

WILLIAMS, R. M., Jr (1964), *Strangers Next Door*, Prentice-Hall.

Part Three
Religion as a Social Attitude

Another approach to the dimensionality of religion has come from the analysis of social attitudes, and not with explicitly religious material. A factor in general social attitudes, usually called religionism, has been consistently identified, and there are several social issues on which a religious position can be identified. These relate to areas like the control of sexual behaviour, including abortion and divorce, capital punishment, race and attitudes to war: or in the most general terms to *good* behaviour. Religion itself is a social object and attitudes to it have been assessed with propositions or attitude statements like, 'Religion is a source of trouble in the world.' Agreement or disagreement is readily expressed to statements like this, and it was with such statements that Thurstone first used the scaling methods of psychophysics to measure attitudes to the Church in 1929. These methods were later developed and applied to the measurement of attitudes to other religious objects. Thurstone's original scale is reproduced in Part Four. A recent study is to be found in Eysenck (1971).

Reference
EYSENCK, H. J. (1971), 'Social attitudes and social class', *Brit. J. soc. clin. Psychol.*, vol. 10, pp. 201-12.

8 M. Sanai

An Empirical Study of Political, Religious and Social Attitudes

M. Sanai, 'An empirical study of political, religious and social attitudes', *British Journal of Psychology* (*Statistical Section*), 1952, vol. 5, pp. 81–92.

Problem
Generality and specificity

In the study of social attitudes one of the most fundamental issues is their degree of generality or specificity. Many writers appear to hold that attitudes are always narrow in their range, each representing a highly specific tendency to make a particular response to a particular situation; others, however, believe that certain attitudes arise from emotional dispositions of a fairly general type, and are thus liable to extend over wide fields of opinion or behaviour. If, in spite of long-drawn-out discussions, no decisive conclusion has been reached, that may perhaps be attributed to two main reasons: first, the lack of any clear formulation of what is meant by 'generality', and secondly, the neglect to use any rigorous technique by which alone such questions can be solved.

The terms in which the problem is commonly debated are reminiscent of a similar controversy that arose years ago in the sphere of cognitive assessment, when Spearman maintained that the results of intellectual tests were due to a single general ability, while Thorndike contended that they were highly specific. Thanks to the adoption of Pearson's method of component analysis, enabling both general and bi-polar (or group) factors to be verified when present, this question seems now virtually settled. It is natural to suppose that the same technique might enable us to deal with an analogous problem in the field of social studies.

History of factorial investigations. A few investigators have already attempted to apply factorial methods to the study of attitudes. But the number of published researches is surprisingly small, and (so far as our present problem is concerned) decidedly inconclusive. In Britain the earliest inquiries along these lines were carried out by Burt, and dealt chiefly with children's attitudes towards different subjects of the school curriculum, books, games, and future careers (Burt, 1937): he inferred that the factors so discovered were the effects partly of temperamental tendencies, and partly of social influences operating chiefly through parents, teachers, and school companions. Later, a succession of inquiries were carried out under his direction at the National Institute of Industrial Psychology and at the Psychological Laboratory, University College, in which similar methods were used to investigate the attitudes of adults (Burt, 1943). Pelling and Bulley, for example, studied the attitudes of men and women of different social classes towards the aesthetic appearance and utilitarian value of various saleable commodities (Burt, 1937, 1939). Johnson (1942) factorized results from a questionnaire on moral, religious, political and economic problems distributed to 234 adults, and obtained two suggestive factors: the first was identified with the tendency towards traditional authoritative or conservative views as contrasted with dissentient or radical views, and the second with a tendency to take a realistic or rational attitude as contrasted with an emotional or sentimental attitude – factors closely resembling those already noted by Burt in the fields of personal and aesthetic preferences. Flugel and Hopkins (1944) circularized more than 700 adults with a questionnaire dealing with dissentient or unorthodox views over a wide range of topics – pacifism, vegetarianism, antivaccination, euthanasia, psychoanalysis, etc. Eysenck (a former research student in the same department) factorized the results, and obtained three factors – one general and two bi-polar (1944). In a later inquiry (1947) he has obtained a general factor which he terms 'radicalism–conservatism' and a bi-polar which he identifies with James' contrast between 'tough-' and 'tender-minded' types. In America, factorial methods have been adopted by Thurstone (1934), Carlson (1934), and Ferguson (1939). Whereas British writers have commonly found at least one general factor, American writers usually report a number of separate group factors. The techniques employed by American writers, however, differ appreciably from those developed in this country; and in any case, owing to the differences in social background, it would manifestly be unsafe to assume that the conclusions reached in such inquiries also hold good of Londoners, much less of the English population as a whole (Sanai, 1951).

Objections to factorial procedures

Several writers have objected that, even if factorial methods are applicable to the results of cognitive abilities or mental tests, they are not appropriate to the study of emotional dispositions or of opinions and behaviour resting on judgements of value. In general, the criticisms urged follow much the same lines as those advanced in other fields of inquiry. First, it is contended that an attitude is essentially a qualitative characteristic, and as such is not amenable to quantitative treatment: here as elsewhere, we are continually told, statistical psychologists are content to publish tables and numerical analyses without giving any thought to the postulates on which all quantitative treatment must depend. Secondly, it is said, even granting the correctness of the procedure, the statistical factors found to underlie attitudes could not possibly have the real or concrete existence that is claimed for them (Chambers, 1943; Penrose, 1950).

Such objections result largely from a misunderstanding of what the factorist is proposing to do. Arguments which are much better informed have recently been put forward by Guttman in a paper discussing the relative merits of analysis by factorization and analysis by scaling (1951).

Factor analysis and scale analysis

Guttman doubts the validity of applying to the problems of social attitudes a procedure 'borrowed straight from the field of mental testing'. Such a proposal, he contends, is tantamount to 'trying to treat qualitative data as though they were quantitative'. His own 'reluctance to attempt a fully fledged conventional factor analysis', he adds, 'stems from the growing evidence of both theoretical and practical inadequacies of current formulations. Current techniques for extracting factors usually stop at three or four, or some similarly limited number; whereas an infinite number exists whose presence can be revealed only by an entirely different approach.'

In reply it may perhaps be pointed out that, in the early stages of an inquiry, an investigator may well be satisfied if he can establish the 'three or four' most important factors in the field he is studying. As regards 'current formulations', it would seem that Guttman has chiefly in mind the formulations favoured by American psychologists. With much of what he says British writers would probably agree; and there can be no question that his own procedure is likely to prove at once suggestive and fruitful, especially at later stages of the work. But the problems attacked are somewhat different; and there seems room for both methods.

The investigation of structure

The object of factor analysis is not so much to discover 'real or concrete entities', as to study the structure of a mass of complicated data. Burt quotes Bertrand Russell's remark: 'the essence of individuality baffles description; but the consequent perplexities may be largely avoided if the importance of *structure*, and the difficulty of getting behind structure, are realized' (1940, p. 220). By structure is meant 'the scheme or pattern of relations exhibited by the members of a class, regardless of their concrete nature' (Burt, 1937); and the dispute about the relative generality or specificity of attitudes is merely the first and most obvious problem that arises in the study of their 'structure' in this sense. Those writers who hold that the mind, unlike the body, is 'comparatively structureless' (Thomson, 1946, pp. 311–12) naturally favour the hypothesis that all attitudes are highly specific. Those, on the other hand, who adopt McDougall's hierarchical theory of mental structure[1] contend that mere consistency of behaviour is bound to impose some degree of generality; and, since an individual's behaviour in certain limited fields is likely to be more highly consistent than the whole range of his behaviour, they will expect to find, not only one broad general factor, but also supplementary factors of diminishing generality. Thus, as Allport observes, 'the issue involved in this lively controversy is of the greatest practical and theoretical significance, for upon its solution depends not only a proper choice of methods for the investigation of attitudes, but likewise the theory of mental organization and the structure of personality itself' (1935).

Methods
Methodological assumptions

The applicability of factorial methods to qualitative data as such has been fully discussed in a paper to which Guttman does not refer (Burt, 1950a). However, in the investigation to be reported here, a more indirect approach was adopted, which, it is

1. See McDougall's discussion of 'affective-conative attitudes' (1912, ch. 3, 'The structure of the mind,' especially pp. 111ff.); and his diagram representing 'The structure of character' (1936, p. 440).

believed, may to some extent avoid the difficulties to which he and other critics refer.

A questionnaire was drawn up containing thirty statements or opinions dealing directly or indirectly with familiar political, social or religious issues. To be comparable with other inquiries, a number of items were taken over from the lists drawn up by previous workers – Burt, Flugel, Johnson, Vernon and others. Where necessary, the phrasing was modified to suit the particular procedure contemplated and (in certain cases) the current form which the issues touched upon seemed to be taking. The final list was submitted to 250 students of both sexes studying at the University or at LCC classes or Extension Courses; and each was asked to indicate the degree to which they agreed or disagreed with each statement.

In defence of this procedure[2] it may be argued that, to any proposition of the type included in our list, considered in reference to any person in the sample, there can be attached what Russell[3] has termed a 'degree of credence'.[4] This will vary with different persons, and might be defined as his impressionistic assessment of the probability that the statement in question is true or untrue. As thus defined it is a characteristic that can give rise to all the relations necessary for quantitative measurement (Burt, 1940, pp. 129ff.). As a result we have what Russell calls 'a scale of doubtfulness'. By means of such a scale we may measure each person's attitude to the idea or belief expressed in the statement submitted to him. If the person neither agrees nor disagrees, the amount of credence is evidently nil; and can therefore be ex-

2. The statement of methodological assumptions which follows is condensed from Burt's discussion in his notes on 'The study of attitudes'. See also Burt (1952).

3. 'Everything we feel inclined to believe has a "degree of doubtfulness" or inversely a "degree of credibility". … There is a cognate subjective conception, namely, the degree of conviction that a man feels about any of his beliefs; but "credibility", as I mean it, is the degree of credence a *rational* man would give' (*Human Knowledge*, p. 359). Since it is impossible to separate men into two mutually exclusive classes, the rational and the non-rational, Burt suggests that credibility should be defined as a weighted average of the degrees of credence attached by an appropriately defined population.

4. Strictly we ought to add 'in reference to any person at any given time'; and '*the* degree of credence' (with no qualification added) should be the average of a number of judgements given by the person on different occasions. This would lead to a consideration of the "reliability" of such judgements; but that would take us too far afield in what is avowedly only a preliminary exploratory study.

pressed by zero. If he is perfectly convinced that the statement is absolutely true or untrue, the amount can be indicated by $+1.00$ or -1.00 respectively.

In practice it proves to be at once convenient and feasible to recognize three degrees of strength in both the positive and the negative direction. Accordingly, when replying to the questionnaire, every person was requested to mark the extent of his agreement or disagreement on a seven-point bi-polar scale, in which the degrees were carefully defined (for details, see Sanai, 1951).

But for our particular purpose a further set of assumptions seems required. We are proposing to investigate attitudes to a number of *different* topics or statements. If we assume that, for all these different statements, credibility or credence remains a homogeneous property, we can regard the various statements as indicating 'the dimensions of a given class', and represent them by lines in one and the same multidimensional space, all passing through a common zero point. Now to apply factorial methods we must be able to resolve an attitude into its components, and to combine these components into a resultant. If we are to adopt the methods originated by Pearson, a supplementary assumption seems necessary to which perhaps insufficient attention is commonly paid. We have to assume that the attitudes form tendencies which can be combined or resolved like forces in accordance with the parallelogram law:[5] in other words, that they can be represented by vectors which obey (at least to a first approximation) the law of vector addition.[6]

5. This, in Mill's phrase, amounts to assuming that the psychology of attitudes conforms to the 'law of the homogeneous mixture of effects'. Mill it will be remembered, held that this assumption was *not* warranted in dealing with mental characteristics: unlike mechanical forces, which obey the principle of the '*composition* of causes', but like chemical properties, which obey the principle of the '*combination* of causes', mental characteristics (so he contends) produce new and unpredictable properties on combination (*System of Logic*, bk 3, ch. 6). For a more rigorous definition of the two alternative assumptions, and the logical importance of the distinction, see Johnson, 1921, pt 2, p. 236). The need for making some such assumption in applying factor analysis to subjective data is admirably seen in the oldest and simplest case of factor analysis, namely, the attempt to determine the 'primary colours'. It was an appreciation of the difficulties mentioned in the text that led the mathematician Grassmann to introduce the newer formulation of the 'laws of colour mixture', in place of the more naïve statements dating back to Newton (Wundt, *Grundzüge*, II, p. 160).

6. It is not easy to verify the accuracy, or rather the approximate accuracy, of the vector law in the case of mental measurements. As Burt observes, probably the most satisfactory confirmation is the fact that it enables fairly correct predictions to be made (1937).

Statistical procedure

To ensure that, for purposes of correlation, all responses should be measured in the same direction, namely, in that of the 'unorthodox' view (as we may call it), the signs were changed for certain items, namely, those numbered 1, 3, 4, 5, 6, 7, 9, 10, 11, 14, 24, 26, 27 and 29. With seven-fold ratings either product-moment, tetrachoric, or point correlations may be calculated. However, in order that the coefficients obtained should be comparable with those computed by recent workers in the same field (as well as for other reasons) the tetrachoric method was chosen.[7] The large correlation table has been published in a previous article (Sanai, 1951, p. 250); it is therefore unnecessary to reprint it here.

The correlations were factorized by the Method of Simple Summation. Burt's 1917 formula was used. As is well known, this yields saturations similar to those obtained with Thurstone's later 'centroid method': the differences, which are seldom very large, are due chiefly to the fact that Thurstone determines the self-correlations or 'communalities' on the basis of rank rather than significance, estimates them from the largest coefficient in the column, and introduces a special procedure of his own for reflecting the negative signs: he then rotates the factor-matrix to secure a 'simple structure' of positive group factors only. Here it seemed essential to adhere to Burt's original procedure, and to obtain the self-correlations by successive approximation. Further, his method of rearranging the matrix of residuals, before reversing signs, appeared not only more illuminating, but quicker and more accurate.

Results

Significance of factors

To determine the significance of the factors as each was extracted, Burt's criterion was adopted: a factor cannot be regarded as significant unless it is based on a set of correlations or residuals among which more than one in twenty exceeds twice the standard

7. The obvious objection to the use of a tetrachoric procedure is that (as will be shown in a moment) the frequency distributions on the rating scale tend to be bimodal rather than unimodal. In defence it is usually contended that the *underlying* tendency would probably show a normal distribution. In point of fact, with distributions like the present the chief effect of using the product-moment method would be that the absolute size of the coefficients would be increased (some would say exaggerated) while their relative size would remain much the same.

error of the observed coefficient. Judged on this basis, the first four factors were found to be significant, and the fifth was not. The saturations were calculated to three decimal places; for simplicity, however, only the first two figures are given in Table 1. The items have been rearranged to indicate the classification revealed by the analysis; and a detailed examination of the table will suggest the general nature of the factors found.

First factor

The first factor has positive saturations for all the thirty statements, and is thus a 'general' factor. It contributes 25 per cent to the total variance, that is, more than any other significant factor, or indeed than the other three put together. Over half the statements obtain saturations exceeding 0·50. On examining those showing the highest saturations, it would seem that this factor indicates a tendency for individuals to break away from traditional and accepted doctrines in favour of views arising out of new movements or new trends.

The generality of the factor implies that in any individual this non-compliant tendency (or the reverse) is, as it were, an habitual standpoint affecting his views in all the fields covered by the questionnaire – political, social, and religious. In a description of *Victorian England*, G. M. Young has drawn attention to a contrast in social tendencies which is very similar to the contrast here implied. 'If,' he says, 'we range the forces operating on society at any moment into the Conformist and the Dissident, or the Stabilizing and the Exploratory, and apply this canon to the development of Victorian England, we shall remark how singularly detached they are from the traditional alignment of parties. There is one pattern of ideas and another of parties, and of the ideas neither party seems to be more or less receptive than the other' (p. 175).

The names usually adopted by statistical psychologists – e.g. 'liberalism' or 'radicalism' – seem unsuitable for two main reasons. First, they are primarily political terms with definite technical associations, whereas the factor is of a more general nature. Secondly, even in the field of politics they do not convey quite the same meaning as the saturations would suggest, and moreover have different meanings in American and British politics. Some term that is both ethically and politically neutral would be preferable. Professor Burt has suggested that in their general form the tendencies might be termed 'alterationism'

Table 1 Factor-saturations

No.	Statements	Factors			
		I	II	III	IV
I*A*					
6	(No personal God)	0·58	0·34	0·31	0·29
14	(No loving God)	0·60	0·23	0·28	0·07
10	(Christ not divine)	0·62	0·28	0·19	0·19
4	(No survival after death)	0·47	0·47	0·19	0·06
12	(Good life without religion)	0·50	0·25	−0·08	0·03
8	(Sterilization approved)	0·16	0·37	−0·45	0·05
19	(Revolution approved)	0·32	0·05	−0·42	0·38
I*B*					
28	(Complete freedom of speech)	0·42	0·23	−0·16	−0·35
17	(Divorce by consent)	0·43	0·42	−0·10	−0·17
30	(Companionate marriage)	0·63	0·28	−0·21	−0·07
15	(Abortion approved)	0·65	0·30	−0·18	−0·26
21	(Birth control encouraged)	0·54	0·22	0·08	−0·26
3	(Extra-marital relations)	0·63	0·18	0·26	−0·10
1	(No divine creation)	0·74	0·36	0·26	−0·12
II*C*					
2	(Rich and poor not equal)	0·27	−0·06	−0·24	0·32
13	(Immorality of capitalism)	0·69	−0·31	−0·25	0·31
25	(Giving up of sovereignty)	0·59	−0·31	−0·06	0·32
20	(Class conflict)	0·69	−0·11	−0·39	0·30
23	(Complete nationalization)	0·68	−0·18	−0·36	0·15
7	(Socialism not bureaucratic)	0·57	−0·34	0·12	0·20
5	(C.O.s not traitors)	0·40	−0·39	0·62	0·19
29	(No corporal punishment)	0·36	−0·08	0·09	0·17
II*D*					
22	(Jews as good citizens as others)	0·30	−0·40	−0·15	−0·55
18	(Equality of sexual freedom)	0·14	−0·23	−0·16	−0·34
27	(Women not inferior)	0·26	−0·04	0·19	−0·38
26	(Jews not too powerful)	0·48	−0·27	0·07	−0·14
24	(Coloured people not inferior)	0·24	−0·38	0·07	−0·05
9	(Mixed marriages)	0·50	−0·30	0·11	−0·19
16	(Lenient treatment of criminals)	0·51	−0·36	0·07	−0·03
11	(No wide differences in intelligence)	0·22	−0·22	0·27	−0·12
	Contributions to variance (per cent)	25·4	8·3	6·2	5·7

and 'preservationism,' and, in reference more particularly to attitudes and opinions, 'heterodoxy' and 'orthodoxy'.[8]

Second factor

The second factor is a bi-polar factor; about half the statements have positive saturations and half negative. It contributes just over 8 per cent to the variance. A study of the items having positive and negative saturations suggests that it distinguishes statements representing unorthodox ethical or religious views from those representing unorthodox political or social views. It might therefore be termed a factor of *ethico-religious* versus *politico-social alterationism*. To avoid these rather clumsy designations, let us describe it more simply as referring to *personal* versus *political* topics.

Sections I and II of Table 1 show the nature of this division. In other connections Burt has reported a factor very similar to this which he calls a factor for 'humane' or 'sentimental' versus 'efficient or realistic' judgements. It represents a dichotomy that cuts across all party lines. Once again it is easy to find outstanding examples of the contrast in British history. In politics, for example, statesmen like Stafford, aiming at a policy of 'thorough', become supporters of traditionalist or authoritarian views; romantic writers like Lytton eventually reach much the same views because they favour all that is ancient both for its own sake and for the sake of the emotional associations that cluster round it. Among the opposite party, the radicalism of Bentham is of the efficient kind, that of Charles Dickens and William Morris of the sentimental kind (Barker, 1947, p. 190).

8. He writes: 'The contrast is much wider than that between liberalism or the reverse. It is suggestive of the opposing tendencies that the old evolutionists regarded as essential to all life and growth – the tendency to *preserve* what has already persisted as contrasted with the tendency to *alter* or deviate – an opposition which they have described by phrases like "permanence" and "variation", "anabolism" and "katabolism", etc. Since the reference is here more particularly to opinions or *doxæ*, we might perhaps speak of 'palæodoxy" and "kainodoxy". These terms would avoid the suggestion of praise or blame, or of particular spheres of doctrine. However, to avoid uncouth neologisms, I think we may provisionally be content with the natural terms "orthodoxy" and "heterodoxy". The prefix "ortho-" however, must be interpreted, not as meaning "correct" opinions, but opinions continuing in the same "straight" line as before, i.e. in the line of tradition or authority; "hetero-" will then mean opinions deviating in a *different* direction. This is consistent with the dictionary definitions: e.g. for "orthodox" the O E D gives (amongst other explanations) "holding currently accepted opinions, not independent-minded or original".'

Fourth factor

The third and fourth factors (second and third bi-polar) contribute almost equally to the variance, namely, 6·2 and 5·7 per cent, respectively. A rough attempt at weighted summation suggests that with continued approximation the fourth factor would emerge as the more important of the two. However, the low values of the factor-saturations as compared with their standard errors render it scarcely worth while at this stage to carry out a more laborious analysis. It seems clear that a larger sample of persons and a larger variety of questions would be needed to reach any conclusive decision on this point.[9]

The fourth factor can be readily interpreted. It divides the positive half of factor II into (A) items concerned mainly with religious topics or topics on which religious persons have strong views (e.g. sterilization) and (B) items concerned mainly with matters of personal morality, especially sex morality; it divides the negative half of factor II into (C) items concerned mainly with relations within the group and (D) items concerned mainly with relations between groups.

Third factor

Within these four sections the third factor may be considered to introduce a still finer sub-classification, by dichotomizing each section. However, with only thirty items each of these narrower classes necessarily contains very few items; and hence the grouping must largely depend on the accidental content of just two or three related items in each case. Any systematic interpretation is therefore bound to be somewhat speculative and artificial.

A. The first of the sections indicated by factor IV appears to be subdivided into (i) *theological* doctrines that depend directly on a religious standpoint, e.g. the existence of a personal God (4, 6, 10, 14), and (ii) *ethical* judgements of a type likely to be strongly influenced by religious preconceptions, e.g. sterilization (8, 12, 19).

B. The second is subdivided into (i) statements on personal conduct favouring a *moderate* degree of freedom, particularly in

9. It is possible that part of the difficulty arises from the fact that the ordinary method of bi-polar analysis assumes that the principle of subdivision introduced by any later factor is the same throughout all sections of the previous factors. Were the data based on sufficiently large samples, it might be instructive to attempt an analysis by *subdivided* bi-polars, which would allow the principle of subdivision to be different for the positive and the negative sections of the previous factor (Burt, 1950a).

matrimonial affairs, e.g. divorce by consent (15, 17, 28, 30), and (ii) statements that would be regarded by most people as demanding an *unusual* amount of freedom, e.g. extra-marital sex relations (1, 3, 21).

C. The third section is divided into (i) statements relating mainly to the question of *state* versus *private* (*capitalistic*) *enterprise* (2, 13, 20, 23, 25) and (ii) statements *deprecating severity* in the treatment of conscientious objectors and children, and in bureaucratic control (5, 7, 29).

D. The last section is subdivided into (i) statements insisting on the *equality* of groups (Jews and non-Jews, women and men) (18, 22), and (ii) statements deprecating the *humiliation* of certain groups (Jews, women, coloured folk, criminals) (9, 11, 16, 24, 26, 27). The former maintain that the supposedly inferior groups have equal rights; the latter that they deserve equal treatment. The distinction may perhaps seem a subtle one. But, as it happens, two of the statements in the questionnaire (both relating to Jews) appear among those used by Eysenck; and Guttman draws attention to precisely the same contrast in the two sets to which, in his view, they belong. One set (which includes such statements as 'Jews are as valuable as any other group'), he says, 'scales a person positively if he thinks the Jews are the *same* as anybody else'; the other (which includes such statements as 'Jews have too much power and influence') scales him positively 'if he *dislikes* the Jews' (1951, p. 118). Trivial as the point may appear, it illustrates the fact that both factor analysis and scalogram analysis may lead to precisely the same distinctions.

Hierarchical classification

It will thus be seen that, without any need for rotation, the bipolar analysis reveals a hierarchical classification and subclassification of attitudes, dividing them into species, sub-species, and so on, the whole being covered by one generic factor. The nature of the classification will be clear from Figure 1, where, following a device introduced by Burt, the scheme indicated by the factorial analysis is exhibited in the form of a 'genealogical tree'.

The distinctions between 'superuniverses', 'universes' and 'subuniverses', to which scalogram analysis leads, are, on the surface at any rate, not unlike the distinctions here suggested where attitudes are classified by successive stages or levels according to degree of specialization. However, Guttman himself criticizes at some length any attempt to base a hierarchical classification on the results of factor analysis – an idea which he apparently attributes to Eysenck. 'Even in the field of mental

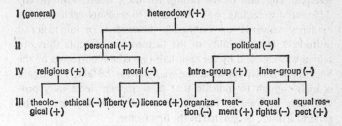

Figure 1 Hierarchical scheme of classification inferred from factors

testing', he says, 'there is no universal acceptance of such a hierarchical theory. . . . Thurstone has a theory of "simple structure" which is quite different from Eysenck's hierarchical one. . . . One can *always* fit a hierarchical theory like Eysenck's to any correlation matrix: it is a pure exercise in arithmetic' (1951, pp. 104–5). The last statement is certainly true. Take a set of correlations between thirty sets of random numbers (representing chance ratings) which have been derived from samples so small that the standard errors, and therefore the non-significant coefficients, are quite large; then factorize them by simple summation: the result will be a succession of bi-polar factors, with a sign pattern superficially resembling a hierarchical classification. But there will be two clear differences. First, the factor matrix *will not be unique:* at each stage there will, as a rule, be no one best way of reversing signs. Secondly, the factor-saturations *will not be significant.* My contention therefore is not only that we here have a hierarchical classification, but that the saturations which specify it are uniquely arranged and for the most part statistically significant.

Finally, the answer to our main problem is clear. Attitudes show both generality and varying degrees of specificity. They display a relational structure; and that structure is hierarchical. Of the factors discovered, the general factor contributes most to the variance; but the bi-polar factors (or the group factors which could be derived from them) are also indicative of genuine differences.

Group differences in the general factor

To measure the general attitude indicated by the first factor the sixteen items having the highest saturations with this factor were selected. The sum of the ratings for these items, without any differential weighting, was then taken to measure each person's tendency towards an habitually heterodox or alterationist attitude.[10] The reliability of the factor-measurements thus obtained was assessed by the split-half procedure, corrected by the Spearman–Brown formula, and was found to be 0·88. This figure is high enough to indicate that these sixteen items may provisionally be used to form a reasonable scale for testing the general attitude designated by the first factor.

Table 2 shows the mean, standard deviation, and coefficient of variability for the two sexes and for the various political parties to which the persons questioned stated that they belonged.

Socialists have the highest factor-measurement; Conservatives the lowest; Liberals fall between the two, being, if anything, nearer to the Conservatives.

Table 2 **Factor-measurements for the various groups**

Group	Mean	Standard deviation	Coefficient of variation
Conservatives	46 ± 2·59	10·68 ± 1·83	23
Liberals	58 ± 2·87	17·00 ± 2·02	29
Socialists	76 ± 1·82	17·46 ± 1·30	22
Non-political	57 ± 3·78	22·98 ± 2·67	40
Men	71 ± 2·78	22·38 ± 2·02	31
Women	62 ± 1·81	19·51 ± 1·28	31

The differences between the mean of the Conservative and Liberal groups and again between the mean of Socialists and those of the Conservative, Liberal and non-political groups were significant at the 1 per cent level. The difference between the Conservative and non-political groups is significant at the 5 per cent level only. The difference between Liberal and non-political groups is not significant.

The men are more heterodox in their attitude than the women; and the difference is significant at the 1 per cent level. This agrees

10. Provided the weights are all moderately high, the use of differential weighting makes little difference to the sum obtained: cf. Burt (1950b).

with the results of somewhat similar inquiries carried out in America. Thus Katz and Allport (1931) conclude that 'the differences between the sexes increase as the degree of orthodoxy diminishes'; Harris, Remmers and Ellison (1932), Johnson (1942), Stagner (1940), and Vetter (1930) all report much the same conclusion.

Judged by the coefficient of variation, the Conservative and Socialist groups appear more homogeneous than the Liberal and non-political group. Uniformity of response may indicate either the influence of a well-formulated and comprehensive political philosophy or else an intellectual inertia and an uncritical acceptance of well-established modes of thinking. It will be noted that a high degree of heterodoxy does not necessarily connote a high degree of original or independent thought on the part of the individual. The further relations between the general attitude thus measured and other traits of temperament and personality form a more speculative problem, and have been discussed in another paper Sanai (1952).

Distribution of degrees of certainty

In a suggestive study, Thouless has reported that most of his subjects, when asked to express an opinion regarding religious questions, displayed a marked bias towards certainty in either a positive or a negative direction: a suspended judgement was rare. As a result, the frequency-distribution of responses formed a U-shaped curve. On the other hand, when the same persons were asked their opinions on alleged assertions of empirical fact (e.g. 'Tigers are found in China'), or on pronouncements in regard to chance occurrences, the frequency-distributions conformed to the normal curve. He argued that the causes of this difference are primarily the presence or absence of a practical implication in various statements: 'in the region of action we must adopt one alternative or the other; scepticism and doubt belong only to thought divorced from action; and of this most people are little capable' (1935).

To examine this conclusion, the responses of 183 persons (a) to the six statements in the questionnaire which related to religion and (b) to the ten statements which related to politics were selected for study, and the frequency-distributions of the averaged replies were plotted in the form of graphs.

For the statements on religious topics the distributions (with one exception) show three peaks – higher values in the middle and at either extreme. The one exception (no. 12) shows a U-shaped rather than a W-shaped curve. So far, therefore, the results do not support Thouless's finding. If we accept his general assumption that 'in the region of action' most people find it difficult to adopt an attitude of neutrality or indifference, it would follow that religious doctrines are today no longer considered to belong to the practical field. The exception (no. 12) concerns the possibility of a good life without religion, and here the form of the statement may be regarded as bringing it within the practical sphere.

For the statements on political topics the majority of the distributions exhibit a U-shaped curve. According to Thouless's principle this result would indicate that, in the minds of those who replied, political issues *do* come within the region of conduct. However, a still more probable explanation is conceivable: in this country (except perhaps among the highly sophisticated or the highly educated) an intermediate position between the two main opposing parties has little interest or support. Burt has also suggested that, as regards political and social questions, the newspaper habitually read may further tend to 'consolidate opinions into firm beliefs'. Three statements (nos. 5, 19 and 28) produced J-shaped distributions: the vast majority of those who replied were definitely of the opinion that conscientious objectors are not traitors to their country, that revolution is not necessary to progress in capitalist societies, and that unrestricted freedom of discussion is strongly desirable. Allport (1934) has drawn special attention to this type of distribution, and has pointed out that 'in any field of conforming behaviour, the distribution of measurable variations of that behaviour is in the shape of a steep unimodal J-shaped curve'.

The occurrence of these non-normal distributions certainly raises important problems for those who desire to measure the degree of concomitant variation between attitudes in the fields here studied. In my view they do not necessarily invalidate the results achieved by the adoption of the usual correlational and factorial techniques; but they may mean that those results can be regarded as no more than a first approximation. For methodological reasons we have provisionally assumed that the qualitative characteristics indicated by the replies are functions of some underlying quantitative variable (or variables) whose distribution is approximately normal; but this is admittedly an assumption for which empirical evidence is desirable.[11] It is hoped in a later investigation to attempt a more intensive inquiry into the use of alternative procedures, notably that of scalogram analysis.

Summary

1. A questionnaire of thirty statements on social, political, and religious topics was given to 250 men and women, who expressed their agreement or disagreement with each on a 7-fold scale. The correlations were factorized by Burt's Method of Simple Summation.

2. Four significant factors were found. The first proved to be a general factor with positive saturations throughout, and was identified with a general tendency towards *heterodoxy* ('alteration-ism') or the reverse. The second factor was bi-polar, and appeared to distinguish *personal* from *political* problems. Of the remaining factors one appeared to divide the positive section of the first bi-polar into *religious* and *moral* subsections, and the negative into *inter-group* and *intra-group* subsections; the other appeared to introduce numerous finer subdivisions whose nature seemed to depend largely on the accidental relations in the questions selected. The whole indicates a *hierarchical classification of attitudes* by factors of increasing specialization.

3. To measure the general tendency towards heterodoxy, the sixteen items most highly saturated with the first factor were treated as forming a provisional scale. The results showed significant differences between the sexes and between the chief political groups.

4. The distributions for the replies to religious questions showed a W-shaped distribution, and for the replies to political questions a U-shaped distribution (with a few minor exceptions). It was inferred that, for those who replied, political questions have a greater practical interest than religious questions.

11. Guttman asserts that, by ignoring the risks attending an uncritical acceptance of such assumptions, 'Eysenck has arrived at nonsensical relations among his hypothetical quantities, namely, a correlation matrix which is not Gramian and partial multiple correlations greater than unity'; as a result, he 'has come a cropper in his own work' (1951, p. 108). We hope that the more conservative procedure we have adopted in calculating our correlations has escaped these graver sources of error.

References

ALLPORT, F. H. (1934), 'The J-curve hypothesis of conforming behaviour', *J. soc. Psychol.*, vol. 5, pp. 141–83.

ALLPORT, G. W. (1935), 'Attitudes', in C. Murchison (ed.), *Handbook of Social Psychology*, Oxford University Press.

BARKER, E. (1947), *Political Thought in England, 1848–1914*, Oxford University Press.

BURT, C. (1937), 'The study of attitudes', unpublished memorandum.

BURT, C. (1939), 'The factorial analysis of emotional traits', *Char. Pers.*, vol. 7, pp. 285–99.

BURT, C. (1940), *The Factors of the Mind*, University of London Press.

BURT, C. (1943), 'An inquiry into public opinion regarding educational reforms', *Occup. Psychol.*, vol. 17, pp. 157–67, vol. 18, pp. 13–23.

BURT, C. (1950a), 'Subdivided factors', *Brit. J. Psych.*, Stat. Sect. 2, pp. 41–63.

BURT, C. (1950b), 'The influence of differential weighting', *Brit. J. Psychol. Stat. Sect.*, vol. 3, pp. 105–25.

BURT, C. (1952), *The Contributions of Psychology to Social Problems*, 22nd Hobhouse Memorial Lecture.

CARLSON, H. B. (1934), 'Attitudes of undergraduate students', *J. Soc. Psychol.*, vol. 5, pp. 202–13.

CHAMBERS, E. G. (1943), 'Statistics in psychology', *Brit. J. Psychol.*, vol. 33, pp. 189–99.

EYSENCK, H. J. (1944), 'General social attitudes', *J. Soc. Psychol.*, vol. 19, pp. 207–27.

EYSENCK, H. J. (1947), 'Primary social attitudes', *Int. J. Opin. Att. Res.* vol. 1, no. 3, pp. 49–84.

FERGUSON, L. W. (1939) 'Primary social attitudes', *J. Psychol.*, vol. 10, pp. 199–205.

FLUGEL, J. C., and HOPKINS, P. (1944), 'A study of social and political attitudes among members of propagandist societies', *J. Soc. Psychol.*, vol. 20, pp. 195–231.

GUTTMAN, L. (1951), 'Scale analysis, factor analysis, and Dr Eysenck', *Int. J. Opin. Att. Res.*, vol. 5, pp. 103–20.

HARRIS, A. J., REMMERS, H. H., and ELLISON, C. E. (1932), 'The relation between liberal and conservative attitude in college students and other factors', *J. soc. Psychol.*, vol. 3, pp. 320–35.

JOHNSON, M. (1942), 'A preliminary study of social attitudes', *Brit. J. Educ. Psychol.*, vol. 12, p. 183.

JOHNSON, W. E. (1921–4), *Logic*, Cambridge University Press.

KATZ, D., and ALLPORT, F. H. (1931), *Students' Attitudes*, Craftsman Press.

McDOUGALL, W. (1912), *Psychology: The Study of Behaviour*, Methuen.

McDOUGALL, W. (1936), *Social Psychology*, 23rd edn., Methuen.

McNEMAR, Q. (1946), 'Opinion attitude methodology', *Psychol. Bull.*, vol. 43, pp. 289–374.

PENROSE, L. S. (1950), 'Factor analysis as a statistical technique', *J. Roy. Stats. Soc.*, vol. 4, p. 90.

SANAI, M. (1950–51), 'An experimental study of politico-economic attitudes', *Int. J. Opin. Att. Res.*, vol. 4, pp. 563–7.

SANAI, M. (1951), 'An experimental study of social attitudes',
  J. Soc. Psychol., vol. 34, pp. 235–64.
SANAI, M. (1952), 'The relation between social attitudes and
  characteristics of personality', *J. Soc. Psychol.*, vol. 36, pp. 3–13.
STAGNER, R. (1940), 'The cross-out technique as a method in public
  opinion analysis', *J. Soc. Psychol.*, vol. 2, pp. 79–90.
THOMSON, G. H. (1946), *The Factorial Analysis of Human Ability*,
  University of London Press.
THOULESS, R. H. (1935), 'The tendency to certainty in religious belief',
  Brit. J. Psychol., vol. 26, pp. 16–31.
THURSTONE, L. L. (1934), 'Vectors of the mind', *Psychol. Rev.*,
  vol. 41, pp. 1–32.
VETTER, C. G. (1930), 'The measurement of social and political
  attitudes and related personality factors', *J. abnorm. soc. Psychol.*,
  vol. 25, pp. 149–89.

Part Four
Measurement

Sound methods of measurement are needed to improve our knowledge of psychology and religion. In general they require tasks on which a person's performance can be assessed and compared with that of others. There are also methods that rely on responses to many different kinds of questioning. This section gives further examples of common scales, and leads to measures that have been derived from a theory, like Piaget's developmental psychology, Osgood's theory of semantic meaning, and the psychoanalytic assumption that a person expresses aspects of himself whenever he describes what he sees in a vague or ambiguous stimulus or classifies statements. These methods have all been developed within general psychology, and applied to religious material. Their broad aim is to place individuals along a specified dimension.

Some common attitude scales are set out in detail in Robinson and Shaver (1969), and in Shaw and Wright (1967).

References

ROBINSON, J. P., and SHAVER, P. R. (1949), 'Religious attitudes', in *Measures of Social Psychological Attitudes*, Institute for Social Research, University of Michigan.

SHAW, M. E., and WRIGHT, J. M. (1967), *Scales for the Measurement of Attitudes*, McGraw-Hill.

9 William James

Answers to Pratt's Questionnaire

William James, *The Letters of William James*, Longman, 1926, edited by
his son, Henry James, pp. 212–15.

The following document is a series of answers to a questionnaire
upon the subject of religious belief, which was sent out in 1904 by
Professor James B. Pratt of Williams College, and to which
William James filled out a reply at an unascertained date in the
autumn of that year.

Questionnaire (James's answers are printed in italics)

It is being realized as never before that religion, as one of the
most important things in the life both of the community and of
the individual, deserves close and extended study. Such study can
be of value only if based upon the personal experiences of many
individuals. If you are in sympathy with such study and are willing to assist in it, will you kindly write out the answers to the
following questions and return them with this questionnaire, as
soon as you conveniently can, to James B. Pratt, 20 Shepard
Street, Cambridge, Mass.

   Please answer the questions at length and in detail. Do not give
philosophical generalizations, but your own personal experience.

1. What does religion mean to you personally? Is it
   (1) A belief that something exists? *Yes.*
   (2) An emotional experience? *Not powerfully so, yet a social
       reality.*
   (3) A general attitude of the will toward God or toward right-
       eousness? *It involves these.*
   (4) Or something else?

If it has several elements, which is for you the most important?
*The social appeal for corroboration, consolation, etc., when things
are going wrong with my causes (my truth denied)*, etc.

2. What do you mean by God? *A combination of Ideality and
    (final) efficacity.*
   (1) Is He a person – if so, what do you mean by His being a

person? *He must be cognizant and responsive in some way.*

(2) Or is He only a Force? *He must* do.

(3) Or is God an attitude of the Universe toward you? *Yes but more conscious. 'God', to me, is not the only spiritual reality to believe in. Religion means primarily a universe of spiritual relations surrounding the earthly practical ones, not merely relations of 'value', but agencies and their activities. I suppose that the chief premise for my hospitality towards the religious testimony of others is my conviction that 'normal' or 'sane' consciousness is so small a part of actual experience. What e'er be true, it is not true exclusively, as philistine scientific opinion assumes. The other kinds of consciousness bear witness to a much wider universe of experiences, from which our belief selects and emphasizes such parts as best satisfy our needs.*

How do you apprehend his relation to mankind and to you personally?

If your position on any of these matters is uncertain, please state the fact. } *Uncertain.*

3. Why do you believe in God? Is it

(1) From some argument? *Emphatically, no.*

Or (2) Because you have experienced His presence? *No, but rather because I need it so that it 'must' be true.*

Or (3) From authority, such as that of the Bible or of some prophetic person? *Only the whole tradition of religious people, to which something in me makes admiring response.*

Or (4) From any other reason? *Only for the social reasons.*

If from several of these reasons, please indicate carefully the order of their importance.

4. Or do you not so much *believe* in God as want to *use* Him? *I can't use him very definitely, yet I believe.* Do you accept Him not so much as a real existent Being, but rather as an ideal to live by? *More as a more powerful ally of my own ideals.* If you should become thoroughly convinced that there was no God, would it make any great difference in your life – either in happiness, morality, or in other respects? *Hard to say. It would surely make some difference.*

5. Is God very real to you, as real as an earthly friend, though different? *Dimly (real); not (as an earthly friend).*

Do you feel that you have experienced His presence? If so, please describe what you mean by such an experience. *Never.*

How vague or how distinct is it? How does it affect you mentally and physically?

If you have had no such experience, do you accept the testimony of others who claim to have felt God's presence directly? Please answer this question with special care and in as great detail as possible. *Yes! The whole line of testimony on this point is so strong that I am unable to pooh-pooh it away. No doubt there is a germ in me of something similar that makes response.*

6. Do you pray, and if so, why? That is, is it purely from habit, and social custom, or do you really believe that God hears your prayers? *I can't possibly pray – I feel foolish and artificial.*

Is prayer with you one-sided or two-sided – i.e. do you sometimes feel that in prayer you receive something – such as strength or the divine spirit – from God? Is it a real communion?

7. What do you mean by 'spirituality'? *Susceptibility to ideals, but with a certain freedom to indulge in imagination about them. A certain amount of 'other worldly' fancy. Otherwise you have mere morality, or 'taste'.*

Describe a typical spiritual person. *Phillips Brooks.*

8. Do you believe in personal immortality? *Never keenly; but more strongly as I grow older.* If so, why? *Because I am just getting fit to live.*

9. Do you accept the Bible as *authority* in religious matters? Are your religious faith and your religious life based on it? If so, how would your belief in God and your life toward Him and your fellow men be affected by loss of faith in the *authority* of the Bible? *No. No. No. It is so human a book that I don't see how belief in its divine authorship can survive the reading of it.*

10. What do you mean by a 'religious experience'? *Any moment of life that brings the reality of spiritual things more 'home' to one.*

10 L. L. Thurstone and E. Chave

Attitude toward the Church

L. L. Thurstone and E. Chave, 'Attitude toward the church', reprinted in
M. E. Shaw and J. M. Wright (eds.), *Scales for the Measurement of
Attitudes*, McGraw-Hill, 1967, pp. 544–6.

Scales in this section have been designed to measure attitudes toward religious institutions (i.e. the church). Scales measuring attitudes toward other religious referents must be sought in other chapters (attitudes toward God are included in chapter 6, attitudes toward Sunday observance and religious practices in chapter 3, attitudes related to religious and philosophical issues are contained in chapter 4). Persons interested in a scale for hostility toward the church should see Funk's battery of scales in chapter 7.

Attitude toward the church
Exhibit 10-15

Description. This is a twenty-four-item scale developed by Thurstone and Chave (1929). It has been used extensively since that time. The items are not at all dated. The content of the scale deals with the social, personal and moral significance of the church. Unfortunately, there are no equivalent forms for the scale, and the Q values for the items could not be located.

Subjects. The sample on which the scale was originally constructed is unknown, but it is assumed to have been University of Chicago undergraduate students.

Response mode. Persons respond by placing a check mark beside those items with which they agree and a cross beside those with which they disagree; they place a question mark beside the items about which they are undecided.

Scoring. The person's score is the median of the scale values of the items which he endorses as 'agree'. A high score indicates an unfavorable attitude toward the church.

Reliability. Nelson (1956) reports a good degree of consistency on a test–retest type of study of changes in attitudes of ex-college students over a period of fifteen years (1936 to 1950), based upon N of 893. In his study, he reports that 51 per cent of the subjects showed no shift in attitude. Of the remaining 49 per cent, 35 per cent shifted toward a more favorable attitude toward the church, and 14 per cent shifted against the church. The two distributions of scores for the 1936 and 1950 testings of this sample are impressively similar.

Validity. Nickols and Shaw (1964) have found this scale to correlate 0·39 (a high saliency group) and 0·76 (a low saliency group) with the semantic differential measurement of attitude toward the church. Diggory (1953) reports the following correlations of this scale with the Thurstone scale measuring attitude toward God, based upon a sample of seventy-five men and 103 women: male, 0·78; female, 0·90. This finding would seem to show a high degree of construct validity. Osgood *et al.* (1957) report correlations ranging from 0·74 to 0·84 between Thurstone and semantic differential measurements of attitudes toward this and other referents.

Comments. This scale seems a relatively valid measuring instrument for purposes of group testing and has been widely used. Evidence is available on which to infer reliability, but further estimates of its reliability are required. For another study using this scale, see Telford (1934).

Exhibit 10-15
Attitude toward the church

This is a study of attitudes toward the church. Below there are twenty-four statements expressing different attitudes toward the church. Put a check mark ($\sqrt{}$) if you agree with a statement. Put a cross ($\times$) if you disagree with a statement. If you cannot decide about a statement, you may mark it with a question mark. This is not an examination. People differ in their opinions about what is right and wrong on a question. Please indicate *your own attitude* by a check mark when you agree and by a cross when you disagree.

Scale value		
3·3	1	I enjoy my church because there is a spirit of friendliness there.
5·1	2	I like the ceremonies of my church but do not miss them much when I stay away.
8·8	3	I respect any church-member's beliefs but I think it is all 'bunk.'
6·1	4	I feel the need for religion but do not find what I want in any one church.
8·3	5	I think the teaching of the church is altogether too superficial to have much social significance.
11·0	6	I think the church is a parasite on society.
6·7	7	I believe in sincerity and goodness without any church ceremonies.
3·1	8	I do not understand the dogmas or creeds of the church but I find that the church helps me to be more honest and creditable.
9·6	9	I think the church is a hindrance to religion for it still depends upon magic, superstition and myth.
9·2	10	I think the church seeks to impose a lot of worn-out dogmas and medieval superstitions.
4·0	11	When I go to church I enjoy a fine ritual service with good music.
0·8	12	I feel the church perpetuates the values which man puts highest in his philosophy of life.
5·6	13	Sometimes I feel that the church and religion are necessary and sometimes I doubt it.
7·5	14	I think too much money is being spent on the church for the benefit that is being derived.
10·7	15	I think the organized church is an enemy of science and truth.
2·2	16	I like to go to church for I get something worth while to think about and it keeps my mind filled with right thoughts.
1·2	17	I believe the church is a powerful agency for promoting both individual and social righteousness.
7·2	18	I believe the churches are too much divided by factions and denominations to be a strong force for righteousness.
4·5	19	I believe in what the church teaches but with mental reservations.
0·2	20	I believe the church is the greatest institution in America today.
4·7	21	I am careless about religion and church relationships but I would not like to see my attitude become general.
10·4	22	The church represents shallowness, hypocrisy and prejudice.

1·7	23	I feel the church services give me inspiration and help me to live up to my best during the following week.
2·6	24	I think the church keeps business and politics up to a higher standard than they would otherwise tend to maintain.

References

DIGGORY, J. C. (1953), 'Sex differences in the organization of attitudes', *J. Person*, vol. 22, pp. 89–200.

NELSON, E. N. P. (1956), 'Patterns of religious attitude shifts from college to fourteen years later', *Psychol. Monogr.*, vol. 70, no. 17, (whole no. 424).

NICKOLS, S. A., and SHAW, M. E. (1964), 'Saliency and two measures of attitude', *Psychol. Rep.*, vol. 14, pp. 273–4.

OSGOOD, C. E. *et. al.* (1957), *The Measurement of Meaning*, University of Illinois Press.

TELFORD, C. W. (1934), 'An experimental study of some factors influencing the social attitudes of college students', *J. soc. Psychol.*, vol. 5, pp. 421–8.

THURSTONE, L. L., and CHAVE, E. J. (1929), *The Measurement of Attitude*, University of Chicago Press.

11 D. Elkind

Piaget's Semi-Clinical Interview and the Study of Spontaneous Religion

D. Elkind, 'Piaget's semi-clinical interview and the study of spontaneous religion', *Journal for the Scientific Study of Religion*, 1964, vol. 4, no. 1, pp. 40–47.

For research purposes it is convenient to distinguish between the spontaneous and the acquired religion of the child. The child's spontaneous religion consists of all those ideas and beliefs that he has constructed in his attempts to interpret religious terms and practices that are beyond his level of comprehension. For example, upon hearing that God was everywhere, a boy refused to occupy his favorite chair for fear of 'sitting on God' and thus revealed his spontaneous conception of God's omnipresence. In contrast to these spontaneous mental constructions there are many religious ideas and beliefs that the child acquires directly from adults either through imitation or through instruction. A child's recitation of the standard definition of theological terms or of particular prayers would thus reflect acquired rather than spontaneous religion.

It is fair to say that by far the majority of research on religious development has concerned itself with acquired rather than with spontaneous religion. For example, in many of the studies dealing with the God conception (Barnes, 1892; Bose, 1929; Mac-Lean, 1930; Mathias, 1943; Tanner, 1906), questionnaires were employed which either asked children to choose among standard conceptions of the Deity or required them to complete sentences which strongly suggested the standard conceptions (e.g. 'God, where is he?'). While such studies of acquired religion are of value for assessing the degree to which children profit from religious education, they do not reveal the full nature of religious development. Indeed, they can be misleading! In all of the studies mentioned above none of the investigators noted any marked age differences in the God concept even when a considerable age span (four to fourteen) was sampled in the study. Yet, developmental psychology has repeatedly shown (Piaget, 1928, 1929, 1930, 1952; Reichard, Schneider and Rapaport, 1944; Welch and Long, 1940a, 1940b, 1940c;) that children's spontaneous conceptions follow a regular sequence from concrete to abstract conceptualization between early (four to six) and late childhood (ten to twelve).

This is not to say that results from the traditional questionnaire studies of religious development are wrong but only that the acquired religion revealed by these results does not follow the same developmental course as spontaneous religion. Since even the young child can memorize definitions of religious terms, it is not surprising that when children are tested on these definitions the young children do about as well as the older children do. If, on the other hand, the *understanding* of these definitions were to be evaluated, it is likely that significant age differences would be found because the understandings would reflect the child's spontaneous and not his acquired ideas. Only the child's spontaneous ideas follow the sequence from the concrete to the abstract that we have come to expect in developmental studies of concept formation.

As yet, however, we have little information about the spontaneous religion of the child, and the purpose of the present paper is to describe and illustrate (by means of a completed investigation) a method for exploring the child's own interpretations of religious terms and practices. The method to be described is the semi-clinical interview devised by the Swiss psychologist, Jean Piaget.

The semi-clinical interview
Background of the method

Piaget was one of the first investigators to realize that the child's spontaneous remarks were more than amusing errors and that they reflected forms of thought that were different from those used by adults. In order to investigate children's spontaneous thought Piaget was forced to devise his own method in as much as this aspect of thought had not been previously recognized, much less explored. The specifications for such a method, however, were exceedingly stringent and apparently contradictory. For what Piaget required was a method with sufficient flexibility to enable him to follow the meandering stream of any particular child's thought and yet with sufficient standardization to enable him to reach the same destination with many different children at different age levels.

The only method which met the first of these specifications was the psychiatric interview, while the only method which met the second specification was the mental test This being the case, Piaget combined the standard questions of the mental test with the free inquiry of the psychiatric interview and labeled the result the semi-clinical interview. The union of standard question and free inquiry was a happy one and led to the now classic findings concerning children's conceptions of physical causality (1930) of the world (1929) and of judgement and reasoning (1928).

Despite the proven fruitfulness of the semi-clinical interview, however, it has seldom been employed by American psychologists and with one exception (Elkind, 1961, 1962, 1963) has never been brought to bear on the study of religious development. The reasons for this neglect of Piaget's method are several, including the amount of time and skill required of the examiner and the difficulty involved in interpreting the obtained data. While these objections are well taken, they do not outweigh the potential value of the method for exploring spontaneous religion.

In the first place, although the interview is more time consuming than the questionnaire, the obtained data will be much more complete and therefore more revealing than that obtained by more rapid group testing procedures. In the second place, while skill in conversing with children is required, most investigators dealing with children have the basic requirements for a good interviewer: a liking for children, a respect for their individuality, and patience. As for the difficulty in interpreting responses, this is present no matter what method is used and, in fact, Piaget has given particular attention to this problem and has worked out techniques and criteria for discriminating between the significant and the trivial in children's verbalizations. So, on this point the Piaget method is actually superior to the questionnaire wherein no such discriminations can be made. There are then no really good reasons for not using the interview techniques in studying religious growth.

Construction of interview questions

Since the construction of appropriate questions is one of the most difficult features of the semi-clinical interview, an illustration of how the author proceeds in formulating such questions might be helpful to prospective investigators. In general one begins with a remark that suggests the presence of a spontaneous conceptualization For example, after the tragic death of President Kennedy the author heard a child say, 'Are they going to shoot God too?' This remark suggested that the child identified God with famous persons in high offices and opened up a whole new path of inquiry. If we desire to follow this lead we might begin formulating some questions about God and high offices. For example we might ask, 'Can God be president of the United States? Why or why not?' Furthermore we might ask about how God obtained his position. For example one might ask, 'Who chooses the president? Who chooses God, or how did God become God?'

If this line of inquiry proved unfruitful we might go back to the original remark and note that it also suggests that God is conceived as a person. This notion leads to quite another line of questioning (Can God dance, talk French?, etc.). Should this line of inquiry prove barren we might approach the problem from the fact that the term 'God' is a name and ask such things as 'How did God get his name? Does God have a first name?', etc. The only requirement in formulating questions is that they be so absurd, to the adult way of thought, that one can be reasonably certain children have not been trained one way or the other regarding them. Trial and error with various questions proposed to one's own or to neighbors' children will soon reveal which questions are the most productive of unstereotyped, spontaneous replies.

Interview technique

Once a group of related questions about a given topic has been gathered, the actual interviewing can begin. The child should be seen in a quiet place where there are few distractions and at a time when he does not desire to be somewhere else. As soon as the examiner has won *rapport* with the child – most easily accomplished by asking the youngster a few questions about himself – he can begin putting his interview questions. After the child has replied, it is usually necessary to ask additional questions to clarify the meaning of the response. It is in this free inquiry part of the interview that the most skill is required because the examiner must direct the child's thought without, at the same time, suggesting an appropriate answer. There is no better preparation for this part of the examination than a course in Rorschach testing because in the Rorschach examination non-suggestive questioning is developed to a fine art.

Interpretation of results: validity

Both during the examination and afterwards, in analysing the data, the most important question is to what extent the child's response truly reflects his own mental constructions. To this end Piaget has described five types of response that need to be distinguished in any examination of the child. When the child is not at all interested in the question and is bored or tired, he may simply answer with anything that comes into his head just to be relieved of the burden of having to answer. Piaget speaks of such responses as *answers at random*. When a child fabricates or invents an answer, without really reflecting about the question, Piaget speaks of *romancing*. On the other hand, when the child does attend to the question but his answer is determined by a desire to please the examiner or is suggested by the question, Piaget speaks of *suggested conviction*.

In contrast to the three foregoing types of reply, which are of little value to the investigator, the following two types are of very great significance. When the child reflects about a question which is new to him and answers it from the reservoirs of his own thought, Piaget calls this *a liberated conviction*. And when the child answers quickly, without reflection, because he has already formulated the solution or because it was latently formulated, it is called by Piaget a *spontaneous conviction*.

Since the investigator is primarily interested in the liberated and the spontaneous conviction, it is important to have ways of separating them from answers at random, romancing and suggested convictions. This can be done at two points in the investigation, one during and the other following the interview. If, during the interview itself, the examiner suspects that a reply is other than a spontaneous or a liberated conviction, he can check this in several ways. First, he can offer counter suggestions to determine how firmly rooted the idea is in the child's thought. A true liberated or spontaneous conviction will withstand counter suggestion whereas romancing, suggested convictions and answers at random are easily changed by counter suggestions. Secondly, he can ask about related issues. If the idea is truly a conviction of the child's, it will fit a pattern or system of ideas that follow a general principle or rule which Piaget calls a *schema*. If the child's response fits the general trend or schema of his thought, this is a good indication that it is either a spontaneous or liberated conviction.

The second point at which one can determine whether or not replies obtained in the interview represent genuine convictions occurs after the data have been collected and age trends can be examined. First of all, if the majority of children at the same age level give similar replies, this is evidence that the responses reflect a form of thought characteristic of that age. If the answers were random, suggested or romancing, there would be no reason to expect such uniformity. Secondly, if the responses show a gradual evolution with age in the direction of a closer approximation to the adult conception, this is another evidence that the replies reflect a true developmental trend. Finally, a valid developmental sequence must give signs of continuity in the sense that traces of concrete ideas held at early age levels (adherences) are present among the abstract conceptions of older children and in the sense that foreshadowings of abstract ideas typical of older children (anticipations) are present among the concrete expressions of the young children.

The use of counter suggestion and varied questioning during the interviewing of individual children and of the three group criteria during the analysis of the data from all children provides a good basis for determining whether the obtained responses are indeed liberated or spontaneous convictions. Piaget has thus provided several means for checking the validity of the data obtained by his semi-clinical interview.

Interpretation of results: reliability

Although Piaget has always been concerned about the validity of his observations he has almost ignored the question of their reliability, i.e. their repeatability. A possible reason for this neglect is that Piaget's training in biological science has led him to assume that a characteristic found in the individual can automatically be taken as characteristic of the species. Such a position is less defensible for the complex human species than it is for lesser organisms, however, and reliability measures probably should be made when using the Piaget method. Two such measures are needed. One is a measure of the consistency with which individual children respond to interview questions at different times. This measure can be obtained by retesting each of the subjects, preferably not before a month and not later than six months after the original examination. The correlation of initial and retest responses will provide an index of response reliability.

The second index of reliability that should be obtained relates to the categorization of responses into stages or sequences of development. That is to say, it is necessary to determine whether the responses are sufficiently distinctive that independent workers will classify them in similar ways. If several persons independently categorize the responses and a measure of their agreement is determined, this measure will serve as an index of the reliability of the categorization. These steps to insure the reliability of response, together with the fulfilment of Piaget's criteria for determining validity, should suffice to insure that investigations employing the semi-clinical interview will be acceptable to even the most hard-headed experimentalist.

To make the use of the semi-clinical interview concrete, a study in which the method was applied to the development of religious identity will be briefly described and summarized.

The development of religious identity

Religious identity can be defined in terms of the spontaneous meanings children attach to their religious denomination. A developmental study of these meanings was undertaken by the writer who investigated the growth of religious identity among Jewish (Elkind, 1961), Catholic (Elkind, 1962), and Congregational Protestant (Elkind, 1963) children.

In these studies the children were individually interviewed and asked six novel questions about their denomination. The questions were, with the appropriate denominational term inserted:

1. Is your family ... ? Are you ... ? Are all boys and girls in the world ... ?

2. Can a dog or cat be ... ?

3. How do you become a ... ?

4. What is a ... ?

5. How can you tell a person is ... ?

6. Can you be ... and American at the same time?

In order to clarify the meaning of the child's responses and to ensure that these were firmly rooted in his thought, additional questions, following no set pattern, were asked.

These questions had their origin in a child's spontaneous question which the author happened to overhear. The child asked whether a dog that ate kosher food became Jewish. From this remark it was clear that the child did not really understand the word 'Jewish' in the adult sense but had his own spontaneous conception, namely, that you became Jewish by eating kosher foods. It seemed to the author that such spontaneous religious conceptions were probably not unique to this child and that an exploration of age changes in the child's spontaneous conceptions of his denomination might reveal material of interest to the developmental psychology of religion. Since a denominational term is basically a class concept, it seemed reasonable to frame questions which would tap various aspects of this class notion but in ways novel to the majority of children. Accordingly, questions 1, 2 and 5 get at the child's understanding of the extension of the concept, i.e. the groups to which it is appropriately applied and the external signs by which group membership can be recognized. Questions 3 and 4, on the other hand, tap the child's grasp of the intension of the concept, i.e. the property or properties that distinguish members belonging to a particular group. Finally, question 6 was designed to test the child's conception of multiple group membership.

In each denominational group at least thirty children at each age level from five to eleven (among the Jewish children) and six to twelve (among the Protestant and Catholic children) were interviewed so that more than 700 children were examined. No attempt was made to control for liberal/conservative status, church attendance, etc., in the belief that uniformities which appeared despite a great deal of uncontrolled variation would be further support for the view that maturation as well as experience plays a part in religious development.

Piaget's (1929) criteria for interpreting children's responses as liberated or spontaneous convictions were applied to the interview materials. The results met all three criteria and there was:

1. Uniformity of ideas at a given age level which often extended over several year levels.

2. An increasing correctness (conformance with adult conceptions) of children's ideas with increasing age.

3. Adherences of ideas from an earlier year level as part of, or added to, the more advanced ideas given at a later age level and also anticipations of later conceptions in the remarks of younger children.

Analysis of the age changes in response made it possible to distinguish three well-marked stages in the attainment of religious identity which held true of Jewish, Protestant and Catholic children.

At the first stage (usually ages five to seven) the child had only a global, undifferentiated conception of his denomination as a kind of proper name. Although he acknowledged being a Jew, Protestant or Catholic, he confused these names with the terms for race and nationality, for example:

Sid (6–3) What is a Jew? 'A person.' How is a Jewish person different from a Catholic? 'Cause some people have black hair and some people have blond.'

Mel (5–9) What is a Jew? 'A man.' How is a Jewish person different from a Catholic? 'He comes from a different country.' Which one? 'Israel.' Furthermore, at this stage the child regarded having a denominational name as incompatible with possessing a racial or national designation. For example, it was common for the child at this stage to reply, in answer to the question about being an American and a Jew (Protestant, Catholic) at the same time, 'You can't have two.' That is to say, because you can't have two names.

Children at the second stage (usually ages seven to nine) had a concretely differentiated conception of their denomination. Their conception was concrete in the sense that they used observable features or actions to define their denomination, and their conception among different behaviors in order to distinguish persons belonging to different denominations. For example:

Mae (7–9) What is a Jew? 'A person who goes to Temple or Hebrew school.'

Bill (8–10) What is a Catholic? 'He goes to mass every Sunday and goes to Catholic school.'

Ron (7–9) Can you be a Catholic and a Protestant at the same time? 'No.' Why not? 'Cause you couldn't go to two churches.'
Unlike the first-stage children, young people at the second stage said they could be an American and their denomination at the same time. The reasons given in explanation were concrete and personal to the effect that 'You can live in America and go to church' or 'I'm an American and I'm a Protestant.'

Third-stage children (usually ages ten to twelve) demonstrated an abstract, differentiated conception of their denomination. It was an abstract conception in the sense that these children no longer defined their denomination by mentioning names or observable activities but rather by mentioning non-observable mental attributes such as belief and understanding. For example:

Bi (12–0) What is a Catholic? 'A person who believes in the truths of the Roman Catholic Church.' Can a dog or a cat be Catholic? 'No, because they don't have a brain or intellect.'

Sed (11–10) What is a Jew? 'A person who believes in one God and doesn't believe in the New Testament.'

When third-stage children were asked the question as to whether they could be American and their denomination at the same time, they replied that one was a nationality and the other was a religion and that they were two different things.

In summary, the results of this study dealing with children's conceptions of their religious identity have shown that identity is at first vague and undifferentiated and has no more significance than a proper name. Gradually the child comes to think of his religious identity in terms of certain religious practices and sacred objects, and since these differ from religion to religion, he now has a means for discriminating between children of different religions. It is only at the age of eleven or twelve, however, that a majority of children come to think of their religious identity in terms of particular beliefs for it is only at this age that the child can reflect on his own thought. To the writer it seems that these interesting findings regarding the development of religious identity would not have been found if a pencil-and-paper technique had been used.

Potential applications

The foregoing sections have described a method for exploring the spontaneous religion of children and the results of a study in which this method was applied to the problems of religious identity. In this concluding section it remains to suggest the range of problems to which the method might be applied and also to suggest the importance of the findings which could result.

With regards to the problems to which the semi-clinical interview could be appropriately applied, they are the traditional ones of the developmental psychology of religion. Conceptions of God, of belief, of prayer, of sin, of morality and many others all deserve to be looked at from the point of view of spontaneous religion. It would be fascinating too, if someone were to undertake a study of children's theologies and cosmologies; of children's confusions between magic and ritual and of children's attempts at integrating moral and religious ideas. For the study of these issues and of many more like them, the semi-clinical interview is a necessary starting point.

The results to be obtained from the study of such issues will be of more than theoretical interest and will pertain directly to religious education. A knowledge, for example, of the erroneous interpretations children are likely to attach to religious conceptions at different age levels would suggest ways of teaching these concepts so that they would not be misunderstood. More importantly, perhaps, the educator's awareness of the ideas children inevitably associate with religious terms and practices will change his orientation. The awareness of spontaneous religion carries with it the implication that teaching must be more than writing on a *tabula rasa*; and that it must be instead the replacement of the correct for the incorrect, the substitution of the proportionate for the exaggerated and the inculcation of the essential in lieu of the trivial. To attain this orientation the religious educator must be conversant with the spontaneous thought of the child.

There are then potent reasons for exploring the spontaneous religion of children and hence for the use of the semi-clinical interview in the study of religious development.

References

BARNES, E. (1892), 'Theological life of a California child', *Pedagog. Semin.*, vol. 2, pp. 442–8.

BOSE, R. S. (1929), 'Religious concepts of children', *Relig. Educ.*, vol. 24, pp. 831–7.

ELKIND, D. (1961), 'The child's conception of his religious denomination I: The Jewish child', *J. genet. Psychol.*, vol. 99, pp. 209–25.

ELKIND, D. (1962), 'The child's conception of his religious denomination II: The Catholic child', *J. genet. Psychol.*, vol. 101, pp. 185–93.

ELKIND, D. (1963), 'The child's conception of his religious denomination III: The Protestant child', *J. genet. Psychol.*, vol. 103, pp. 291–304.

MACLEAN, A. H. (1930), *The Idea of God in Protestant Religious Education*, Columbia University Press.

MATHIAS, W. D. (1943), *Ideas of God and Conduct*, Columbia University Press.

PIAGET, J. (1928), *Judgment and Reasoning in the Child*, Routledge & Kegan Paul.

PIAGET, J. (1929), *The Child's Conception of the World*, Routledge & Kegan Paul.

PIAGET, J. (1930), *The Child's Conception of Physical Causality*, Routledge & Kegan Paul.

PIAGET, J. (1952), *The Child's Conception of Number*, Routledge & Kegan Paul.

REICHARD, S., SCHNEIDER, M., and RAPAPORT, D. (1944), 'The development of concept formation in children', *Amer. J. Orthopsychiat.*, vol. 14, pp. 156–62.

TANNER, A. E. (1906), 'Children's religious ideas', *Pedagog. Semin.*, vol. 13, pp. 511–13.

WELCH, L., and LONG, L. (1940a), 'The higher structural phrases of concept formation in children', *J. Psychol.*, vol. 9, pp. 59–95.

WELCH, L., and LONG, L. (1940b), 'A further investigation of the
higher structural phases of concept formation', *J. Psychol.*, vol. 10,
pp. 211–20
WELCH, L., and LONG, L. (1940c), 'The genetic development of the
associational structures of abstract thinking', *J. genet. Psychol.*,
vol. 56, pp. 175–206.

12 Morven O. Nelson and E. M. Jones

An Application of the Q-Technique to the Study of
Religious Concepts

Morven O. Nelson and E. M. Jones, 'An application of the
Q-technique to the study of religious concepts', *Psychological Reports*,
1957, vol. 3, pp. 293–7.

The scientific investigation of religious problems has frequently
been stifled because of the lack of suitable research instruments.
Some bold attempts to apply the scientific method to the investigation of problems in this field have met with considerable success, e.g. the classic works of William James (1902), Starbuck
(1901), and Coe (1900). Sigmund Freud (1912) and a number of
other psychoanalysts have provided a great deal of insight into
the unconscious motives involved in religious experience by use
of clinical procedures. Allport (1950) applied the scientific method
to the study of the nature of individual religious experience. In
the main, however, most studies seem lacking in specific techniques for obtaining objective data needed in gaining a scientific
description of religious factors.

Problem

The problem for the present investigation was to study the extent
to which the Q-technique might be adapted as an instrument for
the investigation of religious concepts. The specific area of religious concepts selected for investigation was that relating to the
idea of God. It had been noted that Freud, on the basis of clinical
data, suggested that the God concept is formed by the projection
of attitudes and feelings toward one's earthly father into a pattern that could be thought of as a supernatural father, or God
(1938, p. 915). This study attempts to apply an adaptation of the
Q-technique to the investigation of certain aspects of Freud's
hypothesis.

Procedure
Subjects

The group of Ss used in this investigation was composed of sixteen persons of Protestant faith. Among the group were eight
men and eight women, ranging in age from eighteen to forty-four.

Of this number, fifteen were between the ages of eighteen and twenty-seven. Three of the group were married and thirteen were single. With the exception of one woman forty-four years of age, all Ss were students in a church-related college of liberal arts.

Construction of instruments

A list of sixty statements was constructed following the pattern of the Q-technique described by Stephenson (1953). Each question was so worded that it could be used to complete any one of the following sentences: 'When I think of God I ...;' When I think of Jesus I ...;' When I think of Father I ...'; When I think of Mother I ...' The statements were designed to describe feelings, ranging from very positive ones to very negative ones, which might be precipitated by the sentences to be completed. The statements included items such as the following: '....have a feeling that I am understood;' '... feel this is someone who holds nothing against me;' '... have a feeling that I am not always accepted;' '... feel that this is someone who sometimes loves me and sometimes does not love me;' '... feel that this is someone on whom I can never depend;' and, '... have a sense of something being held against me.' Each statement was typed on a separate 3 × 5 card which was numbered on the reverse side.

Nine spaces to accommodate the 3 × 5 cards were drawn on a 54 in × 18 in strip of white cardboard. The spaces were assigned values ranging from zero to eight. The values were written above their respective spaces. At the 'zero' end of the scale was printed the statement: 'Most like I feel', while at the 'eight' end of the scale was printed the statement: 'Least like I feel'. Below each of the spaces was placed a number designating the number of cards to be placed in that space. These numbers were arranged to force a normal distribution of cards ranging from the categories zero to eight, as follows:

	Most like I feel				Least like I feel			
Scale	0	1	2	3	4	5	6	7	8
No. of cards	1	2	6	12	18	12	6	2	1

Administration of the test

Each S was asked to sort the statements four times, placing them in the appropriate position on the scale. Only the designated number of statements were allowed for each space. During the first sorting an 8 in × 6 in card bearing the incomplete sentence 'When I think of God I ...' was placed above the scale so that the cards could be sorted as statements completing that sentence. During the second, third, and fourth sortings, the incomplete sentences referring to Father, Jesus and Mother were respectively used instead of the sentence referring to God.

Statistical treatment

After each sorting the position on the scale for each statement was recorded as the score for that statement. The scores were then used to compute product-moment correlations for six pairs of factors formed by pairing each of the four sortings of statements with each of the other sortings.

In order to discover the degree to which negative or positive feelings were expressed toward Father and Mother, the statements were separated into three groups of twenty statements, each representing those considered by the Es to be expressions of positive, negative, neutral, or ambivalent feelings, respectively. By placing all of the positive statements at the 'Most like I feel', end of the scale and the negative statements at the 'Least like I feel' end, the cards with positive statements would obtain a score of forty-seven and the ones with negative statements a score of 113. By ascertaining the algebraic sum of the scores obtained by the two groups of cards, after having assigned negative and positive values to the two scores respectively, a feeling or 'F-index' was obtained which was used to group the 'S in terms of preference for Father or Mother'.

In treating the results obtained by correlating the paired factors for each S, the coefficients of correlation for all Ss were averaged so that a composite picture of the sixteen Ss could be obtained in terms of an *r* for each of the paired factors. The sixteen Ss were then grouped according to sex to compare male and female *r*s and according to F-index preference for Father and Mother. Group means were obtained for the *r*s of each pair of factors for each of the groups. The *r*s for each of the sixteen Ss appear in Table 1 along with the means for all cases for and the sub-groups.

Results

The results showed the mean *r* for the pair 'God–Jesus' to be positive and well above the 1 per cent level of confidence, the *r*s for individuals ranging from 0·34 to 0·95. Thus, while God and

Jesus seemed to precipitate similar feelings in most cases, some persons appeared to differentiate between the two.

The rs for Mother–Father ranged from 0·67 to 0·81 with the mean for the entire group being 0·225, falling below the 5 per cent level of confidence. This suggests that several persons experienced contrasting feelings toward Mother and Father while only a few experienced feelings that were the same or similar toward the two.

The correlations between God and Father showed individual rs ranging from −0·64 to 0·76, with the mean for the group being 0·153, well below the 5 per cent level of confidence. The rs for Mother–God were somewhat more consistent, though the range for individuals was from 0·29 to 0·89, the mean for the group being 0·427, which is well above the 1 per cent level of confidence. Thus, for the group, the r for Mother and God is much higher than that for Father and God.

While the range of rs for Father–Jesus was from −0·57 to 0·80, the mean for the group was 0·331, slightly above the 1 per cent level of confidence. Thus, for the group, the feelings regarding Father were somewhat more like those regarding Jesus than like those regarding God. The rs for Mother–Jesus, on the other hand, were slightly lower than between Mother–God, though in both cases they were positive and well above the 1 per cent level of confidence.

When Ss were divided on the basis of sex and attitudes toward Father and Mother by use of the F-index as shown in Table 1, quite a different pattern of mean rs was obtained.

The mean rs for the eight male Ss, on the Mother–Father, Father–God, and Father–Jesus factors dropped to a level approaching zero correlation, while the rs for Mother–God and Mother–Jesus remained positive and above the 1 per cent level of confidence. For the eight female Ss, the rs for God–Jesus, Mother–Father, God–Mother, Father–Jesus, and Mother–Jesus were all positive and well above the 1 per cent level of confidence. The r for God–Father was positive, but below the 5 per cent level of confidence.

By the use of the F-index, the sixteen Ss were divided into three groups: those who preferred Father, those who preferred Mother, and those who had no preference or were ambivalent toward both parents. The mean rs were obtained for each of these groups, although the number of Ss in each group was very small. The results were as follows.

For those who preferred Father, only two pairs showed rs

Table 1 Product-moment coefficients of correlation for paired concepts: God–Jesus, Mother–Father, God–Father, God–Mother, Father–Jesus and Mother–Jesus

Case no.	Age	Sex	Parent pref.	G–J	M–F	G–F	G–M	F–J	M–J
101	21	M	M	0·95*	0·47*	0·29**	0·470	0·22	0·54*
102	18	F	N	0·51*	0·14	−0·11	−0·05	0·04	−0·44**
103	21	M	M	0·84*	−0·63*	−0·51*	−0·66*	−0·53*	0·70*
104	24	M	M	0·84*	0·21	−0·25	0·43*	−0·06	0·54*
105	20	M	M	0·73*	−0·67*	−0·61*	0·56*	−0·57*	0·54*
106	21	F	N	0·94*	0·74*	0·76*	0·89*	0·74*	0·88*
107	20	F	N	0·34*	0·63*	0·42*	0·31**	0·69*	0·44*
108	22	M	N	0·48*	0·63*	0·72*	0·68*	0·36*	0·46*
109	27	F	F	0·78*	−0·34*	−0·64*	0·37*	0·75*	0·42*
110	19	F	M	0·74*	0·31**	0·42*	0·78*	0·55*	0·54*
111	18	F	N	0·86*	0·81*	0·67*	0·77*	0·80*	0·65*
112	23	M	N	0·51*	0·42*	0·38*	0·14	0·58*	0·25
113	44	F	F	0·48*	0·07	0·26**	0·55*	0·45*	0·33*
114	20	M	M	0·54*	0·31**	0·26**	0·26**	0·34*	0·20
115	25	F	N	0·57*	0·60*	−0·20	0·31**	0·33*	0·32**
116	22	M	F	0·52*	−0·09	0·60*	−0·29**	0·61*	−0·31**

Mean rs for all cases	0·664*	0·225	0·153	0·427*	0·331*	0·378*
Means for sub-groups:						
Males	0·676*	0·081	0·11	0·363*	0·118	0·365*
Females	0·652*	0·37*	0·197	0·491*	0·543*	0·392*
Prefer Father (F)	0·593*	−0·12	0·073	0·21	0·603*	0·146
Prefer Mother (M)	0·773*	0·000	−0·066	0·526*	0·008	0·510*
No preference (N)	0·60*	0·567*	0·377*	0·435*	0·505*	0·365*

df, 58; 5% level of confidence: 0·255; 1% level of confidence: 0·330.
*Significant at 1 per cent level; **significant at 5 per cent level.

above the 5 per cent level of confidence. These were God–Jesus and Father–Jesus, both of which were above the 1 per cent level of confidence. For those who preferred Mother, the God–Jesus, God–Mother, and Mother–Jesus pairs showed *r*s which were positive and above the 1 per cent level of confidence. The other *r*s for this group were approximately zero. For the six Ss who showed no F-index preference for Father or Mother, all mean *r*s were positive and well above the 1 per cent level of confidence.

Discussion

While the number of Ss in this investigation was too small to warrant drawing any conclusions about the relationship between the various concepts correlated, so far as the group means were concerned, some trends were noted. In the total-group means as well as in the means for the sub-groups, the God concept had a higher positive correlation with the Mother concept than with the Father concept. In all groups but one, the concepts God–Father showed *r*s below the 5 per cent level of confidence. This one group was made up of those who showed no F-index preference for either Father or Mother. The Mother–Jesus concepts for all groupings had mean *r*s which were positive and above the 1 per cent level of confidence. Should these trends be confirmed by a larger number of cases, it would appear that the Mother concept is more influential in the formation of the deity concepts than is the Father concept, except where the concepts of Father and Mother indicate no preference between the two.

On the basis of the trends indicated by the data of this investigation, it appears that the adaptation of the Q-technique used may have some value for further investigation of religious concepts.

Summary

An adaptation of the Q-technique was applied to the study of the Christian deity concepts of God and Jesus as compared with the parent concepts of Mother and Father. The correlations obtained for sixteen Ss indicated: (a) that the deity concepts were more closely related to the Mother concept than to the Father concept for Ss investigated; and (b) that the adaptation of the Q-technique used may have value for further study of religious concepts.

References

ALLPORT, G. W. (1950), *The Individual and his Religion*, Macmillan.
COE, G. A. (1900), *The Spiritual Life*, Eaton & Mains.
FREUD, S. (1912), *Totem and Taboo*, in *The Basic Writings of Sigmund Freud*, Modern Library, 1938.
JAMES, W. (1902), *The Varieties of Religious Experience*, Longman.
STARBUCK, E. D. (1901), *The Psychology of Religion*, Scribner.
STEPHENSON, W. (1953), *The Study of Behavior: Q-Technique and its Methodology*, Chicago University Press.

Part Five
Developmental Studies

The first four parts have treated religion in general terms: the next parts concern specific religious issues and objects, showing the ways in which they have been examined psychologically.

Developmental studies are concerned with the acquisition of a positive religious stance, and have dealt most often with age-related changes in religious concepts and in the knowledge of religious material, or with the effects of religious training or judgements about morally acceptable behaviour. Differentiation and increased sophistication are the main developmental processes, and these changes lead to religious expressions in which the forms of assent and the meaning of material may be quite different from those at an earlier stage. Questions about the continued stability or the changes in religion into later life have not yet been adequately handled.

The brevity of this section belies the attention that has been given to developmental studies. Lawrence's paper shows that readily available information may be interpreted within a theoretical frame, and the others relate to quite separate aspects of development. Too often it is forgotten that developmental change continues through the life-span.

13 P. J. Lawrence

Children's Thinking about Religion: A Study of
Concrete Operational Thinking

P. J. Lawrence, 'Children's thinking about religion: a study of concrete operational thinking', *Religious Education*, 1965, vol. 60, pp. 111–16.

Introduction

A child's question may indicate genuine concern or casual curiosity; it may arise because of some particular experience or event in which the child is involved, or it may have no obvious antecedents: whatever the context, the question in itself is worthy of study as giving some indication of the child's level of understanding. In the investigation of children's concepts of religion it is particularly difficult to assess the level of understanding without at the same time contaminating the data with material which is influenced by their *expectations* of what it is right or appropriate to say, or which merely reflects what has been learned but not necessarily understood. Children brought up by parents who are church members become familiar with a number of fundamental religious concepts – such children are likely to have a more sophisticated understanding of these concepts than children who come from non-church homes. Yet this sophistication is limited by the level of cognitive functioning which a particular child has reached, and in the case of children at the elementary school stage (up to about the age of twelve years) this level is likely to reflect what Piaget has called *concrete* rather than *formal* modes of intellectual operation. Concrete operations are limited to the organization (e.g. classification, ordering) of concrete phenomena, the actual, the here and now; formal operations extend to the *possible* as well as the *actual*, and depend upon hypothetico-deductive propositional thinking which greatly expands the generality, abstractness and flexibility of thought.[1] Religious concepts, beyond the elementary Bible-story stage, may be simple and easily understood, but they may also be rich in symbol,

1. Piaget's analysis of intellectual development is penetrating and fruitful and is being confirmed, in general, by the many studies which have been stimulated by his work. See Inhelder and Piaget (1958) or, for a recent sympathetic exposition, Flavell (1963).

allegory, metaphor, abstraction and theological subtlety. In the years prior to adolescence, although the child is moving out of this Bible-story stage, he is not yet able to rise above the limits of concrete operational thinking: he is thus in a very difficult transitional stage – difficult for himself because his concrete mode of thinking makes him a thorough-going realist, and difficult for his parents or religious teachers because they have the task of preparing him for a deeper and richer understanding of already familiar but inadequate concepts.[2]

The present study arises from an awareness of the methodological and developmental problems discussed above. In order to avoid some of the contamination implicit in the use of such tools as the questionnaire or the interview, the *spontaneous* questions of children were recorded; in order to throw some light upon the relationship between the understanding of religious concepts and a concrete level of operational thinking, the pre-adolescent age group was studied.

Method and sample

Spontaneous questions which might give some indication of the level of, or the difficulties in children's understanding of, religious concepts are not likely to occur frequently. Between the naïve questions of the pre-school child and the serious questionings of the adolescent there is a period when the elementary school child is relatively latent in the religious as well as in the sexual sense, therefore his questions may be very infrequent. Furthermore, the usual context within which religious instruction takes place emphasizes the learning and accepting rather than the questioning of doctrine and of relevant historical events. Because of these factors, it was decided to rely upon parents' recollections of questions asked by their children, and also upon a diary of questions asked over a six-month period as recorded by parents (and a small number of Sunday-school teachers). Fifty parishes[3]

2. Edith F. Hunter (1956) illustrates some of these difficulties very vividly. That religious educators are also concerned with this difficulty is illustrated by the nature of some of the research projects formulated at the Religious Education Association's Workshop on Religious and Character Education (Cook, 1962).

3. These parishes were Presbyterian. The study reported here arose from a request from the Doctrine and the Education Committees of the Presbyterian Church of New Zealand. The Director of the Christian Education Department provided clerical facilities, and the initial invitation to parents to co-operate in the project went out under his name and office.

were chosen at random from proportionally representative lists of rural, city, and suburban churches in New Zealand. An initial letter which explained the purpose of the project asked each minister to invite parents to cooperate. Those parents who indicated their willingness to cooperate were sent an explanatory letter, a record form (for recollected questions), and a diary form (for a six-month period). A small number of teachers (in Sunday schools) who wished to join in the project were sent appropriate parallel forms. The crucial direction on the record form was:

Please list below any questions of a religious nature asked by your children between the ages of about eight to eleven years. If you cannot remember particular questions, you may at least remember topics or problems of a religious nature which have been discussed, or which you found difficult to explain or difficult for the child to grasp.

On the diary forms, the crucial direction was: '... this is a diary of *spontaneous questions....* Sometimes the child may not ask a direct question but may say something which implies a question ....' Very few of the forms sent out to cooperating parents were returned, despite reminders; but it became clear, from the comments made on those forms which were returned or in letters from parents, that one of the main reasons for the poor return was the extreme paucity of questions asked by children at this level. It was pointed out that most of the questions recollected occurred before the age of seven. If this is so, then this fact is in itself of some significance even although it is not surprising (i.e. because of the latency of religious development during the elementary years).

Forms were returned, with comment, by sixty families and eleven teachers. Of the sixty families, fifty-one reported questions (ranging from one to eight, with an average of between three and four per family) and nine reported no questions asked. The total number of questions asked was 225 (134 at home, recollected by parents; forty-three at home, noted in diary forms; forty-eight at Sunday school noted by teachers). The 177 questions asked at home came from eighty-seven children, distributed as follows:

Age	7	8	9	10	11	12
Number of children	14	24	14	18	12	5

The proportion of boys and girls in each group was approximately equal. The eleven classes reported on by the teachers were spread over a similar age range.

From these figures it can be seen that although the total sampling of children's questions is very small, it is representative of the elementary school age range for both boys and girls. An inspection of 'father's occupation' responses indicates that the families represented a typical cross-section of middle-class urban and rural society.

Results

It could be argued that it would be misleading to regard this small sample as representative, and from a statistical point of view this may be so. There are, however, reasons for believing that a much larger sample would have yielded a similar distribution of questions – because the questions illustrate very clearly the general principles of intellectual development characteristic of the seven-to-twelve-year age group; and because from family to family there was a consistency in the types of question asked.

In the first instance, questions were grouped into several broad categories:

Subject of question	Percentage
I Deity: the nature of	35·6
II Suffering and death	28·0
III The churches and the word	21·8
IV Manifestations of the supernatural	12·9
V Miscellaneous	1·7
	100·0

This classification was not imposed upon the data but represented an empirical (and easily applied) grouping of questions: the broad categorization is not, however, as significant as the more detailed analyses. A further breakdown of the four main categories yielded the following:

I Deity: the nature of	total of 80 questions
i God	43
ii Jesus	18
iii Spirit	12
iv Trinity	7
II Suffering and death	total of 63 questions
i Heaven	25
ii Death	24
iii Suffering	14

III The churches and the
    word   total of 49 questions
    i The Bible   22
   ii Church customs   18
  iii Differences between
       churches   9
IV Manifestations of the
    supernatural   total of 29 questions
    i Creation   11
   ii Prayer   6
  iii Miracles   5
  iv Devil   4
   v Angels   3

A cursory inspection of these figures makes it clear that the questions are mainly doctrinal, but in order to bring out the *nature* of the questions it is necessary to specify the types of questions asked under each of the subheadings above. In each case a typical question is given: this conveys something of the general tenor of the children's thinking as they deal with complex doctrinal issues.

Topic	No. of questions
I i *God*	
Origin of	(13)
Typical question: Who made God?	
Nature of	(9)
Typical question: What is he like?	
Omnipresence of	(5)
Typical question: How can he see everyone all the time?	
Invisibility of	(4)
Typical question: Why can't we see God?	
Omniscience of	(4)
Typical question: How can he know what we are doing?	
Location of	(3)
Typical question: Where is God, is he just in Heaven?	
Existence of in time	(3)
Typical question: Is God still living?	
Omnipotence	(2)
Typical question: How does God do everything?	

	Topic	No. of questions
I ii	*Jesus*	
	Present nature of	(8)
	Typical question: Where is Jesus now? Would he still be on earth today?	
	Divinity of	(4)
	Typical question: How can Joseph and God both be Jesus's father?	
	Necessity of His death	(4)
	Typical question: Why did God let his son die?	
	Resurrection and return	(2)
	Typical questions: How did Jesus go to Heaven?	
I iii	*Spirit*	
	Nature of	(7)
	Typical question: What is the Holy Spirit?	
	Nature of soul	(5)
	Typical question: What is your soul?	
I iv	*Trinity*	
	Nature of	(7)
	Typical question: What does it mean to say 'Three in One'? Are God and Jesus the same person?	
II i	*Heaven*	
	Nature and location of	(11)
	Typical question: Where is Heaven now we know so much about space?	
	Mechanism of entry	(7)
	Typical question: Do you get to Heaven through some sort of funnel?	
	Criteria for entrance	(4)
	Typical question: Do black children go to live with God when they die?	
	Animals in	(3)
	Typical question: Do dogs and cats go to Heaven too?	
II ii	*Death*	
	Mechanisms of transition from life to	(12)
	Typical questions: How do children who have been burned in a fire go to Heaven? How do babies get out of the coffin?	
	Nature of after-life	(8)
	Typical questions: Will we meet people in Heaven when we die? What will happen when I die?	
	Nature of body after	(4)
	Typical questions: What will we look like when we rise from the dead?	

Topic	No. of questions
IV ii *Prayer*	
Answers to	(3)
Typical question: Why does God let children die after we have prayed for them?	
Amen	(2)
Typical question: Why do we say 'amen'?	
Direction of	(1)
Typical question: Why do we sometimes pray to God and sometimes to Jesus?	
IV iii *Miracles*	
Truth and explanation of	(5)
Typical questions: Why don't miracles happen today? Did they manage to cross the Jordan because the river was blocked further up?	
IV iv *Devil*	
Nature of	(4)
Typical questions: What does he look like? Does he lay traps for people?	
IV v *Angels*	
Nature and truth of	(3)
Typical questions: What are they? Are they true?	

Discussion

The majority of the questions are doctrinal in nature: the application or implication of religious belief in everyday life does not appear at all. If it can be assumed that the parents' records are representative of the full range of questions asked, then the lack of ethical questions is of interest. It may be due to the fact that – at least for children – the codification of morals (e.g. the Commandments, the simple commands of Jesus, the Beatitudes) is less puzzling than the traditional statements of Christian belief. Moreover, the biblical stories present numerous concrete examples of right actions and attitudes, and Jesus himself used the concrete situation to illustrate the abstract principle.

From the category heading alone, it might appear that children are deeply interested in the fundamental religious concepts of Christianity. But as soon as the specific classifications are given and, even more, as soon as the typical questions are read, it becomes clear that this interest is not metaphysical but, indeed, very matter-of-fact and materialistic. The outstanding characteristic of the questions is their realism: a realism which arises from an attempt to translate highly abstract ideas into the experience, homely morality, cause and effect, and mechanistic interpretation of everyday life.[4] That the children may be misinformed about some matters of church procedure or biblical information is relatively unimportant; but their very reasonable puzzlement about what must seem to many to be an enigmatic religious belief – half fact and half fiction, sometimes contradictory and suggesting the operation of magic – is of the greatest significance.

In the light of our knowledge of children's thought processes, the tenor of the questions is not really surprising. Between eight and eleven or twelve years of age the child has the capacity to classify, order, see cause–effect relationships, and use the basic tools of logic – *but in a concrete setting*. He does not yet appreciate the force of a concept which signifies a set of abstract relationships or points to the underlying qualities abstracted from a set of events. This capacity, more characteristic of middle adolescence, develops gradually – but for the average child it is not available before this time. An adolescent can appreciate the logical necessity or the logical coherence of a set of abstract concepts (e.g. as in algebra) because he can accept the conventions of propositional reasoning (if ... then, or 'as–if' reasoning). The younger child finds it difficult to reason in this way, his reasoning is not so much 'as–if', but 'as–*is*'. It is because of this characteristic that the child's questions are brutally matter-of-fact, and show a questioning mind which can ask penetrating and sometimes shrewd questions – *but at a concrete level*. 'Who made God?' 'Are God and Jesus the same?' 'Why does God intervene at some times and not at others?' These are the realistic but searching questions which probe to the heart of theology, but *the child's mind is not yet prepared for the theological answers to them*.

The religious educator faces a dilemma – he must deal in abstract concepts, yet his pupils cannot be given really satisfying abstract definitions. If he does attempt to do so, the eight- to eleven-year-old child will doubtless learn the definitions by rote, but he will not understand them. Occasionally one hears of the individual who, remembering from childhood some memorized

4. Statements listed for the seven-to-twelve-year group in the Union College Character Research Project (1959) on children's religious concepts, parallel some of the questions listed above. Many of these statements, however, reflect what has been taught rather than what the child would like to know.

but, at the time, poorly understood verse, suddenly has insight into its full implications. Doubtless such things happen, but unfortunately the experience of generations of teachers (and of research workers in the field of learning) is that, in most cases, material which is memorized but not understood is quickly forgotten. Some churches have made use of junior catechisms in an attempt to give the child at least a set of religious truths which can be committed to memory and can thus become fundamental assumptions in his thinking. But a catechism, by its very nature, is a formal presentation – in reality a definition – of certain central truths. To give definitions of concepts such as God, Jesus, Trinity, Suffering, Resurrection, Prayer, and so on, can only result in a memorized but poorly understood set of ideas. A definition cannot be concerned with concrete implications, concrete analogies, and translations into the child's realistic experience: this is the task of the skilled teacher or story-writer. But only as these concepts are dealt with at this concrete level will they become satisfying and meaningful to the child. The implication seems clear: a catechism at this age level is likely to be largely ineffective, and may even be a hindrance to later religious development because a premature formalization of developing understandings and insight may block further development. That such a premature 'hardening' of religious ideas – with little understanding of them – is not only possible but widespread is exemplified in surveys of the religious beliefs of adolescents.[5]

There is, of course, no way of ensuring an easy transition from concrete to formal operational thinking in religious education, nor is it the purpose of this paper to explore ways of facilitating the transition. But at least the educator should be fully aware of the concreteness of the elementary school child's religious thinking and of the need to translate his ideas into more sophisticated theological concepts. It is often assumed that the difficulty in coping with this transitional stage – at least from the point of view of the religious educator – is primarily a pedagogical difficulty, to be overcome by the use of better teaching materials and techniques. Doubtless there is much room for improvement in teaching, but it could be argued that the major problem con-

5. For example, see Kuhlen and Arnold (1944). Allport, Gillespie and Young (1948), in a similar survey, report: 'We conclude that fully half the students who, in some sense, lead religious lives do so without firm doctrinal convictions.' Similar findings have been reported by Sandhurst (1946), Ross (1950) and to a lesser extent, Loukes (1962).

cerns the doctrinal content of religious teaching. Theological concepts, when reduced to doctrine, take on a firmer and sharper form than the thinking upon which they are based. The 'edges' of doctrine are blurred at the highest level of theological discussion: the task of the religious educator is to convey both the doctrinal form and the 'growing edges' of this form. But adolescents and adults carry vestiges of concrete operational thinking into their understanding of religious (and non-religious) concepts,[6] and these vestiges limit the attainment of the greater abstractness, generality, and flexibility of the more mature level of formal operational thinking. This limitation may result in the rejection of doctrines which are inadequately understood, or the suppression of any questioning of doctrines because of uneasiness concerning their adequacy. In the latter case, acceptance without questioning is a means of defense, and like other defense mechanisms may engender hostility or anxiety if brought to the surface.[7]

The child, like the theologian, asks the question: 'What is God like?' and the answer will go on growing in his mind as he develops from child to young adult. It is the task of the religious educator to understand the phases, the limits, and the possibilities of this growth. Part of this development is dependent upon the transition from concrete to formal operational thinking: it has been the purpose of this brief study to draw attention to the significance, in religious education, of this transition.

6. Ross (1950), in his survey of the religious beliefs of almost two thousand young people, concluded that from interviews with a representative group it was apparent that 'only about one in six possessed a conception of God in which he had both confidence and faith' (p. 142) and that about three quarters of his subjects were not at all clear about the nature of God – '... most of them can only describe him in terms they learned in Sunday school many years ago ...' (p. 143).

7. In the writer's experience many adolescents and adults, far from *questioning* religious concepts, feel guilty about discussing them because the very concreteness and immaturity of their understanding can only be preserved by unquestioning acceptance.

References

ALLPORT, G. W., GILLESPIE, J. M., and YOUNG, J. (1948), 'The religion of the post-war college student', *J. Psychol.*, vol. 25, pp. 3–33.

COOK, S. W. (ed.) (1962), *Research Plans Formulated at The Research Planning Workshop on Religious and Character Education*, Mimeographed Report, New York, Religious Education Association.

FLAVELL, J. H. (1963), *The Developmental Psychology of Jean Piaget*, Van Nostrand.

HUNTER, E. F. (1956), *The Questioning Child and Religion*, Beacon Press.

INHELDER, B., and PIAGET, J. (1958), *The Growth of Logical Thinking from Childhood to Adolescence*, Basic Books.

KUHLEN, R. G., and ARNOLD, M. (1944), 'Age differences in religious beliefs and problems during adolescence', *J. genet. Psychol.*, vol. 65, pp. 291–300.

LOUKES, H. (1962), *Teenage Religion*, SCM.

ROSS, M. G. (1950), *Religious Beliefs of Youth*, Association Press.

SANDHURST, B. G. (1946), *How Heathen is Britain?*, Collins.

UNION COLLEGE CHARACTER RESEARCH PROJECT (1959), *Children's Religious Concepts*, Mimeographed, Schenectady: Union College.

14 R. J. Goldman

Researches in Religious Thinking

R. J. Goldman, 'Researches in religious thinking', *Educational Research*,
1964, vol. 6, no. 2, pp. 139–55.

Introduction

The psychology of religion as an accepted discipline has never
really flourished and has produced only intermittent research
during the sixty years of its existence. Much of the writing in
this subject has suffered from two liabilities, one being the
tendency for philosophy and metaphysics to be the major emphasis and the other being the use of anecdotal psychology
rather than findings based upon authentic research methods.
Religion, of course, is not an easy subject for psychological
examination and the reasons for the sparsity of work in the
psychology of religion are outlined clearly by Allport (1951) and
Argyle (1958). Two major reasons stand out. The first is the fear
that psychology will be used to discredit the validity of religious
belief. The attack upon religion by Freud, who characterized it as
a projection of infantile needs, reinforced such a fear. Leuba
(1917) lent support to this view by trying to show religious phenomena to be a natural, or rather, a primitive activity of man, so
hoping to demonstrate religious belief to be both infantile and
crude. The more positive attitude of Jung to religion is frequently
unknown. Flugel (1945), writing of the psychoanalysts, reiterated
the view that psychology must only describe human behaviour
objectively and suggested that religion was extremely significant
in that psychology demonstrated the fundamental and natural
basis of the needs underlying religion. The second major reason
for the neglect of the psychology of religion is the widely held
view that religion is neither analysable nor measurable in the
statistically quantitative manner which research methods demand. This is a legitimate misgiving, but must be modified when
we recognize that it is not 'religion' which is the subject of
investigation but religious behaviour. This is as legitimate a field
of psychological inquiry as is political behaviour, the reading
habits of adolescents or the developing social behaviour of

children. Most writers conclude that while psychological research can tell us nothing about the truth, validity or usefulness of religious phenomena, we can learn a great deal about human behaviour in relation to religion. Religious bodies may use such knowledge to bring about conditions which may help people to become religious. This latter point has been, in fact, the stimulus to much recent activity in this field, especially in Britain, since the religious requirements of the 1944 Education Act focused attention upon the need to know more about the religious development of pupils in our schools.

The educational problems set by agreed syllabuses

According to the Act, the teaching of religion in state schools must be in accordance with the agreed syllabus, the three parties 'agreeing' to the syllabus being the Protestant Churches, the teachers and the local education authority of every area. From the beginning the syllabuses of religious instruction posed many problems to the educator, since they appeared to be based upon a quantitative assumption about intellectual growth, namely, that as a child grows older he becomes capable of dealing with a greater amount of Biblical material. The syllabuses seemed based upon what the committees felt children of various ages ought to know, rather than upon the religious concepts they were able to understand. It is this quantitative emphasis, rather than a qualitative one, which has provoked an interest in many quarters in religious thinking. Some syllabuses, such as the Cambridgeshire (1949), specifically state: 'No attempt should be made to present religious ideas which are beyond the child's powers of apprehension.' The problem in stating this precept, is to know what is within the child's apprehension, for some of the material suggested in the Cambridgeshire syllabus would appear to be beyond the age groups for which it is specifically recommended. The story of the Exodus, for example, is recommended for seven to nine year olds. When we consider the concepts of time alone demanded by these stories, we wonder what the young junior child will make of it. The call of the child Samuel is a favourite in syllabuses for infants because it is a story of a young boy, but it poses severe difficulties in terms of a sensible understanding of the narrative. In these two instances, research informs us that the children cannot cope intellectually with their meanings until much later than the syllabuses suggest.

As a final example, we may note that the parables of Jesus are regarded as suitable for children of five to seven years by many syllabuses. On this very problem Ainsworth (1961) wrote that 'in the light of Piaget's work, the young child's understanding of the parable is questionable. Since the significance of the parable is abstract rather than concrete, is it possible that the child will understand this before he has reached the formal stage in this development?' Her answer, based upon research into children's thinking about the parables, is that only the beginnings of under- standing the simplest parables appeared by the age of ten years. Several researches in the last four years report the dissatisfaction of teachers with much of the material recommended by syllabuses. Notable among these is the survey published by the University of Sheffield Institute of Education (1961) into the religious know- ledge attainments of secondary-school leavers. These pupils, after ten years of agreed-syllabus teaching, show that results were so poor and so disturbing that there is a call for a complete revision of existing syllabuses.

The need for knowledge of religious development

It must in fairness be pointed out that some local authorities have experimented with material and attempted to produce a psychological rather than a biblical framework for their syllabuses. Hewitt in a symposium discussing the present writer's research mentioned several such syllabuses which have made brave at- tempts to present their content in the light of what they consider to be the child's needs. Nevertheless, too little is known about the child's religious development and the nature of his thinking powers when applied to religion. Many questions must still be asked. Upon what assumptions about religious thinking in child- hood and adolescence should reforms of syllabus material be based? Are the assumptions we are making at the moment testable or verifiable in any way as a guide to teachers? There has been in the past a dearth of factual information from research relevant to this particular problem.

Before we explore what has been ascertained to date, we must first of all ask what is meant by the term religious thinking? The view maintained by the writer is that religious thinking is no different in mode and method from non-religious thinking. Religious thinking is a shortened form of expressing the activity of thinking directed towards religion, not a term involving a separate rationality or faculty. Smith (1941) puts it succinctly: 'A child is non-religious at birth as he is non-moral, non-aesthetic, non-thinking. He inherits none of these qualities in a functional form but acquires them gradually through experience.' For a meaning of the term religion we take William James's (1902) classic definition: 'the feelings, acts and experiences of individual men ... so far as they apprehend themselves to stand in relation to whatever they may consider the divine'.

If, then, religious thinking is thinking directed towards what human beings understand as the divine, and religious thinking does not differ as a rational process from thinking applied to other fields, it is important to pursue the question of whether or not there are stages of development to be seen in religious thinking. The role of the intellect in religious development may be minimized by some, but for the teacher it is central because teaching involves the communication of ideas in such a way as they can be grasped intellectually by the learner. The religious teacher is aware that religious truth must be compelling intellectually, not only emotionally, and is continually pressed to ask how his pupils form concepts of God, of the Church, of moral rightness; are there sequences or patterns of religious thought to be discerned with increasing chronological mental age and are there limits of religious understanding imposed by age, immaturity, attitudes of parents and other factors? Teachers for long conversant with reading readiness and number readiness are now asking is such an idea as religious readiness a valid one.

Four categories of religious thinking

Since thinking applied to religion is an important ingredient of the religious development of children and adolescents, it is useful to explore at a deeper level what categories of thinking will help us. Russell (1956) outlines clearly the essential ingredients of thinking as fourfold. First, there are the materials of thinking. These are sensations of the external world which are selected by perception and stored in images and memories, gradually formed into concepts, as categories of thought about groups of objects or experiences. When language develops it greatly facilitates the use of these materials of sensation, perception and conceptual thought. Secondly, there are the processes of thinking. These are patterns of activity seen in selecting, eliminating, searching, manipulating and organizing, beginning with crude undirected thinking through to inductive thinking, problem-solving and creative thinking. Thirdly, there are motives for thinking, the feelings, attitudes and habits of thought acquired at an emotional level, which help initiate and determine the direction of thinking. Finally, there are abilities in thinking, which are the habits, techniques and guides to thinking, which to some extent may be acquired and developed but which may be limited by natural capacity.

Since these categories of thinking receive a fairly wide measure of agreement, we shall use them as the means of looking systematically at what research to date has revealed about religious thinking.

The materials of religious thinking

Thinking applied to religion appears to have the same ingredients or materials involving sensation, perception and conceptualizing activity, with one major distinction. That distinction is evident at the outset of the child's life in terms of sensation. Religious percepts and concepts are not based upon direct sensory data, but are formed from other perceptions and conceptions of experience. The mystics, who claim to have direct sensations of the divine, are exceptions.

Clearly, religion and life in the early years are so interwoven that they are indistinguishable. The child has his first sensory experience of the material world in which people are at first undifferentiated. He then forms general percepts and concepts based upon these experiences, symbolizing them, first in images and later, when he learns to use language, in verbal images or words. The whole structure of religious thinking is, therefore, based upon what Havighurst (1953) calls 'vicarious' experience. There are no definite religious sensations and perceptions separate from the child's other sensations and perceptions. Religious thinking is the process of generalizing from various experiences, previous perceptions and already held concepts to an interpretative concept of the activity and nature of the divine. Because of this it is not possible to supply specific first steps in the religious experience of the young child, other than by enriching his general experience.

This is reflected in the literature of religion, especially in the Bible, where the language is almost entirely based upon analogy and metaphor, inferring from other non-religious experience the nature of the divine and supporting such concepts upon previously acquired concepts. The beginning of the twenty-third Psalm makes this secondary use of concepts obvious. Where 'The Lord is my shepherd' is proclaimed, the whole concept of

God as a personal and caring God is based upon the analogy of the function of a shepherd caring for his sheep. For the child to grasp this concept in any way, he must have some concept of sheep-farming. To see it clearly he must know something of the conditions of the Palestinian sheep-farmer (this psalm would have a limited application in Westmorland or Australia), the heat and need for water, the barren soil and the constant moves from pasture to pasture. Many adults, of course, do not make this transition in analogy completely, but they have sufficient experience of the sensory, perceptual and conceptual factors upon which the analogy is based to grasp, even if partially, the religious concepts involved.

Religious thinking is, therefore, dependent upon understanding the original experience upon which the analogy or metaphor is based. When the child hears 'God is a father', we are pursuing certain concepts of fatherhood which the child has experienced directly. But children, we know, have varied experiences of their fathers. Deprived, deserted, cruelly treated, beaten or hostile children will have different foundations upon which the inference is built. Smith (1949, p. 2) supports this in maintaining that 'The term "God" is best used sparingly and for the young child should not be pressed on the child's attention. The experience which corresponds with the term is far more important than the mere word.'

Once formed, these religious concepts are very dependent upon general experience, verbal association and verbal interpretation. It is inevitable, as in other areas of learning, that the labels are used without the substance of the concept being attained. Serra (1952) further emphasizes 'the more direct the experience on which the concept is built, the greater will be the individual's knowledge and understanding of that concept. . . . Concepts that can be traced back only to verbal language or to symbols acquired through language result in mere verbalism.' The danger of verbalizing in religious thinking, which may be used to manipulate words which are not understood, is as real as in the young child manipulating number symbols in calculation without having formal concepts of quantity or seriation (Churchill, 1958).

If we may use the concept of God as an illustration, which in itself is composed of many varied concepts such as concepts of power, omnipresence, authority, justice and goodness, we may parallel in religious terms the summary of concepts made by Vinacke (1951):

1. Concepts of God are not direct sensory data but something resulting from the elaboration, combination and interpretation of sensory data such as 'my father', 'my home', 'the natural world'.

2. Concepts of God depend upon the previous experience of the child, not merely in naming the data of this experience but in understanding its component and significant features.

3. Concepts of God are responses which tie together or link, or combine discrete sensory experiences such as 'father is strong, big, all-powerful, cares for me, earns money for me'. 'Jesus is like that and he cares for all children.' 'God is a big Daddy up in the sky.'

4. It may be inferred that such ties or links are symbolic in nature, the same response standing for a variety of data. This response, 'God', is usually a word. It is a word which perhaps unifies all experience of what is thought to be best in human relationships. It may, of course, equally be a word symbolizing all that is worst in human relationships, such as anger, deceit, unpredictability and arbitrary punishment.

5. On the side of internal processes in the child, concepts of God represent selective factors, as for example, when God is identified with good and not evil, with something sacred, special and holy.

Two problems raised by Vinacke are: how can we explain and describe concepts?; and what concepts characterize various stages in the development of children's thinking powers? Little is known of the first problem in religious thinking, but the present writer (1962) in a research summary and in a recent lecture (1963) has attempted to describe how religious concepts appear to develop. On the second problem, more is written later in this paper.

The processes of religious thinking

Little application of the processes of thinking has been made to religion. It is evident at once, however, that the crudities and confusions of much that is seen in children's religious concepts, can be accounted for in terms of pre-operational limitations, and even by the later limits set by concretization of data. Jahoda (1951), quoting Piaget, remarks that 'thought is very largely sense tied, hence the high level abstractions abounding in religion are well above the mental horizon of the small child'. Ainsworth's work (1961) on parables is also appropriate to mention here. Taking a group of six to ten year olds, she points out the difficulties caused by parables due to their demand for propositional thinking. 'It is likely', she concludes, 'that until nine or ten years of age, any story heard by a child will probably be interpreted literally, and that the details of the text and incidents of the story will be of paramount importance to the child' (p. 42).

Hebron (1957) finds that the majority of 'C' stream pupils in secondary modern schools reach their twelfth year of mental age during the third year of their secondary-school course. This age is commonly recognized, she reports, through the work of Piaget, 'as the level of mental maturity necessary for generalization with some degree of abstraction'. This must, therefore, considerably limit their grasp of religious ideas.

Kenwrick (1949), using Spearman's concepts of education of relations and correlates as criteria, reports that with eleven and twelve year olds the power to recognize the relevance of an idea to new situations is greatly limited. There was a high percentage of failure in understanding the relevance of such widely accepted parables as the Good Samaritan.

The writer applied the criteria of Piaget's operational thinking stages to the responses of 200 children and adolescents discussing three Bible stories, and found that Piaget's sequences of thinking applied when the scores were scaled by means of the Guttman Scalogram technique. It was very evident that pre-operational and intuitive thought was used by children up to about seven or eight years mental age, that concrete operational thinking was used from seven/eight mental years until about thirteen/fourteen mental years, and that formal operations was the general mode of thought from thirteen/fourteen mental years on. These age boundaries were very approximate and should not be regarded as fixed or the results only of maturational limitations. It may be that with the avoidance of premature material and the introduction of a programme designed to stretch the child's religious thinking, these age boundaries could be lowered. The child tries to think as systematically, consistently and operationally as his own development and the religious material with which he is presented will allow. Methods of thinking, of course, cannot be divorced from their content and it is interesting to see that when first questions were evaluated by psychologists on an operational scale and then quite independently evaluated by theologically trained scorers on a theological scale there was a very high correlation between the two sets of scores (the co-efficients of correlation ranged from 0·78 to 0·89). This supports the view that logic and theology are closely related. Once the act of faith is made in terms of belief in God, logical forms are used, in much the same way as in other areas of experience. It is clear, therefore, that because the forms of thought used by children are childish and immature, children's religious concepts will be childish and immature. We should not expect anything other than this. A great deal of religious thinking is propositional and can only be dealt with at a formal operational level of thought if it is to be intellectually satisfying. If thirteen to fourteen is the mental age at which this level in religious thinking is generally achieved, a great deal of time and effort may be wasted by instruction in religious ideas which are beyond the comprehension of the child.

Implicit in the application of a structural process of thinking in children's religious thinking is the idea of a developmental series of stages. Some, such as Allport (1951), tend to reject the idea of children passing through discernible stages of religious development, since religious experience is so varied between one child and another.

Many of those who suggest the possibility of religious developmental stages have little or no experimental data upon which to base their assumptions. Reik (1955), for example, draws from his psychoanalytic experience and discusses three stages in a child's developing view of prayer. He talks of the state of magic – 'My will be done'; the stage between magic and religion – 'My will be done, because I am God'; and the stage of religion – 'My will be done, if it be God's will.' Another is Johnson (1957) who uses theological stages borrowed principally from Martin Buber, and posits four stages of religious thinking in terms of relationships. These are the relationships of I–Me, I–It, I–We and I–Thou. Johnson envisages the child's spiritual growth as a series of concentric circles or relationships each one encompassing the previous ones.

The only clearly defined series of religious stages based upon sound research is that of Harms (1944). Because he felt the intellectual content of religion to be only a small ingredient of religious experience he devised non-verbal methods for exploring religion in the child. Taking a large sample of children from three years up to early adolescence he asked the children to imagine God or the 'highest being they thought to exist'. He then asked them to draw or paint what they imagined. In criticism of this method we could cite Johnson (1961) who found six year olds very reticent in drawing pictures of God. The children taken by Harms were further asked to write any comments on the back of the picture, or with younger children their spoken comments were written for them by the teacher. In the three- to six-year group, 800 children's pictures were evaluated; from seven to twelve years a similar number; and more than 4000 were assessed for those above twelve years of age. No attempt was made to evaluate the results in terms of the religious background or the ability of the children and we have no information of the sampling taken other than that they were children from both private and state schools in the United States.

From his analysis Harms claimed to discern a threefold structure of development.

Stage 1 (3–6 years) The fairy tale stage of religion.
Stage 2 (7–12 years) The realistic stage.
Stage 3 (12+ years) The individualistic stage.

The first stage showed greater uniformity than later stages, portraying God as a king, as a 'Daddy of all children', living in a house resting in clouds, or made of clouds, or as a cloud in the form of an animal floating in the sky with G O D written upon it. All these pictures are commented on in fairy tale language and as fantasized experience. God is in the same category as dragons and giants – all are regarded as equally valid. God is only different in so far as he is greater and bigger and held accordingly in greater awe by the child. At the realistic stage, approximating roughly to our junior age range, Harms claims that the greater emotional stability of these years is reflected in the pictures. The child is more able to adapt himself to institutional religion and he is much more realistic in his portrayal. Symbols appear and God as a father, even with angels or saints, is not shown in mystical fashion but as a human figure in real life. Children in the individualistic stage in adolescence show a wide variety of interpretations from the conventional to the creative and mystical.

In discussing the implications for religious education Harms suggests that religious teaching for the younger child is too rational, attempting to make him 'understand' God. Adults are often misled by the apparently profound questions asked in infancy and childhood. Rational and instructional ideas should be delayed because 'the entire religious development of the child has a much slower tempo than the development of any other field of his experience'. This, we would assume, is a natural accompaniment of recognizing religious experience as secondary and dependent upon the development of many other concepts before religious concepts can develop.

Loomba (1944), a research worker in India, reported similar findings to Harms, showing a gradual transition with increasing age 'from a religion of pure externals to one of the inner life'. He reports earlier deification of parents, gradually broadening out to portray a man in general, all-knowing, and all-powerful, who made the sun, moon and stars. At about seven years the child's more realistic ideas of the natural world no longer attribute time, wind, sun and other physical phenomena to the personal power of God.

Yeaxlee (1939) also supports the Harms three-stage structure, not from direct experimental data of religious expression but from Griffiths's (1935) work on imagination. Her work is of parallel interest since, in play, children from three to seven years in London and Brisbane revealed much religious expression. Before three years thought is of as a pre-religious stage in which the child is absorbing basic intellectual and emotional patterns. From three to seven years is the age of fantasy (similar to Harms's 'fairy-tale' stage) followed by the post-seven years' stage of realism, the continuous questing, 'Is it true?' In these stages the major emphasis, says Yeaxlee, is for the first three years emotional knowing, from three to seven years it is fantasized knowing (a blend in play form of emotion and intellect) and from seven onwards it is predominantly intellectual knowing, early adolescence being the period of intellectual exploration and of the formation of the religious sentiment.

Gesell and Ilg (1946), in their studies of the child from five to ten years, summarize interesting reactions. The five year old, they suggest, is innocent of causal and logical relationships – his views are strongly tinged with animisms. Clouds move because God pushes them; when God blows it is windy. At six years Gesell and Ilg report that the child more easily grasps the idea of God as the creator of the world, of animals and of beautiful things. Prayers become important and a certain awe enters into worship. The seven year olds, they report, are becoming more sceptical and are leaving behind a naive view of God. Such questions arise as 'Can you see heaven?', 'Does God live in a house?', 'How can God be everywhere and see everywhere?'

These observations, however, like many from the Yale Clinic of Child Development, are rather generalized and appear to present too simplified a picture in terms of a given year age group.

Finally, Piaget (1929) yields extremely stimulating material in his investigations into how the child thinks of the natural world in the years from four to seven. His work on physical causality (1930) is interesting and shows the function of animism in children's religious development. In the former work, however, Piaget examines what he terms 'Artificialism' in the life of the child. Artificialism he defines as the child's tendency to 'regard things as the product of human creation'. By human, he means both the idea of God seen as a powerful man, and the power of human beings to whom are attributed divine qualities.

Piaget suggests that the child explains the origin of sun and moon, clouds, the sky, storms and rivers, in roughly three stages. First, origins are attributed to human or divine agency, as for example, when the six year old sees the sun as originating in God, who lit a fire in the sky with a match. This Piaget terms 'mythological artificialism', extending roughly from four to seven years of age. Then comes an intermediate stage when a natural explanation is joined with an artificial solution as, for example, when the child suggests that the sun and moon are due to the condensation of clouds, but these clouds originate from God or from the smoke from men's houses. This is the stage, from about seven to ten years, named 'technical artificialism'. Finally, there is the stage where human and divine activity are seen as having no connection with these origins and they are conceived in purely natural terms, which a child may reach sometime after approximately ten years of age.

In a concluding chapter on the meaning and origins of child artificialism, Piaget discusses the role of religious education as a stimulant to the child's interest in artificial solutions. He suggests that artificialism is a natural stage in the child's view of the world. 'We have been struck by the fact that the majority of children only bring in God against their will, as it were, and not until they can find nothing else to bring forward. The religious instruction imparted to the children between the ages of four and seven often appears as something foreign to the child's natural thought.' He concludes, 'the child's real religion, at any rate during the first years, is quite definitely anything but the over-elaborated religion with which he is plied'.

The first stage of mythological artificialism receives some

support from the writer's own limited research. But it does not substantiate Piaget's second stage, when, in fact, the junior child may become more artificialist than the infant child even if this view is more refined, and a definite theological artificialism is apparent. There seems to be a tendency in the child to use dual methods of looking at the world, which are not seen in contradiction. One is theological and allows for supernatural interventions especially when thinking of Biblical events, and the other is artificialist-scientific gradually giving way to 'natural' explanations. A major problem of religious education is to bring these separate worlds together so that when the scientific view gains ascendancy the theological view is not invalidated in the child's experience.

To relate the details of all the researches carried out with adolescents would be too lengthy. Work by Moreton (1944), Bradshaw (1949), Walker (1950), Dawes (1954), Rixon (1959), Hilliard (1959), Loukes (1961) and Hyde (1963), to name some of the more important researches in Britain, reveals that children do, in fact, appear to carry through into adolescence developing concepts of God, becoming less anthropomorphic in their thinking about deity. Most pupils are able gradually to refine their ideas about religion. Most researchers agree that adolescence is not a time of increased religious activity. Argyle (1958), in summarizing research into adolescent religious development, suggests that intellectual doubts start at about a mental age of twelve years, followed by emotional stress. By sixteen these conflicts appear to be resolved either by conversion to religion or by a decision to abandon the religion of childhood.

Motives for religious thinking

Because religion is fundamentally a pattern of belief, and not an intellectual formula, the emotional aspect of religious thinking is of great importance. Whilst theoretically it is quite possible to have well-developed concepts about certain subjects in which we disbelieve, in practice it is rarely possible, since negative emotional behaviour interferes with our thinking. The influence of racial prejudice, attitudes to the other sex, beliefs about the authority of the Bible, for example, may lead quite intelligent persons to the most astonishing conclusions, in defiance of a great deal of evidence against their point of view. Further, the amount of intellectual effort we are prepared to expend on a subject will depend upon the level of our interest or motivation in relation to that subject. This is not merely a quantitative matter but also a qualitative one, and may account for the many varied levels of insight on any one subject seen in a single one-year age group in school.

We should clearly recognize this influence in religious thinking. Research reveals that motivation is dependent upon the attitudes of pupils to religion and to the subject of religious teaching in church and school. This is further dependent upon the attitudes of the pupil's family, and especially of his parents. Social psychology indicates that group attitudes, especially in adolescence, affect individual attitudes and levels of aspiration. A great deal of work has been done on the relationship of attitudes to religion and other factors, especially in America, and we shall here sample a few of those most relevant to the problems of religious thinking. Most of this research by its dependence on questionnaires and other written techniques is confined to the adolescent and student population, who are not only more mature but capable of reflecting upon their experience in sufficiently abstract and propositional terms.

Thurstone and Chave (1929) developed their attitude scale dealing with attitudes to Church, which has been adapted and used many times. Glassey (1945) found, among secondary grammar school pupils, that as the pupils moved up the school, their attitudes expressed towards religion became less favourable. He also found, as many other investigators have done, that the attitudes of girls to religion are much more favourable than boys.

Hyde (1963) drew up an attitude scale and applied it to 2500 pupils in secondary schools in Birmingham and then compared the results with their religious concepts. His results clearly indicate that conceptual growth appeared to take place only where there was a degree of religious interest. Where children lacked interest no increase in scores with age was observed. He noted also that lower interest was observable more in senior than in junior forms, in secondary modern than in secondary grammar, and in boys more than in girls. Daines (1949), Rixon (1959) and others support some of these findings. In a study of sixth-form boys in grammar schools, Wright (1962) found in general a serious and searching attitude towards religion. The religious influence of school appeared to be small, but that of parents tended to be great, upon the boys' religious beliefs. A later work of Daines (1962) with teachers in training reflects similar findings of positive attitudes towards religion, despite a decline in church allegiance. Both Wright's and Daines's samples are, of course, from populations not typical of adolescents in general.

Loukes (1961) reports secondary-school senior pupils as very critical of religious teaching, many finding the subject boring and childish, not primarily because of the content, but mainly because of the didactic manner of presentation.

The importance of home and parental influence in many aspects of religious behaviour is brought out by many studies. Here the attitude of parents to religion appears to be the most important factor. Newcomb and Svehla (1937) found a 0·6 correlation between attitudes of children and their parents in 548 cases when both parents and children were tested on the Thurstone scales. Gorer (1955) found that the religious practices of parents affected whether they taught their children to pray, but had little effect on whether they sent them to Sunday school. Chesser (1956) discovered that about half the married women in his sample imposed their own church-going habits on their children, the rest either sent them more than they went themselves (25 per cent) or less often (16 per cent). Hyde and Goldman both report the importance of parental sympathy and support in religious activities.

Abilities in the development of religious concepts

Some of the relevant work in this category was reviewed when 'processes of religious thinking' were dealt with. It is apparent that if our definition of religious thinking is a valid assumption, the ability to form religious concepts and to think operationally about religion will, given a positive motivation, increase with age and experience as children develop in other areas of growth. The writer's research (1962) was planned to explore this hypothesis and to discover what sequences or patterns of concepts, if any, were to be seen in the development of children's and adolescents' religious thinking. Some aspects of this research have already been mentioned, but more detail may be of interest to the reader together with further details of the research design. As the age range to be covered by 'The Picture and Story Religious Thinking Test' was from six to eighteen years, a standardized procedure was planned for interviewing each pupil personally. Three pictures showing children in religious situations were presented as a projective device, the child answering questions after each picture and discussing them with the interviewer. Three Bible stories, selected as common to most agreed syllabuses, but recommended as suitable for a wide variety of ages, were played from a tape recording, and these were similarly discussed. The three pictures show a child about to enter a church, a child kneeling by the bedside and a child looking at a mutilated Bible. The three Bible stories were simplified narratives of Moses and the Burning Bush, the Red Sea Crossing and the Temptations of Jesus. This material was selected from five pictures and eight stories after trial testing indicated the material best suited for examining religious concepts.

The standardized interview procedure was administered to a pilot sample of children and adolescents. After a few adjustments the final form was administered to a sample of two hundred school pupils aged six to eighteen years. This number was judged to be large enough to make statistical results sufficiently valid, but not too large to make scoring unwieldy. Twenty children were tested from each year age group, each one of which was comparable to other age groups in distribution of sex, ability, religious habits and social background. The age range of fifteen to eighteen years was slightly less representative in terms of ability. With this one exception the sample was taken as a random stratified sample representative of British born and bred children, normally exposed to the requirements of the 1944 Education Act. Pupils came from many different schools in the Midlands and Southern England, all in an urban environment.

The results of each section were scored separately on agreed psychological and theological criteria by the investigator and independent judges. All items, with two exceptions, proved capable of objective scoring, the coefficients of correlation (product-moment) between the scores of judges varying from 0.78 to 0.94, showing a high degree of agreement. The scores were then subjected to a Guttman Scalogram analysis. By this method, coefficients of reproducibility were used as indicators of sequences of thinking and conceptual development. In all items, except those involving moral judgements, mental age scaled better than chronological age. Since some forty items were scaled, only the most general results can be indicated here.

The results of the Picture and Story Religious Thinking Test

Bible concepts. No real awareness of the nature of the Bible is grasped until well into the secondary-school course, and even here many regard the Bible as authoritative in a strongly literal sense. It appears that pupils are frequently unaware of the possibility of a critical but reverent approach to the scriptures. Concepts of the authorship of the Bible are extremely confused until mid-adolescence. All concepts discussed are impeded by a literalism from which the adolescent is achieving some liberation.

Until the later junior years are attained the Bible is a book of almost magical veneration, written by God or a powerful adult, unwaveringly true in every point because of its holy origins, but relating to matters of long ago and far away, because God has died or returned to heaven. These crude ideas move on towards venerating the Bible as an ancient and true book, because it contains holy stories about God and Jesus and because adults teach from it. Old and New Testaments are confused, but still literal accuracy is assumed. While many pupils see it as dealing with past events only, a few are moving towards the view that the Bible speaks of truths relevant for today. By the second year of secondary education real insights begin to emerge but only progress to a higher realistic level among those of higher ability in the top end of the grammar schools.

Concepts of God's nature. A remarkably consistent picture of God concepts emerges from the investigation. Infant children think of God very crudely in physical terms as a man, with the physical characteristics of a human being, clad in Palestinian type clothes, invariably bearded and old. He speaks in physical tones, often with a harsh and loud voice, living remotely in heaven in the sky. When he visits the earth it is for a specific purpose in a physical form. In some ways the picture strongly resembles the Greek deities and the myths of Genesis. The junior child is not so crude in his concepts but he is still strongly anthropomorphic, thinking of God as superman rather than man, with special magic qualities of power and with supernatural signs to symbolize this power. There is some confusion about divine communication as simple explanations of a physical voice are seen to be unsatisfactory. The first two years of secondary schooling are still an extension of junior concepts of God, revealing something of an intermediate stage where childish concepts are uncertainly held. Thereafter, the physical interpretations are left behind and the deity tends to be thought of symbolically and then abstractly. God is unseen and unseeable because he is non-physical in nature. When adolescents use human terms to describe God, on the whole they are recognized as analogies, not accepted or meant literally. Divine communication also is now non-physical, proceeding by telepathy, inner thoughts or the operation of conscience. Many adolescents, especially those backward or disinterested in religion, tend to retain cruder anthropomorphic thinking much longer than the twelfth and thirteenth years.

Concepts of God in the natural world. Infant and junior children equate miracle and magic and see God intervening directly and physically in the natural world. This intervention tends to be arbitrary, spectacular and artificialist. Late juniors and secondary-school pupils tend to produce dualistic systems of thought, one theological where God intervenes in the manner described above, and the other, where emerging logical-scientific concepts lead to regarding the natural world as subject to cause and effect. Some interpenetration between the two systems may occur but not a great deal.

Concepts of God's concern for men. Infants and juniors share fairly similar misunderstandings about God in his dealings with men. God's love for all men is denied, because he cannot possibly love naughty people, or the universalism is accepted as a mere verbalism which breaks down in the case of the Egyptian army. Love, for the primary-school child, yields second place to vengeance and God is seen as mainly concerned with retribution. Because God can do anything he can be unfair, and divine behaviour is unpredictable. In the Exodus story, the contenders are seen in terms of white and black, 'goodies' and 'badies', favoured and non-favoured, loved and unloved. Group judgements about Israelites and Egyptians are quantitative and corporate. Some of these concepts continue into secondary schooling, but on the whole a consistent view of God's universal love is expressed by the second year of secondary school. Love and Justice are seen as compatible and God himself must be fair in order to be a consistent being.

Concepts of Jesus. These concepts are far from clear in terms of sequences of developing ideas. One thing is sure, however, that until about nine years old, the child's view of Christ is extremely confused and the problem of evil is only being seen realistically from about twelve years onwards. Infants tend to see Jesus as a good man, juniors see him as a magical worker, sometimes confused with God but not until mid-secondary schooling is his mission beginning to be understood.

Concepts of prayer. These appear to develop in three stages, characterized as magic, semi-magic and non-magic, rather similar to Reik's (1955) findings. This latter stage tends to emerge between twelve and thirteen years of age.

Discussion of results

Despite the fact that only a partial summary of researches has been given here, there is a broad general agreement about religious development and the intellectual problems posed by religious education for children and adolescents.

1. There is a need to examine concepts central to understanding Bible material before we pronounce it suitable for any age group. Plainly a great deal of Bible material suggested is unsuitable for primary children at an instruction level. This is a fertile area for further research.

2. Severe limits to religious thinking are set by limited experience and mental maturation. The major limitations appear to be literalism and concretistic thinking until early adolescence. Much teaching before this may only reinforce crudities of thinking and childish concepts.

3. Concepts introduced too soon may lead to progressive thinking in religion and not only retard later insight but may prevent them developing at all.

4. Twelve to thirteen years appears to be the time when childish concepts can be relinquished and more mature ideas are demanded, but the divergence between his theological and his scientific thinking creates a problem for the pupil, which may only be solved by adhering to a childish literalism or perhaps abandoning religion altogether. Religious education must provide a coherent system of thinking which can reconcile the two worlds.

5. Adolescence is the time for decision, not necessarily in an evangelical sense, but in terms of an intellectual choice. Where negative attitudes develop, poor concepts tend to form and religious thinking may regress.

6. The need for a radical reform of most agreed syllabuses is indicated, particularly in changing Bible-centred material for juniors into more child-centred material. Such a reform should recognize the qualitative changes in thinking in child development.

7. At a time when adolescents begin to be capable of higher levels of religious insight, their changing attitudes may inhibit religious

thought. A much more problem- or adolescent-centred form of religious education in secondary schools is advocated by many writers.

8. While the school and church, where the latter is attended, exercise some influence, there is clear evidence that it is the home, and particularly parents, who most strongly influence the attitudes to religion of children and adolescents. This also affects the willingness to think in religious terms and so directly affects levels of religious concepts achieved by the young.

References

AINSWORTH, D. (1961), 'An aspect of the growth of religious understanding of children aged between five and eleven years', unpublished Dip. Ed. dissertation, University of Manchester.

ALLPORT, G. W. (1951), *The Individual and His Religion*. Constable.

ARGYLE, M. (1958), *Religious Behaviour*, Routledge & Kegan Paul.

BRADSHAW, J. (1949), 'A psychological study of the development of religious beliefs among children and young people', unpublished M.Sc. dissertation, University of London.

CHESSER, E. (1956), *The Sexual, Marital and Family Relationships of the English Woman*, Hutchinson.

CHURCHILL, E. M. (1958), 'The number concepts of young children', *Researches and Studies* (University of Leeds Institute of Education), nos. 17 and 18.

DAINES, J. W. (1949), 'A psychological study of the attitudes of adolescents to religion and religious instruction', unpublished Ph.D. thesis, University of London.

DAINES, J. W. (1962), *An Enquiry into the Methods and Effects of Religious Education in Sixth Forms*, University of Nottingham Institute of Education.

DAWES, R. S. (1954), 'The concepts of God among secondary-school children', Unpublished M.A. thesis, University of London.

FLUGEL, J. C. (1945), *Man, Morals and Society*, Duckworth.

GESELL, A., and ILG, F. L. (1946), *The Child from Five to Ten*, Hamish Hamilton.

GLASSEY, W. (1945), 'The attitude of grammar-school pupils and their parents to education, religion and sport', *Brit. J. educ. Psychol.*, vol. 15, pp 101–4.

GOLDMAN, R. J. (1962), 'Some aspects of the development of religious thinking in childhood and adolescence', Research summary, Dept of Education, University of Reading.

GOLDMAN, R. J. (1963), 'Readiness for religion' (with R. Batten, F. H. Hilliard and G. Hewitt), a symposium in *Learning for Living*, vol. 2, no. 5.

GORER, G. (1955), *Exploring English Character*, Cresset.

GRIFFITHS, R. (1935), *Imagination in Early Childhood*, Routledge & Kegan Paul.

HARMS, E. (1944), 'The development of religious experience in children', *Amer. J. Sociol.*, vol. 50, no. 2, pp. 112–22.

HEBRON, M. E. (1957), 'The research into the teaching of religious knowledge', *Studies in Education*, University of Hull.

HILLIARD, F. H. (1959), 'The influence of religious education upon the development of children's moral ideas', *Brit. J. Educ. Psych.*, vol. 29, pp. 50–59.

HYDE, K. E. (1963), 'Religious concepts and religious attitudes', *Educ. Review*, vol. 15, nos. 2 and 3, pp. 132–41, 217–27.

JAHODA, G. (1951), 'Development of unfavourable attitudes towards religion', *Q. Brit. Psychol. Soc. Bull.*, vol. 2, pp. 35–6.

JAMES, W. (1902), *The Varieties of Religions Experience*, Longman.

JOHNSON, J. E. (1961), 'An enquiry into some of the religious ideas of six-year-old children', Unpublished Dip. Ed. dissertation, University of Birmingham.

JOHNSON, P. E. (1957), *Personality and Religion*, Abingdon Press.

KENWRICK, J. G. (1949), 'The training of the religious sentiment', Unpublished Ph.D. thesis, University of London.

LEUBA, J. H. (1917), 'Beliefs in God and immortality', *Psychol. Bull.*, vol. 14, pp. 405–7.

LOOMBA, B. M. (1944), 'The religious development of children', *Psychol. Abstracts*, vol. 345, no. 35.

LOUKES, H. (1961), *Teenage Religion*, SCM.

MORETON, F. E. (1944), 'Attitudes to religion among adolescents and adults', *Brit. J. educ. Psychol.*, vol. 14, pp. 69–79.

NEWCOMB, T. M., and SVEHLA, G. L. (1937), 'Intra-family relationships in attitudes', *Sociometry*, vol. 1, pp. 180–205.

PIAGET, J. (1929), *The Child's Conception of the World*, Routledge & Kegan Paul.

PIAGET, J. (1930), *The Child's Conception of Causality*, Routledge & Kegan Paul.

REIK, T. (1955), 'From spell to prayer', *Psychoanalysis*, vol. 3, no. 4, pp. 3–26.

RIXON, L. D. (1959), 'An experimental and critical study of the teaching of scripture in secondary schools', unpublished Ph.D. thesis, University of London.

RUSSELL, D. H. (1956), *Children's Thinking*, Ginn.

SERRA, M. C. (1952), 'How to develop concepts and their verbal representations', *Elem. School J.*, vol. 53, pp. 275–85.

SHEFFIELD UNIVERSITY INSTITUTE OF EDUCATION (1961), *Religious Education in Secondary Schools*, Nelson.

SMITH, J. J. (1941), 'The religious development of children', in Skinner and Harrison (eds.), *Child Psychology*, Macmillan Co.

SMITH, J. W. D. (1949), *An Introduction to Scripture Teaching*, Nelson.

THURSTONE, L. L., and CHAVE, E. G. (1929), *The Measurement of Attitudes*, University of Chicago Press.

VINACKE, W. E. (1951), 'The investigation of concept formation', *Psychol. Bull.*, vol. 48, pp. 1–31.

VINACKE, W. E. (1952), *The Psychology of Thinking*, McGraw-Hill.

WALKER, D. J. C. (1950), 'A study of children's conceptions of God' unpublished B.Ed. thesis, University of Glasgow.

WRIGHT, D. S. (1962), 'A study of religious belief in sixth-form boys', *Researches and Studies*, vol. 24, pp. 19–27.

YEAXLEE, B. L. (1939), *Religion and the Growing Mind*, Nisbet.

15 D. O. Moberg

Religiosity in Old Age

D. O. Moberg, 'Religiosity in old age', *Gerontologist*, 1965, vol. 5, pp. 78–87.

Geriatricians and gerontologists hold divergent opinions about the importance of religion in the later years of life. The differences reflect a combination of facts and personal biases. Religious persons tend to praise the influence of religious faith and practice and to believe that people become more religious as they approach death, while secularists are prone to believe religiosity declines and to condemn the 'ill effects' of both personal and organized religion.

There is no question about the relative importance of the church among voluntary association memberships of the aged. Study after study in various parts of the nation and in different types of communities have found that the aged (like most younger people) are more apt to be church members than members of any other one type of voluntary organization and, indeed, than of all other associations together. Disagreements arise, however, on several topics: What are the trends of personal religion over the life cycle? (Are the aged more likely to be church members than middle-aged and young adults? What is their comparative rate of participation in the church?) What are the effects of church participation? (Does it promote personal adjustment or does it reflect a search for security by maladjusted persons?) What are the characteristics of religious faith among the elderly? (Do they revert to the religion of their childhood? Are they progressively emancipated from traditional religion?)

Contradictory answers to questions of these kinds are based not only upon the personal opinions of experts but also upon empirical data from research surveys of behavioral scientists. The confusion that results leads to both traditionalistic attempts to perpetuate past practices and radical proposals that religion be drastically changed or else ignored entirely in geriatric programs.

The confusion of gerontologists about the role of religion is readily transferred to geriatricians, for scientific generalizations eventually influence practical action.

After considerable study and research, I have concluded that the confusion and contradictions about religion in old age are a product of more than a simple lack of research on the subject. The concept of 'religion' is very broad, and it is defined in the research operations of social scientists in a variety of ways. The 'religiosity' of scientist A is so greatly different from the 're-ligiosity' studied by scientist B that they are not dealing with the same subject even though the same words may be used in their reports. Examination of the 'operational definitions' (questions asked and other techniques used to describe and classify people's religious behavior) of relevant research projects reveals several types of 'religiosity'.

The best analysis of this conceptual problem is the five-fold classification of 'dimensions of religiosity' developed by Professor Glock of the Survey Research Center at the University of California (Berkeley). I shall briefly describe each of his five modes or types of religious expression and then summarize some findings on each dimension from studies about religion in old age.

Dimensions of religiosity

Glock's (1962) analysis of the score dimensions of religiosity, within which 'all of the many and diverse manifestations of religiosity prescribed by the different religions of the world can be ordered', provides the most satisfactory extant frame of reference for studying and assessing religion scientifically.

1. The *experiential* dimension reflects the expectation that religious persons 'will achieve direct knowledge of ultimate reality or will experience religious emotion', although the emotions deemed proper or experienced may vary widely from one religion or one person to another. Subjective religious experience or feeling is difficult to study but may be expressed chiefly in terms of 'concern or need to have a transcendentally based ideology', cognition or awareness of the divine, trust or faith, and fear.

2. The *ideological* dimension concerns beliefs that the followers of a religion are expected to hold (official doctrine), the beliefs they actually hold, the importance or saliency of beliefs, and their functions for individuals.

3. The *ritualistic* dimension has to do with the religious practices of adherents to a religion. It includes public and private worship, prayer, fasting, feasting, tithing, participation in sacraments, and the like.

4. The *intellectual* dimension deals with personal information and knowledge about the basic tenets and sacred writings of one's faith. Again, official expectations and the actual achievements of constituents tend to diverge considerably and need to be clearly distinguished from each other. Misconceptions, intellectual sophistication, and attitudes toward both secular and religious knowledge are important aspects.

5. The *consequential* dimension 'includes all of the secular effects of religious belief, practice, experience and knowledge on the individual'. It includes all specifications of what people ought to do and to believe as a result of their religion. In Christianity it emphasizes the theological concept of 'works' and especially Christian perspectives on man's relationships to other men, in contrast to his relationships to God. Rewards and punishments, expectations and obligations, commandments and promises are all aspects of this measure of religiosity.

Obviously, there are distinctions both in kind and in degree within each of the five dimensions. Just as religiosity itself is not a unilateral concept, each of its major dimensions may also be complex and multidimensional. The areas of religious commitment are all inextricably bound up with each other in real life; none can be studied effectively without recognition of and consideration for the others.

The attempt to clarify the present status of knowledge about religion in old age through use of Glock's dimensions is not simple, as we shall see in the following summary. A wide variety of techniques has been used. Measuring instruments and operational definitions of concepts have not been the same; therefore the actual phenomena studied are not identical even when presented under the same terms. The studies have had divergent objectives and in many additional ways have not been directly comparable. Can order be introduced into such a conglomeration of findings and interpretations?

Religious feelings

On the basis of her twenty-five years of medical practice, Dr Nila Kirkpatrick Covalt (1960), Director of the Kirkpatrick Memorial

Institute of Physical Medicine and Rehabilitation in Winter Park, Florida, stated that she found no evidence to support the common assumption that people turn to religion as they grow older. Patients do not talk with their physicians about religion. The religious attitudes of most old people are those they grew up with. Patients' thoughts, visions and dreams when regaining consciousness are often given a spiritual significance, Dr Covalt stated, but

> I recall no person who called out to God or audibly prayed when he was dying. Usually these persons are exerting every bit of energy in a struggle to keep alive.

At least the overt manifestations of their feelings do not indicate a high degree of experiential religiosity.

Contrary evidence is also available, however. The panel of persons in the Terman Gifted Group apparently had greater interest in religion in 1960 (at their median age of fifty-six) than they had in 1940 and 1950 (Marshall and Oden, 1962). Over half (54·1 per cent) of 210 people past age sixty-five in a Chicago working-class area said religion had become more helpful over the preceding decade; 30·1 per cent said that it had not become more helpful, and 6·2 per cent said that there had been no change (9·6 per cent gave no answer) (O'Reilly and Pembroke, n.d.).

Jeffers and Nichols (1961) found in their study of 251 persons in North Carolina past age sixty that religion means more to most Ss as the years go by and the end of life approaches and that this is especially true of disabled persons for whom the end is more imminent. Similarly, 57 per cent of 140 retired Negroes in South Carolina reported that religion and the church held more meaning since retirement than they did before; 42 per cent reported that they held the same meaning, and only two persons said they held less meaning (Lloyd, 1955).

A large study of 1700 elderly Minnesotans found that only from 7 to 19 per cent of the subcategories of men and from 2 to 5 per cent of the women reported that religion did not mean much to them. In contrast, 52 to 55 per cent of the men and 66 to 71 per cent of the women reported religion was the most important thing in their lives (Taves and Hansen, 1963, p. 172). Among the 143 older people in a rural New York community, the church and clergy were much more important than formerly to thirty-four persons, somewhat more important to twenty-eight, about the same to fifty-six, somewhat less important to ten, and much less important to only seven. Corresponding answers about the meaning of God and religion ranged from forty-six who said they held much more meaning than formerly, through twenty-five, fifty-nine and three in the respective intermediate categories, to only one who said they held much less meaning (nine gave no response). Yet only thirteen mentioned religion as one of the things that provided them the greatest satisfaction (Warren, 1952, pp. 155-66).

Wolff's (1961) summary of psychological aspects of aging includes the statement that geriatric patients have ambivalent feelings toward life and death and may turn toward religion, which 'gives them emotional support and tends to relieve them from the fear that everything soon will come to an end'.

The contrasting results of studies which refer to religious feelings of the aged may result from a basic difficulty in scientific research on religious feelings. American societal expectations hold that religion is helpful in any time of trouble. Anyone who expresses a perspective contrary to the position that religion helps the aged may feel that he is in danger of being socially rejected for his seemingly heretical views. With the fear of such reprisals, biased responses to questions about religious feelings may distort the results of questionnaire as well as interview studies. A type of self-fulfilling prophecy mechanism also may be at work: the expectation that religion will help may lead the person to receive genuine help through religious channels or at least to feel as if he had.

While the bulk of the evidence available to date indicates that religious feelings increase for more people than those for whom they decrease, we must retain an open mind on this subject while awaiting additional research.

Religious beliefs

There is some evidence from public opinion survey data that belief in life after death may increase with age; at least a higher proportion of old people than of younger generations believe that there is a life after death. Older people also are more certain that there is a God and apparently are more inclined to hold to traditional and conservative beliefs of their religion (Gray and Moberg, 1962).

A study of 496 persons in New York City, 325 of whom were Jewish, found that the proportion who believed in a life after death (heaven) increased from 30·1 to 40·5 per cent from ages thirty to thirty-five to ages sixty to sixty-five. Non-belief for the same age categories diminished from 36·1 to 25·1, with the remainder uncertain (Barron, 1961). The nationwide *Catholic Digest* (Anon, 1952) survey revealed that 81 per cent of the respondents aged sixty-five and over compared to 79 per cent of all and 76 per cent of those aged forty-five to fifty-four thought of God as a loving Father. Belief in God was held the most certainly by persons aged sixty-five and over, and a somewhat higher proportion of the aged (56 per cent) than of the total sample (51 per cent) believed one should prepare for life after death rather than be concerned with living comfortably. This lends some support to the opinion of Starbuck (1911), the pioneer in the psychology of religion, that religious faith and belief in God grow in importance as the years advance. His research data were skimpy and his highest age category was 'forty or over', but his conclusion has been adopted so widely that Maves (1960, pp. 698–749) has called it a 'part of the folklore of the psychology of religion'.

Surveys have revealed that older people as a whole tend to have more conservative religious perspectives than younger adults. Indirect evidence of this also comes from St Cloud, Florida, where more than half the population in the mid-1950s was aged sixty and over. Its churches were generally more fundamentalistic than was usual in peninsular Florida, and over one-third were evangelical and sectarian (Aldridge, 1956).

Whether the differences in religious beliefs between the generations are a result of the aging process or of divergent experiences during the formative years of childhood and youth, which are linked with different social and historical circumstances, is unknown. Longitudinal research might reveal considerably different conclusions from the cross-sectional studies which provide the foundation for current generalizations about age variations in the ideological dimension of religion.

Religious practices

The ritualistic dimension has received considerable attention from social scientists, perhaps because the observation of most religious practices is relatively simple. The findings are not wholly consistent, however.

All American studies which have come to my attention indicate that more of the formal social participation of the elderly, as well as of other age groups, is in the church than in all other voluntary community organizations together. This holds true whether measured by membership, attendance or other indicators. For example, 87 per cent of 1236 persons aged sixty and older in two Kentucky communities participated in the church, 35 per cent in Sunday school, and 8 per cent in other church activities. The next highest participation was six per cent in 'service and welfare organizations'. As also is consistently true, women participated in the church to a somewhat greater extent than men, 94 per cent compared with 85 per cent of the men in a Lexington sample and 93 and 73 per cent, respectively, in a Casey County sample (Youmans, 1963).

The highest Chapin social participation scores for religious participation among the heads of households in four rural New York communities studied in 1947–8 were found among men aged seventy-five to seventy-nine, followed closely by those aged forty-five to fifty-four. Among homemakers in the same study, the highest scores were found among those aged seventy to seventy-four and seventy-five to seventy-nine, with women aged sixty to sixty-four in third place and forty-five to fifty-four fourth. Female participation in religious organizations exceeded that of the males at every age, but male participation exceeded that of the females in non-religious organizations (Taietz and Larson, 1956). (Chapin scores are based upon a combination of membership, attendance, financial contributions, committee positions, and offices held.)

The peak of intensity of social participation, based on Chapin's scale among 1397 persons aged ten and over in two North Carolina localities, came at ages fifty-five to fifty-nine with a sharp drop thereafter. Four-fifths of this participation was in religious activities, and six-tenths of the persons participated only in churches and their auxiliary organizations (Mayo, 1951).

Some studies have revealed increases in religious practices in old age. Public opinion poll data indicate consistently higher figures for church attendance, Bible reading, and prayer among persons aged fifty and over than among younger groups (Toch, 1953). Age among 597 institutionalized women aged sixty-five or older living in Protestant homes for the aged was positively correlated with increased religious activities as well as with increased dependence upon religion (Pan, 1954). Contrasting evidence from other samples of older people suggests that the relative youthfulness of the 'over fifty' group compared to samples with a higher minimum age and the unusual environmental circumstance of residents in Protestant church homes, which facilitate participation in organized religious activities, may account for the variation between these two studies and others reported below.

A survey of one hundred first admissions of persons aged sixty and over to a county hospital found evidence which was interpreted tentatively as contrary to the common assumption that people become more interested in religion as they grow older. Several were found to attend church less frequently than at age fifty, and few attended more often than before (Fiske, 1961). (The report sensibly qualifies the finding by suggesting that a change in behavior does not necessarily imply less concern with spiritual matters. It refers to a University of Chicago study which found that the decrease in church attendance among aging persons is accompanied by increased listening to religious programs on radio and television.)

In the 'Back of the Yards' Chicago study (O'Reilly and Pembroke, n.d.) approximately equal proportions of men attended church more (34 per cent) and less (32 per cent) than they did before the age of sixty-five, but among women the respective figures of 27 and 46 per cent indicate a decrease in attendance. Increasing age among Catholics in Fort Wayne, Indiana, was associated with decreasing church attendance, chiefly because of poor health (Theisen, 1962). Fichter's (1954, pp. 83–93) study of 8363 active white Catholic parishioners found that the percentage who received monthly Communion diminished fairly consistently in each ten-year category from age ten to sixty and over. However, a higher percentage of the eldest category (86·6) made their Easter duties (confession and Holy Communion) than any other age except the youngest (ages ten to nineteen, 92·1 per cent), and only the youngest exceeded the elderly in the percentage attending Mass every Sunday (92·8 versus 90·9 per cent). Physical disabilities may account for differences. Although variations over the total life span cannot be accounted for solely on the basis of age, both the young and the old were significantly more religious as measured by these practices than persons aged thirty to thirty-nine, who had the lowest record for both sexes (63·4 per cent made their Easter duties, 69·3 per cent attended Mass every Sunday, and 31·6 per cent received monthly Communion).

Only 4 per cent of a representative stratified sample of people aged sixty-five and over studied in 1948–9 in a small midwestern city rejected religion and the church, but an additional 18 per cent had no church affiliation and no attendance, and 15 per cent had only a passive interest. The other 63 per cent participated in religious activities frequently and actively. Most people evidently continued to carry on the religious habits of their middle years, but they also customarily dropped gradually out of church leadership positions after the age of sixty (Havighurst and Albrecht, 1953, pp. 201–3). In a metropolitan Kansas City study (Cumming and Henry, 1961, pp. 91–4) the proportion of persons aged fifty and over who seldom attended church was lowest at age sixty to sixty-four in both sexes and reached its highest figure among those aged seventy-five and over (64·3 per cent of the men and 75·0 per cent of the women).

Senior citizens surveys of a cross-section of the population aged sixty-five and over in Long Beach, California (McCann, 1955), and Grand Rapids, Michigan (Hunter and Maurice, 1953, pp. 62–3) indicated a definite tendency of the aged to attend church less often than they did ten years earlier, and increasing non-attendance accompanied increasing age. Problems of physical mobility and finances were among the most significant factors related to declining attendance. Listening to religious services on radio or television and 'lost interest' followed health or physical condition in importance among the reasons respondents gave for attending church less often than they had a decade earlier; where the former is a major reason for decreased attendance (17·1 per cent of the Long Beach and 33·9 per cent of the Grand Rapids sample), non-attendance can hardly be accepted as an indicator of a loss of religiosity.

Fifty-five per cent of 131 aged members of two urban Baptist churches in Minnesota attended church every Sunday. The percentages ranged from 71·4 among the fourteen persons aged eighty to eighty-four to 20 among the five aged eighty-five to eighty-nine. Nearly half (45·6 per cent) of the persons aged seventy-five and over attended church every Sunday, compared with 64·5 per cent of those aged sixty-five to sixty-nine and 60·5 per cent of those aged seventy to seventy-four. The evidence pertinent to attendance at other church activities clearly supported the hypothesis that participation declines in old age. This decline was even more pronounced in regard to holding lay leadership positions, which reached its peak in both churches at the age of twenty-five to forty-four. Only 4·6 per cent said that they were more active in the church now than they were in their fifties, but

72·5 per cent said that they were less active than in their fifties (Moberg, 1965).

The survey (Barron, 1961) of 496 residents of New York City (325 of whom were Jewish, ninety-eight Roman Catholic, sixty-five Protestant, and eight of other or no faiths) found only insignificant differences between the age categories thirty to thirty-five, forty to forty-five, fifty to fifty-five, and sixty to sixty-five in the proportion that attended church or synagogue 'often' in contrast to 'sometimes' and 'hardly ever' or 'never'.

The strongest criticism of the 'contemporary folklore that "older" people are more religious than others ..., and that there is a turning to religion in old age' comes from Orbach's (1961) interpretations and research. In support of his position, Orbach appealed to sociological interpretations of the functions of religion in our 'youth-centered society', evidence of the significance of religious beliefs, feelings and conversion among the young rather than the aged, and empirical findings from studies like those mentioned above which indicate that participation in religious activities decreases in old age.

Since other studies are weak on the levels of both sampling and the analysis of relevant sociological variables other than sex, Orbach made a careful analysis of five probability samples of 6911 adults aged twenty-one and over who resided in the mid-1950s in the Detroit Metropolitan Area. Church attendance on a five-point scale from once a week to never was related to age in five-year intervals with sex controlled. Age *per se* was found to be unrelated to changes in church attendance; there was no indication of an increase in attendance in the later years, although the data suggest that there is a polarizing effect in which intermediary categories of 'casual' and 'cursory' churchgoers tend to shift into a dichotomous distribution of regular church attenders and non-attenders.

When the data were grouped into four age categories (twenty-one to thirty-nine, forty to fifty-nine, sixty to seventy-four, seventy-five and over), the most striking finding was the constancy of attendance in all age groupings, with the one exception of significantly increased non-attendance among the oldest group, which can be attributed at least partly to the effect of age on physical health. Multivariate analysis of church attendance in relationship to age with religious preference, sex, and race as control variables found only Protestant Negro males and Jewish males and females to show increased attendance with age. The small number of cases of Negro males in the oldest age category and the historical decline of Jewish orthodoxy, which is directly reflected in the age groupings, may account for these exceptions to the general pattern of declining attendance as age increases. When other sociological variables were controlled, the relationships between age and attendance were mixed and inconsistent and lent no support to the hypothesis that religiosity increases with age.

The bulk of reliable evidence thus indicates that church attendance of people generally remains fairly constant but tends to decline in the later years compared with younger ages. It is hazardous, however, to assume that church attendance is anything more than a crude indicator of religiosity; it is only one subdimension of religious practices, which themselves comprise but one of Glock's five major dimensions of religious commitment.

Orbach (1961) states that 'participation in religious bodies through attendance and involvement in ceremonial worship is perhaps the most crucial and sensitive indicator of overt religiosity'. This may apply satisfactorily to the most sacramentally oriented religions – those which believe that the religious institution is the channel of God's grace and that salvation is bestowed upon the individual only through institutionalized participation in church rituals. It probably does not apply to nonsacramental Protestants and to Jews. Orbach (1961) also wisely reminds us that 'objective criteria such as attendance cannot replace study of the area of religious beliefs and attitudinal changes or approximate the subjective aspect of inner religious feelings'. Attendance is easier to study, but it should be used as a measure of religiosity only provisionally and with a clear recognition of attendant dangers.

Although church attendance tends at most to remain constant with increasing age in cross-sectional studies of the population and more often to decline, regular listening to church services and other religious broadcasts on the radio and reading from the Bible at least weekly have been found to increase among the elderly with advancing age (Cavan, Burgess, Havighurst and Goldhammer, 1949, pp. 58, 198). Evidently religious practices outside the home diminish while those within the home increase. Physical condition may be the chief intervening variable responsible for such trends. Comparative studies reveal that participation in other social organizations declines at a much more rapid rate than participation in the church.

Religious knowledge

Relatively little research has been done on age differences in the intellectual dimension of religiosity among older adults. I have been unable to locate any published research which bears directly upon this topic.

Effects of religion

Although many of the other dimensions of religiosity have been only crudely defined, they have been used as independent variables in research designed to discover the effects of religion upon other aspects of personal and social life. Examples of some of these explorations of the consequential dimension of religion will be presented here.

A number of studies have demonstrated that church members hold a larger number of memberships in voluntary community associations and other organizations than those who are not members and that lay leaders in the church are more active in non-church organizations than are other church members (Moberg, 1962, pp. 393–5, 414–18), but relatively little attention has been given to age variations in this pattern.

A national survey of adults (Lazerwitz, 1962) in the spring of 1957 related the age of persons with Protestant and Catholic religious preference to the number of voluntary association memberships they held. It was found that the lowest membership levels prevailed among Protestants in the youngest (twenty-one to twenty-four) and oldest (sixty to sixty-four and sixty-five and over) categories and the highest membership rates at ages thirty to fifty-nine. Among Catholics the highest percentage of persons with no organizational memberships was at ages sixty-five and over and forty-five to forty-nine, with the greatest number of memberships at ages thirty-five to forty-four. Most of the Protestants and Catholics who seldom or never attended church also lacked membership in voluntary associations, while most of those who attended faithfully had one or more such memberships.

Other studies support the conclusion that there is a positive correlation between church participation and other formal social participation at all ages. It is not unreasonable to think that associating with people in church-related activities and organizations contributes to knowledge of other voluntary organizations; friendships in the church with persons who are members of other groups may lead to social participation in them. The lower organizational membership levels of Catholics hence could result from their lesser stress upon 'fellowship' in the church as compared to Protestants, as well as from their somewhat lower position in the social class structure of American society.

Barron's (1961) New York City study included a question about the respondent's self-image, 'Would you say you are a religious person, or doesn't religion mean very much to you?' Of all the respondents, 44·7 per cent responded affirmatively and 25·2 per cent expressed an irreligious self-image. Among the 116 persons aged sixty to sixty-five, however, the respective percentages were 55·1 and 19·9 (25·0 per cent were undecided compared with 30·1 per cent in the total sample).

The most significant aspect of the chronological age distribution in answer to this question was the steadily increasing proportions of the religious self-image and the steadily declining proportions of indecision regarding the self-image in the ascension of chronological age.

The relationship of religion to personality problems has been observed and commented upon by a number of behavioral scientists. Religion was the preferred topic of discussion in group therapy sessions with geriatric patients at a state hospital. Religious beliefs and faith in God helped disorganized members to overcome their grief when unhappy, lonesome and despondent. They were eager to discuss a better life after death; other members sensed the support religion gave them because they themselves also received greater 'ego strength' from religion. Delusions and hallucinations involving religious symptoms were, however, not accepted by other members of the group as true and correct; when they occurred the possibility of a mistake or incorrect interpretation was discussed (Wolff, 1959a).

Elderly patients who have ambivalent feelings toward life and death often want to die, since they believe they have nothing for which to live. Yet as they sense death is approaching, they may become disturbed and insecure, want others near at all times, and fear the dark. They may attend church more often than previously, confess, and ask that their sins be forgiven. They thus turn toward religion, which gives them emotional support and relief from the fear that everything soon will end (Wolff, 1959b, p.75).

Fear of death was one topic probed in a study of 260 community volunteers aged sixty and over in North Carolina. Such fear was found to be significantly related (at the 1 per cent level of confidence) to less belief in life after death and less frequent Bible reading (Jeffers, Nichols and Eisdorfer, 1961). Swenson's (1961) psychological study of 210 Minnesota residents aged sixty and over similarly found a significant relationship between death attitudes and religiosity as measured by both religious activity and the M M P I religiosity scale, a measure of devotion to religion.

Persons with more fundamental religious convictions and habits look forward to death more than do those with less fundamental convictions and less activity. Fearful attitudes toward death tend to be found in those persons with little religious activity... it seems logical to infer that the eschatologically oriented person contemplates death in a positive manner.

These findings support the conclusion that a sense of serenity and decreased fear of death tend to accompany conservative religious beliefs. This does not necessarily prove, however, that religious faith removes the fear of death. It is conceivable that attitudes toward death of the religiously faithful differ from those of nonreligious people because of differences in their social integration (Treanton, 1961); the religious have a reference group that gives them support and security and the nonreligious are more likely to lack such social support. Swenson's finding that fear of death is related to solitude supports this hypothesis; social isolation may be an intervening variable explaining the observed relationships.

The traditional cultural definition of death complicates research on this subject among people of Christian convictions. The faithful believer is expected so to rest upon the promise of his salvation that he has no fear of death; he is expected to see death as a portal to immortality. His affirmation that he does not fear the advent of death could be an expression of a neurotic personality which disguises death and pretends that it is not a basic condition of all life (Fulton, 1961). Feifel (1956) has hypothesized that 'certain older persons perceive death as the beginning of a new existence for the purpose of controlling strong anxieties concerning death'. While this hypothesis may be perceived by some religious people as an impudent attack upon the genuineness of religious faith, it may also be viewed as a compliment to it. If the hypothesis is verified, one of the social-psychological functions commonly attributed to religion by even the most faithful when they seek comfort in biblical teachings about the resurrection will have received scientific support.

Happiness was significantly related to frequency of church attendance among both Catholics and non-Catholics in the Chicago 'Back of the Yards' study. The 'very happy' attended church the most frequently, the 'moderately happy' the next most frequently, and the 'less happy' persons attended the least of all. Lonely Catholics tended to be less active in the practice of their religion, but the relationship was not statistically significant (O'Reilly and Pembroke, n.d.).

Feelings of satisfaction and security were provided in older persons by religion and church participation in a small midwestern community studied by McCrary (1956). Yet in her general medical practice in Muncie, Indiana, Covalt (1958, pp. 78–90) observed little or no relationship between religion and good adjustment to illness. The patient who brought a Bible to the hospital with him thereby gave the physicians a sign of anticipated trouble, for the stable, secure person did not bring a Bible. These insecure individuals often were members of fringe-type religious sects. They were uncooperative, did not carry out instructions, fought the nurses, complained about even the most minor matters, and unpleasantly hindered their own recovery.

Contradictory evidence thus emerges on the matter of whether religion performs such functions as promoting happiness, increasing personal security, combating loneliness and removing the fear of death. Several of these concepts are reflected in studies of personal adjustment or morale in old age. To discuss the techniques and findings of these in any detail is impossible in the short space available here, but a brief summary of some of the major studies will help to illuminate this aspect of the consequential dimension of religion. More thorough surveys are found in Gray and Moberg (1962, pp. 41–3, 153) and Maves (1960).

These studies generally have found that there is a direct relationship between good personal adjustment and such indicators of religiosity as church membership, church attendance, Bible reading, regular listening to radio church services, belief in an after life and religious faith. Yet a carefully planned experimental design to explore this relationship further, with the use of the Burgess–Cavan–Havighurst Attitudes Inventory as the measure of personal adjustment, revealed that controlling other factors which also are linked with good adjustment removed the correlation between adjustment and church membership (Moberg, 1953a). The relationship observed in cruder studies must be a result of linking with church membership certain other factors which contribute to adjustment rather than a result of church membership in and of itself.

Further analysis (Moberg, 1956) through additional experimental designs demonstrated that religious activities (church attendance in the past and present, lay leadership in the church, grace at meals, reading from the Bible and other religious books, family prayers, etc.) were significantly correlated with high adjustment scores. It was concluded that either those who are well-adjusted engage in many religious activities, or else engaging in many religious activities contributes to good adjustment in old age.

Similarly, an experimental design (Moberg, 1953b) to analyse the relationships between adjustment and leadership in the church, as indicated by office-holding and committee work in the past and present, revealed that personal adjustment was positively related to lay leadership. An investigation (Moberg, 1958) of Christian beliefs about sin, prayer, the future, the Bible, and Jesus in relationship to personal adjustment also revealed a positive relationship between holding conventional Christian beliefs and good adjustment in old age when other factors were controlled. The evidence from these experimental designs, based upon institutionalized persons in homes for the aged, a county home and a soldiers' home, supports the conclusion that religious beliefs and activities, in contrast to church affiliation *per se*, contribute to good personal adjustment in old age.

This conclusion is supported by additional studies of elderly people. The most significant of these (Moberg and Taves, 1965) involves over 5000 persons aged sixty years and over interviewed in five surveys in four midwestern states. It was found that the adjustment scores of church 'leaders' (church officers and committee men), other church members, and non-church members were significantly different, with the leaders consistently highest and non-members lowest. Cross-tabulations of the data for 1340 urban respondents in one of the states demonstrated that these differences remained

statistically significant at the 0·001 level when analysed within categories of sex, age, education, marital status, home ownership and type of residence, participation in civic, social, and professional organizations, organizational activity levels compared to those during the respondents' fifties, self-rating of health, and self-identification of age. Only in the area of employment were the variations non-significant, but even these were in the anticipated direction.

so the hypothesis that church participation is related to good personal adjustment in old age was overwhelmingly supported by the evidence.

A study (Oles, 1949) of Orthodox Jews aged sixty-five and over also found that adjustment was related to religious adherence. No non-religious persons were in the well-adjusted category; all were intensely or fairly religious. Three-fourths of the fairly adjusted group were intensely or fairly religious, but only 35 per cent of the poorly and very poorly adjusted group were.

Religious beliefs and activities seem, on the basis of these and other studies, to be positively related to good personal-social adjustment in old age. Contrary evidence, but on a somewhat different basis, comes from Barron's (1961, pp. 161–83) New York City study. Only 39 per cent mentioned that religion and the church gave them the most satisfaction and comfort in their lives today. This was exceeded by being home with the family, keeping house, 'doings things I like to do by myself at home', having relatives visit, and spending time with close friends. Worry about getting older was significantly less among these who found religion comforting only for the age group forty to forty-five; the comparative figures for all ages indicate that 37 per cent of those who derive comfort from religion worry about aging compared with 40·6 per cent of those who do not find religion comforting. Both of these measures of religiosity are very limited, but this finding suggests the need for further research before making sweeping generalizations about the impact of religion upon personal adjustment.

Another consequential aspect of religion is the large number of retirement homes and communities, nursing care facilities, social clubs, literary projects, counseling centers, volunteer services programs, educational activities, and other programs by and for the aged which are under church sponsorship (Culver, 1961). While these, like all human behavior, are based upon a wide range of economic, social, political, psychological and humanitarian interests, the very fact that religiously based institutions are their sponsors demonstrates this to be a consequence of organized religion. Religious beliefs, feelings, knowledge and practices undoubtedly are an underlying factor in much of the humanitarian work that is done through other institutional structures as well. The educational and inspirational work of the church often is directly oriented toward such goals; to whatever extent it is effective, it serves as an enlightening and motivating influence in society, and more often produces change through its constituents than through formal institutional action. This aspect of the consequential dimension of religious commitment is obviously very difficult to study empirically because it is so intricately woven into the total fabric of society.

Interrelations of the dimensions

Some studies have shown both the interconnectedness and the relative independence of various dimensions of religious commitment. The biserial correlation coefficient between the religious activity and religious attitude scores in the Chicago Activities and Attitudes Inventories by Burgess, Cavan and Havighurst, for example, was significant at the 0·001 level of confidence in a North Carolina study (Jeffers and Nichols, 1961). The correlation coefficient between attitudes toward religion and frequency of attendance at religious services in the original Chicago study was 0·55 among 1024 males and 0·37 among 1894 females (Cavan et al., 1949, pp. 58, 198). In a study (Moberg, 1951, p. 105) of 219 institutionalized aged persons, the product-moment correlation of a religious activities score and a religious belief score was 0·660 with a standard error of 0·038.

Such relationships are the kind one would expect; if a person has religious faith, he is more apt to participate in the personal and social activities which simultaneously nourish that faith and are consequences of it. Belief in life after death thus is significantly associated with more frequent church attendance, more frequent Bible reading, a greater number of other religious activities, a feeling that religion is the most important thing in life, less fear of death, and stronger religious attitudes than are found among those who lack such a belief (Jeffers et al., 1961).

Nevertheless, it is a fallacy to assume that *all* dimensions of religiosity are highly intercorrelated. Hospitalized old people, we know, are somewhat more likely than the elderly in the community to identify with a religious group, but they also are considerably less likely to attend religious services than non-hospitalized old people (Fiske, 1960, p. 13). To judge the totality of the religiosity of a person on the basis of one of the five major dimensions of religious commitment or, as is a common practice, of but one subdimension thereof, can lead to serious errors. Religious preference, church attendance, religious self-identification, and other simple indicators of religiosity must be used with great caution of interpretation. Religious commitment is a complex phenomenon with many ramifications. Until research has demonstrated the ways in which and the extent to which the experiential, ideological, ritualistic, intellectual and

D. O. Moberg 203

consequential dimensions of religious commitment are inter-correlated, it is wise to refrain from jumping to conclusions about any of them on the basis of evidence only from another.

Summary and conclusions

Research to date seems to indicate fairly conclusively that ritualistic behavior outside the home tends to diminish with increasing age, while religious attitudes and feelings apparently increase among people who have an acknowledged religion. To use Kuhlen's (1962, p. 23) words in his summary of research findings on adult religion,

in all studies examined, with the exception of those relating to church attendance, trends indicate an increased interest in and concern about religion as age increases, even into extreme old age.

In other words, religion as a set of external extradomiciliary rituals apparently decreases in old age, while the internal personal responses linked with man's relationships to God apparently increase among religious people. Thus both disengagement from and re-engagement with religion are typical in old age!

We have seen that some religious practices decline in the later years, but religious feelings and beliefs apparently increase. These contrasting tendencies account for most of the apparently contradictory statements about the place of religion in old age. The use of non-comparable 'indicators' or 'measures' of religiosity has led to confusion. More research is needed on the major dimensions of religiosity; it will have implications for the specialist in geriatrics as well as for churchmen and gerontologists.

This distinction is related to the age-old contrast between faith and works. Most of the objective practices ('works') of religion become increasingly difficult to perform in old age as the body and mind gradually show the effects of the aging process. Yet in his 'spirit' the religious person may remain devout; his religious beliefs and feelings can become more intense even though his institutionally oriented religious practices diminish.

Recognition of these distinct dimensions of religiosity thus helps to resolve differences of opinion about the role of religion among the elderly. Research can clarify the subject further; it also can lead to more realistic and wholesome relationships between clergymen and psychologists, social workers, and medical personnel and to keener awareness of the religious implications of geriatric practice.

References

ALDRIDGE, G. J. (1956), 'The role of older people in a Florida retirement community', *Geriatrics*, vol. 11, pp. 223–6.

ANON (1952), 'Do Americans believe in God?' *Cath. Digest*, vol. 17, pp. 1–5.

BARRON, M. L. (1961), *The Aging American: An Introduction to Social Gerontology and Geriatrics*, Crowell.

CAVAN, R. S., BURGESS, E. W., HAVIGHURST, R. J., and GOLDHAMMER, H. (1949), *Personal Adjustment in Old Age*, Sci. Res. Assoc., Chicago.

COVALT, N. K. (1958), 'The meaning of religion to older people – the medical perspective', in D. L. Scudder (ed.), *Organized Religion and the Older Person*, University of Florida Press.

COVALT, N. K. (1960), 'The meaning of religion to older people', *Geriatrics*, vol. 15, pp. 658–64.

CULVER, E. T. (1961), *New Church Programs with the Aging*, Association Press.

CUMMING, E., and HENRY, W. E. (1961), *Growing Old: The Process of disengagement*, Basic Books.

FEIFEL, H. (1956), 'Older persons look at death', *Geriatrics*, vol. 11, pp. 127–30.

FICHTER, J. H. (1954), *Social Relations in the Urban Parish*, University of Chicago Press.

FISKE, M. (1960), *Some Social Dimensions of Psychiatric Disorders in Old Age*, Langley Porter Neuropsychiatric Institute (mimeo.).

FISKE, M. (1961), 'Geriatric mental illness: methodologic and social aspects', *Geriatrics*, vol. 16, pp. 306–10.

FULTON, R. L. (1961), 'Symposium: death attitudes. Comments', *J. Geront.*, vol. 16, pp. 63–5.

GLOCK, C. Y. (1962), 'On the study of religious commitment', *Relig. Educ.*, vol. 57, pp. 98–110.

GRAY, R. M., and MOBERG, D. O. (1962), *The Church and the Older Person*, Wm. B. Eerdmans, Grand Rapids.

HAVIGHURST, R. J., and ALBRECHT, R. (1953), *Older People*, Longman.

HUNTER, W. W., and MAURICE, H. (1953), *Older People Tell Their Story*, University of Michigan Press.

JEFFERS, F. C., and NICHOLS, C. R. (1961), 'The relationship of activities and attitudes to physical well-being in older people', *J. Geront.*, vol. 16, pp. 67–70.

JEFFERS, F. C., NICHOLS, C. R., and EISDORFER, C. (1961), 'Attitudes of older persons toward death: a preliminary study', *J. Geront.*, vol. 16, pp. 53–6.

KUHLEN, R. G. (1962), 'Trends in religious behavior during the adult years', in L. C. Little (ed.), *Wider Horizons in Christian Adult Education*. University of Pittsburgh Press.

LAZERWITZ, B. (1962), 'Membership in voluntary associations and frequency of church attendance', *J. sci. Study Relig.*, vol. 2, pp. 74–84.

LLOYD, R. G. (1955), 'Social and personal adjustment of retired persons', *Sociol. soc. Res.*, vol. 39, pp. 312–16.

MARSHALL, H., and ODEN, M. H. (1962), 'The status of the mature gifted individual as a basis for evaluation of the aging process', *Gerontologist*, vol. 2, pp. 201–6.

MAVES, P. B. (1960), 'Aging, religion, and the church', in C. Tibbitts (ed.), *Handbook of Social Gerontology*, University of Chicago Press

MAYO, S. C. (1951), 'Social participation among the older population in rural areas of Wake County, North Carolina', *Soc. Forces*, vol. 30, pp. 53–9.

MCCANN, C. W. (1955), *Long Beach Senior Citizens' Survey*, Community Welfare Council, Long Beach, pp. 50–52.

MCCRARY, J. S. (1956), *The Role, Status and Participation of the Aged in a Small Community*, Ph.D. thesis, Washington University, St Louis.

MOBERG, D. O. (1951), *Religion and Personal Adjustment in Old Age*, Ph.D. thesis, University of Minnesota.

MOBERG, D. O. (1953a), 'Church membership and personal adjustment in old age', *J. Geront.*, vol. 8, pp. 207–11.

MOBERG, D. O. (1953b), 'Leadership in the church and personal adjustment in old age', *Sociol. soc. Res.*, vol. 37, pp. 312–16.

MOBERG, D. O. (1956), 'Religious activities and personal adjustment in old age', *J. soc. Psychol.*, vol. 43, pp. 261–7.

MOBERG, D. O. (1958), 'Christian beliefs and personal adjustment in old age', *J. Amer. Sci. Affil.*, vol. 10, pp. 8–12.

MOBERG, D. O. (1962), *The Church as a Social Institution*, Prentice-Hall.

MOBERG, D. O. (1965), 'The integration of older members in the church congregation', in A. M. Rose and W. A. Peterson (eds.), *Older People and Their Social World*, F. A. Davis, Philadelphia.

MOBERG, D. O., and TAVES, M. J. (1965), 'Church participation and adjustment in old age', in A. M. Rose and W. A. Peterson (eds.), *Older People and Their Social World*, F. A. Davis, Philadelphia.

OLES, E. S. (1949), *Religion and Old Age, A Study of the Possible Influence of Religious Adherence on Adjustment*, Thesis, Bucknell University, Lewisburg, Pa.

ORBACH, H. L. (1961), 'Aging and religion: church attendance in the Detroit metropolitan area', *Geriatrics*, vol. 16, pp. 530–40.

O'REILLY, C. T., and PEMBROKE, M. M. (n.d.), *Older People in a Chicago Community*, Loyola University, Chicago, n.d. (survey made in 1956).

PAN, J. S. (1954), 'Institutional and personal adjustment in old age', *J. gen. Psychol.*, vol. 85, pp. 55–8.

STARBUCK, E. D. (1911), *The Psychology of Religion*, 3rd edn, Walter Scott, New York.

SWENSON, W. M. (1961), 'Attitudes toward death in an aged population', *J. Geront.*, vol. 16, pp. 19–52.

TAIETZ, P., and LARSON, O. F. (1956), 'Social participation and old age', *Rur. Sociol.*, vol. 21, pp. 229–38.

TAVES, M. J., and HANSEN, G. D. (1963), 'Seventeen hundred elderly citizens', in A. M. Rose (ed.), *Aging in Minnesota*, University of Minnesota Press.

THEISEN, S. P. (1962), *A Social Survey of Aged Catholics in the Deanery of Fort Wayne, Indiana*, Ph.D. thesis, University of Notre Dame, Indiana.

Toch, H. (1953), 'Attitudes of the "fifty plus" age group: preliminary considerations toward a longitudinal study', *Publ. Opin. Q.*, vol. 17, pp. 391–4.

Treanton, J. R. (1961), 'Symposium: death attitudes. Comments', *J. Geront.*, vol. 16, p. 63.

Warren, R. L. (1952), 'Old age in a rural township', in *Old Age Is No Barrier* N. Y. State Jt., Legis. Com. on Problems Aging, Albany.

Wolff, K. (1959a), 'Group psychotherapy with geriatric patients in a state hospital setting: results of a three-year study', *Group Psychotherapy*, vol. 12, pp. 218–22.

Wolff, K. (1959b), *The Biological, Sociological and Psychological Aspects of Ageing*, Thomas.

Wolff, K. (1961), 'A coordinated approach to the geriatric problem', *J. Amer. Ger Soc.*, vol. 9, pp. 573–80.

Youmans, E. G. (1963), 'Aging patterns in a rural and an urban area of Kentucky', *Univ. Ky agric. Exp. Sta. Bull.*, no. 681, p. 45.

Part Six
Experimental Studies

Experimental and quasi-experimental procedures set out to produce refined control over the effects of religious materials on judgement and behaviour, and to test predictions about these effects. Some experiments use religious material to study basic psychological processes like intolerance of ambiguity or the effects of group membership. Other experiments have tested specific theories about religious functioning, like Welford's test of the theories that prayer depends either on affect or on frustration. Despite the difficulties in carrying out experiments in religion, the experimental approaches have covered a broad range and are an important contribution that psychologists can make to the study of religion.

16 A. T. Welford

Is Religious Behavior Dependent upon Affect or Frustration?

A. T. Welford, 'Is religious behavior dependent upon affect or frustration?', *Journal of Abnormal and Social Psychology*, 1947, vol. 42, no. 3, pp. 310–19.

Religion, both as a social institution and as a branch of individual behavior, has from time to time aroused considerable interest among social and abnormal psychologists. A number of studies have been made of religious attitudes, especially since the publication of the Thurstone–Chave scale for measuring attitude toward the church (1929), and the Vernon–Allport test for personal values (1931), but, except for the investigations into religious conversion following the pioneer work of Leuba and Starbuck, studies of religious *behavior*, particularly laboratory experimental studies, have been relatively few. The lack of these would seem to be due to the difficulty of obtaining genuine religious behavior in the laboratory, and the almost equal difficulty of introducing controlled conditions in situations where religious behavior does occur, such as at church services. The experiment to be described here represents a further attempt on the author's part (Welford, 1946) to introduce experimental techniques into this field.

Any adequate discussion of the psychological processes involved in the motivation and functioning of religion must take into consideration at least five problems:

1. The nature of religious as compared with other types of behavior.

2. The individual and environmental factors which accompany and seemingly produce religious behavior.

3. The nature and origins of the concepts used in religion.

4. The effect of these concepts impinging upon the individual and the manner in which they are used by the individual.

5. The way in which these concepts become institutionalized, and the functioning of religion as a social institution.

All these problems interlock so that any one study, while it may deal mainly with one or two, will almost always deal to some extent with the others as well.

The present study deals mainly with the second, but touches upon the first and fourth of these problems. It takes its rise from the theories of the analysts and Flower. Among the former, Freud (1928, 1933) and Jung (1921, 1938) regard religious behavior as essentially a response of men and women to features of their environment, either natural or social, to which they fail to adjust in a normal manner. Such maladjustment leads to a sense of inadequacy and a tendency to seek a substitute for the parental care enjoyed in early childhood. The concepts used in religion are, for Freud and Jung, built up around God as a substitute parent. For Adler (1938) the general picture is similar except that the emphasis is on the individual's struggle, not for adjustment, but for perfection, and on God as representing the omnipotence and perfection which are the goals of the individual's striving. It is important to realize that the views about religion put forward by the analysts may, to a considerable extent, be considered apart from the rest of their systems.

Flower's theory (1927) bears some similarity to these, but is based on concepts taken from experimental psychology. For him, any situation which presents features with which the individual is unable to deal adequately by means of existing reaction tendencies is clothed with images and analogies which aim at bringing it within the scope of these tendencies. There is, in short, what Bartlett has termed 'effort after meaning' (1932, p. 20). If the work of image and analogy is successful, the result is what we know as rational thought. If it is unsuccessful, a religious response may result in which the reaction is made, not to the original situation, but to the images with which it has been clothed. Flower distinguishes between a religious response and a 'neurotic' one by holding that in the former the images, although they fail to bring the situation fully 'under control', are nevertheless truly representative of that situation and are reacted to as such, whereas in neurotic responses they are not. The fantasies projected by religion are not mere escapes from a 'reality' which is displeasing: they are constructions around a reality which is baffling' (1927, p. 196).

These theories have in common the postulate that religious behavior arises on a basis of frustration, and seem to presume that it will be in some way bound up with affect. This is in line with much that can be observed in everyday experience, in some of the behavior of men and women under the stress of battle or bombing, and in the topics dealt within Christian prayer books. Exactly what is the relation of religious behavior to frustration and affect – and how far its relation to each is determined by the relationships that frustration and affect are commonly supposed to bear to each other – is, however, not clear. Also, the analysts do not always make it clear to what extent they regard religious behavior as a response to individual frustration, and to what extent as a response to those frustrations which, while they affect society in general, may impinge themselves only slightly upon the consciousness of any particular individual. The essential difference between the theories of the analysts and that of Flower is that the former, especially Freud, tend to regard religion as due to man's helplessness in the face of 'fate' and 'culture', leading to the projection of his struggles on to a substitute parent, while Flower postulates that a lack of adequate existing response mechanisms leads to religious behavior as a new mode of response capable of dealing with the situation and relieving the affective tension which results from the frustration. He makes no postulate regarding the form and content of religious concepts.

The present experiment was designed to study the relationships of religious behavior to frustration and affect at the individual level, in particular with a view to testing the plausibility of Flower's hypothesis.

Method

There were sixty-three subjects, all university or theological seminary male students between eighteen and twenty-five years of age, and all church-goers – mostly Presbyterians and Episcopalians.

In seeking to make the stimuli as 'real' as possible under experimental conditions, questions of the questionnaire type were abandoned in favor of short anecdotes describing concrete situations into which the subjects were instructed to introject themselves. The anecdotes were written in a way which left them a little vague, in the hope that the subjects would be the more able to link them to actual experiences. Remarks made by the subjects indicated that this hope was realized in a large number of cases. The anecdotes used were as follows:

1. The wind had been rising all night and the sea was rougher than ever in the morning; at times the towering waves surrounded

the little ship with a wall of dark water. He had just come out on deck when suddenly this wall seemed to rush upon the vessel like a wild thing. The man staggered forward and clutched at the rail, but even as he did so he felt his fingers slipping.

2. It was an anxious group that gathered round the bedside in that little room; the doctor shook his head gravely at their whispered questions and stood for a while in silence; then picking up his bag, he went quietly downstairs. As soon as he had gone, the father slipped away from the others into the parlor. The fire had burned low, and the one candle lit up the room but dimly. . . .

3. Business had been getting steadily worse for many months past and just recently it seemed to have been falling off more than ever. He was sitting at his desk as usual when the manager came up to him: 'I hate to have to tell you', he said, 'but we've come to the conclusion the only thing is to close up. I'm sorry, and it'll be tough on you, specially after the way you've worked here. We shall be able to pay you a month's salary which will keep you going for a little while, and give you the chance of looking round for another job, but at your age it's a bit difficult.'

When he reached home that evening the future seemed very black. He went quietly up to his bedroom. . . .

4. He sat down at his desk with some hesitation, and at first could think of nothing to write. However, after a time his ideas began to flow, and soon he was writing busily with but little effort. Just as the clock outside chimed half past four he put down his pen, and with a gentle sigh of satisfaction, gathered together the sheets lying scattered about his desk into a neat pile. 'Well, that's that done', he said, 'now for a cigarette.'

5. It was one of those late spring days when the boisterous sky and fresh wind seem to brace even the most lethargic of us to go out into the country for a long walk. As he strode along, the carpet of moist grass under foot, the bright green of the hedges and trees and the smell of the damp soil around him, a sensation of renewed vigor came over him and he felt supremely happy.

6. He had now been waiting over two weeks and still had heard nothing. Eagerly he watched every mail to see if it contained the fateful letter which would mean so much to his future. He found the suspense was trying him very hard; all the previous night he had lain in a restless half-waking state, wondering what his chances of getting it might be.

The postman pushed the letters into the mail-box in the usual nonchalant manner. Concealing his excitement with some difficulty, he looked them through. At last, there it was! He opened the envelope quickly and scanned the note inside: yes, it really was all right! A thrill of intense happiness ran through him, and for a few seconds he was speechless with joy.

Of these anecdotes, 1, 2 and 3 will be referred to as depicting *unpleasant* situations; 4, 5 and 6, as depicting *pleasant* ones.

The religious behavior used for the study was *prayer*. It was assumed that this is a fairly representative religious activity, although no definite evidence justifying this assumption was available. How far prayer is representative could well be a matter for further research.

For the majority of the subjects the experiment was conducted as a group experiment, using the following procedure. Each subject was given the six anecdotes, each on a separate slip of paper (the slips arranged in random order), and three blank slips on which to record results. The subjects were then instructed to read the anecdotes and to introject themselves into them ('imagine the man in the anecdote is *you*'), supplying from their imagination anything which they found vague or lacking in them. They were then told to arrange the anecdotes in the order in which the situations described would stir their emotions, taking 'emotions' in a wide sense to cover all kinds of feelings. This 'popular' use of the term 'emotions' was intentional since hardly any of the subjects were familiar with more exact terminology. Each subject recorded his order on one of the blank slips, which was then collected.

The subjects were next told to arrange the anecdotes in an order based upon the extent to which the situations would present features with which they felt it would be beyond their power to deal except, perhaps, by praying. In order to force the subjects to make a real rearrangement of the anecdotes, they were instructed to put *first* the situation to which they felt they could react most completely and effectively, and *last* the one to which they felt they could make the least complete and effective reaction. This order of placing was recorded on another of the blank slips, which was then collected.

The subjects were then told to arrange the anecdotes in the order in which they felt they would be likely to pray in the situations described. Again a rearrangement was forced by requiring them to put *first* the one in which they felt they would be most likely to pray. It was explained that the term 'pray' was to be taken in a wide sense to cover all forms of address to the deity. After this order had been recorded on the third blank slip, the subjects were asked to indicate in which of the situations they probably would, and in which they probably would not, pray. They were then further asked to state any reasons they could as to why they would be more likely to pray in some situations than in others.

With sixteen of the subjects the procedure was a little different. The subjects were examined individually or in pairs; the anecdotes were shuffled by the experimenter after each order of placing had been made; the order for prayer was asked for first instead of last; and the subjects were not asked to state reasons for prayer.

By these procedures, orders of placing were produced by each subject according to three factors which, for convenience, we shall refer to as *affect* (indicated by A), *frustration* (indicated by F), and *prayer* (indicated by P). The quantitative results of the experiment are concerned with the rank correlations between these orders.[1]

Quantitative results

As the number of pairs in the rank correlations was the same for each subject, the group results can conveniently be presented in terms of mean rank correlations. These are summarized in Tables 1 and 2. All the coefficients shown in these tables attained the 1 per cent significance level except the last in Table 2 ($\tau_{PF.A}$ for pleasant situations) which attained the 5 per cent level.[2]

1. In working out the rank correlations, a new coefficient, τ, due to Kendall (1938, 1945), was used in place of Spearman's ρ. τ has several important advantages over ρ: in particular, a sampling distribution which rapidly approaches normal as the number of pairs is increased, the possession of a formula which permits the application of Yule's formula for partialing, and considerably greater ease in calculation. This coefficient should prove a valuable statistical tool in psychological work. In interpreting τ it is important to remember that, except when close to unity, it is numerically lower than ρ for any given degree of association When the number of pairs is large, ρ is approximately equal to $3\tau/2$ over most of its range
2. The significance of the coefficients in Table 1 was assessed on the probability that, in a universe where all possible rankings occur an equal number of times, the means of samples of τ will be normally distributed with a standard deviation of $\sigma_\tau \sqrt{m}$, where m = the number of individuals in the sample, and $\sigma_\tau = \dfrac{\sqrt{2}(2n+5)}{9n(n-1)}$, and n = the number of pairs in each individual τ.

In assessing the significance of the mean partial correlations shown in

Table 1 **Mean correlations**

	Mean τ	σ
I. *Between prayer and affect*		
(mean τ_{PA})		
A. All anecdotes (mean τ_{PA})	0·51	0·29
B. Unpleasant anecdotes	0·58	0·35
C. Pleasant anecdotes	0·51	0·35
II. *Between prayer and frustration*		
(mean τ_{PF})		
A. All anecdotes	0·59	0·32
B. Unpleasant anecdotes	0·59	0·34
C. Pleasant anecdotes	0·40	0·35
III. *Between affect and frustration*		
(mean τ_{AF})		
A. All anecdotes	0·38	0·30
B. Unpleasant anecdotes	0·42	0·34
C. Pleasant anecdotes	0·34	0·34

It will be seen that the mean correlations between prayer and affect and between prayer and frustration (I.A and II.A of Table 1) are very substantial, and are in both cases higher than the corresponding correlation between affect and frustration (III.A). The fact that the instructions to the subjects called for rankings on the three factors – prayer, affect and frustration – independently makes it reasonable to regard the first two of these correlations as reliable in spite of the presence of the third. For the most rigorous treatment of the data, however, it is necessary to work out for each subject a partial correlation between prayer and affect, keeping frustration constant; and between prayer and frustration, keeping affect constant. The mean partial correlations are given in Table 2 (I.A and II.A). It will be seen that they remain substantial.

It will also be seen from Tables 1 and 2 that the mean correlations and partial correlations remain positive, and in most cases substantial, when calculated for unpleasant *and also for pleasant*

Table 2, 'Student's' *t* was used in the manner usual for testing the significance of means. Results obtained by the use of this statistic must be interpreted with caution as nothing is yet known about the sampling distribution of partial τ.

Table 2 **Mean partial correlations**

	Mean τ	σ
I. *Between prayer and affect with frustration held constant* (mean $\tau_{PA.F}$)		
A. All anecdotes	0·33	0·35
B. Unpleasant anecdotes	0·25	0·47
C. Pleasant anecdotes	0·25	0·47
II. *Between prayer and frustration with affect held constant* (mean $\tau_{PF.A}$)		
A. All anecdotes	0·47	0·39
B. Unpleasant anecdotes	0·21	0·48
C. Pleasant anecdotes	0·14	0·48

situations separately. It seems clear that both affect and frustration have substantial independent correlations with prayer, and that both these factors are operative, not only in unpleasant situations, but in pleasant ones as well.

The measure of independence that affect and frustration have of one another in relation to prayer may be seen from the differences between τ_{PA} and τ_{PF} (Figure 1), and even more clearly in the differences between $\tau_{PA.F}$ and $\tau_{PF.A}$ (Figure 2), for the individual subjects. It seems clear that there is a bipolarity between a tendency to pray according to the degree to which affect is aroused and a tendency to pray according to the amount of inability to deal adequately with the situations. Some individuals incline strongly to the one tendency, some to the other. As is the case with most such polarities, however, the majority of individuals fall between the two extremes and manifest both tendencies to a certain extent.

Qualitative reports

From the reasons given for prayer, the following points were clearly seen:

1. With a few intermediate cases, the subjects divided about equally into two groups in regard to their reaction to the unpleasant situations. One group tended to view prayer more as a means of modifying the objective situation, the other tended to view it more as a means of modifying their own subjective attitude

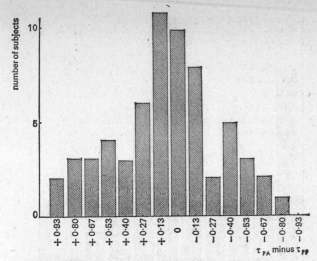

Figure 1 Distribution of differences between τ_{PA} and τ_{PF} for individual subjects

to the situation. No relationship could be found between these groups and the degree to which prayer was correlated with affect rather than frustration (or vice versa).

2. The more objective group laid stress on prayer as something which occurs when human abilities fail and there is a need for *help* in dealing with the situation:

[1, 2 and 3] are issues in which man is helpless in the face of great odds. In them he needs the help of a power greater than himself.

I would be most likely to pray in the situations which are beyond human help.

I would pray because I believe God could and will help me achieve the aim which I have in each case.

The importance of the feeling that helplessness leads to prayer was further indicated by statements that subjects would not pray when the situation was such that they could, or should, deal with it adequately by their own ability:

I would feel that it rested more on me than on God what the results ... were. [6]

The situation in which I should be least likely to pray is a matter of self-discipline and concentration upon a given task.

I feel I could cope with this situation [4] best by myself.

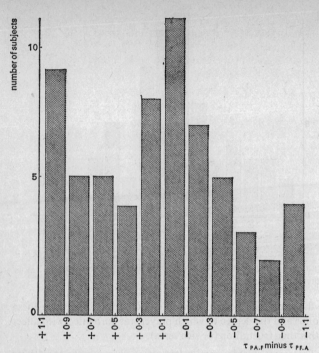

Figure 2 Distribution of differences between $\tau_{PA.F}$ and $\tau_{PF.A}$ for individual subjects

3. It is noteworthy that prayer tended to be regarded as a *last resort*:

[2] seems to be a . . . situation in which medical intelligence has spent itself. . . . The remaining hope is in God.

It would be only after successive failures to achieve a new job that I should pray in 3.

[I should pray in 2] from the realization that all human help had failed – all now depends on God.

4. The more subjective group, while mentioning the need for help, also stressed the function of prayer as bringing peace of mind, emotional stability, and relief of tension:

[I should pray in 2 because of a] need for comfort and assurance, [and in 1 because I should] need relief from terror.

I would want some sense of assurance that my loves and hopes are not meaningless.

Suspense is difficult in my life. I have a tendency to worry unduly over trivial matters. Without depending on God it seems to me the strain would be too much for me.

I believe that I would be more likely to pray in the first three cases [1, 2 and 3] because of an element of fear that is involved.

[3] I would tend to implore God and get him to help me to overcome the feeling of void I would probably feel.

I think prayer is most efficacious when emotions are involved. I feel that prayer will not particularly affect the course of physical events. Therefore prayer seeking emotional stability seems most successful.

5. In both groups of subjects there was shown a tendency for prayer to occur in unusual situations rather than in everyday ones. Especially was this the case in situations containing an emergency or involving death:

Things that are ordinary require less praying than situations when emergencies arise.

In sample 4 I don't feel the need for prayer because it is one of the ordinary daily tasks. . . . If the task were an extraordinary one, then perhaps a prayer of thanks at its completion.

I would feel most like praying in the hour of death because I believe that only prayer can carry you through such a time.

Having stood at the brink of life many times in combat flying, I have always consciously or unconsciously found myself praying with vigor for my life.

6. From the quotations we have given it seems clear that a religious response to a distressing situation tends to be given only when there is a feeling present that the frustration it produces is something which no human ingenuity could have averted. This attitude holds not only in the case of anecdotes 1 and 2, where the frustration is due to 'natural' causes, but also in 3, where human failure would seem to some a sufficient cause for the business concern's having fallen upon hard times.

7. In the pleasant situations the dominant immediate cause given for prayer was gratitude:

I would feel a profound sense of gratitude for the solution. [6]
I would feel thankful for benefits received.

In these pleasant situations other immediate causes for prayer, such as the sense of the revelation of God in nature, were given in only a very few cases.

8. Several subjects said they would pray only in situations where

there was time for reflection – i.e. where no immediate activity was possible:

[2 is] a situation remediable by the power of God, and there is time for reflection, leading to prayer. [1 is] an equally serious situation, but motion so rapid that prayer might be momentarily neglected.

I feel that I would probably pray in the first instance [2] mainly because there would be time to think things over.

In sample 1 I don't believe prayer would come foremost, I would rather grasp at the railing.

I do not think I would pray in a moment when extreme physical activity would be required.

9. The reasons given for prayer suggest that, while all the subjects were making use of very much the same religious concepts, they were making use of them in very different ways.

Conclusion

We may repeat that the quantitative results indicate that both affect and frustration have substantial independent correlations with prayer, and that both these factors are operative, not only in unpleasant situations, but in pleasant ones as well. While there is considerable variation among individuals (as is shown by the size of the standard deviations listed in Tables 1 and 2) and some individuals show results which run counter to the general trend, three assertions seem to be justifiable:[3]

1. Any simple hypothesis which regards prayer as a response merely to *distressing, threatening* forces in the environment is inadequate.

2. To some extent, an hypothesis which regards prayer as a response to *thwarting* or *frustration* accounts for prayer, not only in unpleasant, but also in pleasant situations.

3. Neither frustration nor affect alone is adequate to account for prayer. Together they appear to account for a large part of the covariation in this experiment.

3. In obtaining subjects, education, age, and sex were held constant. Previous studies (Cantril, 1943; Ferguson, 1944; Homrighausen, 1944; Kingsbury, 1937; Moreton, 1944; Vernon and Allport, 1931) have demonstrated differences of religious belief and behavior going with all these variables. For results which would fully justify general statements, the investigation would have had, therefore, to be extended to take all these into account, and should probably also have had regard to differences of religious denomination. The previously observed differences seem for the most part small, however, in comparison to the results obtained in this study.

The qualitative reports stress prayer as a means of active adjustment to situations, especially those of an unusual or baffling nature in which other responses have been tried and have failed or seem useless. We see that a prayer response is more likely if there is time for reflection. As in the quantitative results, we find considerable individual differences among the subjects.

With regard to the two types of theory outlined in the introduction, the evidence as a whole seems to point to prayer as part of the process of building an active response to a baffling situation, and not as a mere 'escape'. It thus supports Flower's hypothesis, at least in a general way. Support for the analysts' viewpoint is furnished by the fact that the large majority of the subjects who gave reasons for prayer regarded it as a means of obtaining *help* from some being or force more powerful than themselves. Not one protocol, however, mentioned God as a 'father', in spite of the stressing of this concept in the prayers used in churches.

Much further work will have to be done before any comprehensive statement can be made, but it seems reasonable to suggest tentatively that the analysts' theories accord well with many of the concepts used in religion, while Flower's theory gives a plausible explanation of the way in which these concepts are used which is in line with general trends of theory in other fields of psychology.[4]

References

ADLER, A. (1938), *Social Interest*, trans. J. Linton and R. Vaughan, Faber.

BARTLETT, F. C. (1932), *Remembering*, Cambridge University Press.

CANTRIL, H. (1943), 'Educational and economic composition of religious groups', *Amer. J. Sociol.*, vol. 48, pp. 574–9.

FERGUSON, L. W. (1944), 'Socio-psychological correlates of the primary attitude scales', *J. soc. Psychol.*, vol. 19, pp. 81–98.

FLOWER, J. C. (1927), *An Approach to the Psychology of Religion*, Routledge & Kegan Paul.

FREUD, S. (1928), *The Future of an Illusion*, trans. W. D. Robson-Scott, Liveright and the Institute of Psycho-Analysis, New York.

FREUD, S. (1933), *New Introductory Lectures on Psychoanalysis*, trans. W. J. H. Sprott, Norton.

HOMRIGHAUSEN, E. G. (1944), 'The social status of religious constituencies', *Theology Today*, vol. 2, pp. 543–5.

JUNG, C. G. (1921), *Psychology of the Unconscious*, trans. B. M. Hinkle, Moffat Yard.

4. For additional data obtained in the course of this experiment see Welford (1947).

JUNG, C. G. (1938), *Psychology and Religion*, Yale University Press.

KENDALL, M. G. (1938), 'A new measure of rank correlations', *Biometrika*, vol. 30, pp. 81 ff.

KENDALL, M. G. (1945), *The Advanced Theory of Statistics*, vol. 1, Griffin.

KINGSBURY, F. A. (1937), 'Why do people go to church?' *Religious Educ.*, vol. 32, pp. 50–54.

MORETON, F. E. (1944), 'Attitudes to religion among adolescents and adults', *Brit. J. educ. Psychol.*, vol. 14, pp. 69–79.

THURSTONE, L. L., and CHAVE, E. J. (1929), *The Measurement of Attitude*, University of Chicago Press.

VERNON, P. E., and ALLPORT, G. W. (1931), 'A test for personal values', *J. abnorm. soc. Psychol.*, vol. 26, pp. 231–48.

WELFORD, A. T. (1946), 'An attempt at an experimental approach to the psychology of religion', *Brit. J. Psychol.*, vol. 36, pp. 55–73.

WELFORD, A. T. (1947), 'A psychological footnote to prayer', *Theology Today*, vol. 3, pp. 498–501.

17 A. Siegman

An Empirical Investigation of the Psychoanalytic Theory of Religious Behavior

A. Siegman, 'An empirical investigation of the psychoanalytic theory of religious behavior', *Journal for the Scientific Study of Religion*, 1961, vol. 1, pp. 74–8.

The interest of psychoanalysis in the psychology of religion dates back to the writings of Freud on this topic. In *The Future of an Illusion* (1928) and again in *Civilization and its Discontents* (1946) Freud suggests that God was invented by primitive man when he found himself overwhelmed by life's inevitable difficulties and frustrations. In response to these difficulties many an individual regressed and wished that he were a child again and could appeal and be helped by his all-powerful father; thus emerged the concept of an omnipotent God. But a father is not only a source of help and support but also, as a result of the castration complex, a fear inspiring figure. Consequently, God too is both loved and feared. Moreover, Freud clearly implies that this theory is not only intended to explain the religious behavior of primitive man, but also the religious behavior of all men.

It is important, however, to distinguish two aspects in Freud's theory of religious behavior, namely, a philosophical and a psychological. It is a philosophical theory in the sense that it purports to explain the nature of God. It is also, however, a psychological theory in the sense that it identifies psychological variables which supposedly are causally related to individual differences in religious behavior. As a philosophical theory it can be criticized on many counts, but primarily for its reductionism (Siegman, 1959). The present paper, however, is only concerned with the psychological aspect of this theory. As such it has the advantage of generating a number of testable deductions or hypotheses.

One obvious deduction from this theory is that a person's feelings and concepts about God should resemble his feelings and concepts about his father. Another deduction, based on the theory that fear of God is a projection of castration fears, is that there should be more fear of God among men than women, since according to Freudian theory castration fears are most prevalent among men.

Freud's theory on religion was elaborated by his students and later followers who placed relatively greater emphasis on internal frustrations or intra-psychic conflicts, rather than on environmental frustrations, as the source of the belief in God (Fenichel, 1945). According to Flugel (1945), for example, religious prohibitions and injunctions are a projection of the super-ego onto God. With this projection one externalizes the conflict between the instincts and the super-ego, and thus one reduces the severity of the conflict. This theory generates the obvious deduction that religious people should have a greater tendency to project. As a matter of fact most of the theories advanced by psychoanalytically oriented writers about the dynamics of religious behavior, in so far as they are rooted in psychoanalytic theory, center around the concept of projection.

Thus, the present study tested the following three hypotheses.

1. The more religious in belief and observance have a greater tendency to project.

2. There is a positive correlation between Ss' feelings and concepts concerning God and their feelings and concepts concerning their father.

3. Males have a greater tendency than females to perceive God as a punishing figure.

Subjects and procedure

Subjects

Hypothesis 1 was tested in two different groups. One consisted of sixty female and twenty-five male undergraduate students at Bar-Ilan University, Israel. All Ss in this group were of the Jewish faith. A second group consisted of fifty-seven male, first-year medical students at the University of North Carolina (US group A). All Ss in the US group were of the Protestant faith.

Hypothesis 2 was tested in the same Israeli group, and in a group of seventy-nine male, first-year medical students at the University of Maryland (US group B). Ss in this US group were roughly equally divided between the Protestant, Catholic and Jewish faiths.

Hypothesis 3 was only tested in the Israeli group.

Measures

The degree of Ss' religious belief and observance, in the Israeli group, was determined respectively by Thurstone's Attitude Toward God Scale (Thurstone and Chave, 1929) and Foa's Sabbath Observance Scale (1948). In US group A, Thurstone's Attitude Toward God Scale was used as an index of Ss' religious belief, and Thurstone's Attitude Toward the Church and Sunday Observance Scales as indices of Ss' religious observance. Self-ratings on a ten-point religiosity scale were used in US group B as a general index of Ss' religiosity. In a previous study, such self-ratings correlated (r) 0·86 with a general religious behavior scale (Siegman, n.d.). The test–retest reliability of such self-ratings in a group of eighty Israeli college students was $r - 0·91$.

Ss' tendency to project, which in the present context is used in its widest sense and includes denial and externalization, was evaluated by means of the Paranoia and Schizophrenia scales of the MMPI, an objective psychodiagnostic test (Dahlstrom and Welsh, 1960), and Welsh's R-scale (Welsh, 1956). The extra-punitiveness score of Rosenzweig's Picture Frustration Test (Rosenzweig, Fleming and Clark, 1947), and Fould's Extra-punitiveness scales (Foulds, Caine and Creasey, 1960) provided additional indices of projection in the Israeli group.

Finally, Osgood's Semantic Differential (SD) (Osgood, Suci and Tannenbaum, 1957) was used to test hypotheses 2 and 3. The SD grew out of Osgood's factor analytic studies of meaning, in which he discovered three primary factors, namely, an evaluative factor, a potency factor, and an activity factor. With the SD one can rate any word on various scales which have high and relatively pure loadings on each of the factors (e.g. good–bad, strong–weak, fast–slow). Ss in the Israeli group rated the words *God* and *Father* on three evaluative scales (good–bad, unpleasant–pleasant, fair–unfair), three potency scales (heavy–light, small–large, loud–soft) and three activity scales (active–passive, relaxed–tense, hot–cold). Ss of the United States group B rated the words *God* and *Father* on six evaluative scales (good–bad, cruel–kind, pleasant–unpleasant, unfair–fair, happy–sad, worthless–valuable) two potency scales (strong–weak, light–heavy) and two activity scales (passive–active, fast–slow). According to hypothesis 2 one should expect significant positive correlations between Ss' ratings of *God* and *Father*.

Finally, a comparison was made between the male and female

Ss of the Israeli sample in relation to their ratings of the word *God* on the following scales: cruel–kind, angry–good natured, punishing–forgiving. According to hypothesis 3 the male Ss should show a greater tendency to perceive God as a punishing figure.

Table 1 Correlations between Ss' ratings of the words God and Father on three semantic factors

Group	N	Factors		
		Evaluative	Potency	Activity
United States	79	0·17	0·15	0·35*
Israeli	85	0·20	0·18	0·03

*Significant beyond the 0·01 level.

Results and discussion

The correlations (r) between the indices of religious belief and observance and the various indices of projection were all less than 0·10 and clearly not significant. It has to be admitted that none of the tests which were used in the present study to measure projection are completely satisfactory. Each of the tests, however, measures some aspect of projection with some degree of validity. The fact that not a single test was related with any of the indices of religious belief and observance certainly raises some doubts about the validity of the projection hypothesis.

Table 1 lists the correlations between Ss' ratings of the word *God* and their ratings of the word *Father* in relation to the evaluative, potency and activity dimensions of these two words. The positive correlation, in the United States group B, between S' activity ratings of *Father* and *God* was the only statistically significant correlation.

Thus the results of the present study provide only very attenuated support for the hypothesis that there is a correlation between a person's feelings and concepts concerning God and his feelings and concepts concerning his father. Although this finding is consistent with the projection hypothesis, such an interpretation is contraindicated by some of the other findings of this study.

1. Contrary to the projection hypothesis, the male Ss in the Israeli group did not show a greater tendency than the female Ss to perceive God in punishing and fear inspiring terms. As a

matter of fact, there was a significant difference between the two groups, but in the opposite direction from that which was predicted from the Freudian theory (Table 2). The greater tendency

Table 2 A comparison of the Israeli male and female Ss in relation to their ratings of God on three 'fear of God' scales

Group	Mean	SD	t	p
Females	2·70	1·84	2·26	<0·05
Males	1·82	1·48		

among females to perceive God as a punishing figure may be related to the greater religiosity of females, which has been reported by many investigators and/or to the greater general fearfulness of women (Garwood, 1960).

2. According to the projection theory the resemblance between one's feelings and concepts about God and one's feelings and concepts about one's father should be most pronounced among Ss who believe in God. In order to test this hypothesis, US group B was divided into two subgroups. One subgroup consisted of thirty-two Ss with the lowest religiosity self-ratings (1–4), and the second subgroup consisted of thirty-two Ss with the highest religiosity self-ratings (7–10). Whereas in the former group all the correlations between Ss' rating of *Father* and *God* in relation to the three semantic factors were significant at the 0·10 level or better, none of the correlations in the latter group reached similar levels of statistical significance. This finding is clearly in the opposite direction from that which one would expect on the basis of the projection hypothesis.

Some of the basic principles of the perceptual and learning process, however, may provide a much more parsimonious explanation for the findings of the present study. According to some of these principles one would expect some transfer or generalization from one's feelings and concepts about one's father to other authority figures and symbols, especially in the initial contact with such a figure. With increasing contacts, however, the authority figure or symbol should be increasingly more perceived in terms of its own stimulus properties. Or to state the same principle differently, the more ambiguous the figure the greater the generalization. With a decrease in its ambiguity, due to increased experience or other factors, there should be less generalization. In applying these principles to the perception of God, one would expect the least generalization or transfer in people to whom God is unambiguous, i.e. in the most religious. Similarly one would expect the most generalization in relation to the most ambiguous factor, namely, the activity factor. The findings of the present study are generally consistent with these deductions.

Table 3 The correlations between Ss' ratings of Father and God on three semantic factors in a group of high religiosity scorers and in a group of low religiosity scorers

Group	N	Factors		
		Evaluative	Potency	Activity
High religiosity	32	−0·19	0·00	0·18
Low religiosity	32	0·33[1]	0·34[1]	0·38[2]

1. Significant at 0·10 level.
2. Significant at 0·05 level.

Summary and conclusions

The present study was undertaken in order to test the following hypotheses which were derived from the Freudian theory of religious belief and observance.

1. The more religious in belief and observance have a greater tendency to project.

2. There is a positive correlation between a person's feelings and concepts concerning God and his feelings and concepts about his father.

3. Males have a greater tendency than females to perceive God as a punishing figure.

The results of the present study are clearly inconsistent with hypotheses 1 and 3, but provide some support for hypothesis 2. It was suggested that the positive results can be best explained in terms of basic perception and learning principles.

References

DAHLSTROM, W. G., and WELSH, G. S. (1960), *An MMPI Handbook*, University of Minnesota Press.

FENICHEL, O. (1945), *The Psychoanalytic Theory of Neurosis*, Norton.

FLUGEL, J. C. (1945), *Man, Morals and Society*, International Universities Press.

FOA, U. G. (1948), 'An equal interval scale for the measurement of Sabbath observance', *J. soc. Psychol.*, vol. 27, pp. 273–6.

FOULDS, G. A., CAINE, T. M., and CREASY, M. A. (1960), 'Aspects of extra- and intra-punitive expression in mental illness', *J. Ment. Sci.*, vol. 106, pp. 559–611.

FREUD, S. (1928), *The Future of an Illusion*, Liveright.

FREUD, S. (1946), *Civilization and its Discontents*, Hogarth Press.

GARWOOD, K. W. S. (1960), 'Three problems in one psychology of human fears', *Int. J. Soc. Psychiat.*, vol. 6, pp. 58 66.

OSGOOD, C. E., SUCI, G. J., and TANNENBAUM, P. H. (1957), *The Measurement of Meaning*, University of Illinois Press.

ROSENZWEIG, S., FLEMING, E. E., and CLARK, H. J. (1947), 'Revised scoring manual for the Rosenzweig picture frustration study', *J. Psychol.*, vol. 24, pp. 165–208.

SIEGMAN, A. W. (1959), 'Psychologia, Psychoanalysa Vehadet', *Deiot*, vol. 12, pp. 28–32.

SIEGMAN, A. W. (n.d.), 'The relationship between introversion, extraversion and religious behavior', ms.

THURSTONE, L. L., and CHAVE, E. J. (1929), *The Measurement of Attitude*, Chicago University Press.

WELSH, G. S. (1956), 'Factor dimensions A and R', in G. S. Welsh and W. G. Dahlstrom (eds.), *Basic Readings on the MMPI in Psychology and Medicine*, Universiy of Minnesota Press.

18 N. T. Feather

Acceptance and Rejection of Arguments in Relation to
Attitude Strength, Critical Ability and
Intolerance of Inconsistency

N. T. Feather, 'Acceptance and rejection of arguments in relation to
attitude strength, critical ability and intolerance of inconsistency',
Journal of Abnormal and Social Psychology, 1964, vol. 69, pp. 127–36.

Several models which are relevant to the problems of attitude
organization and change have recently appeared in the psychological literature. In spite of differences, these models share
the common assumption that man has a 'preference for consistency'. For example, Osgood and Tannenbaum (1955) develop
a congruity model of attitude change, and Festinger (1957)
assumes that the individual strives to reduce dissonance between
his cognitions. In a recent volume Rosenberg and Hovland
(1960) assume that the components of an individual's attitude
(cognitive, affective and behavioral) tend toward consistent
interrelationships, and this focal assumption is common to the
different models elaborated in that volume (Brehm, 1960;
McGuire, 1960; Rosenberg, 1960; Rosenberg and Abelson,
1960). Cartwright and Harary (1956), Heider (1958), and Newcomb (1959) also present models involving the assumption that
disequilibrium or inconsistency will initiate change in the
direction of a restoration of balance.

One important and rather neglected issue implied by these
various models is the degree to which this assumed tendency to
maintain consistency is related to personality variables. This
issue has been discussed in the literature. For example, Hovland
and Rosenberg (1960) suggest that there is a need to investigate
the correlation between strength of the tendency to maintain
response consistency, degree of general neurotic anxiety, and
response to inconsistency-producing communications. Brehm
and Cohen (1962) discuss the problems involved in investigating
individual differences in reactions to dissonance-arousing
situations, on the assumption that personality factors may play
a role in the dissonance process. However, possibly because of
procedural difficulties, there has been a notable lack of controlled
investigation of the relationship between this tendency to main-

tain consistency and personality variables. The present study is an attempt to explore this relationship in terms of three personality variables, viz. attitude strength, critical ability and intolerance of inconsistency.

In the present investigation, subjects who differ in the strength of their religious attitude are required to evaluate the logical validity of arguments about religion which are presented to them in syllogistic form. Half of these arguments are in favor of religion; the remaining half are opposed to religion. In addition, half of the pro-religious arguments are logically valid and half are logically invalid. Similarly, half of the anti-religious arguments are logically valid and half are logically invalid.

We are interested in the degree to which a subject accepts, as logically sound, those arguments which are consistent with his attitude and rejects, as logically unsound, those arguments which are inconsistent with his attitude. This tendency to evaluate arguments in a manner consistent with attitude is considered in relation to the strength of the subject's religious attitude, his ability to see the logical implications of an argument, and the degree to which he is intolerant of inconsistency.

Three hypotheses are investigated.

1. The tendency to evaluate arguments in a manner consistent with attitude will be *positively* related to the strength of the attitude. When an individual's attitude is intense, his evaluation of relevant arguments is more likely to be modified by his attitude in the direction of consistency with the attitude. For example, we predict that, as the pro-religious attitude becomes more intense, subjects will tend to accept more pro-religious arguments as logically sound and to reject more anti-religious attitudes as logically unsound.

2. The tendency to evaluate arguments in a manner consistent with attitude will be *negatively* related to the level of critical ability. By critical ability we mean the ability to judge the soundness of the logic with which the conclusion of an argument is drawn. Subjects who have a high level of critical ability should be less likely to be dominated by their attitude in evaluating the soundness of an argument, and should be more influenced by its logic.

3. The tendency to evaluate arguments in a manner consistent with attitude will be *positively* related to intolerance of inconsistency. We assume that subjects may differ in their ability to

tolerate inconsistency. Those subjects who are especially intolerant of inconsistency should be more likely to evaluate arguments in line with their attitude.

In short, we expect that subjects with a strong attitude, a low level of critical ability, and high intolerance for inconsistency will be likely both to accept arguments consistent with the attitude and to reject arguments inconsistent with the attitude. In contrast, we expect that subjects with a weak attitude, a high level of critical ability, and low intolerance for inconsistency will be less likely both to accept arguments consistent with the attitude and to reject arguments inconsistent with the attitude.

There is a lot of evidence in the research literature which supports hypothesis 1. Hovland, Harvey and Sherif (1957), for example, arguing in terms of 'assimilation' and 'contrast' effects, show that reactions to a communication will become less favorable as the discrepancy between the subject's own stand and the position advocated in the communication increases. Feather (1963) has shown that whether an individual is a smoker or a non-smoker will affect his evaluation of evidence about the cigarette smoking/lung cancer relationship. A number of early studies indicate that the evaluation of an argument is influenced by the desirability of its conclusion (for example, Janis and Frick, 1943; Lefford, 1946). Thouless (1959) has recently shown that, in a small group of adult students, judgements of the soundness or unsoundness of arguments are influenced by whether or not individuals agree or disagree with the conclusions. He presents an index showing the influence of prejudice in determining a subject's judgement as to soundness or unsoundness. McGuire (1960), in a syllogistic model of cognitive relationships, assumes that 'wishful thinking' will produce a deviation from logical thinking.

There is, however, a dearth of information relevant to hypotheses 2 and 3, although there are suggestions from the literature that personality factors such as critical ability and intolerance of inconsistency may be important in understanding an individual's reactions to communications. For example, Thouless (1959) was unable to find evidence of the effects of prejudice on reasoning in a graduate group. This suggests that superior education, test sophistication, and high intelligence might moderate the influence of attitude on evaluation. Janis and Hovland (1959), commenting upon the failure to discover a relationship between persuasibility and level of general intelligence, suggest that differentiated measures of various types of intellectual ability may yield significant relationships. They consider that evaluative abilities, 'the set of abilities that make for careful scrutiny of the truth and cogency of arguments and appeals and of the logic with which the main conclusions are drawn [p. 258]', will tend to interfere with the acceptance of persuasive communications. This suggestion is consistent with our prediction of a negative relationship between the tendency to evaluate arguments in a manner consistent with attitude and level of critical ability. Finally, a discussion by Festinger (1957) of differences in the degree to which individuals are able to tolerate states of cognitive dissonance is relevant to our prediction that subjects high in intolerance of inconsistency would be more likely to evaluate arguments in a manner consistent with attitude. Festinger suggests that people who are described as 'authoritarian personalities' and 'intolerant of ambiguity' may be intolerant of cognitive dissonance. We assume that this intolerance may become evident in a tendency to make 'black' or 'white' judgements which are in accordance with a firmly established attitude, to be extreme in evaluation, and not to tolerate intermediate or completely opposed positions.

The present study takes up these suggestions and provides a procedure which enables us to explore the separate influences of attitude strength, critical ability and intolerance of inconsistency on a subject's tendency to evaluate arguments in a manner consistent with his attitude.

Method

Subjects were 165 male, external students enrolled in the introductory course in psychology and attending a vacation school at the University of New England in 1962. None of these subjects had previously undertaken courses in formal logic. Subjects completed a reasoning test consisting of forty syllogisms. For each syllogism, they were asked to check whether they thought the argument was sound, i.e. the conclusion follows logically from the premises, or unsound, i.e. the conclusion does not follow logically from the premises. The instructions indicated: 'You may or may not agree with the premises. What is important is to determine whether the argument is logically sound or logically unsound.'

Twenty-four of the syllogisms concerned religion. They included six valid syllogisms with pro-religious conclusions, six invalid syllogisms with pro-religious conclusions, six valid syllogisms with anti-religious conclusions, and six invalid syllogisms with anti-religious conclusions. The pro-religious and anti-religious syllogisms were matched for length of argument and for logical form to control for 'atmosphere effect' (Woodworth and Sells, 1935). Mean number of pro-religious syllogisms correct for all subjects ($M = 7.38$, $SD = 1.53$) did not differ significantly from the mean number of anti-religious syllogisms correct ($M = 7.09$, $SD = 1.56$), thus attesting to the success of the matching.

A syllogisms-evaluation score was computed for each subject from his answers to the twenty-four religious syllogisms. This score was defined as the number of pro-religious syllogisms marked sound plus the number of anti-religious syllogisms marked unsound. A subject who was completely accurate in evaluating the syllogisms would obtain a score of twelve. A subject who disregarded logic and answered every syllogism in accordance with his pro-religious attitude would obtain a score of twenty-four. A subject who disregarded logic and answered every syllogism in accordance with his anti-religious attitude would obtain a score of nil.

The syllogism-evaluation score had the essential advantage of permitting the evaluation of direction and degree of bias. However, it did not provide information about accuracy of judgement. A subject who answered all syllogisms incorrectly would obtain the same syllogism-evaluation score as a subject who was completely accurate in his answers, viz. a score of twelve. Therefore, two error scores were also computed for each subject from his answers to the twenty-four religious syllogisms. One of these, called the pro-religious error score, was defined as the number of pro-religious syllogisms incorrectly marked sound plus the number of anti-religious syllogisms incorrectly marked unsound. The other, called the anti-religious error score, was defined as the number of anti-religious syllogisms incorrectly marked sound plus the number of pro-religious syllogisms incorrectly marked unsound. The pro-religious error score therefore indicated the number of errors made in the pro-religious direction. The anti-religious error score indicated the number of errors made in the anti-religious direction. A high pro-religious error score and a low anti-religious error score would determine a high syllogism-evaluation score. A low pro-religious error score and a high anti-religious error score would determine a low syllogism-evaluation score.[1]

The remaining sixteen syllogisms were of a neutral character, unrelated to religion and covering a variety of topics. Of these syllogisms, eight were valid and eight were invalid. The neutral syllogisms were included in the reasoning test to provide a measure of critical ability. The critical-ability score was defined as the number of neutral syllogisms a subject judged correctly, and had a range from 0 to 16. Both neutral syllogisms and syllogisms concerning religion were distributed randomly throughout the test which most subjects completed within forty minutes ($M - 25.64$, $SD = 6.81$). Examples of the different types of syllogisms used in the reasoning test are presented in Table 1.

A religious-attitude scale was administered to subjects one week after they had completed the reasoning test.[2] This test consisted of the conclusions of the twelve pro-religious and twelve anti-religious syllogisms presented as an attitude scale in the same order in which they appeared in the reasoning test. Subjects were required to check the extent to which they agreed or disagreed with each statement using numbers $+1$, $+2$, $+3$ in the direction of increasing agreement, and -1, -2, -3 in the direction of increasing disagreement. Since this scale contained an equal number of positively and negatively worded items, it should not be influenced by acquiescence response set. For each subject the scale was scored in the direction of a *pro-religious* attitude. The range of possible scores on this test was from $+72$ to -72.

Two tests were administered to subjects on the assumption that each provided a measure of intolerance of inconsistency. The first test was Form E of the dogmatism scale developed by Rokeach (1960). It consisted of forty items designed to make sure the degree to which a person's belief systems are 'closed' rather

1. The syllogism-evaluation score and the two error scores for each subject are related as follows: syllogism-evaluation score $-12 =$ pro-religious error score $-$ anti-religious error score. Because of the balanced nature of the test the Thouless (1959) index of the effect of bias is equal to $100/12$ (pro-religious error score $-$ anti-religious error score) for each subject.

2. The decision to administer the religious-attitude scale *after* the reasoning test was determined by the need to minimize other effects. Had the attitude scale been administered first, subjects may have guessed the purpose of the experiment when later they worked at the syllogisms, and this may have affected their judgements (cf. Thouless, 1959).

Table 1 **Examples of syllogisms used in reasoning test**

Type	Number of items	Examples of syllogisms
Pro-religious valid	6	People who are without religion are spiritually devoid and need the Christian teachings to show them the true way of life. Atheists and agnostics are people without religion and devoid of spiritual life. Therefore, atheists and agnostics need Christian teachings to show them the true way of life.
Invalid	6	A charitable and tolerant attitude towards mankind helps to bring people together in love and harmony. Christianity always helps to bring people together in love and harmony. Therefore, a consequence of Christianity is a charitable and tolerant attitude towards mankind.
Anti-religious valid	6	The reality of any phenomenon is established by scientific investigation and treatment. The existence of God is not established by scientific investigation and treatment. Therefore, the existence of God is not real.
Invalid	6	If thorough scientific investigation cannot prove that the Christian religion is superstition then belief in Christian miracles is justified. But thorough scientific investigation is able to prove that the Christian religion is superstition, so it follows that belief in Christian miracles is not justified.
Neutral valid	8	All members of the finance committee are members of the executive committee. No members of the library committee are members of the executive committee. Therefore, no members of the library committee are members of the finance committee.
Invalid	8	Some artists are unconventional and all portrait painters are known to be artists. It follows, therefore, that some portrait painters are unconventional.

than 'open'. The range of possible scores on this test was from 40 to 280. The second test was a measure of 'intolerance of ambiguity' developed by Budner (1962). It consisted of sixteen items designed to measure the degree to which a person perceives ambiguous situations as sources of threat and unambiguous situations as desirable. The range of possible scores on this test was from 16 to 112.

Analyses of data were performed separately for subjects with a *positive* score on the religious attitude scale (the pro-religious group) and for subjects with a *negative* score on the religious attitude scale (the anti-religious group). There were 131 subjects in the pro-religious group and their religious attitude scores ranged from +2 to +66. The remaining thirty-four subjects constituted the anti-religious group and their religious-attitude scores ranged from −3 to −55. Unfortunately, the size of the anti-religious group was quite small and there were very few large negative scores (quartile deviation = 12·50). Hence we are more confident in the analysis of results for the pro-religious group, where the sample was large and there were a number of subjects with high pro-religious attitude scores (quartile deviation = 14·88).

Table 2 **Intercorrelation of scores for pro-religious group**

	Syllogism evaluation	Religious attitude	Critical ability	Dogmatism
Religious attitude	0·22***			
Critical ability	−0·24***	0·03		
Dogmatism	0·08	0·21*	−0·12	
Intolerance of ambiguity	0·21**	0·12	−0·20*	0·14

Note: $N = 131$.
　　*$p < 0·02$, two-tailed test.
　　**$p < 0·01$, one-tailed test.
　　***$p < 0·005$, one-tailed test.

Results
Analysis of results for pro-religious group
Table 2 presents the intercorrelations between syllogism-evaluation scores, religious-attitude scores, critical-ability scores, dogmatism scores, and intolerance-of-ambiguity scores, for the pro-religious group.

The results of particular interest in Table 2 are those

correlations which involve the syllogism-evaluation scores. Table 2 shows that there is a significant positive correlation between syllogism-evaluation and religious-attitude scores ($p < 0.005$), a significant negative correlation between syllogism-evaluation and critical-ability scores ($p < 0.005$), and a significant positive correlation between syllogism-evaluation and intolerance-of-ambiguity scores ($p < 0.01$). These three correlations are consistent with the predictions in hypotheses 1, 2 and 3, respectively. They indicate that the degree to which subjects with a pro-religious attitude check pro-religious syllogisms as logically sound and anti-religious syllogisms as logically unsound increases as the pro-religious attitude becomes stronger, decreases as critical ability becomes more evident, and increases as subjects are more intolerant of ambiguity. In short, evaluation of the syllogisms in a manner consistent with a pro-religious attitude is positively related to intensity of the attitude, negatively related to level of critical ability, and positively related to intolerance of inconsistency (assuming that the intolerance of ambiguity scores reflect this variable). Table 2 shows that syllogism-evaluation and dogmatism scores are not significantly related. There is, however, a significant positive correlation between dogmatism scores and religious-attitude scores ($p < 0.02$). The negative correlation between intolerance-of-ambiguity scores and critical-ability scores is also significant ($p < 0.02$).

The partial correlation of syllogism-evaluation and religious-attitude scores with critical-ability and intolerance-of-ambiguity scores controlled is 0.21. The partial correlation of syllogism-evaluation and critical-ability scores with religious-attitude and intolerance-of-ambiguity scores controlled is -0.23. The partial correlation of syllogism-evaluation and intolerance-of-ambiguity scores with religious-attitude and critical-ability scores controlled is 0.15.

Table 3 presents mean error scores of subjects classified as high in pro-religious attitude and subjects classified as low in pro-religious attitude, using a median split[3] in the distribution of attitude scores for the pro-religious group. The results of a Type I analysis of variance (Lindquist, 1956) are presented in the lower portion of Table 3.

3. The sixty-six subjects classified as high had religious-attitude scores exceeding 32. The sixty-five classified as low had religious-attitude scores of 32 and below but in the positive range. Note that high and low refer to a classification in terms of strength of pro-religious attitude.

Table 3 shows that there is a highly significant tendency for pro-religious error scores to exceed anti-religious error scores in the pro-religious group ($F = 115.23$, $df = 1/129$, $p < 0.001$). Subjects with positive religious-attitude scores tend to make errors in the pro-religious direction rather than in the anti-religious direction, i.e. their errors tend to be those in which pro-religious syllogisms are incorrectly judged sound and anti-

Table 3 **Mean error scores of subjects high and low in pro-religious attitude**

Strength of pro-religious attitude	Type of error Pro-religious	Anti-religious	Row means
High	6.06	3.42	4.74
Low	5.75	4.15	4.95
Column means	5.91	3.79	

Analysis of variance

Source	df	MS	F
Between subjects	130		
Attitude (A)	1	2.93	1.06
Error (b)	129	2.77	
Within subjects	131		
Type of error (B)	1	294.98	115.23**
A × B	1	17.59	6.87*
Error (w)	129	2.56	
Total	261		

*$p < 0.01$.
**$p < 0.001$.

religious syllogisms are incorrectly judged unsound. Table 3 also shows that the difference between the mean pro-religious error score and the mean anti-religious error score is greater for those subjects classified as high in pro-religious attitude. The interaction of type of error with strength of religious attitude is statistically significant ($F = 6.87$, $df = 1/129$, $p < 0.01$). Subjects are therefore more likely to make errors in the pro-religious direction when their positive religious-attitude scores are relatively high. Their higher syllogism-evaluation scores are due to this tendency to make relatively more errors in the pro-religious direction.

Table 4 **Intercorrelations of scores for anti-religious group**

	Syllogism evaluation	Religious attitude	Critical ability	Dogmatism
Religious attitude	0·13			
Critical ability	−0·26	−0·30		
Dogmatism	0·15	−0·08	−0·12	
Intolerance of ambiguity	0·35*	0·44**	−0·27	0·18

Note: $N = 34$.
*$p < 0·05$, two-tailed test.
**$p < 0·01$, two-tailed test.

Analysis of results for anti-religious group

Table 4 presents the intercorrelations between syllogism-evaluation scores, religious-attitude scores, critical-ability scores, dogmatism scores, and intolerance-of-ambiguity scores, for the anti-religious group.

Table 4 shows that the correlation between syllogism-evaluation scores and intolerance-of-ambiguity scores is positive and would be significant using a two-tailed test ($p < 0·05$). This relationship is not in the direction we would expect for subjects with an anti-religious attitude. Rather, if these subjects evaluate the syllogisms, in a manner consistent with their attitude, they would tend to judge pro-religious syllogisms as logically unsound and anti-religious syllogisms as logically sound. We would expect this tendency to be especially evident in subjects high in intolerance of inconsistency. This implies that, for subjects with an anti-religious attitude, low syllogism-evaluation scores should tend to accompany high intolerance-of-ambiguity scores (i.e. a negative relationship). But instead the results indicate a positive relationship. When differences in religious-attitude and critical-ability scores are controlled, the partial correlation between syllogism-evaluation and intolerance-of-ambiguity scores is 0·30. None of the other correlations involving syllogism-evaluation scores is statistically significant.

Table 4 also shows that, for the anti-religious group, there is a significant positive correlation between religious-attitude scores and intolerance-of-ambiguity scores ($p < 0·01$). Since the religious-attitude scale is scored in the pro-religious direction, this correlation implies that subjects low in anti-religious attitude tend to be high in intolerance of ambiguity.

Table 5 presents mean error scores of subjects classified as high

Table 5 Mean error scores of subjects high and low in anti-religious attitude

Strength of anti-religious attitude	Type of error Pro-religious	Anti-religious	Row means
High	3·88	4·12	4·00
Low	5·18	4·71	4·94
Column means	4·53	4·41	

Analysis of variance

Source	df	MS	F
Between subjects	33		
Attitude (A)	1	15·06	4·16*
Error (b)	32	3·62	
Within subjects	34		
Type of error (B)	1	0·24	
A × B	1	2·12	1·37
Error (w)	32	1·55	
Total	67		

*$p < 0.05$.

in anti-religious attitude and subjects classified as low in anti-religious attitude, using a median split[4] in the distribution of attitude scores for the anti-religious group. The results of a Type I analysis of variance (Lindquist, 1956) are presented in the lower portion of Table 5.

In contrast to the results in Table 3 for the pro-religious group, Table 5 shows that there is no tendency in the anti-religious group for pro-religious error scores to exceed anti-religious error scores. In fact, the results show that the reverse tendency occurs among subjects who are relatively high in anti-religious attitude, viz. the mean anti-religious error score exceeds the mean pro-religious error scores. Hence there is a tendency for subjects with relatively high negative religious-attitude scores to make more errors in the anti-religious direction. This result is in the predicted direction, but the interaction of type of error with strength of religious attitude is not statistically significant ($F = 1·37$, $df = 1/32$, ns).

4. The seventeen subjects classified as high had religious-attitude scores of −24 and below. The seventeen subjects classified as low had religious-attitude scores above −24 but in the negative range. Note that high and low refer to a classification in terms of strength of anti-religious attitude.

Table 5 also shows that the mean of the combined error scores is significantly less ($F=4\cdot16$, $df=1/32$, $p<0\cdot05$) for subjects classified as high in anti-religious attitude. Subjects who are relatively high in anti-religious attitude tend to make fewer errors in judging the validity of the religious syllogisms than do subjects who are relatively low in anti-religious attitude. This result is consistent with the negative correlation ($r=-0\cdot30$) between religious attitude scores and critical-ability scores for the anti-religious group.

Difference between pro-religious and anti-religious groups

Table 6 presents mean syllogism-evaluation scores, mean number of religious syllogisms correctly answered, mean critical-ability scores, mean dogmatism scores, and mean intolerance-of-ambiguity scores for the pro-religious and anti-religious groups.

Table 6 indicates that the mean syllogism-evaluation score is lower in the anti-religious group than in the pro-religious group. The difference in means is statistically significant ($t=4\cdot70$, $df=163$, $p<0\cdot001$) and is consistent with hypothesis 1. The difference indicates that subjects in the pro-religious group tend to judge more pro-religious syllogisms as logically sound and more anti-religious syllogisms as logically unsound than do subjects in the anti-religious group. In fact, the mean syllogism-evaluation score of $12\cdot12$ for the anti-religious group implies that their evaluation of syllogisms is relatively unaffected by their attitude. This interpretation is further supported by the low correlation of $0\cdot13$ in Table 4 between religious-attitude and syllogism-evaluation scores for these subjects, which is in the predicted direction but is not statistically significant. The anti-religious group also has a significantly higher mean critical-ability score ($t=2\cdot08$, $df=163$, $p<0\cdot05$) and a significantly lower mean intolerance-of-ambiguity score ($t=3\cdot10$, $df=163$, $p<0\cdot01$) than the pro-religious group. There is no significant difference between the groups in mean dogmatism scores, or in mean number of religious syllogisms correctly answered.

Discussion

The results from subjects with a pro-religious attitude provide clear support for our predictions. They show that the tendency to accept or reject relevant arguments in a manner consistent with attitude is positively related to the strength of the attitude, negatively related to level of critical ability, and positively related to intolerance of inconsistency (if we assume that the measure of in-

Table 6 Mean scores and standard deviations for pro-religious group ($N=131$) and anti-religious groups ($N=34$)

Group	Syllogism evaluation		Religious syllogisms correct		Critical ability		Dogmatism		Intolerance of ambiguity	
	M	SD	M	SD	M	SD	M	SD	M	SD
Pro-religious	14·11	2·30	14·31	2·35	11·76	1·88	155·31	24·60	51·60	9·94
Anti-religious	12·12	1·75	15·06	2·78	12·50	1·72	146·12	31·61	45·71	9·45

tolerance of ambiguity reflects this variable). It should be noted, however, that the obtained correlations are quite low.

In contrast, the results from subjects with an anti-religious attitude do not support our predictions. It is likely, however, that this group does not provide a satisfactory test for the predictions. Quite apart from its small size, there are few members of this group who are intensely anti-religious. In fact, the results suggest that this group is mainly composed of members who are mildly anti-religious, and who are higher in critical ability and tolerance of inconsistency than their pro-religious counterparts. One might expect differences of this nature in such a group, since those people who arrive at an anti-religious position would do so in opposition to a strong cultural attitude. It is likely that such opposition would be facilitated by critical ability and tolerance of inconsistency. We expect, however, that our predictions would be supported in a study involving a group containing members who are strongly committed to an anti-religious attitude. Such a group may not be easy to find in our culture, but this possibility could be further investigated. Perhaps, also, attitudes other than the religious attitude could be studied to test the generality of our hypotheses.

One deficiency in the present study is the lack of a test specifically designed to measure intolerance of inconsistency. We have assumed that Rokeach's Dogmatism Scale and Budner's Intolerance-of-Ambiguity Test provide measures of this variable. The results indicate, however, that the correlation between dogmatism scores and intolerance-of-ambiguity scores for *all* subjects is positive and significant but very low ($r=0.17$, $df=163$, $p<0.05$). Moreover, while syllogism-evaluation scores correlate positively with intolerance-of-ambiguity scores, as predicted for the pro-religious group, they are unrelated to dogmatism scores. These two tests appear to have a more general rationale than would a test of intolerance of inconsistency. Each is developed on the basis of theoretical considerations not specifically concerned with reactions to inconsistency. Budner's test defines intolerance of ambiguity in terms of reactions to situations involving novelty, complexity and insolubility. Rokeach's measure of dogmatism is based on a theoretical analysis of the nature of 'closed' and 'open' belief systems. The development of a more specific measure of the degree to which persons are intolerant of inconsistency provides a challenge to future research. The success of this venture will depend upon detailed specification of the different types of inconsistency which may confront individuals and the possible reactions to these. The conceptualization of cognitive dissonance by Brehm and Cohen (1962) and Festinger (1957), and the discussion by Hovland and Rosenberg (1960) of problems involved in the measurement of degree of inconsistency, should provide useful leads to future investigation.

The main contribution of the present investigation is the finding that personality variables influence the tendency to evaluate arguments in a manner consistent with attitude. The evidence that attitude intensity influences evaluation is consistent with previous research and is not a novel finding. Of greater significance is the indication that critical ability and intolerance of inconsistency are variables affecting the evaluation of arguments. As we have noted variables similar to these have been previously suggested in the literature as factors affecting a person's reaction to communications, but there has been a lack of systematic investigation of their influence. In fact, most attention appears to have been focused upon demonstrating the effect of attitude on evaluation. We should now move beyond such demonstrations to the investigation both of variables (such as critical ability) which may *moderate* the effect of attitude upon evaluation, and of variables (such as intolerance of inconsistency) which may *amplify* this effect. It appears that attitude may 'set' or bias valuation in a direction consistent with the attitude, but other variables may moderate or amplify the degree to which the attitude dominates evaluation. We need detailed investigation of such variables. The present results are consistent with the suggestion by Hovland and Janis (1959) that persuasibility might be related to more differentiated measures of intellectual abilities than the type of measure obtained from a general intelligence test. They are also consistent with Festinger's (1957) suggestion that subjects 'intolerant of ambiguity' may be intolerant of cognitive dissonance. Finally, it is apparent that the research design developed in the present study permits controlled investigation of other personality variables which may influence acceptance or rejection of arguments.

References

BREHM, J. W. (1960), 'A dissonance analysis of attitude-discrepant behavior', in C. I. Hovland and M. J. Rosenberg (eds.), *Attitude Organization and Change*, Yale University Press, pp. 164–97.
BREHM, J. W., and COHEN, A. R. (1962), *Explorations in Cognitive Dissonance*, Wiley.

BUDNER, S. (1962), 'Intolerance of ambiguity as a personality variable', *J. Pers.*, vol. 30, pp. 29–50.

CARTWRIGHT, D., and HARARY, F. (1956), 'Structural balance: a generalization of Heider's theory', *Psychol. Rev.*, vol. 63, pp. 277–93.

FEATHER, N. T. (1963), 'Cognitive dissonance, sensitivity, and evaluation', *J. abnorm. soc. Psychol.*, vol. 66, pp. 157–63.

FESTINGER, L. (1957), *A Theory of Cognitive Dissonance*, Harper & Row.

HEIDER, F. (1958), *The Psychology of Interpersonal Relations*, Wiley.

HOVLAND, C. I., HARVEY, O. J., and SHERIF, M. (1952), 'Assimilation and contrasts effects in reactions to communication and attitude change', *J. abnorm. soc. Psychol.*, vol. 55, pp. 244–52.

HOVLAND, C. I., and JANIS, I. L. (1959), 'Summary and implications for future research', in C. I. Hovland and I. L. Janis (eds.), *Personality and Persuasibility*, Yale University Press, pp. 225–54.

HOVLAND, C. I., and ROSENBERG, M. J. (1960), 'Summary and further theoretical issues', in C. I. Hovland and M. J. Rosenberg (eds.), *Attitude Organization and Change*, Yale University Press, pp. 198–232.

JANIS, I. L., and FRICK, F. (1943), 'The relationship between attitudes toward conclusions and errors in judging logical validity of syllogisms', *J. exp. Psychol.*, vol. 33, pp. 73–7.

JANIS, I. L., and HOVLAND, C. I. (1959), 'Postscript: theoretical categories for analysing individual differences', in C. I. Hovland and I. L. Janis (eds.), *Personality and Persuasibility*, Yale University Press, pp. 255–79.

LEFFORD, A. (1946), 'The influence of emotional subject matter on logical reasoning', *J. gen. Psychol.*, vol. 34, pp. 127–51.

LINDQUIST, E. F. (1956), *Design and Analysis of Experiments in Psychology and Education*, Houghton Mifflin.

MCGUIRE, W. J. (1960), 'A syllogistic analysis of cognitive relationships', in C. I. Hovland and M. J. Rosenberg (eds.), *Attitude Organization and Change*, Yale University Press, pp. 65–111.

NEWCOMB, T. M. (1959), 'Individual systems of orientation', in S. Koch (ed.), *Psychology: A Study of a Science*, Vol. 3. *Formulations of the Person and the Social Context*, McGraw-Hill, pp. 384–422.

OSGOOD, C. E., and TANNENBAUM, P. H. (1955), 'The principle of congruity in the prediction of attitude change', *Psychol. Rev.*, vol. 62, pp. 42–55.

ROKEACH, M. (1960), *The Open and Closed Mind*, Basic Books.

ROSENBERG, J. M. (1960), 'An analysis of affective-cognitive consistency', in C. I. Hovland and M. J. Rosenberg (eds.), *Attitude Organization and Change*, Yale University Press, pp. 16–64.

ROSENBERG, M. J., and ABELSON, R. P. (1960), 'An analysis of cognitive balancing', in C. I. Hovland and M. J. Rosenberg (eds.), *Attitude Organization and Change*, Yale University Press, pp. 112–63.

ROSENBERG, M. J., and HOVLAND, C. I. (1960), 'Cognitive, affective, and behavioral components of attitudes', in C. I. Hovland and M. J. Rosenberg (eds.), *Attitude Organization and Change*, Yale University Press, pp. 1–14.

THOULESS, R. H. (1959), 'Effects of prejudice on reasoning', *Brit. J. Psychol.*, vol. 101, no. 50, pp. 289–93.

WOODWORTH, R. S., and SELLS, S. B. (1935), 'An atmosphere effect in formal syllogistic reasoning', *J. exp. Psychol.*, vol. 101, no. 18, pp. 451–60.

19 G. K. Morlan

An Experiment on the Recall of Religious Material

G. K. Morlan, 'An experiment on the recall of religious material',
Religion in Life, 1950, vol. 19, pp. 589–94.

No minister or religious leader can ignore the way people feel and
respond to his message. He needs to know their reactions in order
to direct his sermons effectively to their problems and interests.
He must reach the minds of his listeners if he is to succeed in influencing their attitudes and behavior, and it occurred to me
some years ago that an analysis of what people remember of sermons might give a clue for reaching more effectively the thinking
of laymen.

It was not assumed that what people remembered was the sole
criterion of what they had learned. They may have been influenced in
a significant way by sermons they no longer can recall, but what they
can recall is one measure, at least, of what they have learned.

To get at this remembered material, I asked 191 people from
various walks of life to tell me as much as they could recall of the
sermon that stood out most vividly in their minds, which they had
heard more than two weeks previously. An analysis of this data
revealed that word pictures were best retained; next, those that
concerned the problems and interests of people; third, those that
shocked, and, least of all, sermons that 'stuck to religion'.

There was overlapping between these categories, as can be
found in the teachings of Jesus, but this evidence indicated that
ideas expressed in vivid pictorial form reach the minds of people
and are retained much better than are abstract ideas.

There is a *clue* here for getting at the minds and memories of
people, but since there was no control over the character of the
sermons that the people heard, any conclusion was somewhat
equivocal. The purpose of the following experiment was to subject
the four hypotheses derived from the previous investigation to
more rigorous scientific test by controlling the character of the
sermons that a given group would hear.

Three published sermons and a selection of equivalent length
from John Stuart Mill's *The Idea of God in Nature* were read to

two sections of Springfield College students in educational psychology. In one section, the selection from Mill was read first, and the sermons in the following order: Ernest Fremont Tittle's 'The obligation to be intelligent' (1931), Harry Emerson Fosdick's 'Winning the war of nerves' (1941), and John Henry Newman's 'The religion of the day' (1926). In the second section the order was reversed.

There was no structuring to obtain a set to remember. The students were merely told to listen and attend to what followed as they would in a real-life situation – as soon as they recognized what the situation was. They were told they would not be graded on the experiment, but that their cooperation would be appreciated. It was necessary that all should hear, and since too much talking would interfere with the results of the experiment, they were asked not to talk. Nevertheless, there was some whispering and talking, but probably little, if any, more than occurs in the average middle-class church where young people attend.

The situation differed from a church setting in a number of significant ways. There was no religious mood cultivated through sacred music, prayer, or devotional atmosphere resulting from church architecture, or the feeling of there being something special because of Sunday clothes. In passing it may be noted that it is an unproved theory that the setting of the sermon in the midst of religious symbols, sacred music, prayer, and the like makes the mind more receptive to the sermon. The quiet of a plain Quaker service may well be far more impressive than any elaborate ritual or theatrical service. It is not only possible, but there is a real probability, that the place of the sermon at the end of the long introductory service of music, Bible reading, offertory, prayer is psychologically unsound. Jesus never drowned his message under a plethora of other things. There should be some experimentation in placing the sermon at the beginning of the service, for it is a reasonable hypothesis that after a long introduction, the people are too worn out, sleepy, or resistant to listen further.

In order to equate the presentation of the material, the experimenter read all four selections himself. In each instance he tried to read the material as effectively as possible, but the ideas, words and sentence structure were that of others, and his presentation was undoubtedly not as effective as the original authors could have made it. On the basis of my experience in this experiment, I am now more dubious of a suggestion made by a Westchester organist that had seemed to me to merit trying out. He had declared that it would be folly to require church organists to play only music of their own composition. Wasn't it equally fallacious to expect ministers to give only their own original thoughts? He advocated that churches should 'allow, encourage, or even require that their preachers deliver the best sermons of other preachers, as well as their own best and most inspired ones' (Morlan, 1938, p. 29).

Requiring preachers to produce a stimulating, inspiring sermon every week is unrealistic, but I am sure that my own presentation was uninspired; and until clergymen are trained as thoroughly as organists are in presenting the works of others, reading a great sermon by another hardly seems to be the solution to the difficulty.

Preceding the reading of the first selection, the instructions to each group were as follows: During this term I wish to perform an experiment that is relevant to this course, and I believe is potentially important for many fields. In order to approximate the conditions of real life, I shall not tell you what my purpose is, nor discuss any aspect of the experiment until it is completed, but when it is completed, the instructor will discuss any aspect of it that you wish discussed. Your only instructions are to listen as carefully as you would under the conditions that you would normally hear the following discourse.

Actually, ministers and teachers often tell the purpose they wish to achieve in their presentations, but they do not usually try to measure what is retained, as I proposed to do. If a congregation were told that the amount that they retained was to be measured, the result would likely differ from what I found in the earlier investigation, as well as in this more recent one.

Two weeks after the final selection had been read, students were asked to tell as much as they could recall of the four selections. The instructions were as follows:

During the first four class periods, your instructor read to you on each day a different selection. Please write out, as completely as you can, what you recall of the four selections. If there is any reason why any particular part stuck in your mind, indicate in the margin your reasons. You may have as much time as you need. (Use the remaining space on this page and the space on the other side if you need it.)

Your name is not wanted, but the following information would be appreciated if you are willing to give it.

Denomination of Church you belong to or prefer – (Check one).

Protestant	( )
Catholic	( )
Jewish	( )

You attend – (Check one).

Frequently	( )
Occasionally	( )
Rarely	( )
Never	( )

There were ninety-four returns. Of these, fifty could not retell anything definite enough to be tabulated, and forty-four were able to tell something of one or more of the selections.

Could not remember – 50	Could remember – 44
Protestant – 36	Protestant – 33
Catholic – 11	Catholic – 11
Jewish – 3	Jewish – 0
Attend frequently – 21	Attend frequently – 20
Attend occasionally – 20	Attend occasionally – 17
Attend rarely – 7	Attend rarely – 7
Never attend – 2	Never attend – 0

The selections by Mill and Newman were both concerned with religion itself, but there was a great difference in the character and approach in the two selections. Mill's views generally come as a shock, whereas Newman's views are likely to strike those with inquiring minds as pious, but very nice humbug. Since a fairly high percentage of college students have inquiring minds, Mill made a deeper impression than Newman. There was also a significant difference between the results of the two series where Mill was read first in one and Newman first in the other.

Section one reported recall on a total of forty-one sermons; section two, a little more than half as much, or twenty-five. Fewer students were enrolled in section two, but the difference in enrollment was not great enough to account for the difference in amount recalled. A tentative hypothesis that needs further experimentation is that Mill's essay was so stimulating that the students were more receptive and alert to the sermons that followed. Newman's sermon, on the other hand, was boring (though included in a volume modestly called *Great Sermons of the World*), and the unfavorable mindset created in the beginning of the series affected the attention and interest in the rest.

Sermons recalled

Section one:	Mill 19	Tittle 10	Fosdick 10	Newman 2
Section two:	Newman 5	Fosdick 16	Tittle 2	Mill 2

Totals for two groups:

Mill 21	Tittle 12	Fosdick 26	Newman 7

The number who recalled something of Fosdick's sermon in the second series does not appear to fit this hypothesis. Nevertheless, what many recalled was the shocking language quoted from Walt Whitman. Eight who remembered something from 'Winning the war of nerves' mentioned Walt Whitman's words 'God damn war!' Many of the boys had been in the armed services and shared these sentiments about war, but they also frequently commented that the use of this language in the situation was startling, and the eight responses might be totaled with the twenty-one who recalled something from Mill. Furthermore, psychologically, Tittle's sermon and Fosdick's might be classified together in that they both were related to the thinking and problems of these students. The results would then be totaled as follows:

Shock	Problems	Religions alone
Mill and Whitman 29	Tittle and Fosdick 30	Newman 7

These figures are not quite adequate. So far as subject matter is concerned, Mill and Newman might be classed together. Both concern essentially religious problems. In both there is a minimum of relating religion in a meaningful way to the problems that these students meet in everyday life. Mill was dealing with theology, and the number who recalled something of Mill is strikingly different from the results of the earlier investigation. In the earlier investigation, the number who recalled sermons on distinctively 'religious' subjects ran a poor fourth. The earlier conclusion that sermons that 'stick to religion' are the least effective in getting at the minds of people must be modified. On the basis of this experimental evidence, it would appear that it is the dullness of the usual sermonic approach that is psychologically unsound. A fresh treatment that can be recognized as honest and courageous thinking did get the attention of this sample of college students, with the result that they were able to retell more about this selection than from any of the others, if Whitman's quotation is excluded.

Discussion and conclusions

Two conclusions of the previous investigation, namely, about the effectiveness of (1) shock, and (2) sermons that deal with the problems and interests of listeners, are confirmed in this experiment, but there is marked difference in the data as regards the effectiveness of word pictures.

Are students so different from the average church population? Could it be that they are much less impressed by vivid word imagery? This is doubtful, for out of the 191 interviewed in the previous investigation, a considerable number were students, though they were not as mature as those in the experiment that included many veterans. It is possible that mature students are less impressed by adornment than is the average sample of our population, but a reanalysis of the entire data suggests a different answer. There were some word pictures in all four selections, but none was rich in imagery or word pictures. None was equivalent to Merson S. Rice's dramatic 'So what?' lecture, that a number of laymen remembered vividly in the previous investigation. For this reason, we are not justified as yet in drawing any categorical conclusion about the effectiveness of word pictures.

We are justified, however, in concluding that the daring method Jesus used of shocking audiences out of their complacency is still an effective technique for getting at the minds of modern people. Nor can there be any doubt that sermons that deal with the interests and problems of people hit home. Furthermore, theological problems are among the issues that college students are thinking about, and if presented honestly and with courage, students will listen and remember.

References

FOSDICK, H. E. (1941), 'Winning the war of nerves', in *Living Under Tension*, Harper & Row.

MORLAN, G. K. (1938), *Laymen Speaking*, R. R. Smith.

NEWMAN, J. H. (1926), 'The religion of the day', in C. E. Macartney (ed.), *The Great Sermons of the World*, Stratford Co., pp. 399–411.

TITTLE, E. F. (1931), 'The obligation to be intelligent', in E. M. McKee (ed.), *What Can Students Believe?*, Richard S. Smith, pp. 43–57.

20 J. E. Dittes

Justification by Faith and the Experimental Psychologist

J. E. Dittes, 'Justification by faith and the experimental psychologist',
Religion in Life, 1959, vol. 58, no. 4, pp. 567–76.

Religion, according to the man in the street or the woman in the
pew, is almost always defined in terms of creeds, practices, codes
or institutions. Yet most of those whom the people in the street
and pew revere as their teachers and saints have insisted that such
things are as likely to be the marks of irreligion as of religion.
Their position has been that creeds, codes, and practices frequently become but scrambling, desperate grasping for a religious certainty and security which is not only illusory but is rendered
unnecessary by what, in the heritage of Paul and the Reformers,
has been called justification by faith.

Confronting the perennial religious questions, there are those
who rest uneasy until supplied with certain and positive answers.
How can I be assured of God's favor? There are sacramental
forms and sectarian tests guaranteed to remove all doubt. What
shall I believe? There are scriptural literalists and dogmatists of
every kind ready with an unambiguous answer. How shall I
behave? There have always been legalists with specific rules for any
situation. Ambiguity and uncertainty in the face of such questions are too terrifying to tolerate.

But ambiguity and uncertainty are terrifying, Paul and the
Reformers seem to say, only if one somehow has the feeling that
his salvation, integrity, self-image – or whatever terms he uses for
that which renders fundamental worth and value to his existence –
is critically dependent on having clear answers to such questions.
When one discovers within a faith relationship that this fundamental worth and value is basically assured, then all frantic efforts to
grasp both at the supposed evidence and at the supposed means
of justification lose their desperate imperative. Clarity and un-
ambiguity are not to be disparaged, but they are not sought for
and clung to at all costs, including too often the cost of incomplete, inadequate and inapplicable formulations.

Such a theological assertion may arouse the interest of an

experimental psychologist because it seems to point to a more general theory about the relation of certain psychological conditions and because it may be put in a form not wholly inaccessible to experimental investigation. This paper is a report of just such an attempt to deal in the psychological laboratory with the kind of psychological relations proposed by the theological affirmation. As such, it may be a novel venture. Familiar as contemporary theologians and ministers may be with the speculations and insights of clinical psychology, there is little precedent for undertaking to bring to bear on theology the more plodding labors of the experimental psychologist.

What the experimentalist has to contribute to the theologian is not verification or validation of propositions, but rather the encouraging of more precise definition and conceptualization. It is the empirical operations, not the statistical outcome, that is of chief importance. For the experimentalist to deal with any assertion, he must determine precisely what manipulations to perform and what questions to ask, and these all must be specified clearly in advance of the experiment as part of his theoretical labors, not settled in an ambiguous *ad hoc* fashion after he has recourse to the data. The psychologist does not expect that his experimental results will induce the theologian to reaffirm, abandon or modify the theological assertion. But the psychologist can submit his operations and ask the theologian, 'Is this one of the operations to which your concept can refer?' If so, maybe he has helped the theologian better understand what he himself means. If not, the theologian's efforts to explain why not may further help to clarify, specify, and make more precise the concept involved. The recourse to experimental operations may serve to demonstrate, sharpen and give substance to the theological insight, in a way which is, for some at least, more dramatic than otherwise possible.

Dogmatic creedal formulations, legalistic codes, confidence-building good works and sacramental assurances – these are some of the devices practised in the name of religion to make the ambiguities of life seem less than they are. One who experiences a profound sense of support within the very scheme of things in his universe is less likely than one without such experience to search out and cling to such signs of certainty. Such is the proposed theory, still in language familiar to the theologian.

In more general psychological terms, the formulation may go

something like this: persons whose self-esteem is enhanced or guaranteed by supporting agents or conditions are less likely to display an impulsiveness of closure and more likely to tolerate ambiguity in making any kind of judgement.

In making their way through life, people spend a good deal of effort in trying to make conceptual sense out of the environment. In some of these groping attempts to comprehend and cope with the universe in which man finds himself, traditional religious concepts are used. In much of it, they are not. One may simply be trying to predict the weather, form an impression of another person, judge political issues, or make the innumerable decisions of daily routine. Some persons may regard some of these instances as part of their religious quest. Others would choose different experiences. Some will designate only a limited core of such searchings as religious. Others will regard a much broader compass as religious. In any case, however, the groping is all of a piece. One is constantly trying to find coherence, meaning or structure in the face of a largely ambiguous environment.

What is of interest here is the readiness with which people impose a meaning or coherence on the available information, to impose a 'closure' – by analogy with the parliamentary act of ending deliberation. Some seem able to tolerate ambiguity and to hold out for more adequate information and further deliberation. Others seem ready to impose closures impulsively even at the risk of an inferior, inadequate judgement.

Any one person probably behaves much in the same way in his different areas of groping for meaning. The person who jumps to conclusion on one problem probably tends to do so on all. In the experiments to be reported, several conclusion-forming tasks are used as a measure of impulsiveness. It may be that none of these tasks should properly be regarded as part of a person's religious searching. But it is assumed that such coping with the environment as is represented in these tasks is at least continuous with that groping which is religious. When we see how fearful of ambiguity a person is and how impulsively he grasps at positive answers on these tasks, we also have some indication of his approach toward trying to discover the person and will of God in the events around him and in the records of the past.

Such impulsiveness doubtless has many determinants, but the important one here under investigation concerns the extent to which a person resorts to 'having the answers' as a compensating means of enhancing an otherwise faltering sense of self-esteem.[1] When the supports and props on which a person's self-esteem depends are weakened, is he more likely, as he tries to deal with his world, to make judgements more impulsively; is he less able to bear the threat of ambiguity and confess uncertainty?

The psychologist can neither measure nor manipulate the ultimate sources of a person's sense of well-being and self-esteem. These are inaccessibly rooted in the outreachings of Divine grace and the religious intuitions of a man. But the psychologist can deal with circumstances which approximate these ultimate groundings of well-being. He can deal with circumstances on which personal self-esteem depends very highly, if not absolutely and ultimately.

One major source of a person's self-esteem is the regard of important persons in his life. The child's sense of worth depends largely on his parents' attitudes toward him. As he grows, so too does the circle of those on whose esteem his own self-esteem depends. For the late adolescent perhaps the most important source is the regard of his peers. It was this that was varied in one of the experiments about to be described. The subjects of the experiment, college freshmen, were made to feel, for a period of up to an hour, that they were regarded either highly or poorly by a group of their fellow students. Under these conditions, their tendency to search impulsively for positive meaning or their willingness to delay judgement and tolerate ambiguity could be measured. Could persons be made to grasp more quickly for certainty by being made to feel less well accepted among a group of peers?

Another important source of personal self-esteem is the experience of successful achievement. Especially for graduate students, who were the subjects of the second experiment to be described, esteem seems to ride hard on the sense of personal mastery

1. There are important subsidiary problems in this hypothesis. The psychologist – to satisfy his own needs for clarity or to improve the esteem of his colleagues – may try to fill in some of the implied details. Chief among these is the question of how closure may come to have properties of enhancing self-esteem. In brief, it may be proposed that in repeated early experiences, closure, even in cases as simple as learning to name objects, tends to be rewarded by association with basic gratifications such as approval of parents, out of which self-esteem is evolved. A more technical discussion of these problems and of the procedures of Experiment 1 may be found in the *Journal of Abnormal and Social Psychology* for May 1959. The report of Experiment 2 appears in the same journal in 1960.

and accomplishment. In the second experiment, subjects were made to feel, for a temporary period, that they had succeeded or failed on a test which allegedly measured abilities on which they highly depended. Could persons be made to grasp more quickly for certainty by having their sense of professional and intellectual competence threatened?

While it is true that these manipulations of peer acceptance and personal competence are not equivalent with the sense of Divine acceptance which is talked about as the faith experience, it is believed that there is a certain relevant continuum between the two. Subjectively, the experience of being accepted or not accepted by important persons in our lives may be so profound, intense and personality-shaking that it is difficult to imagine how this experience may differ psychologically in its impact from one described as a sense of ultimate acceptance by the very ground of being. Similarly, the sense of support which one derives from repeated daily signs of his own ability to get along in the world and to achieve his goals may not differ, except perhaps quantitatively, in psychological impact from other signs available to him of more ultimate support.

In general, we are dealing with the psychological question of whether a person is more able to withstand the ambiguities of his life and avoid premature certainties when he has other grounds for feeling more or less 'at home' in his environment. This is an important psychological problem. It also seems part of and continuous with the theological assertion.

Slightly more than one hundred students took part in the first experiment, meeting in groups of five or six at a time. So far as these subjects knew (until the actual procedures were disclosed at the end of the experiment), each of these groups was simply a model discussion panel, convened by social scientists to observe how a group of persons who were not previously acquainted with each other would behave in discussing a variety of issues. When they met, they were given questions to discuss, such as juvenile delinquency, and the discussion was recorded on tape, as though for future analysis. This discussion was interrupted several times to ask each group member to appraise the group's performance and, on especially prepared rating scales, to rate each other person's desirability within such a group. These ratings were collected by the experimenter, as though for his own purposes, and the group discussion proceeded.

When the discussion had finished, the critical part of the experiment, from the experimenter's point of view, was about to begin. The discussion was turned to the appraisals the group members had made of each other. Without exception, each group became interested in seeing these ratings, and the experimenter 'agreed' to distribute the forms so that each person could see privately the appraisals that had been made of him by others in the group. However, the forms distributed were not the actual ratings which had been made by the students, but were fictitious ratings which had been prepared in advance by the experimenter and substituted for the genuine forms. No student doubted the genuineness of the ratings he saw. Each believed that he had here a record of how he was regarded by four or five of his fellow students.

The fictitious ratings were used to induce, at random, different feelings of acceptance among the subjects. Some of the students found in these ratings that they were apparently very highly regarded by their fellows, and that their fellow members indicated that this opinion was stable and unconditional; they were confident about their high regard and it was unlikely to change regardless of future events. Others found ratings indicating that their peers, had at the moment, a high regard for them but that this opinion was tentative and very likely subject to change. Still others found a low regard indicated in the ratings. In summary, three different feelings were introduced at random among the subjects: feelings of being highly and unconditionally accepted by peers, feelings of being highly but tentatively accepted, and feelings of being poorly accepted. Questionnaire responses near the end of the session indicated that these manipulations were fully successful. The subjects receiving high stable ratings reported feeling pleased, confident and secure. The others reported feeling disturbed and threatened by the ratings with evidence of considerably reduced self-esteem.[2]

2. All of these procedures were fully disclosed to the subjects before they left the experimental room. Their reactions and their behavior were fully discussed, and care was taken to re-involve each person as an obviously accepted group member. The total experiences clearly tended to be therapeutic, rather than damaging. Subjects typically thanked the experimenter for an instructive experience. One measure of the students' positive feelings about the experience is their full cooperation in maintaining secrecy about the procedures during the remaining weeks in which the sessions were scheduled, in spite of the fact that some men went through the procedure a week or more before their roommates and close friends.

Following this, the subjects were asked to complete three brief tasks, individually and without any further discussion. These tasks were designed to represent typical judgement situations offering possibilities either for making an impulsive effort to find meaning and certainty or for deferring judgement and withstanding the ambiguity. The results with each task will be described separately.

1. A parable in biblical idiom was presented to the subjects, re-presented as a translation of part of a recently discovered scroll, and they were asked to write comments on its meaning. Actually the parable had been especially prepared to be essentially incoherent, although it did contain a large number of familiar religious symbols. Many subjects conceded their inability to find any coherent meaning in the passage as presented. They remarked, for example, that it must be a bad translation, that something must be left out, that it must be read in a larger context, or in the case of one subject, 'If this is the Kingdom of Heaven, then I'm for this world, because I don't get it.' However, other subjects explained the meaning of the parable without qualification or hesitation, even though this meant ignoring parts of the passage and distorting others to fit the supposed meaning, and even though no two subjects ever found the same meaning.

With a difference highly significant statistically, those who conceded the unintelligibility of the passage tended to be those who had been made to feel highly and unconditionally accepted, and those who found clear and unqualified meaning in it were in general those who had been made to feel poorly accepted or highly but unstably accepted. Is it possible that biblical literalists can be produced by conditions of poor social acceptance?

2. On an impression formation task, subjects were given lists of traits which were represented as words used by close friends to describe particular students. The subjects were asked to write their impressions of each student, based on these trait lists. These lists, like the parable, were especially prepared to measure impulsiveness of closure. The list purportedly describing each student consisted of a dominant set of traits, essentially synonyms for each other, and also a subordinate set which was incompatible with the dominant set. One list, for example, was: 'individualist, suspicious, belligerant, considerate, self-concerned, thoughtful, stubborn, tolerant'. The fourth, sixth and last words suggest very different characteristics from the dominant impression of the list,

although the disparity is by no means atypical of actual persons.

Some subjects made an effort to use all the information and to integrate the subordinate set with the dominant set, such as by writing, 'This man probably seems aggressive and inconsiderate until you know him well, then he softens and becomes warm and sympathetic.' Others completely ignored the subordinate, inconsistent traits and formed their impressions exclusively on the basis of the dominant traits.

Those made to feel accepted were the ones who tried to use all the information. Those who were poorly accepted or highly but tentatively accepted tended to form the easier and more impulsive judgement based on the dominant information alone. Conditions of poor social acceptance apparently nourish the soil in which social stereotypes grow.

3. On the 'jammed message' task, a sound tape was played on which a single phrase was repeated twenty times at fifteen-second intervals, with a decreasing amount of masking noise at each repetition; the phrase was completely unintelligible at the first repetition and clearly heard at the end. Subjects listened to the tape and were instructed to write down the phrase as soon as they were quite sure what it was.

The poorly accepted subjects wrote a phrase, on the average, on a much earlier repetition than the well-accepted subjects, and were almost always wrong – this in spite of the fact that they knew that the phrase was about to be repeated more clearly in another fifteen seconds. The well-accepted subjects waited out the noise and unintelligibility, made their guesses much later, and were more frequently correct.

Peer acceptance is only one possible source of self-esteem and only one approximation toward a sense of absolute and ultimate support. Persons vary in the extent to which their esteem is dependent upon this particular source. Some students are more dependent on the esteem of their peers and more vulnerable to such manipulation than others. Some come into such an experiment with their self-esteem well enough assured from other sources – other groups, other persons, other experiences of personal worth – so that the apparent opinion of this particular group has relatively little effect. To check this, a measure of general self-esteem was obtained on a questionnaire before the experiment began. This presumably represented the net total effects of other sources of self-esteem on which the persons relied. The results of the experimental manipulation were then examined separately for those students who reported above-average initial self-esteem and for those below the average in initial self-esteem. Manipulation of acceptance was clearly less effective for those who possessed high initial self-esteem. Differences in apparent acceptance produced the differences in subsequent impulsiveness of judgement among all the subjects, but the effects were clearly much greater among those who entered the experiment with already low self-esteem.

Since Experiment 1 dealt with only one possible source of self-esteem, a source on which not everyone is equally dependent, as just reported, Experiment 2 was designed to assess the effects of a quite different source of self-esteem, the sense of personal worth deriving from experiences of success or failure. A class of graduate students was administered a ten-minute test which, they were led to believe, measured important professional abilities. They scored the test themselves and compared their results with norms supposedly established in previous testing. Actually, two different sets of fictitious answer sheets and norms were distributed at random, so that some students were made to feel that their results were far below acceptable standards, and others that they had performed exceedingly well.

Impulsiveness or deliberation in forming conclusions was measured with the same three tasks used in Experiment 1 – parable, impression formation and 'jammed message'. On all three tasks, those who had experienced the support of successful achievement tended to deliberate and defer judgement as compared with those who had experienced the threat of poor performance, who tended to form their conclusions impulsively.

Behavioral sciences have but recently developed the techniques to deal experimentally with such complex aspects of personality functioning as those reported here. The gain of applying rigorous experimental methods to such a problem is the certainty with which it makes a conclusion possible as to what causes what. Why was one group of students consistently[3] more impulsive in grasping for certainty than another group? The only way in which they differed as groups was that, in Experiment 1, some of them had

3. Statistical tools are available which indicate that the difference in impulsiveness scores between the two groups could happen by chance fewer than two times out of a thousand, and the results may therefore confidently be regarded as a real difference, not a chance one.

seen one kind of rating they thought was made by their fellow students, and others had seen another kind of rating; and, in Experiment 2, some thought that they had done well on a ten-minute test and others that they had done poorly. These differences must be considered as the critical determinants. The random distribution of the high and low ratings and the success and failure papers should have insured that all other differences in personality and other predispositions were about equally distributed between the two experimental groups of each experiment.

The psychological hypothesis here tested seems well confirmed. Threats or assaults on a person's self-esteem can propel him to greater impulsiveness in seeking out certainty of meaning and cognitive clarity.

This psychological finding will seem either more or less intimately related to the theological affirmations which generated the investigation, depending upon the stand one takes on certain theological presuppositions. Here the psychologist can only report the findings of an investigation which he undertook because he believed it to be relevant to the theology. But it remains for the theologian to determine what relevance he is able to grant.

If God, the experience of divine acceptance and grace, and the religious pilgrimage of man in general are taken as things apart, as of qualitatively different categories from other experiences of life, then the findings of this study provide at most an interesting analogy. If, however, the meeting place of the divine thrust and the human searching is seen as within human experience, and not apart from it, then more may be said about such a psychological finding. Then it may be that the facts demonstrated in the experiment are a part of the same reality apprehended in the Reformers' understanding of 'justification by faith'.

21 H. H. Kelley

Salience of Membership and Resistance to Change of Group Anchored Attitudes

H. H. Kelley, 'Salience of membership and resistance to change of group anchored attitudes', *Human Relations*, 1955, vol. 8, no. 3, pp. 275–90.

A basic finding in social psychology is that the attitudes a person holds depend in part upon his social contacts and particularly upon the groups in which he holds membership. At the same time, it is apparent that the typical individual, at least in our own culture, simultaneously belongs to a number of different organizations and is associated with a variety of groups. While these different sources of attitude anchorage sometimes mutually reinforce one another or affect non-overlapping areas of attitudes, they often exert contradictory influences upon the person. This phenomenon, termed 'cross-pressures', has been investigated primarily with respect to political issues (Kreisberg, 1949; Lazarsfeld, Berelson and Gaudet, 1948).

An important problem created by the existence of cross-pressures is whether, as an individual moves from one situation to another, there are concurrent variations in the extent to which his various social affiliations operate to support his attitudes and to determine the opinions he holds. We might expect that at any given moment conformity to a specific group's norms will depend upon the degree to which cues associated with that group successfully compete with other cues in the individual's environment, capture his attention, and arouse his conformity motives. The phenomenon singled out for consideration in the present research has to do with situational variations in whether or not symbols or 'reminders' of a specific group are present for its members and the effects of this variation upon their resistance to communications contrary to the group's norms.

The degree to which, in a given situation, a specific group is present and prominent in a person's awareness is termed the *salience* of that group. In some instances high salience corresponds to presence in the center of the person's attention, but it is not the intention here to restrict the notion to instances where there is a fully conscious or reportable awareness of the group.

Possible differences in the salience of the various aspects of the group or its norms will be disregarded and reference will be made only to general salience of the group, on the tentative assumption that salience of any aspect of the group heightens the tendency to conform to its norms at that particular time.

Several theoretical discussions are pertinent to this problem. In an outline of the psychological consequences of minority group membership, Lewin noted that sometimes a person's belonging to one group is dominant and sometimes his belonging to another. At any given time, the dominant group largely determines the person's feelings and actions. Lewin considered the particular group that dominates in a given situation to be related to the characteristics of that situation (1935). Elsewhere, he took account of the effects of motivational factors upon the relative dominance of different sets of behavioral and attitudinal determinants. In this regard, he postulated that an increase in the intensity of the need related to a certain goal increases the relative potency (read 'salience') of the situation containing that goal (1938, pp. 34–5). Thus, it would seem reasonable to expect persons who are strongly motivated to achieve or maintain membership in a given group to relate controversial questions to its norms, whether or not the group or its symbols are immediately present.

Other related discussions are those which attempt to account for inconsistency in attitudes and behavior (for example, Chein, Deutsch, Hyman and Jahoda, 1949). It is common knowledge that expressed opinions vary from situation to situation and often exhibit apparent self-contradictions. Undoubtedly, some of these variations are due to conformity to the social pressures of the moment and represent a more or less conscious, opportunistic attempt to avoid criticism and obtain approval. However, it is also possible that the apparent disregard for the norms of a group, which at other times and places plays an active part in the determination of attitudes and behavior, reflects its temporary absence as a psychological force.

Recently, Eugene and Ruth Hartley have discussed the problem of 'evoking specific reference groups' (1952, pp. 479–81). They describe several relevant findings, for example, the 'interviewer effects' found in public opinion polling, which can be interpreted in terms of variations in the group roles that respondents assume when confronted by different social situations.

An investigation by Charters and Newcomb (1952) was specifically directed at the problem of the effects of the immediate social situation upon opinions expressed on an attitude questionnaire. They administered the questionnaire to three comparable groups of Roman Catholics under the following conditions:

1. In a large class with many other students.

2. In a small group by themselves, but with no mention of their church membership or of the reason for their being together.

3. In a small group by themselves where, before answering the questionnaire, they were told that they had been called together as Catholics in order to obtain their help in constructing a questionnaire on religious beliefs and were asked to discuss the 'basic assumptions' underlying the opinions of all Catholics.

In the last variation, the common religious affiliation of all subjects in the room was repeatedly emphasized. In all three variations, the subjects anonymously answered a questionnaire that contained, among other items, a number of critical ones related to Catholic norms but so worded that they could also be answered by the subjects in their roles as members of other groups. The results showed that subjects in the third variation answered these critical items more in the manner prescribed for Catholics than did subjects in the other two variations.

There is some ambiguity as to whether this result is, as the authors suggest, due simply to 'heightening the individual's awareness of his membership in the specified group by vivid reminders of this membership' (p. 415). First is the possibility that the initial discussion of 'basic assumptions' in the third variation gave the Catholics new information about their church's values, which enabled them to conform more loosely than did their prior, less clear conceptions of the norms. Charters and Newcomb attempted to minimize this by asking their discussion leaders to avoid discussing what Catholics *should* believe or the opinions they would give on specific issues. Another possibility is that the subjects were motivated to answer as 'good' Catholics. For example, being aware that all persons in the room were Catholics, the subjects may have foreseen the possibility that the data would be examined to determine how uniformly Catholics adhere to their church's norms and the subjects may have wanted to have their religious group make a good showing in this respect. Again, the investigators attempted to eliminate this factor by instructing the subjects to give their own personal opinions.

Charters and Newcomb conclude from their findings that 'an individual's expression of attitudes is a function of the relative momentary potency of his relevant group memberships' (p. 420).

If, as this suggests, situational cues affect the opinions a person expresses, they may also affect his resistance to counternorm communications. It would seem reasonable to assume that the salience of a group determines its availability as a possible source of resistance to change, the strength of the resistance being determined by other factors, such as how highly membership is valued. The purpose of the present experiment was to test the following hypothesis: when group anchored attitudes are exposed to counter-pressures, their resistance to change at the particular time will be greater with high salience of the relevant group than with low. In addition, the procedure was designed so as to determine whether the phenomenon described by Charters and Newcomb would appear under more rigorous conditions than theirs, where subjects are mixed together in terms of their religious affiliation and are not told that this factor is involved in the investigation.

A further purpose of this study was to obtain some initial evidence on the relative permanency of attitudinal changes accomplished under conditions of high and low salience. If it proves to be true that a communication will produce more immediate change when opposing group norms are at a low level of salience than when they are highly salient, this might suggest that where group anchorage is important a communicator would be wise to approach his audience when the pertinent group is in the background and they are preoccupied with other loyalties and interests. However, the problem immediately arises as to the fate, with the passage of time, of changes produced under these conditions. When the group becomes salient in subsequent situations, we might expect the resistance to the communication to be restored and to produce a reversion to the old attitudes. This would reduce the difference in final attitudes between persons initially with low salience and those initially with high. There are still other lines of reasoning that lead one to expect changes produced under conditions fostering low salience to be maintained less well, than those produced under conditions fostering high salience (cf. Discussion page 279).

Procedure

Attitudes of members of the Roman Catholic Church were studied within high school and college age groups. This particular group membership was chosen in order to provide the possibility of comparing the results with those of Charters and Newcomb. The experiment was conducted during regular class sessions when members of all religious faiths were present and when, because of the presence of cues related to competing loyalties and interests, the salience of any particular religious affiliation could be expected to be relatively low. The students were first given short readings, some of them receiving material intended to heighten the salience of Catholic membership and others receiving unrelated 'neutral' material. They then answered an opinion questionnaire containing items that were related to Catholic norms but were carefully selected so as to involve other roles and memberships and to heighten the salience of Catholic membership as little as possible. In addition, two out of every three of the subjects received, as part of the questionnaire, a communication intended to modify their opinion responses. This was done by including for each item in their questionnaire, information purporting to give the opinion of the typical student at the same level in school. The 'typical opinions' were indicated at positions fairly divergent from those most acceptable to Catholics and thus constituted a counter-norm communication for them.

Through appropriate combinations of these materials, two main experimental conditions were created:

1. Communication, high salience.
2. Communication, low salience.

In addition, an experimental condition with no communication and high salience was used in order to check upon the effectiveness of the communication. A random procedure was used for assigning subjects to each experimental variation, so the subjects within the three samples can be assumed to be comparable initially, within the limits of sampling error. The basic data consist of a comparison of the attitudes expressed by members of various religious groups under these conditions, the questionnaire providing an immediate after-test of the experimental treatments.

Three days after the initial testing, most of the subjects were given a delayed after-test. The same questionnaire was re-administered, but this time under the 'no communication, high salience' condition for all subjects. The data from this delayed after-test provide the means for studying the loss of the initial opinion shifts as time passes and church membership becomes salient for all Catholic subjects.

The specific characteristics of the subjects and details of the procedure are as follows:

Subjects

Two hundred and seven third-year students in a public high school and 247 second- and third-year students in a metropolitan university. The experimental procedure was carried out during regular class sessions (high-school English classes and introductory college courses in psychology and sociology) where students of various religious faiths were present. In order to avoid one extraneous possibility of salience arousal, the question of religious affiliation was not raised at any time during the experiment.

For the high-school Ss, identification of religious affiliation (whether 'Catholic', 'Jewish' or 'other') was made on the basis of family names. The judgements as to inclusion in the first two categories were made by two judges independently and with very high agreement. Only those names on which both judges agreed were included among the 'Catholics'. (These consisted mainly of Italian and Irish names and, in a few instances, Polish. Demographic studies of the community in which the high school is located show that over 95 per cent of persons from these national backgrounds are Catholics.) The classification 'Jewish' was established to provide a category that could be assumed to contain virtually no Catholics. The results from the 'Jewish' and 'other' classifications proved to be so similar that they were combined to provide a single category of 'non-Catholics'. Religious affiliation of the college Ss was determined by a direct question asked at the conclusion of the experiment.

Introductory instructions

After being introduced by the class instructor, the experimenter gave instructions, the essence of which is as follows: 'We've been making a study of the opinions of students in this area. With you, we'd like to try a somewhat different procedure from the usual. Before giving us your opinions on these questions, we want you to take your minds off the things you're thinking about now – your class work, things going on here at school, and your friends. To help you do this we want you to read some short articles. These have nothing to do with the questions we're going to ask but are simply articles about well-known men or organizations we thought you might find interesting. While you're reading these, relax and take your minds off the things you're thinking about now. Then we'll ask your opinions on various matters.'

Booklets containing three articles and the questionnaire were distributed and the Ss were asked to give their birthday, sex, and (in the case of the high-school students) name. They were then instructed to begin with the first article and to read rapidly for a short time without turning to the questions.

Reading material

The three articles dealt with either famous men or world organizations. (Classes receiving the 'famous men' series at the first session received the 'world organizations' series at the delayed after-test, and vice versa). Only enough time was allowed for reading the first of the three articles, the content of which was varied in order to produce the high and low salience conditions. The other two articles were similar in content to the low salience reading. In the 'famous men' series, the 'high salience' article dealt with the life of Pope Pius XII and his role as international leader of the Catholic Church; the corresponding 'low salience' reading summarized the life of (then) General Dwight D. Eisenhower. In the 'world organizations' series, the 'high salience' article described the world-wide missionary work of the Catholic Church; the 'low salience' article described the work of UNESCO. (The 'famous men' and 'world organizations' series produced similar patterns of results and hence no distinction is made between them in the presentation of the data.)

All articles were selected from current books and magazines and were edited to ensure student interest. The 'high salience' articles were carefully selected so as to contain no references to the issues raised in the opinion questionnaire. They constituted very favorable pictures of the Catholic Church, its activities, and leader, as drawn by outside observers. They were intended to make a Catholic feel proud of his church and, at the same time, bring his church membership into the forefront of his awareness.

Opinion questionnaire

After most Ss had finished reading the first article, the entire class was stopped and asked to complete the opinion questionnaire. The instructions included strong assurances that their answers would be treated confidentially.

The questionnaire consisted of eighteen critical items, with six irrelevant 'filler' items distributed among them. The critical items dealt with four broad topics, examples of which follow:

1. *Censorship* of books, movies, plays, etc.: 'Censorship of books and movies is *not* good in our country; a truly free people must be allowed to choose their own reading and entertainment.'
2. *Parental control* over children: 'Parents should give their children complete freedom when it comes to deciding about matters like political and religious beliefs.'
3. Traditionalism in *religious practices*: 'Religion should move away from the traditional doctrines and practices and adapt itself to modern life.'
4. *Loyalty* to nation versus loyalty to other organizations: 'A person's loyalty to his country is far more important than his loyalty to any institution or organization of which he is a member.'

Subjects responded to these items by indicating on a rating scale the extent of their agreement or disagreement with each. From the eighteen critical items, a total score was computed for each S, with a *high score representing a high degree of conformity to what the investigator prejudged to be the Catholic norms on these questions.*

Communication

The communication delivered to certain of the Ss consisted of special check marks placed along the rating scales provided for responding to the questionnaire items. On the eighteen critical items, these marks were placed in the half of the scale opposite the end thought to represent Catholic norms. These marks were placed in a standard pattern, which was the same for all subjects receiving the 'communication'.

Before the Ss started answering the questionnaire, the experimenter explained these marks as follows: 'As I said before, we've already given these questions to a number of students in this area. We thought this might be more interesting for you if you could see how other students have answered these questions. So we've placed red check marks in your booklets to show where, *on the average*, other students have answered the questions. I'm sorry we didn't have time enough to put these check marks in all the booklets so some of you may not have them. Those of you who do have them need not pay any attention to them if you don't want to. Just give your own opinions about these matters.'

For Ss given the communication, the initial opinion measurement constitutes a test given *immediately after* the communication since the S presumably responds to each item after reading it and noticing the location of the check mark. The effectiveness of this type of communication has previously been demonstrated. Kulp, for example, studied the effect of opinion responses attributed to various kinds of people (e.g. educators, lay citizens) and found that even unlabeled responses produce some effect (1934).

The three experimental conditions

The various reading materials and the two versions of the questionnaire (with and without the special check marks) were combined into test booklets to produce three different experimental conditions:

1. No communication, high salience.
2. Communication, high salience.
3. Communication, low salience.

The three types of test booklets were intermixed and distributed at random within each classroom. In the remainder of this paper, subjects will be identified in terms of the experimental booklet that they happened to receive during this first session.

Delayed after-test

For all high-school Ss and half of the college Ss, the above procedure was repeated in its major details three days later. However, at this time all Ss received the 'no communication, high salience' set of materials, the purpose being to determine the relative retention under high salience conditions of opinion changes produced initially under different degrees of salience. The re-administration of the procedure was explained to the subjects as an investigation of the variability of responses to the questionnaire. They were requested to try to answer the questions as if they had never seen them before and not to try to remember how they had answered them earlier.

Results
Effects of salience on resistance to change

The results for the high-school students are presented in Figure 1, where high scores represent close conformity to what were prejudged to be Catholic norms. The validity of this prejudgement is apparent from the fact that for the 'no communication, high salience' variation the Catholic subjects showed significantly higher scores than the non-Catholic subjects ($p < 0.01$). Thus, it seems clear that the questionnaire measures attitudinal dimensions on which Catholics differ from non-Catholics.

It is also evident in Figure 1 that the communication was effective in producing changes in attitude responses. The communication presented a more extreme position on the issues raised in the questionnaire than that taken by non-Catholics, so it operated to shift their responses as well as those of the Catholics. The difference between the 'no communication, high salience' variation and the two communication samples is significant at beyond the 1 per cent level of confidence for both religious classifications.

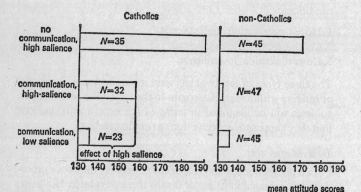

Figure 1 The effects on attitude score of variations in salience of catholic membership for high school students

The expectation of greater resistance to change for the Catholic subjects with high salience of their church than with low salience is borne out by the data in Figure 1. Of the Catholics receiving the communication, those for whom the church was highly salient showed higher attitude scores than those for whom it was not ($p < 0.05$ using a one-tailed test). Subjects of other religious affiliations who received the communication expressed much the same attitudes, whether receiving the salience-arousing materials or not, which is to be expected because the salience of the Catholic Church is not relevant to their attitude anchorage.

Table 1 presents the results for the college students. The evidence for the relevance of the questionnaire and the effectiveness of the communication is similar to that obtained from the high-school students. In the 'no communication, high salience' condition, Catholics score significantly higher than non-Catholics ($p<0.01$). Subjects receiving the communication score lower than those without it, both for the Catholics ($p<0.01$) and non-Catholics ($p<0.01$).

Table 1 **The effects on attitude scores of variations in salience of Catholic membership for college students**

	Catholics		Non-Catholics	
Experimental condition	*N*	*Mean score*	*N*	*Mean score*
No communication, high salience	36	178	42	147
Communication, high salience	32	157	53	123
Communiction, low salience	39	162	45	127

With regard to salience and resistance to change, the results from the college students do not support the hypothesized relationship. Among Catholics receiving the communication, there is little difference between the scores of those in the 'high salience' condition and those in the 'low salience' one. So it appears that the experimental variation intended to produce differences in salience of Catholic membership failed to produce any difference in the Catholics' resistance to the communication.[1]

1. A correlational analysis was made of the college students' data, in which a tentative measurement of salience was substituted for the experimental manipulation. This measure of the degree to which their church membership was salient for Catholic college students in the testing-situation was based on answers to the instructions: 'Write down the first things that come into your mind. Ready? Name two groups or organizations to which you belong.' Catholic subjects who named a church group were considered as having their membership at a high level of salience and were compared with those mentioning other than church groups. The former subjects showed somewhat higher scores both within the samples receiving only the questionnaire ($p=0.06$) and within the samples receiving the communication with the questionnaire ($p=0.28$). These trends were especially marked ($p=0.06$ and $p<0.05$, respectively) for a part-score based only on the questionnaire items dealing with the topic of censorship. (Incidentally, it may be noted that this particular part-score appeared to be more sensitive than the other part-scores to the variations in salience produced experimentally for the high-school students.) In brief, this cor-

Because of the apparent failure of the experimental manipulation of salience with the Catholic college students, only the results from the Catholic high-school students will be considered from the point of view of the effect of salience upon the retention of opinion change. For subjects who were initially in the 'no communication, high salience' condition there was virtually no change from the immediate to the delayed after-test. Since the two tests were given under identical conditions, the absence of any sizeable change indicates that extraneous factors such as practice or intervening events did not systematically affect the results.

For the Catholic high-school students initially receiving the communication, a comparison of the high and low salience samples is shown in Figure 2. (The data for each sample are presented in terms of how much it differs from the 'no communication' group, which serves as a control group.) It can be seen that both samples made large shifts on the delayed after-test in the direction of greater conformity to Catholic norms. The magnitude of this shift over the three-day interval was virtually identical for those given the communication initially under low salience and those exposed under high. In addition, it is apparent that the highs had returned to the level of the control (no communication) sample while the low salience sample still showed a sizeable effect of the original communication. (For the difference between the high and low salience samples at the time of the delayed after-test, $p=0.06$). Thus the results bear out the common observation

---

relational analysis of the data for the college students yields some evidence, although somewhat tenuous, in support of the hypothesis that group members express more conforming attitudes when their membership is salient than when it is not, both when they are merely asked for their opinions and when they are exposed to a counternorm communication.

The trends described above remained even when age and a measure of valuation of membership (reported frequency of attendance at religious services) were taken into account. Both these variables were found to affect resistance to the counternorm communication. The older Catholics were less influenced than the younger ones ($p < 0.01$) and the high-valuation members were less influenced than the low-valuation members ($p < 0.06$, using a one-tailed test). The latter finding is consistent with the finding by Kelley and Volkart (1952) that members' resistance to a counternorm communication is a direct function of how highly they value their membership in the group. Also consistent with that study was the finding that, although high- and low-valuation members apparently differed in their ability to withstand a counter-communication, they tended to express quite similar opinions in the absence of a communication of this type.

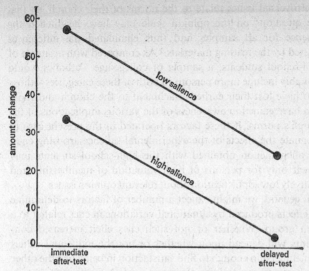

Figure 2 Retention over three-day interval of opinion changes produced under conditions of high and low salience

that the greater the initial change, the greater the opinion change shown on subsequent occasions. There is no evidence that changes induced under conditions of low salience tend to be lost completely or retained to any lesser degree than those produced under high salience.

Discussion

The experimental procedures intended to produce variation in salience of church membership were apparently successful with the high-school students. Although the correlational analysis of the college students' data (cf. footnote 1) suggests that their conformity may be related to salience of church membership, the attempt to vary salience experimentally for this population appears to have been quite ineffective. Several factors might account for this result. One possibility is that the Catholics sampled in a metropolitan college include large numbers who have drifted away from their church and feel little attachment to it. Consequently, heightening the salience of church membership would have little or no effect on their expressed opinions or resistance to counternorm communications. Another possibility is that college students are more sophisticated about how various controversial issues relate to the norms of their church, so that the questions on the opinion scale may have heightened the salience for all samples and thus eliminated the differences created by the reading materials.[2] As compared with a sample of high-school students, a sample of college-age Catholics would probably include more persons in both of these categories – those who have lost their earlier attachment to the church and those who have gained in awareness of the various implications of the church's norms. If these factors operated in the present case to attenuate the effects of the experimental salience-arousing cues, the phenomenon obtained with the high-school students may appear only for persons of high valuation of membership and relatively low sophistication about relevant opinion issues.

In general, we might expect a number of factors to determine the effects produced by situational variations in cues related to a given group. Whether or not such cues elicit increased conformity will depend upon whether or not the individual values his membership enough to find satisfaction in being like the other members and maintaining their approval. A problem for future research is whether the person who places very high value upon membership will be much affected by situational cues: he is more likely to furnish his own cues and to relate controversial questions to the group's norms whether or not it or its symbols are externally present The specific kind of conformity behavior elicited by 'reminders' of membership will be a function of the person's knowledge and beliefs about the kind of behavior that is expected and approved. In short, the effects of situational cues undoubtedly depend upon the various predispositional factors (e.g. valuation of membership, social rank, knowledge of norms) that have been found to affect the degree of conformity to group norms.

Assuming that a person is predisposed to conform to group norms and resist counter-communications when that membership is highly salient, there remains the question of the appropriate

2. A related possibility is that students in college classes, and particularly those taking psychology, are especially aware that experiments often have hidden purposes. Consequently, they become interested in trying to figure out the purpose of any experimental procedure they are asked to follow. Even though they do not deduce the true purpose, their incorrect hypotheses may seriously modify their responses to the instructions. There is no reason to expect the effects of these 'hunches' to cancel out one another and, hence, merely to contribute to the random error. It seems more likely that the various hypotheses will have enough in common to introduce systematic variance into the results.

conditions for observing the effects of increases in salience. It is necessary, of course, that the group membership should exist initially at a low level of salience. This is accomplished, as in the present study, by finding a situation in which competing memberships or interests are aroused and active. Then, if variations in salience are to be detected in the person's expressed opinions, the questions used to elicit these opinions probably must tap areas of conflict between the influence of the group under study and the competing influences. Unless the measured opinions reflect an area of controversy or cross-pressures, there is no particular reason to expect opinions expressed with high salience of group membership to differ from those expressed with low. The existence of cross-pressures is ensured in the procedure of the present study by the use of a counternorm communication. In the absence of such counter-pressures, whether or not there are variations in opinion associated with variations in salience may provide a means of determining the attitudinal areas in which a given group is in conflict with other attitude determinants. In this connection, it may be noted that in the present investigation the censorship items were most affected by variations in salience of Catholic membership. This suggests that, of the topics used in the questionnaire, the issue of censorship represents the most definite area of conflict between Catholic norms and other influences operating in the milieu of our subjects.

Of particular interest for further investigation is the problem of determining the conditions that affect the persistence of opinion changes produced under high and low salience. The above results indicate that in the specific circumstances of the present experiment, the greater immediate change made possible by low salience also appears at a later time. In other circumstances, particularly when group members encounter pro-norm opinions and become sharply aware of their earlier non-conformity, a complete loss of the initial change might be expected.

Several other theories would suggest not merely that the greater change produced under low salience will be completely lost, but that the end result will be a kind of boomerang effect, with the low salience condition giving rise to less persistent change than the high salience condition. One such possibility is that subsequent situations of high salience may produce guilt and anxiety among those persons initially low, if they become aware of having been caught off guard and seduced into deviating markedly from the group norms. One way of alleviating this guilt and of warding off possible social punishment for the non-conformity is to conform more closely to the group norms than ever before. As a result, those persons initially low in salience (and hence most influenced initially by the counternorm communication) would finally be more in conformity with the norms (and less in agreement with the communication) than those initially high.

A second mechanism would have almost the same end effect. If, during the communication situation, the resistance stemming from the group can be aroused and dealt with, then the likelihood is increased that the change will endure through later situations in which the group happens to be salient. The problem becomes one of providing the person with a method either for resolving the conflict between the appeals of the communication and the counter-pressures of the group or for becoming adapted to it. This may involve revaluation of the group, redefining the issue, resigning oneself to a special role or position in the group, and so on. It may also be useful to prepare the individual for the social criticism that his new views will eventually evoke. The assumption here is simply that when a person changes an attitude in full awareness of the norm that has supported the old position, the reorganization produced will tend to have a better chance of enduring than one produced in the absence of the norm. Accordingly, changes produced under high salience would endure more than those produced under low. This and other hypotheses related to the persistence of changes brought about under various conditions of salience require further experimental analysis.

Summary

An experiment was performed to determine whether the degree to which a specific group membership is salient for a person has any bearing on the resistance to change of attitudes supported by the group. Salience of membership in the Catholic Church was studied for high-school and college students. The experiment provides partial confirmation of the hypothesis that, other factors operating at an appropriate level, the resistance to change of group anchored attitudes is directly related to the degree of salience of the group. The results from the experimental procedure indicate that for high-school students, while in their classes, salience of membership in the Catholic Church can be heightened by brief reading materials that describe the Church's leader, symbols and functions. However, the same procedure did not appear to have a similar effect for Catholics obtained in college classes.

A second purpose of the experiment was to investigate the relative permanency, over a short period of time, of changes accomplished under conditions of high and low salience. The results are consistent with the usual finding that the greater the initial change, the greater the amount of change retained at a later time. Those subjects for whom church membership was low in salience showed greater immediate change than the high salience subjects and continued to show greater acceptance of the communication at the time of a delayed after-test. Suggestions are made for a more rigorous test of theories that predict less retention of changes produced under low salience than of those produced with high.

References

CHARTERS, W. W., Jr, and NEWCOMB, T. M. (1952), 'Some attitudinal effects of experimentally increased salience of a membership group', in G. E. Swanson, T. M. Newcomb and E. L. Hartley (eds.), *Readings in Social Psychology* (rev. edn), Holt, Rinehart & Winston, pp. 415–20.

CHEIN, I., DEUTSCH, M., HYMAN, H., and JAHODA, M. (eds.) (1949), 'Consistency and inconsistency in intergroup relations', *J. soc. Issues*, vol. 5, no. 3.

HARTLEY, E. L., and HARTLEY, R. E. (1952), *Fundamentals of Social Psychology*, Knopf.

KELLEY, H. H., and VOLKART, E. H. (1952), 'The resistance to change of group-anchored attitudes', *Amer. soc. Rev.*, vol. 17, pp. 453–65.

KRIESBERG, M. (1949), 'Cross-pressures and attitudes', *Publ. Opin. Q.*, vol. 13, pp. 5–16.

KULP, D. H. (1934), 'II. Prestige, as measured by single-experience changes and their permanency', *J. educ. Res.*, vol. 27, pp. 663–72.

LAZARSFELD, P. F., BERELSON, B., and GAUDET, H. (1948), *The People's Choice* (2nd edn), Columbia University Press.

LEWIN, K. (1935), 'Psycho-sociological problems of a minority group', *Character and Pers.*, vol. 3, pp. 175–87.

LEWIN, K. (1938), 'The conceptual representation and the measurement of psychological forces', *Contr. psychol. Theory*, vol. 1, no. 4.

22. L. B. Brown and D. J. Pallant

Religious Belief and Social Pressure

L. B. Brown and D. J. Pallant, 'Religious belief and social pressure', *Psychological Reports*, 1962, vol. 10, pp. 269–70.

Assuming that religious beliefs constitute a 'cognitive system requiring strong social support for its maintenance' (Brown, 1962), then it should be possible to influence the strength of an individual's beliefs by imposing appropriate social pressure. The present experiment was designed to test this deduction by obtaining scores from a graphic rating scale for strength of belief or disbelief, about the fourteen statements of religious belief previously used by Brown, and repeating the procedure a week later under changed conditions in which accepted or rejected expert opinion was used as the social influence. The rating line ranged from 'True' through 'Uncertain' to 'False'.

Ss were nine males and eighteen females, aged from thirteen to sixteen years ($M = 14.6$), attending Bible Class at a suburban Methodist Church. The self-administered questionnaires were distributed in envelopes on both occasions, and after the first testing Ss were divided into three separate groups, equated only for age and sex, for the re-testing. One group was a control, simply re-tested with the added instruction, 'Make sure that you place your cross at the EXACT position which shows your belief.' On the papers of the first experimental group the following appeared in red, 'The beliefs of *Rev. A. S. Whitehead*, a prominent *Methodist Minister* are shown by a red cross on each line', while the other experimental group had the expert opinion of 'Rev. Father Sullivan, a prominent Roman Catholic priest' shown. For these two experimental groups the pressuring marks were specially prepared for each S by placing the red cross 2 cm either positively or negatively away from his original marking on the 15 cm rating line for each item. For three items no pressure was exerted and S's own rating was repeated. The' beliefs' of the fictitious Roman Catholic priest were used as it was thought that for these Ss there would be prejudice against Roman Catholicism, while the 'beliefs' of the fictitious Methodist should be strongly accepted.

The results showed that the mean change in the control group's markings was 0·56 cm, while the Methodist influence group showed a mean change of 2·14 cm ($t = 3·6$). When the direction of change for the experimental groups is taken into account, the mean of the Methodist influence group is $+1·1$ cm, and the mean of the Roman Catholic influence group is $-0·35$ cm ($t = 3·6$). That the beliefs of a Methodist expert significantly changed the stated beliefs of Methodist adolescents, and that such Ss are more influenced to conformity by a Methodist expert than by a Roman Catholic expert lend further support to the previously drawn conclusion that religious beliefs have a strong social component. This material provides another instance for the application of Festinger's theory of cognitive dissonance (1957), and shows that expressions of religious belief can be influenced like other social attitudes and opinions.

Summary

Measures of religious belief were obtained from adolescents under conditions of positive and negative social pressure. Positive pressure produced a significant change in stated beliefs towards an 'expert's' opinion, showing that religious beliefs are susceptible to social influences, as are attitudes and opinions.

References

BROWN, L. (1962), 'A study of religious beliefs', *Brit. J. Psychol.*, vol. 53, pp. 259–72.
FESTINGER, L. (1957), *A Theory of Cognitive Dissonance*, Harper & Row.

23 Jean-Pierre Deconchy

Boys' and Girls' Choices for a Religious Group

Jean-Pierre Deconchy, 'Sujets feminins et sujets masculins dans un groupe à finalité religieuse', *Archives de Sociologie des Religions*, 1968, vol. 26, pp. 97–110. Translated for this volume by Petra Morrison.

The idea that women are more 'religious' than men is a particularly prevalent assumption. To delve deeper than simple intuition, the idea seems to have a dual origin. On the one hand, some phenomenological or clinical analyses agree with the Jungian approach to the problem of religion and seem to reinforce the argument that 'religious values' have a more 'feminine' character. On the other hand, the sociology of religion has revealed strong differences in the behaviour of men and women. The idea has sprung up that women adopt religious behaviour more readily than do men. It must however be pointed out that this conclusion depends on the socio-cultural environment in which it is made. But in the final analysis, the idea that women are 'more religious' than men is as unsoundly based, philosophically and empirically, as it is apparently self-evident to some people.

I asked myself if in a group composed of both boys and girls, there would be a general over-selection of the girls when the group considered how to perform a task which it regarded as a 'religious' one.

I have discussed elsewhere the usefulness of comparing the specific structures which a group adopts when presented with a series of social tasks, including one that is 'religious' (Deconchy, 1968). Given the absolute ignorance which still prevails about the parameters of 'religion' it is useful to compare other social activities with those which a group defines as specifically 'religious'. The content of 'religion' can then be expressed in terms of the reference set up by the other tasks; and the social structure of a group with a 'religious' purpose can be interpreted through the structures which the group adopts in performing the other tasks.

I will not reiterate the reasons which led me to adopt the classic procedures of sociometric analysis, as I have discussed their advantages and disadvantages elsewhere. On the whole, I took fewer experimental precautions with this study than I was able to take for the rest of my research.

I worked with a group of twenty-five subjects – ten boys and fifteen girls, all about eleven years old and all pupils in the same class of a state school in a major provincial town. They had been brought together by the Catholic chaplain for religious instruction before their first communion. The experiment took place in March, when the group had been together for six months. Their catechetical teaching had been pretty formal, and no small teams had been formed. It is obvious that different results would be obtained with a group of adolescents or adults as subjects.

The twenty-five subjects in the group were presented with three 'tasks', whose wording I must confess was not entirely unequivocal. The first one in particular seems to have encouraged a *ranking* behaviour, rather than to have made the subjects plan an integrated group.

1. *An 'academic' task:* 'If some of you had to represent this group in a competition between different schools, which involved all the main school subjects, and you were asked to set up this group yourself ... whom would you choose and who do you think would not be much use?'

2. *A 'friendship' task:* 'If you were told that during the summer you could take a group of friends on holiday, and could choose them yourself from the boys and girls here ... whom would you choose and whom would you not want to take?'

3. *A 'religious' task;* 'If, in order to prepare for Easter, the boys and girls here formed little groups to talk about God and pray together ... whom would you choose and whom would you refuse for your small group?'[1]

Were the girls over-selected for the religious task?

This question immediately divides into two parts:

1. Were the girls over-selected (by the group as a whole, as well as by each of the two subgroups) for the religious task?

1. These tasks were formulated on the basis of interviews with children of identical age and socio-economic status, who were not themselves tested. The final formulations were adopted after several preliminary trials.

A 'sporting' task had also been proposed, but I left it out when I found that the boys and girls had separate gym lessons. I may say that the boys were massively over-selected for this task.

Jean-Pierre Deconchy 285

2. Did the religious task produce more marked over- or under-selection than did the other tasks?

1. Inspection of the matrices in Table 1 shows that each sub-group has a strong tendency to over-select subjects of the same sex and to over-reject subjects of the opposite sex (except for the academic task). At first sight the religious task shows the same trend.

Table 1

B→indicates number of selections applied by the boys towards . . . .
B↔indicates number of rejections applied by the boys towards . . . .
→B indicates number of selections received by the boys from . . . .
↔B indicates number of rejections received by the boys from . . . .

	Academic				Friendship				Religion		
	→B	→G			→B	→G			→B	→G	
B→	37	10	47	B→	41	2	43	B→	26	11	37
G→	27	48	75	G→	12	61	73	G→	16	51	67
	64	58	122		53	63	116		42	62	104
	↔B	↔G			↔B	↔G			↔B	↔G	
B↔	10	20	30	B↔	5	30	35	B↔	8	16	24
G↔	19	38	57	G↔	23	30	53	G↔	28	34	62
	29	58	87		28	60	88		36	50	86

The number of selections and rejections which each subject could make was unrestricted and the matrices in Table 1 take into account only the first five selections. I had to choose between two arbitrary systems: either to impose a limit on the selections, or to use only the first ones. I opted for the second approach. Although it is an arguable procedure anyway, it created particular difficulties for this study: in the case where each subject perceived the group as being composed of two subgroups, it is possible that each subject might have formed a subgroup of his own sex first, and *then* used the other subgroup. This of course makes it necessary to assess the order in which the selections were made, and to use only the first five choices carries the risk of eliminating the choices made for the opposite subgroup. My procedure probably accentuates the tendency to over-select one's own subgroup.

The experimental group contained fewer boys (ten) than girls (fifteen). If the tendency to select within one's own subgroup is powerful, a boy thus has less of a field from which to choose than does a girl. To take only the first five choices may eliminate this difference.

A simple addition of the first five choices made by different subjects towards different targets poses problems for the analysis. The procedure is made even more suspect in this study by the preceding problem.

We are thus confronted with a collection of difficulties inherent in sociometric procedures, exacerbated by the particular problem that we are studying.

2. Examination of the matrices of Table 1 allows us to identify a tendency to 'endoselection' and 'exorejection' in each subgroup: but it is not easy to measure that tendency. It was shown long ago that indices such as Criswell's *intra-group preference index* (1943), or Proctor and Loomis's *cleavage index* (1961), are not only suspect but basically useless.

It may nevertheless be helpful to see whether the distribution of the scores in the matrices in Table 1 differs significantly from a random or chance distribution. For this purpose Proctor and Loomis suggest a simplified χ^2 formula.[2] For the three tasks, and treating selections and rejections separately, we obtained the following χ^2 results:

Selections	Academic	39·01	Highly significant
	Friendship	67·91	Highly significant
	Religion	21·31	Highly significant
Rejections	Academic	0	
	Friendship	8·23	Highly significant
	Religion	0·99	Non-significant

The tendency to endoselection leads to distributions which are very different from chance. Though the comparison is a relative one, it will be seen that the religious task produces the smallest χ^2: one is tempted to say that the tendency to endoselection is weaker here than for the other tasks, even though we know that

2.
$$\frac{[(B \to B. G \to G) - (B \to G. G \to B)]^2 \, N}{(B \to B + G) \, (G \to B + G) \, (B \to B + G \to L) \, (G \to G + B \to G)}$$

where N is the total number of statements, $B \to B$ is the number of boys selecting boys, and so on.

the χ^2 formula does not measure the divergence between two variables.

The tendency to exorejection is not strong enough to produce distributions which differ significantly from chance, except for the 'friendship' task.

These results do not, in themselves, necessarily show a tendency to endoselection or to exorejection: it is only the preliminary examination of these matrices that led us to interpret the differences in that way. It should also be noted that this χ^2 calculation is not valid when there is an over-selection (or over-rejection) of one of the subgroups: as is the case with the rejections on the academic task.[3]

3. Comparison with theoretical scores

1. To start with and for the sake of illustration, we may begin by *not* presupposing the existence of two subgroups each with a marked tendency to endoselection and to exorejection.

Each of the ten boys can apply his selections (or rejections) to nine boys and fifteen girls, whereas each of the girls can apply hers to ten boys and fourteen girls. The theoretical percentage distribution of the number of selections (or rejections) made by the group as a whole (N) is therefore as follows:

	$\overset{\rightarrow}{\underset{\leftrightarrow}{}}B$	$\overset{\rightarrow}{\underset{\leftrightarrow}{}}G$
$B\overset{\rightarrow}{\underset{\leftrightarrow}{}}$	15%	25%
$G\overset{\rightarrow}{\underset{\leftrightarrow}{}}$	25%	35%

Having calculated the theoretical number of selections (or rejections) for each of the four cells of the matrix, it is then possible to produce an endoselection index and an exorejection index for each subgroup and for each task (Maisonneuve, 1965, p. 247).

If S is the number of selections (or rejections) which a subgroup actually makes from subjects of the same subgroup, 0 the number applied to the subjects in the other subgroup, and S^1 and 0^1 are the corresponding expected frequencies, the index takes the form $S \times 0^1/0 \times S^1$. It will be seen that the tendency to endoselection increases as this index increases and the tendency

3. A χ^2 calculation for the distribution of *all* the selections made (and not just the first five) produces the same results. Nevertheless, as would be expected, the distributions for the first five choices are a little closer to the chance expectation.

to exorejection increases as this index diminishes. We have obtained the following table of indices:

		Endoselection		Exorejection	
Academic	B	6·2		0·84	
	G		1·3		1·44
Friendship	B	34·2		0·28	
	G		3·6		0·93
Religion	B	3·9		0·83	
	G		2·3		0·87

The verdict is clear: endoselection is a general phenomenon. Nevertheless, one notes that among the boys, it applies least to religion. There is less endoselection among the girls than among the boys where it primarily affects friendship and, to a lesser extent, religion.

Among the boys, exorejection is massive for friendship and about equal for the academic task and religion. Among the girls, however, there is endorejection for the academic task, and for this task the boys are over-selected by the group as a whole. Nevertheless, it is for religion that they are most rejected by the girls.

For the moment I will not carry this line of interpretation any further. In fact, it would appear that a comparison of the actual and theoretical distributions has only limited relevance when one studies the distribution of all selections, whichever subgroup makes them. In a group where the two subgroups are not the same size (ten boys and fifteen girls), and where tendencies to endoselection and exorejection intrude so strongly, it is clear that one must work at another level, with the number of selections made by each subgroup. In fact, it is probable that a subject makes more or less selections or rejections according to the subgroup to which he belongs.[4]

The girls regularly make more selections than do the boys. We can thus postulate a simple hypothesis: where the tendency to endoselection is concerned, each of the fifteen girls has a wider

4. A study of the number of *selections* made on average by each subject (not just the first five) produces the following figures:

	Academic	Friendship	Religion
B	6	5·7	5·4
G	7·9	6·8	6·4

field than each of the ten boys, within which to satisfy this tendency.

If one examines the rejections, the hypothesis becomes complicated:

	Academic	Friendship	Religion
B	3·2	4·6	2·8
G	4·1	4·2	4·4

The hypothesis is corroborated for the academic task (endo-rejection among the girls) and for friendship (exorejection among the girls). On the other hand, while exorejection is marked among the girls for religion, they still make more religious rejections than do the boys. I can find no immediate explanation for this phenomenon.

2. We can therefore begin our calculations afresh by hypothesizing different behaviour for each subgroup in relation to the other subgroup.

Each boy can apply his selections to nine boys and fifteen girls: each girl can apply them to ten boys and fourteen girls. For NB (the number of selections made by the boys) and for NG, the expected percentage distributions are as follows:

	$\overrightarrow{+}$B	$\overrightarrow{+}$G	
B$\overrightarrow{+}$	37·5%	62·5%	NB
G$\overrightarrow{+}$	41·6%	58·4%	NG

Table 2 gives the observed percentage distributions and the heavy surround indicates those cells where the observed percentages were higher than the expected percentages.

Among both boys and girls, endoselection and exorejection is a general phenomenon, with one exception: boys and girls agree in over-rejecting the girls for the academic task.

Nevertheless the phenomenon is not unequivocal. *Among the boys*, it is for the religious task that masculine 'prestige' is weakest and the girls' prestige is strongest. Where rejections are concerned, the girls are vigorously rejected from 'friendship', but much less strongly for the academic task and for religion. *Among the girls*, it is for the academic task that feminine 'prestige' is weakest, but girls are over-selected more for the 'friendship'

Table 2

	→B	→G		→B	→G		→B	→G
B→	78·7%	21·3%	B→	95·3%	4·7%	B→	70·1%	29·9%
G→	36%	64%	G→	16·4%	83·6%	G→	23·8%	76·2%

	↦B	↦G		↦B	↦G		↦B	↦G
B↦	33·3%	67·7%	B↦	14·3%	85·2%	B↦	33·3%	66·7%
G↦	33·3%	66·7%	G↦	43·4%	56·6%	G↦	45·1%	54·9%

| *Academic* | *Friendship* | *Religion* |

task than for the 'religious' one. As for rejections, girls over-reject girls for the academic task, but they reject the boys more for the religious task than for the friendship one.

It would appear that we have succeeded in separating out the occasionally contradictory role of two tendencies: first, the tendency to over-select subjects of one's own sex and to over-reject those of the opposite sex; and second, the tendency to see the girls as more 'religious' than the boys.[5] I must however point out that the second of these tendencies is by no means the most powerful, since *when the occasion arises, the second tendency never succeeds in overcoming the first* (for the academic choice the girls over-reject the girls), and it is only by comparing the tasks among themselves that we can infer the existence of this second tendency.

By putting into parentheses the general tendency to endoselection and to exorejection, and by comparing the selections made for the religious task against the other tasks, the tendency to see the girls as more 'religious' than the boys appears on several levels. Among the boys there is a tendency to over-select and to under-reject the girls for the religious task. Among the girls there is a tendency to over-reject the boys for the religious task; the selections they make concerning their own subgroup appear to be more ambiguous.

Nevertheless, we cannot stop at the affirmation that 'the girls

5. The criterion of the girls' 'religiousness' is taken here to be the tendency to select them in preference to boys for the religious task, and to reject them less than the boys for the same task.

are more religious than the boys'. We must try to penetrate deeper into the way that each subgroup views itself and the other subgroup.

Each subgroup's view of itself and of the other subgroup
The groupings of individual selections and rejections

The ϕ coefficient. One subject may apply to another subject several selections or several rejections across the different tasks. It is therefore important to see how frequently a selection made for one task matches up with a selection made for another task. We can make this kind of comparison by means of the ϕ-coefficient, in terms of pairs of selections. This has the advantage of being a simple calculation and is distribution-free.[6]

For our purpose, we need to calculate this coefficient as it applies not only to the groups as a whole, but also to the way the subjects of each subgroup view the subjects both of their own and the other subgroup: this produces the sets of three ϕ-coefficients laid out in Table 3.

Reading the ϕ-coefficients. As might be expected, social attitudes turn out to be highly transferable, i.e. a subject who has selected (or rejected) another subject for a particular task tends to choose him (or reject him) equally for another task.

One cannot compare the value of the ϕ-coefficients from subgroup to subgroup since they are calculated from different data. One can only, within each series of three ϕ, attempt to scale in terms of similarity.[7] The matrix below gives the relationships between the religious selection (or rejection) and to the academic or friendship selections (or rejections). (For example, $F > A$ means that the religious selection is more often linked to a friendship selection than to an academic selection).

6. To see if the presence of a given A and that of a given B are linked, one sets up the following matrix:

	A +	A −
B +	a	b
B −	c	d

The ϕ-coefficient is therefore written:

$$\frac{ad - bc}{\sqrt{[(a+b)\,(c+d)\,(a+c)\,(b+d)]}}$$

The coefficient ranges between −1 and +1.

7. This is perhaps the least suspect of the calculations which can be made with the ϕ-coefficient, which is generally recognized to be ambiguous since it is a kind of balanced version of χ^2.

Table 3

The Ø. coefficients

(A = academic task; F = friendship task; R = religious task)

	Group as a whole		B→B		B→G		G→G		G→B	
	F	R	F	R	F	R	F	R	F	R
A	0.43	0.34	0.37	0.22	0.03	0.03	0.45	0.41	0.37	0.40
F		0.42		0.40		0.03		0.44		0.30

	Group as a whole		B↔B		B↔G		G↔G		G↔B	
	F	R	F	R	F	R	F	R	F	R
A	0.31	0.32	0.07		0.34	0.31	0.48	0.36	0.12	0.44
F		0.29		0.43		0.26		0.34		0.22

	→B	→G
→	$F>A$	$A>F$
B ↔	$F>A$	$A>F$
→	$A>F$	$F>A$
G ↔	$A>F$	$F>A$

For the group as a whole:

$$→ = F>A$$
$$↔ = A>F$$

Interpretation. In spite of the size of certain ϕ-coefficients, notably for B→G, one can interpret these results at two levels: for the group as a whole, the religious selection is more often linked (or perhaps due?) to a friendship selection than to an academic selection. On the other hand, the religious rejection is more often linked (or perhaps due?) to an academic rejection than to a friendship rejection.

Each of the two subgroups links its religious selections and rejections of the other subgroup more with its academic selections and rejections than with its friendship selections and rejections.

Among themselves, the boys link their religious selections and rejections more to their friendship selections and rejections than to their academic selections and rejections. *Among themselves*, the girls link their religious and friendship selections closely, but prefer to link their religious with their academic rejections. Once again, the only deviation from our hypothesis occurs with the rejection of the girls by the girls on the academic task.

A comparison of the above matrix with Table 2 reveals an agreement which is important for the analysis of individual attitudes.

Concerning attitudes towards the same subgroup: the religious selection is always most closely linked to the selection for the task which most favours endoselection; the religious rejection is always most closely linked to rejection for the task which most favours exorejection. Concerning attitudes towards the other subgroup: the religious selection is always most closely linked to the selection for the task where endoselection is weakest; the religious rejection is always most closely linked to rejection for the task where exorejection is weakest.

The idea of a 'more religious' view of the girls – advanced earlier – should thus be qualified. The girls' specific 'religiousness' should not be seen as an identifying characteristic or as a built-in quality which overlays the whole of the social image attributed to them. Rather, it depends on the global view taken of the boys' and girls' different social behaviour. The religious selection is linked to the selection for the task which most reinforces endo-selection, when the same sex is involved, and to selection for the task which most weakens it, when the other sex is involved: religious rejection is linked to rejection for the task which most weakens exorejection, when the same sex is involved, and to rejection for the task which most reinforces it, when the other sex is involved. In other words, in terms of individual attitudes the two tendencies I have isolated (the tendency to endoselection and to exorejection, and the tendency to see a girl as more 'religious' than a boy) are not opposing tendencies, but complementary. One can separate them, as I have done in the first part of this study: but in doing this one breaks up the real psychosocial link which unites the subjects among themselves, both inside and outside their own subgroup.

Comparison of the group's and subgroup's global structures for each task

So far I have examined only the components of the *individual* attitudes. It is now necessary to compare the total distribution of selections: as I have shown elsewhere, this involves two entirely different procedures. For example, it is conceivable that for two tasks A and B a group may form total structures which are very alike, even though each of the subjects may never choose the same subject for both task A and task B. This is the case, for example, when a subject is selected as the *leader* for both tasks A and B, but is selected for task A by a first subgroup and for task B by a second subgroup.

I have only considered the distribution of all the selections made by the twenty-five subjects: and I have done this not in terms of the socio metric scores themselves (number of choices received by each subject), but in terms of the ranks which each subject occupies in the distribution of these scores. The correlations were worked out by means of Spearman's ρ-coefficient.[8]

8. If N is the number of subjects, and D the 'difference between the rankings' which each subject occupies in two distributions, we have:
$$\rho = 1 - \frac{6\Sigma D^2}{N(N^2-1)}.$$
The ρ-coefficient ranges between -1 and $+1$.

The total structure of each subgroup by itself and by the other subgroup. We must start by asking whether, for a given task, a subgroup is organized in the same way:

by the group as a whole;
by the subjects of its own subgroup;
by the subjects of the other subgroup.

The resulting group of correlations is set out in Table 4.

It is immediately apparent that it is for *religion* that a subgroup's organization differs most, according to whether it is organized by the subgroup itself or by the other subgroup (0·26 as against 0·27 and 0·86, 0·27 as against 0·61 and 0·50, 0·21 as against 0·30 and 0·84).[9] Yet where the rejections applied to girls are concerned, it is for religion that the divergence is the least great (0·46 as against 0·36 and 0·17). Again one might be tempted to stop at observing that the religious rejections made by the girls constitute a special case. One can however go further.

We cannot compare the correlations from table to table, since the components differ: we can however state that the correlation for the religious *rejections* applied to girls relates to the other rejections differently from the way it applies to the selections and rejections of boys, and to the selections of girls. Returning now to the matrix on page 294, we can make another point. Where the selections and rejections applied to the boys are concerned, the religious selections and rejections are more closely linked to the friendship selections and rejections made by the boys than they are to the academic selections and rejections made by the girls: with the selections of girls, the religious selection is more closely linked to the academic selection made by the boys, than it is to the friendship selection made by the girls. To the extent that 'link' may imply 'cause', we can say that the religious selections and rejections are made for different reasons according to whether they apply within the subgroup or outside it. On the other hand, the religious rejections of the girls are always more closely linked to the academic rejections, whether they come from boys or from

9. One will note the strong correlation which exists for the academic task between, on the one hand, the distributions of selections of boys by boys and by girls, and, on the other hand, the distributions of rejections of boys by boys and by girls. This is due to the over-selection of boys and the over-rejection of girls for the academic task. This over-selection and over-rejection, applied as it is to a narrow field of ten subjects (out of twenty-five) has the effect of levelling out the distributions and making them correlate strongly.

Table 4

The ρ coefficients

	Distribution of selections applied to boys			Distribution of selections applied to girls			Distribution of rejections received by boys			Distribution of rejections received by girls		
	B→	G→	Σ→	B→	G→	Σ→	B↔	G↔	Σ↔	B↔	G↔	Σ↔
Academic	0·97	0·91	0·86	0·70	0·92	0·50	0·86	0·99	0·84	0·65	0·75	0·17
Friendship	0·83	0·78	0·27	0·63	0·99	0·61	0·66	0·85	0·30	0·86	0·76	0·36
Religion	0·78	0·77	0·26	0·47	0·95	0·27	0·67	0·75	0·21	0·70	0·95	0·46

girls: the girls are thus rejected for religion *for the same reason* by both boys and girls. This difference probably originates in the general over-rejection of the girls for the academic task.

Comparison of the total structures produced by the different tasks. By scaling the sociometric scores, it is possible to compare the structures which the group adopted in turn for its three tasks, and the same can be done for each subgroup according to whether it is organized by itself or by the other subgroup. The resulting series of three ρ are set out in Table 5.

On the whole, then, the total structures reflect the patterns observed in the individual groupings. But with one important exception: the subgroup of girls as organized by the subgroup of boys has a religious structure which is closer to the friendship structure than to the academic structure (with the ϕ-coefficients, the result was $A > F$, for both selections and rejections).

The limited number of components should once again be borne in mind. Out of 106 selections made for the friendship task (of which forty-three were made by the boys), only two $B \rightarrow G$ selections were made: this obviously distorts our scaling of the sociometric scores obtained by the girls on the basis of the boys' selections. But how are we to explain the fact that the rejections, too link religion and friendship for preference? Out of eighty-eight rejections (thirty-five were made by the boys), there were thirty $B \rightarrow G$ ones. One must therefore admit that for the $B \rightarrow G$ area, the ϕ-coefficients do not find their reflection in the ρ-coefficients. In the subgroup of girls as viewed by the boys, the leaders and the scapegoats are the same for both religion and friendship, though one may surmise that they were not named by the same boys. Nevertheless it would be very risky to try and distinguish two subcategories within the very narrow group of $B \rightarrow G$ statements – especially for the friendship task. At all events, I have not found any coherent explanation for this discrepancy between the ϕ and ρ coefficients.

Table 5

The ρ coefficients

	F	R		F	R		F	R		F	R		F	R
A	0·71	0·54		0·64	0·57		0·42	0·03		0·84	0·63		0·85	0·88
F		0·76			0·89			0·63			0·69			0·71
Group as a whole	B→G			B→G			B→G			G→G			G→B	

	F	R		F	R		F	R		F	R		F	R
A	0·49	0·69		0·52	0·52		0·49	0·19		0·63	0·76		0·38	0·75
F		0·40			0·91			0·37			0·61			0·07
Group as a whole	B↔G			B↔G			B↔G			G↔G			G↔B	

References

CRISWELL, J. H. (1943), 'Sociometric methods of measuring group preferences', *Sociometry*, vol. 6, pp. 398–408.

DECONCHY, J. P. (1968), 'Petits groupes à finalité réligieuse: Etude de sociometrie comparee', *Archives de Sociologie des Religions*, vol. 25, pp. 39–79.

MAISONNEUVE, H. (1965), 'Le sociometrie et l'étude des relations preferentielles', in P. Fraisse and J. Piaget (eds.), *Traite de Psychologie Experimentale*, vol. 9, Presse Universitaires de France.

PROCTOR, C., and LOOMIS, C. P. (1961), 'Analysis of sociometric data', in M. Jahoda, M. Deutsch and S. Cook (eds.), *Research Methods in Social Relations*, vol. 2, pp. 561–85, Dryden.

24 W. N. Pahnke

Drugs and Mysticism

W. N. Pahnke, 'Drugs and mysticism', *International Journal o Parapsychology*, 1966, vol. 8, no. 2, pp. 295–314.

The claim has been made that the experience facilitated by psychedelic (or mind-opening) drugs such as LSD, psilocybin and mescaline can be similar or identical to the experience described by the mystics of all ages, cultures and religions. This paper will attempt to examine and explain this possibility.

There is a long and continuing history of the religious use of plants which contain psychedelic substances. Scholars such as Osmond (1957), Schultes (1963) and Wasson (1963) have made valuable contributions to this intriguing field. In some instances, such natural products were ingested by a priest, shaman or witch doctor to induce a trance for revelatory purposes; sometimes they were taken by groups of people who participated in sacred ceremonies. For example, the dried heads of the peyote cactus, whose chief active ingredient is mescaline, were used by the Aztecs at least as early as 300 BC and are currently being employed by over 50,000 Indians of the North American Native Church as a vital part of their religious ceremonies. Both *ololiuqui*, a variety of morning-glory seed, and certain kinds of Mexican mushrooms (called *teonanacatl*, 'flesh of the gods') were also used for divinatory and religious purposes by the Aztecs. These practices have continued to the present among remote Indian tribes in the mountains of Oaxaca Province in Mexico. Modern psychopharmacological research has shown the active chemicals to be psilocybin in the case of the mushrooms, and several compounds closely related to LSD in the case of *ololiuqui*. *Amanita muscaria*, the mushroom which has been used for unknown centuries by Siberian shamans to induce religious trances, does not contain psilocybin. The most important psychologically active compound from this mushroom has not yet been isolated, but promising work is in progress. Other naturally-occurring plants, which are used by various South American Indian tribes in a religious manner for prophecy, divination, clairvoyance, tribal initiation of male adolescents or sacred feasts, are: cohoba snuff, made from the pulverized seed of *Piptadenia*; the drink *vinho de Jurumens*, made from the seeds of *Mimosa hostilis*; and the drink *caapi*, made from *Banisteriopsis*. These last three products contain various indolic compounds which are all closely related to psilocybin, both structurally and in their psychic effects (e.g. bufotenine, dimethyltryptamine, and harmine, respectively). Both LSD and psilocybin contain the indolic ring, and mescaline may be metabolized to an indole in the body.

An experimental examination of the claim that psychedelic drug experience may resemble mystical experience

Some of the researchers who have experimented with synthesized mescaline, LSD or psilocybin have remarked upon the similarity between drug-induced and spontaneous mystical experiences because of the frequency with which some of their subjects have used mystical and religious language to describe their experiences. This data interested the author in a careful examination and evaluation of such claims. An empirical study, designed to investigate in a systematic and scientific way the similarities and differences between experiences described by mystics and those facilitated by psychedelic crugs, was undertaken (Pahnke, 1963, 1966). First, a phenomenological typology of the mystical state of consciousness was carefully defined, after a study of the writings of the mystics themselves and of scholars who have tried to characterize mystical experience. (For example, William James, 1935, was an invaluable pioneer in this area.) Then, some drug experiences were empirically studied, not by collecting such experiences wherever an interesting or striking one might have been found and analysed after the fact, but by conducting a double-blind, controlled experiment with subjects whose religious background and experience, as well as personality, had been measured *before* their drug experiences. The preparation of the subjects, the setting under which the drug was administered, and the collection of data about the experience were made as uniform as possible. The experimenter himself devised the experiment, collected the data, and evaluated the results without ever having had a personal experience with any of these drugs.

A nine-category typology of the mystical state of consciousness was defined as a basis for measurement of the phenomena of the psychedelic drug experiences. Among the numerous scholars of mysticism, the work of W. T. Stace (1960) was found to be the most helpful guide for the construction of this typology. His conclusion – that in the mystical experience there are certain fundamental characteristics which are universal and not restricted to any particular religion or culture (although particular cultural, historical or religious conditions may influence both the interpretation and description of these basic phenomena) – was taken as a presupposition. Whether or not the mystical experience is 'religious' depends upon one's definition of religion and was not the problem investigated. Our typology defined the universal phenomena of the mystical experience, whether considered 'religious' or not.

The nine categories of our phenomenological typology may be summarized as follows:

Unity

Unity, the most important characteristic of the mystical experience, is divided into internal and external types, which are different ways of experiencing an undifferentiated unity. The major difference is that the internal type finds unity through an 'inner world' *within* the experiencer, while the external type finds unity through the external world *outside* the experiencer.

The essential elements of *internal unity* are loss of usual sense impressions and loss of self without becoming unconscious. The multiplicity of usual external and internal sense impressions (including time and space), and the empirical ego or usual sense of individuality, fade or melt away while consciousness remains. In the most complete experience this consciousness is a pure awareness beyond empirical content, with no external or internal distinctions. In spite of the loss of sense impressions and dissolution of the usual personal identity or self, the awareness of oneness or unity is still experienced and remembered. One is not unconscious but is rather very much aware of an undifferentiated unity.

External unity is perceived outwardly with the physical senses through the external world. A sense of underlying oneness is felt behind the empirical multiplicity. The subject or observer feels that the usual separation between himself and an external object (inanimate or animate) is no longer present in a basic sense; yet the subject still knows that on another level, at the same time, he and the objects are separate. Another way of expressing this same phenomenon is that the essences of objects are experienced intuitively and felt to be the same at the deepest level. The subject feels a sense of oneness with these objects because he 'sees' that at the most basic level all are a part of the same undifferentiated unity. The capsule statement 'all is One' is a good summary of external unity. In the most complete experience a cosmic dimension is felt, so that the experiencer feels in a deep sense that he is a part of everything that is.

Transcendence of time and space

This category refers to loss of the usual sense of time and space. This means clock time but may also be one's personal sense of his past, present and future. Transcendence of space means that a person loses his usual orientation as to where he is during the experience in terms of the usual three-dimensional perception of his environment. Experiences of timelessness and spacelessness may also be described as experiences of 'eternity' or 'infinity'.

Deeply felt positive mood

The most universal elements (and, therefore, the ones which are most essential to the definition of this category) are joy, blessedness and peace. The unique character of these feelings in relation to the mystical experience is the intensity which elevates them to the highest levels of human experience, and they are highly valued by the experiencers. Tears may be associated with any of these elements because of the overpowering nature of the experience. Such feelings may occur either at the peak of the experience or during the 'ecstatic afterglow', when the peak has passed but while its effects and memory are still quite vivid and intense. Love may also be an element of deeply felt positive mood, but it does not have the same universality as joy, blessedness and peace.

Sense of sacredness

This category refers to the sense of sacredness which is evoked by the mystical experience. The sacred is here broadly defined as that which a person feels to be of special value and capable of being profaned. The basic characteristic of sacredness is a non-rational, intuitive, hushed, palpitant response of awe and wonder in the presence of inspiring realities. No religious 'beliefs' or traditional theological terminology need necessarily be involved, even though there may be a sense of reverence or a feeling that what is experienced is holy or divine.

Objectivity and reality

This category has two interrelated elements: (a) insightful knowledge or illumination felt at an intuitive, non-rational level and gained by direct experience; and (b) the authoritative nature of the experience, or the certainty that such knowledge is truly real, in contrast to the feeling that the experience is a subjective delusion. These two elements are connected because the knowledge through experience of ultimate reality (in the sense of being able to 'know' and 'see' what is really *real*) carries its own sense of certainty. The experience of 'ultimate' reality is an awareness of another dimension unlike the 'ordinary' reality (the reality of usual, everyday consciousness); yet the knowledge of 'ultimate' reality is quite real to the experiencer. Such insightful knowledge does not necessarily mean an increase in facts, but rather in intuitive illumination. What becomes 'known' (rather than merely intellectually assented to) is intuitively felt to be authoritative, requires no proof at a rational level, and produces an inward feeling of objective truth. The content of this knowledge may be divided into two main types: (a) insights into being and existence in general, and (b) insights into one's personal, finite self.

Paradoxicality

Accurate descriptions and even rational interpretations of the mystical experience tend to be logically contradictory when strictly analysed. For example, in the experience of internal unity there is a loss of all empirical content in an *empty* unity which is at the same time *full* and complete. This loss includes the loss of the sense of self and the dissolution of individuality; yet something of the individual entity remains to experience the unity. The 'I' both exists and does not exist. Another example is the separateness from, and at the same time unity with, objects in the experience of external unity (essentially a paradoxical transcendence of space).

Alleged ineffability

In spite of attempts to relate or write about the mystical experience, mystics insist either that words fail to describe it adequately or that the experience is beyond words. Perhaps the reason is an embarrassment with language because of the paradoxical nature of the essential phenomena.

Transiency

Transiency refers to duration and means the temporary nature of the mystical experience in contrast to the relative permanence of the level of usual experience. There is a transient appearance of the special and unusual levels or dimensions of consciousness as defined by our typology, their eventual disappearance, and a return to the more usual. The characteristic of transiency indicates that the mystical state of consciousness is not sustained indefinitely.

Persisting positive changes in attitude and behavior

Because our typology is of a healthful, life-enhancing mysticism, this category describes the positive, lasting effects of the experience and the resulting changes in attitude. These changes are divided into four groups: (1) toward self; (2) toward others; (3) toward life; and (4) toward the mystical experience itself.

1. Increased integration of personality is the basic inward change in the personal self. Undesirable traits may be faced in such a way that they may be dealt with and finally reduced or eliminated. As a result of personal integration, one's sense of inner authority may be strengthened, and the vigor and dynamic quality of a person's life may be increased. Creativity and greater efficiency of achievement may be released. An inner optimistic tone may result, with a consequent increase in feelings of happiness, joy and peace.

2. Changes in attitude and behavior toward others include more sensitivity, more tolerance, more real love, and more authenticity as a person by virtue of being more open and more one's true self with others.

3. Changes toward life in a positive direction include philosophy of life, sense of values, sense of meaning and purpose, vocational commitment, need for service to others, and new appreciation of life and the whole of creation. Life may seem richer. The sense of reverence may be increased, and more time may be spent in devotional life and meditation.

4. Positive change in attitude toward the mystical experience itself means that it is regarded as valuable and that what has been learned is thought to be useful. The experience is remembered as a high point and an attempt is made to recapture it or, if possible, to gain new experiences as a source of growth and strength. The

mystical experiences of others are more readily appreciated and understood.

The purpose of the experiment in which psilocybin was administered in a religious context was to gather empirical data about the state of consciousness experienced. In a private chapel on Good Friday, twenty Christian theological students, ten of whom had been given psilocybin one and one-half hours earlier, listened over loudspeakers to a two-and-one-half-hour religious service which was in actual progress in another part of the building and which consisted of organ music, four solos, readings, prayers and personal meditation. The assumption was made that the condition most conducive to a mystical experience should be an atmosphere broadly comparable to that achieved by tribes who actually use natural psychedelic substances in religious ceremonies. The particular content and procedure of the ceremony had to be applicable (i.e. familiar and meaningful to the participants). Attitude toward the experience, both before and during, was taken into serious consideration in the experimental design. Preparation was meant to maximize positive expectation, trust, confidence and reduction of fear. The setting was planned to utilize this preparation through group support and rapport, through friendship and an open, trusting atmosphere, and through prior knowledge of the procedure of the experiment in order to eliminate, if possible, feelings of manipulation which might arise.

In the weeks before the experiment, each subject participated in five hours of various preparation and screening procedures which included psychological tests, medical history, physical examination, questionnaire evaluation of previous religious experience, intensive interview and group interaction. The twenty subjects were graduate-student volunteers, all of whom were from middle-class Protestant backgrounds and from one denominational seminary in the free-church tradition. None of the subjects had taken psilocybin or related substances before this experiment. The volunteers were divided into five groups of four students each on the basis of compatibility and friendship. Two leaders, who knew from past experience the positive and negative possibilities of the psilocybin reaction, met with their groups to encourage trust, confidence, group support and fear reduction. The method of reaction to the experience was emphasized (i.e. to relax and cooperate with, rather than to fight against, the effects of the drug). Throughout the preparation, an effort was made to avoid suggesting the characteristics of the typology of mysticism. The leaders were not familiar with the typology which had been devised.

Double-blind technique was employed in the experiment, so that neither the experimenter nor any of the participants (leaders or subjects) knew the specific contents of the capsules, which were identical in appearance. Half of the subjects and one of the leaders in each group received psilocybin (30 mg for each of the ten experimental subjects and 15 mg for five of the leaders). Without prior knowledge of the drug used, or of its effects, the remaining ten subjects and the other five leaders each received 200 mg of nicotinic acid, a vitamin which causes transient feelings of warmth and tingling of the skin, in order to maximize suggestion for the control group.

Data were collected during the experiment and at various times up to six months afterwards. On the experimental day, tape recordings were made both of individual reactions immediately after the religious service and of the group discussions which followed. Each subject wrote an account of his experience as soon after the experiment as was convenient. Within a week all subjects had completed a 147-item questionnaire which had been designed to measure the various phenomena of the typology of mysticism on a qualitative, numerical scale. The results of this questionnaire were used as a basis for a one-and-one-half-hour, tape-recorded interview which immediately followed. Six months later each subject was interviewed again after completion of a follow-up questionnaire in three parts with a similar scale. Part I was open-ended; the participant was asked to list any changes which he felt were a result of his Good Friday experience and to rate the degree of benefit or harm of each change. Part II (fifty-two items) was a condensed and somewhat more explicit repetition of items from the post-drug questionnaire. Part III (ninety-three items) was designed to measure both positive and negative attitudinal and behavioral changes which had lasted for six months and were due to the experience. The individual descriptive accounts and Part I of the follow-up questionnaire were content-analysed with a qualitative, numerical scale by judges who were independent of the experiment and who knew only that they were to analyse twenty accounts written by persons who had attended a religious service.

Prior to the experiment, the twenty subjects had been matched in ten pairs on the basis of data from the pre-drug questionnaires, interviews and psychological tests. Past religious experience, religious background and general psychological make-up were used for the pairings, in that order of importance. The experiment was designed so that by random distribution one subject from each pair received psilocybin and one received the control substance, nicotinic acid. This division into an experimental and control group was for the purpose of statistical evaluation of the scores from each of the three methods of measurement which used a numerical scale: the post-drug questionnaire, the follow-up questionnaire, and the content analysis of the written accounts.

A summary of percentage scores and significance levels reached by the ten experimentals and ten controls, for each category or subcategory of the typology of mysticism, is presented in Table 1. The score from each of the three methods of measurement was calculated as the percentage of the maximum possible score if the top of the rating scale for each item had been scored. The percentages from each method of measurement were then averaged together. A comparison of the scores of the experimental and control subject in each pair was used to calculate the significance level of the differences observed by means of the non-parametric sign test. As can be seen from Table 1, for the combined scores from the three methods of measurement, p was less than 0·020 in all categories except deeply felt positive mood (love) and persisting positive changes in attitude and behavior toward the experience, where p was still less than 0·055.

Although this evidence indicates that the experimentals as a group achieved to a statistically significant degree a higher score in each of the nine categories than did the controls, the degree of completeness or intensity must be examined.

In terms of our typology of mysticism, ideally the most 'complete' mystical experience should have demonstrated the phenomena of all the categories in a maximal way. The evidence (particularly from the content analysis and also supported by impressions from the interviews) showed that such perfect completeness in all categories was not experienced by all the subjects in the experimental group. In the data the various categories and subcategories can be divided into three groups in regard to the degree of intensity or completeness, as shown in Table 2. Criteria were the percentage levels and the consistency among different methods of measurement. The closest approxima-

Table 1 **Summary of percentage scores and significance levels reached by the experimental versus the control group for categories measuring the typology of mystical experience**

Category	Percentage of maximum possible score for 10 Ss		
	Exp.	Cont.	p*
1. Unity	62	7	0·001
(a) Internal	70	8	0·001
(b) External	38	2	0·008
2. Transcendence of time and space	84	6	0·001
3. Deeply felt positive mood	57	23	0·020
(a) Joy, blessedness and peace	51	13	0·020
(b) Love	57	33	0·055
4. Sacredness	53	28	0·020
5. Objectivity and reality	63	18	0·011
6. Paradoxicality	61	13	0·001
7. Alleged ineffability	66	18	0·001
8. Transiency	79	8	0·001
9. Persisting positive changes in attitude and behavior	51	8	0·001
(a) Toward self	57	3	0·001
(b) Toward others	40	20	0·002
(c) Toward life	54	6	0·011
(d) Toward the experience	57	31	0·055

*Probability that the difference between experimental and control scores was due to chance.

tion to a complete and intense degree of experience was found for the categories of internal unity, transcendence of time and space, transiency, paradoxicality and persisting positive changes in attitude and behavior toward self and life. The evidence indicated that the second group had almost but not quite the same degree of completeness or intensity as the first group. The second group consisted of external unity, objectivity and reality, joy, and alleged ineffability. There was a relatively greater lack of completeness for sense of sacredness, love, and persisting positive changes in

Table 2 Relative completeness* of various categories in which there was a statistically significant difference between experimental and control groups

1	2	3
Closest approximation to the most complete and intense expression	Almost, but not quite as complete or intense as (1)	Least complete or intense, though still a definite difference from the control group
Internal unity	External unity	Sense of sacredness
Transcendence of time and space	Objectivity and reality	Deeply felt positive mood (love)
Transiency	Alleged ineffability	Persisting positive changes in attitude and behavior toward others and the experience
Paradoxicality	Deeply felt positive mood (joy, blessedness and peace)	
Persisting positive changes in attitude and behavior toward self and life		

*Based on qualitative score levels and agreement among the three methods of measurement in comparing the scores of the experimental versus the control group.

attitude and behavior toward others and toward the experience. Each of these last eight categories or subcategories was termed incomplete to a more or less degree for the experimentals, but was definitely present to some extent when compared with the controls. When analysed most rigorously and measured against all possible categories of the typology of mysticism, the experience of the experimental subjects was considered incomplete in this strictest sense. Usually such incompleteness was demonstrated by results of the content analyses.

The control subjects did not experience many phenomena of the mystical typology, and even then only to a low degree of completeness. The phenomena for which the scores of the controls were closest to (although still always less than) the experimentals were: blessedness and peace, sense of sacredness, love, and persisting positive changes in attitude and behavior toward others and toward the experience.

The design of the experiment suggested an explanation for the fact that the control subjects should have experienced any phenomena at all. The meaningful religious setting of the experiment would have been expected to encourage a response of blessedness, peace and sacredness. In the case of love and persisting changes toward others and toward the experience, observation by the controls of the profound experience of the experimentals and inter-action between the two groups on an interpersonal level appeared, from both post-experimental interviews, to have been the main basis for the controls' experience of these phenomena.

The experience of the experimental subjects was certainly more like mystical experience than that of the controls, who had the same expectation and suggestion from the preparation and setting. The most striking difference between the experimentals and controls was the ingestion of 30mg of psilocybin, which it was concluded was the facilitating agent responsible for the difference in phenomena experienced.

After an admittedly short follow-up period of only six months, life-enhancing and -enriching effects similar to some of those claimed by mystics were shown by the higher scores of the experimental subjects when compared to the controls. In addition, after four hours of follow-up interviews with each subject, the experimenter was left with the impression that the experience had made a profound impact (especially in terms of religious feeling and thinking) on the lives of eight out of ten of the subjects who had been given psilocybin. Although the psilocybin experience was quite unique and different from the 'ordinary' reality of their everyday lives, these subjects felt that this experience had motivated them to appreciate more deeply the meaning of their lives, to gain more depth and authenticity in ordinary living, and to re-think their philosophies of life and values. The data did not suggest that any 'ultimate' reality encountered had made 'ordinary' reality no longer important or meaningful. The fact that the experience took place in the context of a religious service, with the use of symbols which were familiar and meaningful to the participants, appeared to provide a useful framework within which to derive meaning and integration from the experience, both at the time and later.

The relationship and relative importance of psychological preparation, setting and drug were important questions raised by our results. A meaningful religious preparation, expectation, and environment appeared to be conducive to positive drug experiences, although the precise qualitative and quantitative role of each factor was not determined. For example, everything possible was done to maximize suggestion, but suggestion alone cannot account for the results because of the different experience of the control group. The hypothesis that suggestibility was heightened by psilocybin could not be ruled out on the basis of our experiment. An effort was made to avoid suggesting the phenomena of the typology of mysticism, and the service itself made no such direct suggestion.

Implications for the psychology of religion

The results of our experiment would indicate that psilocybin (and LSD and mescaline by analogy) are important tools for the study of the mystical state of consciousness. Experiences which previously have been possible only for a small minority of people, and which have been difficult to study because of their unpredictability and rarity, are now reproducible under suitable conditions. The mystical experience has been called by many names which are suggestive of areas which are paranormal and not usually considered easily available for investigation (e.g. an experience of transcendence, ecstasy, conversion or cosmic consciousness); but this is a realm of human experience which should not be rejected as outside the realm of serious scientific study, especially if it can be shown that a practical benefit can result. Our data would suggest that such an overwhelming experience, in which a person existentially encounters basic values such as the meaning of his life (past, present, and future), deep and meaningful interpersonal relationships, and insight into the possibility of personal behavior change, can possibly be therapeutic if approached and worked with in a sensitive and adequate way.

Possibilities for further research with these drugs in the psychology of religion can be divided into two different kinds in relation to the aim: (1) theoretical understanding of the phenomena and psychology of mysticism, and (2) experimental investigation of possible social application in a religious context.

The first or theoretical kind of research would be to approach the mystical state of consciousness as closely as possible under controlled experimental conditions and to measure the effect of variables such as the dose of the drug, the preparation and personality of the subject, the setting of the experiment, and the expectation of the experimenter. The work described above was a first step in the measurement of these variables, but more research is needed. The results should be proved to be reproducible by the same and by different experimenters under similar conditions. Such work could lead to a better understanding of mysticism from a physiological, biochemical, psychological and therapeutic perspective.

Several experimental approaches can be envisioned for the second kind of research, to determine the best method for useful application in a religious context. One suggestion would be the establishment of a research center where carefully controlled drug experiments could be done by a trained research staff which would consist of psychiatrists, clinical psychologists and professional religious personnel. Subjects, ideally, would spend at least a week at the center to facilitate thorough screening, preparation and observation of their reactions, both during and after drug experiments. Another suggestion would be the study of the effect of mystical experience on small natural groups of from four to six people who would meet periodically, both prior to and after a drug experience, for serious personal and religious discussion, study and worship. The reactions of a varied range of subjects with different interests could be studied, but perhaps a good place to start would be with persons professionally interested in religion, such as ministers, priests, rabbis, theologians and psychologists of religion.

Such research may have important implications for religion. The universal and basic human experience which we have called mystical is recorded from all cultures and ages of human history, but mysticism has never been adequately studied and understood from a physiological, biochemical, sociological, psychological and theological perspective.

Perhaps there is more of a biochemical basis to such 'natural' experiences than has been previously supposed. Certainly many ascetics who have had mystical experiences have engaged in such practices as breathing and postural exercises, sleep deprivation, fasting, flagellation with subsequent infection, sustained meditation, and sensory deprivation in caves or monastic cells. All of these techniques have an effect on body chemistry. There is a definite interplay between physiological and psychological processes in the human being. Some of the indolic substances in the body do not differ greatly from the psychedelic drugs.

Many persons concerned with religion are disturbed by drug-facilitated mystical experiences because of their apparent ease of production, with the implication that they are 'unearned' and therefore 'undeserved'. Perhaps the Puritan and Calvinistic element of our Western culture – especially in the United States, where most of the controversy about psychedelic drugs has centered – may be a factor in this uneasiness. Although a drug experience might seem unearned when compared with the rigorous discipline which many mystics describe as necessary, our evidence has suggested that careful preparation and expectation play an important part, not only in the type of experience attained but in later fruits for life. Positive mystical experience with psychedelic drugs is by no means automatic. It would seem that the 'drug effect' is a delicate combination of psychological set and setting in which the drug itself is the trigger or facilitating agent – i.e. in which the drug is a *necessary* but not *sufficient* condition. Perhaps the hardest 'work' comes after the experience, which in itself may only provide the motivation for future efforts to integrate and appreciate what has been learned. Unless such an experience is integrated into the on-going life of the individual, only a memory remains rather than the growth of an unfolding renewal process which may be awakened by the mystical experience. If the person has a religious framework and discipline within which to work, the integrative process is encouraged and stimulated. Many persons may not need the drug-facilitated mystical experience, but there are others who would never be aware of the undeveloped potentials within themselves, or be inspired to work in this direction, without such an experience. 'Gratuitous grace' is an appropriate theological term, because the psychedelic mystical experience can lead to a profound sense of inspiration, reverential awe, and humility, perhaps partially as a result of the realization that the experience *is* a gift and not particularly earned or deserved.

Mysticism and *inner* experience have been stressed much more by Eastern religions than by Western. Perhaps Western culture is as far off balance in the opposite direction – with its manipulation of the *external* world, as exemplified by the emphasis on material wealth, control of nature, and admiration of science. Mysticism has been accused of fostering escapism from the problems of society, indifference to social conditions, and disinterest in social change. While the possibility of such excesses must always be remembered, our study has suggested the beneficial potential of mystical experience in stimulating the ability to feel and experience deeply and genuinely with the full harmony of both emotion and intellect. Such wholeness may have been neglected in modern Western society.

The subjects in our experiment who were given psilocybin found the religious service more meaningful, both at the time and later, than did the control subjects. This finding raises the possibility that psychedelic drug experiences in a religious setting may be able to illuminate the dynamics and significance of worship. Increased understanding of the psychological mechanism involved might lead to more meaningful worship experiences for those who have not had the drug experience. The analogy with the efficacy of the sacraments is one example of what would have to be considered for a better psychological understanding of what goes on during worship. Such considerations raise the question of the place of the emotional factor, compared to the cognitive, in religious worship. An even more basic question is the validity of religious experience of the mystical type, in terms of religious truth. Reactions to such religious implications will vary with theological position and presuppositions, but one value of our study can be to stimulate thoughtful examination of the problems.

Although our experimental results indicated predominantly positive and beneficial subjective effects, possible dangers must not be underestimated and should be thoroughly evaluated by specific research designed to discover the causes and methods of prevention of physical or psychological harm, both short term and long term. While physiological addiction has not been reported with psychedelic substances, psychological dependence might be expected if the experience were continually repeated. The intense subjective pleasure and enjoyment of the experience for its own sake could lead to escapism and withdrawal from the world. An experience which is capable of changing motivation and values might cut the nerve of achievement. Widespread apathy toward productive work and accomplishment could cripple a society. Another possible danger might be suicide or prolonged psychosis in very unstable or depressed individuals who are not ready for the intense emotional discharge. If it can be determined that any of these forms of harm occur in certain types of individuals, research could be directed toward the development of pre-test methods to screen out such persons. Our evidence would suggest that research on conditions and methods of administration of the drugs might minimize the chance of harmful reactions. Spectacular immediate advance must be sacrificed for ultimate progress by careful, yet daring and imaginative, research under adequate medical supervision.

The ethical implications also cannot be ignored. Any research which uses human volunteers must examine its motives and methods to make certain that human beings are not being manipulated like objects for purposes which they do not understand or share. But in research with powerful mental chemicals which may influence the most cherished human functions and values, the ethical problem is even more acute. The mystical experience, historically, has filled man with wondrous awe and has been able to change his style of life and values; but it must not be assumed that greater control of such powerful phenomena will automatically result in wise and constructive use. Potential abuse is just as likely. Those who undertake such research carry a heavy responsibility.

This is not to say that research should be stopped because of the fear of these various risks in an extremely complex and challenging area which has great promise for the psychology of religion. But while research is progressing on the theoretical or primary level and before projects for testing useful social applications in a religious context become widespread, serious and thoughtful examination of the sociological, ethical and theological implications is needed without delay.

Not the least of these implications is the fear that research which probes the psyche of man and involves his spiritual values may be a sacreligious transgression by science. If the exploration of certain phenomena should be prohibited, should the mystical experiences made possible by psychedelic drugs be one of the taboo areas? Such restrictions raise several relevant questions. Who is wise enough to decide in advance that such research will cause more harm than good? If such restrictions are applied, where will they end and will they not impede knowledge of unforeseen possibilities? This attitude on the part of religion is not new. Galileo and Servetus encountered it hundreds of years ago. The issue should not be whether or not to undertake such research, but rather how to do so in a way which sensitively takes into consideration the contribution, significance, and values of religion. A better scientific understanding of the mechanisms and application of mysticism has the potential for a greater appreciation and respect for heretofore rarely explored areas of human consciousness. If these areas have relevance for man's spiritual life, this should be a cause for rejoicing, not alarm. If the values nurtured by religion are fundamental for an understanding of the nature of man, then careful and sensitive scientific research into the experiential side of man's existence has the potential for illumination of these values. The importance of such research should be emphasized, especially because of its possible significance for religion and theology.

At present we are a long way from legitimate social use of such drugs in our society. We do not yet have nearly enough adequate knowledge of the long-term physiological or psychological effects. It is true that thus far no organ or tissue damage has been reported in the usual dosage range, and physiological addiction has not occurred. But as in the case of any new drug, deleterious side effects sometimes do not become apparent until years after a drug has been introduced. The social suffering caused by the misuse of alcohol is a major public health problem throughout the Western world. We certainly need to hesitate before introducing a new agent, much more powerful than alcohol and perhaps with a potential for the development of subtle psychological dependence. And yet, paradoxically, these very drugs may hold a promise for the treatment of chronic alcoholism by way of the psychedelic mystical experience (Kurland, Unger and Shaffer, 1965; Kurland *et al.*, 1966; Unger, 1965). Such questions can only be satisfactorily answered by thorough scientific research of the possibilities and by sober evaluation of the results.

Many unknown conscious and unconscious factors operate in the mystical experience. Much investigation is needed in this area, and drugs like psilocybin can be a powerful tool. Experimental facilitation of mystical experiences under controlled conditions can be an important method of approach to a better understanding of mysticism. Better understanding can lead to appreciation of the role and place of such experiences in the history and practice of religion.

If parapsychology is concerned in an interdisciplinary way with the question of the potentials of human experience, then the controlled exploration of experimental mysticism, facilitated by psychedelic drugs, is an important parapsychological research area where psychopharmacology, psychiatry, psychology and theology can meet to mutual advantage.

References

JAMES, W. (1935), *The Varieties of Religious Experience*, Longman.

KURLAND, A. A., UNGER, S., and SHAFFER, J. (1965), 'The psychedelic procedure in the treatment of the alcoholic patient – a research program at the Spring Grove State Hospital', paper presented to the Second Conference on the Use of LSD in Psychotherapy, Amityville, NY, 8–10 May 1965, and published in the *Conference Proceedings*, 1966, Bobbs-Merrill.

KURLAND, A. A., UNGER, S., SHAFFER, J., SAVAGE, C., WOLF, S., LEIHY, R., and MCCABE, O. L. (1966), 'Psychedelic therapy (utilizing LSD) in the treatment of the alcoholic patient: a preliminary report', unpublished paper presented to meeting of the American Psychiatric Association at Atlantic City, N.J.

OSMOND, H. (1957), 'A review of the clinical effects of psychotomimetic agents', *Ann. N.Y. Acad. Sci.*, vol. 66, pp. 418–34.

PAHNKE, W. N. (1963), 'Drugs and mysticism: an analysis of the relationship between psychedelic drugs and the mystical consciousness', Ph.D. thesis, Harvard University.

PAHNKE, W. N. (1966), 'The contribution of the psychology of religion to the therapeutic use of the psychedelic substances', paper presented to the Second Conference on the Use of LSD in Psychotheraphy, Amityville, N.Y., published in the *Conference Proceedings*, Bobbs Merrill.

SCHULTES, R. E. (1963), 'Botanical sources of the new world narcotics', *Psychedelic Rev.*, vol. 1, no. 2, pp. 145–66.

STACE, W. T. (1960), *Mysticism and Philosophy*, Lippincott.

UNGER, S. (1965), 'The current status of psychotherapeutically-oriented LSD research in the US', unpublished paper presented to the New York State Psychological Association, Annual Convention, Grossinger, N.Y., 30 April.

WASSON, R. G. (1963), 'The hallucinogenic fungi of Mexico: an inquiry into the origins of the religious idea among primitive peoples', *Botanical Museum Leaflets, Harvard University*, vol. 19, no. 7, pp. 137–62. Also in *Psychedelic Rev.*, vol. 1, no. 1, 1963, pp. 27–42.

25 R. K. Wallace

Physiological Effects of Transcendental Meditation

R. K. Wallace, 'Physiological effects of transcendental meditation',
Science, 1970, no. 167, pp. 1751–4.

For thousands of years philosophers have held that it is possible
for man to attain 'higher' states of consciousness through
meditation techniques. At present, scientists are investigating the
physiological changes that take place during some of these
practices and the practical applications that they may have.

During the practice of various techniques of meditation, expert
Zen monks decreased their rate of respiration, oxygen consumption and spontaneous galvanic skin response (GSR),
and their pulse rate and blood pH showed a slight increase
(Akishige, 1968). The electroencephalograph (EEG) record was
predominantly alpha-wave activity (even with eyes half open).
The alpha waves progressively increased in amplitude and
decreased in frequency, and occasional theta activity was noted.
When repeated trials of click stimulation were given, there was no
habituation of the alpha blocking response (Kasamatsu and
Hirai, 1966). Studies of autonomic functions in 'practitioners of
yoga' in India showed a lower breath rate, an increase in skin
resistance, and no consistent changes in heart rate and blood
pressure during various practices (Bagchi and Wenger, 1957;
Wenger and Bagchi, 1961; Wenger and Anand, 1961). The electro-
encephalogram of yogis during meditation showed an increase
in alpha-wave amplitude and activity, and in a few of the yogis
studied there was a loss of the alpha blocking response to all
external stimuli (Anand, Chhina and Singh, 1961).

Investigators have reported difficulty in obtaining expert
practitioners of meditation and in taking measurements in a
way that did not interfere with the subjects' contemplative or
concentrative efforts (Wenger and Bagchi, 1961). Transcendental
meditation as taught by Maharishi Mahesh Yogi was investigated
for the following reasons. (i) It is claimed by the proponent that
all practitioners immediately experience beneficial physiological
changes (Mahesh Yogi, 1966, pp. 180–209). (ii) Subjects report

that the technique is easy and enjoyable and does not involve concentration, contemplation, or any type of control, and that they therefore find no difficulty in meditating during the experiment. (iii) A large number of subjects were readily available who had received consistent and uniform instruction through an organization that specializes in teaching this technique.

The technique is defined as 'turning the attention inwards towards the subtler levels of a thought until the mind transcends the experience of the subtlest state of the thought and arrives at the source of the thought' (Mahesh Yogi, 1969, p. 470). The technique involves no suggestion, mental control or physical manipulation (Mahesh Yogi, 1966, pp. 50–59). The instruction is given personally by a teacher qualified by Maharishi Mahesh Yogi. The technique is normally practiced twice a day for periods of fifteen to twenty minutes; during the practice the subject sits in a comfortable position with eyes closed.

A sample of fifteen 'normal' college students (that is, with no mental or physical disabilities), whose practice of the technique had ranged from six months to three years, was arbitrarily selected. Each subject sat quietly with eyes open for five minutes and then with eyes closed for fifteen minutes; he meditated for thirty minutes, continued to sit with eyes closed for ten minutes, and then sat with eyes open for five minutes. Oxygen consumption was measured in nine of the subjects by either the open- or closed-circuit methods (Benedict and Benedict, 1933; Consolozio, Johnson and Pecora, 1963, pp. 1–30). In both cases a large mouthpiece and low resistance nonrebreathing valve were used. In the closed-circuit system air was circulated by an airtight pump operating at 10l per minute. A 6 or 13l Collins respirometer was used to record changes, and O_2 was added periodically to keep the mixture of air slightly above ambient oxygen concentration.

In the open system, gas was collected in a Collins 120l Tisot spirometer, and samples were analysed in triplicate with a Beckman Physiological Gas Analyzer Model 160. The electrocardiograph (ECG) tracing and skin resistance were recorded by a Grass Model 5 polygraph, and the EEG tracing was recorded by a Grass Model 6 electroencephalograph. Beckman silver–silver chloride and Beckman gold-plated electrodes were used. The GSR electrodes were placed across the palm, and the EEG electrodes were placed according to the international 10–20 system at F_p1, C_z, T3, P3, O1, and O2. Recordings were monopolar, with the reference electrode attached to the opposite ear and a ground over the mastoid bone. The E E G recordings were made on an Ampex Model FR1300 tape recorder, digitized by the Data Processing Laboratory of the Brain Research Institute at U C L A, and then submitted to the U C L A Health Science Computer Facility for spectrum analysis by the BMDX92 program. In several of the E E G studies, sound and light stimulation were given at irregular intervals (varying from 20 to 120 sec) to test habituation of alpha blocking.

Oxygen consumption, measured by either the open- or closed-circuit methods, decreased in all subjects within 5 mins after the onset of meditation. The mean decrease was about 45 cm^3/min, or about a 20 per cent decrease from the control period. Oxygen consumption remained low during meditation and rose toward the resting level after meditation (see Figure 1 and Table 1). In measurements made by the open-circuit method there was a mean decrease in total ventilation during meditation of about 11 min.

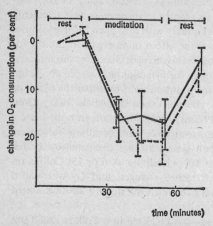

Figure 1 Percentage of change in O$_2$ consumption during control and meditation periods. Each point represents the average change in O$_2$ consumption. The first point was taken as zero per cent change. and all other points are calculated as differences from it. The dotted line represents the mean change in four subjects measured by the open-circuit respiration system. The solid line represents the mean change in five subjects measured by the closed-circuit respiration system. Only nine of the fifteen subjects were tested for O$_2$ consumption changes. The error bars are equal to twice the standard deviation

The respiratory quotient (the ratio of the volume of CO_2 eliminated over the O_2 consumed) was in the basal range and did not change significantly throughout the experiment (Table 1). The observed decrease in total ventilation was caused by either decreased frequency of breath or tidal volume, varying from subject to subject.

Table 1 **Physiological changes during transcendental meditation. The values given represent the mean for all subjects tested. The resting values are typical for normal subjects (24)**

Time sequence	O_2 consumption (cm^3/min)	Respiratory quotient	Minute ventilation (l/min)	Skin resistance (kilohm)
Resting				
10	246·8	0·86	5·90	91·2
20	244·4	0·87	7·56	101·2
Meditation				
35	208·1	0·84	5·25	205·0
45	201·9	0·85	5·28	188·8
55	200·8	0·85	5·55	180·1
Resting				
70	233·1	0·86	5·94	80·2

Skin resistance increased markedly at the onset of meditation, with some rhythmical fluctuations during meditation; it decreased to the resting value after meditation (Table 1). Electrocardiogram recordings were taken on only five subjects. The heart rate of each of the subjects decreased during meditation, with a mean decrease of five beats per minute.

Before meditation, with eyes closed, all subjects showed alpha activity. During meditation the regularity and amplitude of the alpha waves increased in all subjects. In four of the subjects, the alpha waves occasionally changed to a slower alpha wave frequency and in some cases stopped for 2 to 5 min periods and low-voltage theta waves predominated. A time history of alpha-wave intensity (mean square amplitude) for one subject who showed the characteristic increase in alpha-wave activity and the common long trains of theta activity is shown in Figure 2. In almost all subjects, alpha blocking caused by repeated sound or light stimuli showed no habituation. After meditation, regular alpha activity continued when eyes were closed, and irregular alpha activity developed when eyes were open.

There are certain aspects of the respiration equipment that may have caused unwanted side effects and minimized the findings. In the open-circuit system there was a dead space of 120 ml (due to the large non-rebreathing valve and large mouthpiece). This large dead space, coupled with inadequate circulation, could have produced an increase of CO_2 in the dead space, thus stimulating breathing and possibly increasing O_2 consumption. During the rest period the circulation was probably adequate to eliminate most of the excess CO_2, but during meditation, with decreased frequency of breath or tidal volume, it is possible that excess CO_2 periodically built up and stimulated breathing. Respiration during meditation may also have been hindered by the large collection of moisture in the non-rebreathing valve after an hour of continuous use. Despite possible difficulties caused by the

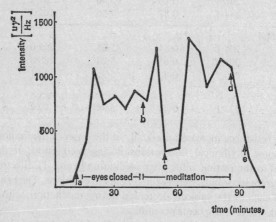

Figure 2 A time history of the intensity (mean square amplitude) of an alpha frequency (9 Hz) for one subject. The intensity was calculated from E E G recordings taken from monopolar lead in the occipital region (C). The alpha frequency of 9 Hz was selected as the most characteristic for this subject because it showed the largest alpha-wave amplitude. This subject showed the characteristic increase in alpha-wave intensity and the less common 2 to 5 minute fall in alpha activity. The 2 to 5 minute period, denoted by arrow c, showed predominantly low-voltage theta activity. Before arrow a the subject's eyes were open; from arrow a to arrow b his eyes were closed. Between arrow b and arrow d the subject was practicing transcendental meditation. At arrow d the subject stopped meditating and kept his eyes closed until arrow e

equipment, the physiological changes recorded during meditation indicate a significant and reproducible decrease in oxygen consumption and metabolic rate.

During sleep there is also a decrease in metabolic rate; the reported decrease in mean O_2 consumption during sleep varies with each investigator (Robin, Whaley, Crump and Travis, 1958; Kreider and Iampietro, 1959; Benedict and Carpenter, 1910, pp. 179–87; Grollman, 1930). These values range from about 20 to 10 per cent, three of them showing less of a decrease over a full night's sleep than that which occurs during 30 mins of transcendental meditation.

The patterns of skin resistance changes during sleep (Tart, 1967; Hawkins, Puryear, Wallace, Deal and Thomas, 1962) are also different from those seen during meditation. In individuals in whom there is a maintained increase in skin resistance during sleep (Tart, 1967), the magnitude and steepness of change is generally less than the change that occurs during meditation.

The EEG pattern during meditation clearly distinguishes this state from the sleeping state. There are no slow (delta) waves or sleep spindles, but alpha-wave activity predominates. A few of the subjects showed EEG patterns similar to those found by Kasamatsu and Hirai in expert Zen meditators (1966). These patterns, which are characterized by large-amplitude alpha waves, by a tendency for the alpha waves to decrease in frequency, and by occasional periods during which alpha activity stops and low-voltage theta activity predominates, are similar to the EEG activity seen in the transition from wakefulness to sleep (Fiske and Maddi, 1961). However, this transitional period of drowsiness is usually short and followed by sleep spindles, slow waves, and the loss of consciousness (Fiske and Maddi, 1961). Kasamatsu and Hirai interpret the Zen monks' EEG pattern and the non-habituation of their alpha blocking response as a 'special state of consciousness in which the cortical excitatory level becomes lower than in ordinary wakefulness but is not lowered as in sleep and yet outer and inner stimulus is precisely perceived with steady responsiveness' (1966). Since this type of EEG pattern was only seen occasionally in four of the subjects, it cannot be said at present whether these subjects were drowsy or in the state postulated by Kasamatsu and Hirai.

The physiological state attained in transcendental meditation is different from states induced by hypnosis or autosuggestion. Conflicting studies characterize hypnotic sleep by either an increase, a decrease, or no change at all in heart rate, blood pressure, skin resistance, and respiration rate (Jana, 1967; Gladfelter and Gonik, 1963; Kleitman, 1963, pp. 329–38; Barber, 1961; Whitehorn, Lindholm, Fox and Benedict, 1932; Jana, 1965). The results of these studies and others indicate that the physiological changes induced during hypnosis vary in the same way as in different emotional states observed during wakefulness. Hypnotic sleep following the suggestion of complete relaxation produces no noticeable change in O_2 consumption (Kleitman, 1963; Barber, 1961; Whitehorn, Lindholm, Fox and Benedict, 1932; Jana, 1965). Many different EEG patterns have been reported during hypnosis, but most are identical with wakefulness patterns and all appear to be different from the patterns observed during meditation (Kleitman, 1963).

Recent evidence suggests that conditioning procedures can also alter autonomic functions and EEG patterns (Hart, 1968; Miller, 1969; Katkin and Murray, 1968). A subject can increase his alpha-wave activity through auditory and visual feedback (Hart, 1968). By instrumental techniques animals can learn to control their heart rate, blood pressure, and some endocrine secretions (Miller, 1969). Studies on humans have produced some evidence that heart rate, GSR and blood pressure can be controlled, but the practical application of such procedures needs further investigation (Katkin and Murray, 1968). Expert practitioners of some meditation processes have been found to have some control over certain 'involuntary' physiological functions (Akishige, 1968; Kasamatsu and Hirai, 1966; Bagchi and Wenger, 1957; Wenger, Bagchi and Anand, 1961; Anand, Chhina and Singh, 1961). Although some of these changes could have practical applications, research has been negligible, owing to the difficulty and impracticality of teaching these processes.

The fact that transcendental meditation is easily learned and produces significant physiological changes in both beginners and advanced students gives it certain advantages over other, more austere techniques. Physiologically, the state produced by transcendental meditation seems to be distinct from commonly encountered states of consciousness, such as wakefulness, sleep and dreaming, and from altered states of consciousness, such as hypnosis and autosuggestion. Subjective reports coupled with the physiological measurements reported above suggest that this state might have applications to clinical medicine. Transcendental meditation has been reported to have practical therapeutic value in relieving mental and physical tension (Vanselow, 1968). Its value in the alleviation of drug abuse has been suggested, and its value in controlling arterial blood pressure is being investigated (Benson, 1969). It could also have other applications – for instance, in space travel and in certain diseases where extended periods of low oxygen consumption that are simultaneous with responsive mental activity would be very useful.

References

AKISHIGE, Y. (1968), *Bull. Fac. Lit. Kyushu Univ.*, vol. 11, p. 1.
ANAND, B. K., CHHINA, B., and SINGH, B. (1961), *EEG clin. Neurophysiol.*, vol. 13, pp. 452.
BAGCHI, B. K., and WENGER, M. A. (1957), *EEG clin. Neurophysiol.*, vol. 7, p. 132.
BARBER, T. X. (1961), *Psychol. Bull.*, vol. 58, p. 390.
BENEDICT, F. G., and BENEDICT, C. G. (1933), *Mental Effort in Relation to Gaseous Exchange, Heart Rate, and Mechanics of Respiration*, Carnegie Institution of Washington.
BENEDICT, F. G., and CARPENTER, T. M. (1910), *The Metabolism and Energy Transformations of Healthy Man during Rest*, Carnegie Institution of Washington.
BENSON, H. (1969), *N. Engl. J. Med.*, vol. 281, p. 1133.
CONSOLOZIO, F., JOHNSON, R. E., and PECORA, L. J. (1963), *Physiological Measurement of Metabolic Functions in Man*, McGraw-Hill.
FISKE, D. W., and MADDI, S. R. (eds.) (1961), *Functions of Varied Experience*, Dorsey, p. 145.
GLADFELTER, J. H., and GONIK, U. (1963), *Tex. Rep. Biol. Med.*, vol. 21, p. 534.
GROLLMAN, A. (1930), *Amer. J. Physiol.*, vol. 95, p. 274.
HART, J. (1968), *Psychophysiol.*, vol. 4, p. 506.
HAWKINS, D. R., PURYEAR, H. B., WALLACE, C. D., DEAL, W. B., and THOMAS, E. S. (1962), *Science*, vol. 136, p. 321.
JANA, H. (1965), *J. appl. Physiol.*, vol. 20, p. 308.
JANA, H. (1967), *Indian J. med. Res.*, vol. 55, p. 591.
KAMIYA, J. (1967), *Psychol. Today*, vol. 1, p. 56.
KASAMATSU, A., and HIRAI, T. (1966), *Folia psychiat. neurol. Jap.*, vol. 20, p. 315.
KATKIN, E. S., and MURRAY, E. N. (1968), *Psychol. Bull.*, vol. 70, p. 52.
KLEITMAN, N. (1963), *Sleep and Wakefulness*, University of Chicago Press, rev. edn.
KREIDER, M. B., and IAMPIETRO, P. F. (1959), *J. appl. Physiol.*, vol. 14, p. 765.
MAHESH YOGI, M. (1966), *The Science of Being and Art of Living*, International SRM, London, rev. edn.
MAHESH YOGI, M. (1967), *Maharishi Mahesh Yogi on the Bhagavad-Gita: A New Translation and Commentary*, Penguin.
MILLER, N. E. (1969), *Science*, vol. 163, p. 434.

ROBIN, E. D., WHALEY, R. D., CRUMP, C. H., and TRAVIS, D. M. (1958), *J. Clin. Invest.*, vol. 37, p. 981.

TART, C. T. (1967), *Psychophysiol.*, vol. 4, p. 35.

VANSELOW, K. (1968), *Hippokrates*, vol. 39, p. 462.

WENGER, M. A., and ANAND, B. K. (1961), *Circulation*, vol. 24, p. 1319.

WENGER, M. A., and BAGCHI, B. K. (1961), *Behav. Sci.*, vol. 6, p. 312.

WHITEHORN, S. C., LINDHOLM, H., FOX, E.L., and BENEDICT, F. G., (1932), *New Eng. J. Med.*, vol. 206, p. 77.

26 K. G. Magni

The Fear of Death: Studies of its Character and Concomitants

K. G. Magni, 'The fear of death: studies of its character and concomitants', in *Death and Presence*, Lumen Vitae, 1971, vol. 5, pp. 129–42.

It is clear that psychologists and sociologists are becoming increasingly interested in studying fear of death. Good accounts of recent investigations have been presented by Ariés (1967), Lester (1967) and Templer (1970). Until now this trend of research has hardly reached the Scandinavian countries.

An examination of the American research projects conducted since the American Psychological Association's 1956 symposium on death and dying and the publication of Feifel's work (1959) does not, however, give the impression that the question has been attacked radically and systematically. Recently scientists have constructed instruments, more or less developed into scales, for measuring various attitudes toward death, and in particular the fear of dying. This is already an advance when one recalls that until now this area had been almost entirely dominated by phenomenological considerations. But we still have to ask ourselves *what researchers have set out to measure* under the heading 'fear of death', *how this concept can escape the confusion* created by its use in popular speech, what *the convergence or the divergence* of the results obtained from the various scales of measurement really signify, and finally what relations emerge between the level of *manifest fears* and that of *latent anxiety*.

These four questions have been borne in mind throughout the investigations which we have pursued during the past three years and will now attempt to outline in this article. Our few preliminary results concern the correlations between the measures provided by three 'fear of death' scales (already published in the United States) and those obtained by what we believe to be an original method of assessing latent anxiety through the time required for the correct perception of pictures illustrating death.

Methodological reflections

Fear of death has numerous potential meanings: interest in the subject varies considerably, depending on whether one is a psychiatrist, a doctor, a surgeon or a pastor. Each of these professions has its own reasons for hoping that the human sciences will provide fuller descriptions and more accurate analyses of the sufficient and necessary conditions for this reaction in the person who is confronted by death or turns his thoughts to it.

But our psychological knowledge of this attitude is still very rudimentary. It has hardly progressed beyond the 'verbal' level, in other words that of common speech. Fear of death is a non-technical term and the layman intuitively believes that he grasps its meaning. But it is not certain that it can be of use to psychological research without undergoing a few transformations of a technical order.

In our view, these transformations follow a step by step procedure corresponding to three ascending degrees of formalization:

1. At first, attitudes toward death are readily accepted as an object of study whose identity and independence are supposedly established. In this case, investigators devise a 'theory of reactions to death' as if they were dealing with a circumscribed entity and before having made any attempt to study it in the global context of general behavior.

2. Assuming that they are willing to discuss these reactions to death within a wider system of behavior, they none the less maintain that this object of study *per se* is one that can usefully be studied separately and in isolation.

3. The ultimate goal should be to envisage this category of reactions on the basis of more fundamental formulations. Although it is not certain that psychology is yet sufficiently mature to avail itself of such formulations, it is to be hoped that sooner or later it will be adequate for the task.

Whatever may be said of the latter objective, we cannot disregard the necessity of examining, even with verbal realities as our starting-point, to what extent our observations tally with the assumptions of the first two steps. Here we are calling the present stage, in which we use scales of measurement formulated in terms of current speech, the 'exploratory' stage. At this preliminary stage, 'fear of death' is an expression that seems to have a specific identity, as one speaks of a child's 'fear of the dark' or 'fear of being left on his own'.

But for the scientific psychologist, a concept like 'fear of death' is a *construct*, a hypothetical model. And his initial task would precisely consist in verifying the unity and validity of this construct. The present investigation envisages three basic tasks:

1. First, the 'scales' devised up to this date do not seem to derive from theoretical notions or a well-defined vocabulary. For example, should we not differentiate between 'fear of death' and 'death anxiety'? And having made this distinction, how should we define death-phobia (or phobias)? Moreover, if we speak of death anxiety should we not make a further distinction between the *state* of anxiety and the (permanent) *trait* of anxiety? Lazarus (1966), Levitt (1968) and Spielberger (1966) have published important discussions on this theme of anxiety as distinct from fear or phobias, and their reports are relevant to our subject. But so far research in this area is incomplete.

2. Second, the degree of correlation between the various observations already made has not been given enough study so far. To discover the degree of 'overlap' between the various measures would be a means of discriminating between the various theories.

The notion of *convergent and discriminant validity* (Campbell and Fiske, 1959) is of special importance here, as well as the methodological observations further proposed by Campbell (1960), Jackson (1969) and Kahn (1968).

We should note, however, that the study of the 'fear of death' is here complicated by the fact of two defence systems whose importance has been demonstrated by Byrne (1961, 1965): *repression* is a defence mechanism used by one type of personality to thrust away anxiety-provoking thoughts or feelings; whereas *intellectualization*, *projection* and *reaction formation* are defence mechanisms used by another type of personality who becomes particularly *sensitized* to anxiety-arousing themes, is fond of discussing them, and feels no apparent need to repress them. Eriksen and Davids (1955) have established a high correlation (0·92) between this type of personality (know as *Pt*, or psychasthenic, in the MMPI test) and results obtained from the Taylor manifest anxiety scale (MAS).

One might expect the 'repressors' to behave very differently from the 'sensitizers' in their response to verbal fear of death scales. And to use samples representing a so-called 'normal' population would risk permanently concealing tendencies that would none the less be extremely divergent.

3. Finally, although certain investigators like Boyar (1964), Lester (1966), Spilka (1963) and Templer (1970) have recently attempted to multiply correlational studies and experimental tests, much still remains to be done in order to ensure that the various measures really apply to the 'construct' of death anxiety and to discover why they entail discrepancies in the results. In our view, questions particularly requiring further study are the interactions between various levels of anxiety, and the correlations between these levels and verbal or social behavior. It is easy to undertake 'wild and undisciplined experiments' in this field, but it is only by establishing theoretically correct and empirically founded hypotheses that investigators can follow a fruitful path of research.

Fear of death: correlation between scales

When we began our investigations in 1968, three instruments for assessing the conscious fear of death provided elementary technical guarantees:

1. *The Lester scale for 'measuring attitudes toward death' (LATD)*. Constructed and analysed in 1966, this scale 'for measuring attitudes toward death' comprises twenty-one propositions whose scale *value* operates along a 'favorability–unfavorability' continuum. Examples:
'Death comes to us as a comfort' (*Value:* 2·81).
'Death is a great mystery' (*Value:* 5·58).
'Death is the final and worst insult to man' (*Value:* 10·19).

This scale has a reliability of 0·58 (with an interval of six weeks). The results showed no statistically significant association either with the idea that dying would be a distressing experience or with the fact of believing in an after-life. However, the results of those who affirmed that they believed in God showed a more favorable attitude toward death (probability = 0·025).

2. *Boyar's questionnaire, the 'fear of death scale' (FODS)*. Elaborated in 1964, this list of eighteen propositions was compiled from sentences noted during interviews on the fear of death, then selected and reformulated by several judges in order to render each proposition suitably unambiguous. This question-

naire requires the respondent to indicate agreement or disagreement with a graded series of six propositions by marking a cross against them.

'Cemeteries leave me fairly indifferent.'

'The thought of an early death has never disturbed me.'

'I find the thought of being buried after my death very distasteful.'

The answers have a reliability of 0·79 (with an interval of ten days).

The internal consistency of the propositions was 0·89.

Validation was obtained by asking two groups, of which one had seen a film on road accidents, to answer the questionnaire twice. An appreciable increase in the 'fear of death' measured by the questionnaire 'was found only in the group who had seen the film.'[1]

3. *The questionnaire devised by Kalish we are calling the 'Kalish death anxiety scale' (K D A S)* although, in fact, it comprises sixteen propositions related to diverse themes: abortion, euthanasia, capital punishment, war, fear of death, birth control, belief in an after-life, and belief in God. This research (1963) involves only two propositions on the 'fear of death', but reveals interesting relationships between variables that are not usually compared (e.g. belief in God, or in an after-life, and agreement with capital punishment).

Sample

For our first test, we obtained the cooperation of fifty-three student nurses preparing for their diploma at the Uppsala School of Nursing. In connection with the experimental procedure described below, these students were asked to answer the three questionnaires we have just discussed, as well as the hysterical (*Hy*) and psychasthenia (*Pt*) subscales of the *Minnesota Multiphasic Personality Inventory* (M M P I) and Allport's series of propositions (adapted by Feagin, 1964) for distinguishing two types of religiosity: the extrinsic and the intrinsic.

1. It should be noted that Templer (1970) has recently constructed and validated a 'death anxiety scale' (D A S) whose interesting features are its conciseness (fifteen propositions) and avoidance of propositions that might induce 'socially desirable' answers (cf. the Marlowe–Crowne Social-Desirability Scale, 1960). There is a high correlation (0·74) between the D A S and the F O D S. One may therefore assume that the F O D S is also free of 'social desirability' as a response-distorting factor.

Table 1 Intercorrelations between death scales with their correlations to MMP 1 scales and extrinsic–intrinsic religiosity scales

Scale	LATD	FODS	KDAS
LATD		0·43**	0·00
FODS	0·00		0·45**
KDAS	0·04		0·45**
Type of personality (MMPI)			
Hy scale	0·09	0·25	0·38**
Pt scale	0·38**	0·69**	0·41**
Type of religiosity (Feagin)			
Extrinsic	0·37**	0·27*	0·37**
Intrinsic	0·38**	0·09	0·21

Table 1 shows the various correlations observed. The correlations significant at the 0·05 level are indicated by a single asterisk (*) and those significant at the 0·01 level by a double asterisk (**).[2]

Comments

1. The results obtained from the Lester scale (LATD) and the Boyar scale (FODS) are significantly related. This is also the case with the FODS and the Kalish questionnaire (KDAS). But there is no correlation between the LATD and the KDAS.

This last fact lends itself to various interpretations. We are already aware that the FODS showed a high correlation with Templer's recent scale (DAS), and that the latter avoids questions capable of inducing 'socially desirable' answers. One might therefore surmise that the FODS is equally free of this response-distorting factor. Since the factor of social desirability has never been controlled for the LATD and the KDAS, it might intervene, to some extent, in the differences observed. But a special point to be considered is the reduced variability of the responses, due to the fact that our population is a restricted and very homogeneous sample. However, since the publications relating to these scales make no comment on the variation typically found

2. With a total of fifty-three subjects, a correlation of 0·27 is significant at the 0·05 level, and a correlation of 0·35 is significant at the 0·01 level.

for the samples, this theoretically plausible explanation cannot be developed further at this stage.

To sum up, our preliminary study reveals no perfect similarity in the range of responses provoked by these three scales. In examining our other correlations, we have therefore retained all three as scales of measurement.

2. Earlier in this article we referred to the interesting hypothesis whereby subjects tending to repress anxiety-provoking themes (the so-called *'repressors'*) react very differently to propositions of the 'fear of death' scales from subjects (known as *'sensitizers'*) who attempt to avoid anxiety by using other defense mechanisms, such as intellectualization, projection and reaction formation. And we mentioned in this connection that high scores on the subscales *Hy* and *Pt* of the MMPI would be useful indications when it comes to distinguishing the 'repressors' (*Hy*) from the 'sensitizers' (*Pt*).

On this basis, one could predict that answers establishing a high 'fear of death' score would be given *more frequently* by the *Pt* (non-repressed 'sensitizers'), whereas the *Hy* (or 'repressors') would correlate negatively with this means of detecting 'fear of death'. A glance at Table 1 shows that this hypothesis is perfectly supported so far as the LATD and the FODS are concerned. The measures obtained from the KDAS behave differently (showing a high correlation for the *Hy* and *Pt* group alike), but, as we have already pointed out, the KDAS cannot be regarded as a system of propositions exclusively oriented toward the 'fear of death', and it is theoretically understandable that here the *Hy* would hardly bring their repressive tendencies into play.

3. When Allport suggested a distinction between two types of religious style and experience (1958), he devised a questionnaire (with twenty-one propositions in the Feagin version, 1964) aimed at distinguishing the adherents of an *extrinsic* religion from those of an *intrinsic* religion. For the first type, religion confers a sense of status and security, and therefore serves a hollow function; but among the second, it is far more internalized, being successfully integrated with the personality and regarded as an end in itself.

On this basis, it could be predicted that the group characterized by *extrinsic* religiosity would manifest a *greater* fear of death, whereas the one distinguished by *intrinsic* religiosity would correlate *negatively* with the same scales. A glance at Table 1 effectively confirms this supposition: markedly significant differences are revealed when the 'fear of death' is assessed by means of the LATD and the FODS. Here again, the KDAS produces differently oriented results, probably for the reasons we have already surmized.

By bringing to light unsuspected relationships between the scores obtained from the scales of *manifest* (or manifested) fear of death and certain personality traits, these few results prompted us to pursue our investigations with the object of assessing *latent* anxiety by means of a method whose main features we will now outline.

Latent death anxiety: an experimental technique

In an article published some years ago on the role of the environment during growth, Hebb (1955) stressed that the more intelligence develops, the more the individual becomes affectively vulnerable. Hebb suggested that in the adult, culture acts as a protective factor, enabling him to conceal his emotive weaknesses more successfully than a five-year-old child. He even maintained that 'a man's emotional stability depends more on *his capacity for effectively avoiding emotional provocations* than on his other personality traits'. Civilized man would be increasingly incapable of protecting himself against real environmental dangers precisely through his inability to recognize them.

This idea of 'successful avoidance', accompanying a system of taboos regarding all death-related things, has provided us with a simple hypothesis, which we are formulating as follows:

If a stimulus suggestive of death is presented it will take longer to be recognized than a neutral stimulus or a series of stimuli not suggestive of death.

Various other hypotheses (or corollaries of the basic hypothesis) would also lend themselves to experimental confirmation. To mention two of these: (a) the simultaneous presence of a 'cheerful' stimulus and a 'death' stimulus will retard the perception of the latter; (b) recent events can sensitize subjects to a swifter perception of the death stimulus.

We should add that in research which we are now pursuing, approximately twelve death stimuli, together with 'cheerful' or 'neutral' stimuli, largely confirm these hypotheses. Here we are only commenting on the results immediately relating to the 'fear of death' revealed by the verbal scales, according to the two types of personality and religiosity already described in the first part of this article.

Apparatus

A projector equipped with a special hydrogen gas lamp and connected to an electric chronometer. Slides were projected on a screen at a distance of five metres from the projector, and shown from 0·04 to seven full seconds, according to the procedure described below.

Pictures

A 'neutral' picture of the English Garden in Munich and a picture of death, showing the mutilated face of a man killed in an accident.

Procedure

The fifty-three student nurses were invited to come, in two successive groups, to the lecture-room of the School of Nursing where we had installed a screen. Each respondent was given a random number to be retained throughout the experiment, so that all answers should be anonymous. Each group knew that it was cooperating in an experiment on perception. The light was dimmed in order to facilitate dark-adaptation.

The first group was shown a neutral picture of the English Garden in Munich, which was projected for 0·04 seconds. After three seconds, the light was half switched on to enable the respondents to write down what they had seen on the screen and to indicate their degree of certainty. For this purpose they were given special leaflets.

When they had filled in these leaflets, the light was switched off and the same picture was projected again, but now for an interval of 0·06 seconds. After this, the subjects were asked to wait for three seconds then to fill in another leaflet bearing their number, but without being told that the same picture had been projected again. We continued in this way, showing a series of flashes with increasing exposure times: 0·08, 0·1, 0·3, 0·5, 0·7 and so on, up to seven full seconds.

The same procedure was used for the second group, but in this case we showed the picture of the 'dead man', with the same gradual increase in exposure time.

Then, five minutes after the end of the first series, we showed each group the picture that it had not seen so far, projecting each picture and gradually increasing the exposure time as before.

Finally, when they had rested for at least ten minutes, the

members of each group were asked to fill in the various scales and questionnaires mentioned above; this work took about fifty minutes. The respondents then wrote their number on each of these leaflets and in this way it was later possible to relate each respondent's scores on the fear of death scales to her answers on the exposure-time leaflets, while respecting her anonymity.

Assessment of the correlations

Having used for each subject the necessary exposure time in milliseconds required for a correct perception of the 'neutral' picture or the picture of the 'dead man', we had to establish correlations with the scores obtained from the other methods of measurement, for example the 'extrinsic' religiosity scores on the Allport–Feagin scale. We discovered that, when plotted on a graph, the scores thus obtained by each of the methods produced a curve if the values were assessed in milliseconds, but a line if we used the logarithm of these values. Moreover, this index of correlation gives the same result whether it is established by starting from the logarithm of the values in milliseconds, or from the logarithm of the values of 'extrinsic' religiosity. The two variables can be reversed without statistical inaccuracy.

Comments

Table 2 shows that very different relationships were established between the variables already shown in Table 1 when these are compared with the *latent times* required for the perception of the 'death' picture. It equally shows that the *latent times* required for the perception of the 'neutral' picture introduce no differential correlation.

Although the threshold of significance (0·27) is rarely reached, one notes that several relationships are reversed when compared to those of Table 1.

First, in Table 2 the latent times correlate *negatively* with the 'fear of death' scores on all the scales, LATD, FODS and KDAS (a very significant difference, at the 0·01 level, when compared with FODS). A very significant correlation (−0·37 in Table 2) therefore indicates that latent anxiety about death, increasing the time required for the perception of the disturbing picture, is generally stronger in subjects who reveal less fear of death in the verbal scales.

Second, *contrary to what occurred in the verbal scales*, one notes that the *Pt* of the MMPI correlates negatively with latent

Table 2 Correlations between measures of the latent time required for the perception of a 'death' picture and a 'neutral' picture, compared with measures relating to 'fear of death' assessed by verbal scales, to M M P I personality traits and to extrinsic–intrinsic religiosity (Allport–Feagin)

	Log. ms for the 'death' picture	Log. ms for the 'neutral' picture
Scales		
LATD	−0·26	0·02
FODS	−0·37**	0·00
KDAS	−0·26	0·03
Traits		
MMPI – *Hy*	0·24	0·03
MMPI – *Pt*	−0·28*	0·01
Religion		
Extrinsic	0·22	0·03
Intrinsic	−0·12	0·04

times for perception. The mechanisms of intellectualization would therefore enable the high *Pt* to decrease their subjects' latent anxiety, yet lead them to be more articulate about their preoccupations with death in their answers to the verbal scales. For the *Hy* subjects, on the other hand, the mechanism of repression, whereby anxiety-provoking thoughts are avoided, would not appear to be effective at the level of latent anxiety.

Finally, the subjects for whom religion is 'extrinsic' continue to maintain a positive, but weaker, relationship with the latent time (the correlation has become non-significant: 0·22), whereas the 'intrinsic' subjects continue to maintain a negative, but much weaker, relationship with the latent time (non-significant correlation: −0·12).

The latter observation doubtless warrants the conclusion that the interesting correlations noted between the two types of religiosity and the 'fear of death' scores mainly concern the manifest (and manifested) level of that fear, and not the phenomena of latent anxiety as revealed by the longer interval required for the correct perception of the 'death' stimulus.

In short, *the phenomenon of successful avoidance* of the 'death' stimulus presented in short flashes is an observable manifestation: it is *distinct from the other observations* provided by the verbal scales and is capable of enriching our knowledge of general *or* specific death anxiety.

Summary and conclusion

We have analysed certain conditions of future research on 'the fear of death', our aim being to progress beyond the purely verbal stage and to establish the validity of these 'constructs' or cultural entities.

In outlining our research, we have shown that the correlations between the three scales of measurement warrant the conclusion that the objects measured are not identical. We have discovered the importance of two types of personality (the 'repressors' and the 'sensitizers', respectively known as *Hy* and *Pt* in the M M P I questionnaire) and have confirmed that they have very different ways of responding to the verbal 'fear-of-death' scales. The religious psychologist in particular will doubtless have been struck by certain significant relationships between two types of religiosity (extrinsic–intrinsic) and the manifest fear of death. Finally, we have suggested a procedure, based on the successful avoidance (or increased latency time) of the perception of a 'death' stimulus and have discovered new relationships between this measure, which manifests a latent attitude, and the measures previously observed. Latent anxiety is thus revealed in numerous subjects who, on the verbal scales, do not seem markedly affected by the fear of death. These are but a few preliminary indications and points of reference for future research. We believe that by multiplying the systems of observable relationships it will be possible to make a truly scientific study of the identification (or distinction) between general anxiety and death anxiety. It might eventually be possible to speak of 'death anxiety'. A failure to establish that death anxiety or fear of death have characteristics different from general anxiety would be regarded with satisfaction. And although Templer's recent findings (1970) seem discouraging in this respect, we will continue to adopt this working hypothesis until such time as accumulated empirical observations, factorially analysed, oblige us to abandon it.

References

ALLPORT, G. (1958), *The Nature of Prejudice*, Doubleday.

ARIÉS, P. (1967), 'La mort inversée. Le changement des attitudes devant la mort dans les societés occidentales', *Archiv. europ. sociol.*, vol. 8, pp. 169–95.

BOYAR, J. I. (1964), 'The construction and partial validation of a scale for the measurement of the fear of death', Ph.D. thesis, University of Rochester (N.Y.).

BRÄNNSTRÖM, A., CARLBERG, A. L., and HOLMLUND, M. (1969), 'Risktagning och dess samband med personlighetsvariabler', Unpublished Ms. Department of Psychology, University of Uppsala.

BYRNE, D. (1961), 'The repression–sensitization scale: rationale, reliability and validity', *J. Personality*, vol. 29, pp. 334–49.

BYRNE, D. (1965), 'Repression–sensitization as a dimension of personality', in B. Maher (ed.), *Progress in Experimental Personality Research*, Academic Press.

CAMPBELL, D. T. (1960), 'Recommendations for APA test standards regarding construct, trait or discriminant validity', *Amer. Psychol.*, vol. 15, pp. 546–63.

CAMPBELL, D. T., and FISKE, D. W. (1959), 'Convergent and discriminant validation by the multitrait, multimethod matrix', *Psychol. Bull.*, vol. 56, pp. 81–105.

CESAREC, Z., and MARKE, S. (1968), *Mätning av psykogena behon med froge formulärsteknik*, Stockholm, Skand., Testforlaget.

CROWNE, D. P., and MARLOWE, D. (1960), 'A new scale of social desirability independent of psychopathology', *J. consult. Psychol.*, vol. 24, pp. 349–54.

ERIKSEN, C. W., and DAVIDS, A. (1955), 'The meaning and clinical validity of the Taylor Anxiety Scale and the hysteria–psychasthenia scales from the MMPI', *J. abnorm. soc. Psychol.*, vol. 50, pp. 135–7.

FEAGIN, J. R. (1964), 'Prejudice and religious types: focused study of Southern fundamentalists', *J. sci. Study Religion*, vol. 4, no. 1, pp. 3–13.

FEIFEL, H. (1959), *The Meaning of Death*, McGraw-Hill.

GUSTAFSSON, B. (1965), *Religionssociologi*, Stockholm, Sv. Bokforlaget.

HEBB, D. O. (1955), 'The mammal and his environment', *Amer. J. Psychiatry*, vol. 111, pp. 826–31.

JACKSON, D. N. (1969), 'Multimethod factor analysis in the evaluation of convergent and discriminant validity', *Psychol. Bull.*, vol. 72, no.1 pp. 30–49.

KAHN, S. B. (1968), 'An internal criterion of test validity', *Psychol. Reports*, vol. 22, pp. 1145–52.

KALISH, R. A. (1963), 'Some variables in death attitudes', *J. soc. Psychol.*, vol. 59, pp. 137–45.

LAZARUS, R. S. (1966), *Psychological Stress and the Coping Process*, McGraw-Hill.

LESTER, D. (1966), 'A scale measuring attitudes toward death: its consistency, validity and use', Unpublished Ms. Brandeis University.

LESTER, D. (1967), 'Experimental and correlational studies of the fear of death', *Psychol. Bull.*, vol. 67, no. 1, pp. 27–36.

LEVITT, E. E. (1968), *The Psychology of Anxiety*, Staples Press.
ROYCE, J. R. (1963), 'Factors as theoretical constructs', *Amer. Psychol.*, vol. 18, pp. 522–8.
SPIELBERGER, C. D. (1966), 'Theory and research on anxiety', in C. D. Spielberger (ed.), *Anxiety and Behavior*, Academic Press.
SPILKA, B., DAILEY, K. A., and PELLEGRINI, R. J. (1963), 'Religion, American values and death perspectives', Conference given to the Congress of the Religious Research Association Columbus, Ohio, 1968; published in *Sociological Symposium*, no. 1, Western Kentucky University Press.
TEMPLER, D. I. (1970), 'The construction and validation of a death anxiety scale', *J. gen. Psychol.*, vol. 82, pp. 165–77.
UNDERWOOD, B. J. (1957), *Psychological Research*, Appleton-Century Crofts.

Part Seven
Pathological and Possibly Related States

Questions about the relationships between religion and
personality are commonly asked of psychologists. They have
been investigated either by finding correlations between measures
of personality and of religion, or by investigating the
characteristics of criterion groups, including those whose
behaviour has become disturbed. Early theories of personality
were based on the classifications of abnormal behaviour, and
responses to the forms of religion were assimilated to these
classifications. This approach led to a general assumption that
religious behaviour is a form of abnormality.

While specific relationships between religion and abnormal
states give little insight to the patterns of normal behaviour,
they help to define the limits of abnormal involvement, and so
can lead to studies of the positive effects of religion. But it is
easier to identify narrowing and destructive effects than to
assess how religion can liberate people and focus adjustment.
Allport's concept of an intrinsic religious orientation has
facilitated some analysis of the constructive aspects of religion,
but this is still an area that is yet to be fully opened up. Further
development through the use of well agreed measures and of
recognized markers is also needed, as well as a more sensitive
analysis of the relationships between different measures, and a
continued application of general theories to religious material
and to the members of religious groups. More detailed studies
of the ways in which religion fits the life styles of individuals,
especially to assess constancy and change in religious patterns
with the aim of differentiating the social from the personal
factors involved, are also required.

27 G. Stanley

Personality and Attitude Correlates of Religious Conversion

G. Stanley, 'Personality and attitude correlates of religious conversion',
Journal for the Scientific Study of Religion, 1964, vol. 4, no. 1, pp. 60–63.

It has been shown in a number of studies that about 30 per cent of religious people report a more or less sudden conversion experience, while the others become gradually more religious as a result of social influences (Argyle, 1958). Religious conversion has often been considered to be caused by a type of temporary neurotic condition, resolution of which results in the establishment of a 'new life'. Definitions of the term 'conversion' generally emphasize this aspect, e.g.:

A genuine religious conversion is the outcome of a crisis. Though it may occur to persons in a variety of circumstances and forms, and though we may find many preparatory steps and long-range consequences, the event of conversion comes to focus in a crisis of ultimate concern. There is in such conversion a sense of desperate conflict in which one is so involved that his whole meaning and destiny are at stake in a life-or-death, all-or-none significance (Johnson, 1959).

To be converted ... (is) the process, gradual or sudden, by which a self hitherto divided, and consciously wrong, inferior and unhappy, becomes unified and consciously right, superior and happy, in consequence of its firmer hold upon religious realities (James, 1929, p. 186).

Hypothesis 1: There is a negative correlation between neuroticism and religious conversion, i.e. people who report conversion tend to have a lower neuroticism score than people who are not converted.

Sargent, in a monograph dealing with the mechanics of indoctrination, brain-washing and thought control, has likened religious conversion to an hysteric neurotic breakdown. Accepting a Pavlovian model to explain differences in breakdown, he considers that 'among the readiest victims of brain-washing or religious conversion may be the simple healthy extravert' (1957).

Hypothesis 2: There is a positive correlation between extraversion and religious conversion.

The religious beliefs of parents have been shown to relate

positively to the subsequent beliefs of their children (Putney and Middleton, 1961). Since religious beliefs are inculcated as part of the general socialization process, it is likely that in those homes where religion is a strong influence they will tend to be emphasized, with a resulting greater likelihood of acceptance on the part of the children (undoubtedly, acceptance-rejection is related to child training in a complex way) (McGann, 1959).

Those who have a strong religious background would have been inculcated with religious beliefs over a long period of time and hence would be less likely to have had a conversion experience, except perhaps where such an experience manifests itself in an institutionalized form (e.g. heightened religious experience at Confirmation). Presumably people who are converted to religion are not likely to have had a strong religious background (Argyle, 1958, p. 62).

Hypothesis 3: There is a negative correlation between the amount of parental religious belief and religious conversion.

Festinger (1957) has produced a theory of personality and attitude functioning based upon the reduction of 'cognitive dissonance': after making decisions people tend to indulge in activities which confirm the wisdom of making that decision and to avoid suggestions or communications indicating that they were wrong. Hence on the basis of this theory one would expect people who have made a definite decision in favour of religion to develop a closed mind in relation to dissonant attitudes and beliefs. Rokeach (1960) has produced an operational measure of closedmindedness (the Dogmatism Scale) which has been shown to differentiate among groups of religious believers.

Hypothesis 4: There is a positive correlation between dogmatism and religious conversion.

Religious groups who hold beliefs which are somewhat incompatible with the general socio-cultural milieu would be expected to manifest a greater incidence of conversion experience among their adherents than other groups (Festinger, Riecken and Schachter, 1956). Fundamentalists accept a very literalistic view of the Bible, a view incompatible with most modern scholarship, both sacred and secular, and thus may be expected to report more conversions than other religious groups. Moreover as they take the Bible literally they may also be more concerned with its commands to convert than liberal believers.

Hypothesis 5: There is a positive correlation between fundamentalism and religious conversion.

Method

Sample

The results to be reported were obtained from questionnaires administered to 347 Australian theological students representing eight different Christian denominations. Questionnaires were completed by the students of ten theological seminaries under supervision of the college authorities who returned them to the author for processing.

The measures

Ss were administered the extraversion and neuroticism scales of the Maudsley Personality Inventory, Rokeach's Dogmatism Scale and measures of conversion, parental religious belief and fundamentalism. The conversion item was:

Of the following please check the statement which most nearly describes your own experience:

(a) I consider that my present religious commitment is a gradual outgrowth of many years of religious instruction and training and that I cannot point to any single event in my life which wrought a definite change from unbelief to belief ( ).

(b) Although there was a time in my life when I had no religious belief, the change from unbelief to belief has been a gradual one ( ).

(c) Although I have always held some religious beliefs I can vividly recall the occasion when I became more vitally committed to these beliefs ( ).

(d) There was a time in my life when religion had no interest for me and I can attribute my present religious commitment to a distinct point in my life at which I made a definite decision in favour of religion ( ).

If the student checked (a) and/or (b) he was called 'non-converted'; if he checked (c) and/or (d) he was called 'converted'.

For purposes of assessing parental religious belief, the S was asked to check two items:

On the whole would you say that your father was

very religious
religious
indifferent to religion
antagonistic to religion
very antagonistic to religion
(*Underline which one applies*)

The second item was identical except that 'mother' was substituted for 'father'. Each item was scored from 0 to 4 (4 representing high religiosity) and a combined score for the two items obtained by addition.

The fundamentalist item was a direct question about the literal truth of the Bible and has been reported elsewhere (Stanley, 1963).

Which one of these two statements most closely represents your own belief? (*Please pick one statement only*.)

(a) I believe in a God to whom one may pray for help, but I do not believe that every word of the Bible should be accepted as literal truth ( ).

(b) I believe in a God to whom one may pray for help and I believe that all of the Bible is divinely inspired and literally true ( ).

People checking item (b) were classified as fundamentalists.

Analysis

Biserial correlations between converted/non-converted and the personality variables and a tetrachoric correlation between the converted/non-converted and fundamentalist/non-fundamentalist were computed.

Results

Table 1 lists the correlations obtained between conversion and the personality and attitude variables.

The correlations are significant and in support of the five hypotheses under consideration. Thus there is a tendency for the converted theological student to be more extraverted, to have a lower neuroticism score (less emotionally unstable?), to be more dogmatic and to come from a less religious home than the non-converted theological student and to be conservative and literalistic in his religious beliefs.

Discussion

A certain degree of caution must be exercised in the interpretation of the results. The correlations are small, although statistically significant because of the large sample used. The correlations between the measures used are similar to those obtained in validation studies and do not suggest the operation of any obvious response bias.

The present findings may be interpreted as supportive of the theories from which the hypotheses were derived. Further research is needed with groups of laity in order to determine the extent to which the results may have been attenuated by sampling factors.

Summary

From a review of the psychological literature on conversion five hypotheses were proposed:

1. There is a negative correlation between neuroticism and religious conversion.

2. There is a positive correlation between extraversion and religious conversion.

3. There is a negative correlation between amount of parental religious belief and conversion.

4. There is a positive correlation between dogmatism and religious conversion.

5. There is a positive correlation between fundamentalism and religious conversion.

These hypotheses were tested on 347 theological students on the basis of their replies to a questionnaire containing the N & E scales of the MPI, Rokeach's D Scale and conversion, parental religious belief and fundamentalism measures. All were confirmed at the 5 per cent level or better. However it was pointed out that the study should be viewed as suggestive rather than definitive: replications with groups of laity are necessary to determine the generality of the results.

Table 1 **Correlations between conversion and personality and attitude variables**

	C	N	E	P	D	F
Conversion (C)	1·00	0·15**	0·11*	0·34**	0·19**	0·33**
Neuroticism (N)		1·00	0·02	0·01	0·26**	0·04
Extraversion (E)			1·00	0·02	0·05	0·20**
Parental Belief (P)				1·00	0·03	0·00
Dogmatism (D)					1·00	0·58**
Fundamentalism (F)						1·00

*$p > 0.05$.
**$p > 0.01$.

References

ARGYLE, M. (1958), *Religious Behaviour*, Routledge & Kegan Paul.

FESTINGER, L. (1957), *A Theory of Cognitive Dissonance*, Harper & Row.

FESTINGER, L., RIECKEN, H. W., and SCHACHTER, S. (1956), *When Prophecy Fails*, University of Minnesota Press.

JAMES, W. (1929), *The Varieties of Religious Experience*, Modern Library.

JOHNSON, P. E. (1959), *Psychology of Religion*, Abingdon Press.

MCGANN, R. U. (1959), 'An empirical study of religious change', *Acta Psychol.*, vol. 15, pp. 510–11.

PUTNEY, S., and MIDDLETON, R. (1961), 'Rebellion, conformity and parental religious ideologies', *Sociometry*, vol. 24, pp. 125–35.

ROKEACH, M. (1960), *The Open and Closed Mind*, Basic Books.

SARGENT, W. (1957), *Battle for the Mind*, Pan.

STANLEY, G. (1963), 'Personality and attitude characteristics of fundamentalist theological students', *Austral. J. Psychol.*, vol. 15, pp. 121–3.

28 O. S. Walters

Religion and Psychopathology

O. S. Walters, 'Religion and psychopathology', *Comprehensive Psychiatry*,
1964, vol. 101, no. 5, pp. 24–35.

Religious faith and practice play a tremendous role in the patterning of the emotional life, the thinking, and the behavior of men.
After declaring this fact, an authoritative psychiatric body
advises the psychiatrist to look most seriously at religion and
learn to take it adequately into account in understanding and
treating sick men (*Psychiatry and Religion*, 1960).

Religion and psychopathology are not infrequently found
together. Religious preoccupation in incipient psychosis is well
known. Religious ideas may also be interwoven with neurosis.
This occasional mingling of religion and pathology makes it
important that the psychiatrist be able to differentiate between
normal and pathologic in religious expression.

Starbuck, one of the earliest students of the psychology of
religion, stated the need of criteria for differentiating between
normal and pathologic.

The value of the study of persons in groups is that it *establishes certain
standards by which to judge individual instances*. To have well-established
types by which to estimate religious phenomena is as important in the
sphere of spiritual things as to have standards of distance in physics and
astronomy, or laws and principles and formulas in mathematics and
chemistry. It is of even greater importance, inasmuch as the data are
intangible (1906, p. 409).

Many students of personality deny the possibility of drawing a
definite distinction between normal and pathologic. Jahoda's
review (1958) recognizes the difficulty of finding a basis for
agreement on the concept of mental health but acknowledges
that the individual's relation to reality is an essential criterion.

Starbuck was aware of the difficulty of establishing criteria of
normality.

No two persons will agree upon the limit at which normal religious experiences pass over into pathological. Where the line of demarcation

will fall depends largely on one's general attitude toward religion, and on one's temperamental attitude toward human experiences, which allows them a wide or narrow range. There are the alienists, too, who are constantly on the lookout for some abnormal tendency, and, consequently, are sure to find it (p. 163).

Varieties of religious psychopathology

The best known study in the psychology of religion is William James's *Varieties of Religious Experience* (1902). James described his Gifford Lectures as 'a laborious attempt to extract from the privacies of religious experience some general facts which can be defined in formulas upon which everybody may agree' (p. 433). After passing in review a large number of widely diverse personal histories, he undertakes 'to reduce religion to its lowest admissible terms' as a basis for broad agreement upon the validity of religious experience (p. 503). James concludes, 'I only translate into schematic language what I may call the instinctive belief of mankind: God is real since he produces real effects' (p. 517).

James had no interest in differentiating between normal and pathologic in religious expression. In the process of cooking down religious experience to determine its essential components, he made no effort to screen out the atypical and bizarre to eliminate the influence of psychopathology upon the final result. Instead, he took as his major premise, 'If there were such a thing as inspiration from a higher realm, it might well be that the neurotic temperament would furnish the chief condition of the requisite receptivity' (p. 25).

Those 'best able to give an intelligible account of their ideas and motives', James contended (p. 3), are the 'religious geniuses' who have invariably been 'creatures of exalted emotional sensibility', subject to melancholy, obsessions, trances, voices, visions and 'all sorts of peculiarities which are ordinarily classed as pathological' (p. 7). Frankly acknowledging his study as a 'pathological programme' (p. 21) James asserts that 'in the psychopathic temperament we have the emotionality which is the *sine qua non* of moral perception (p. 25). . . . We learn most about a thing when we view it. . . in its most exaggerated form. This is as true of religious phenomena as of any other kind of fact' (p. 39). The essence of religious experience, he insists, is most prominent in those which are most one-sided, exaggerated and intense (p. 45).

This selective bias which granted a higher order of authenticity to the more extreme forms of religious expression sprinkled James's pages with psychopathology. These 'violenter' examples were by no means essential to the fulfillment of his objective. He acknowledges in introducing one of the more ordinary of his documents, 'Probably thousands of unpretending Christians would write an almost identical account' (p. 70). James himself asks, 'Why not leave pathological questions out?' In answer, he pleads his own irrepressible curiosity and the dubious premise that a thing is better understood in its exaggerations and perversions (p. 21).

James's logic was sound up to the point of selecting his data. Since religion reports what claim to be facts, it is only proper to examine the evidence. The objective truth of the experience will hinge upon the reliability of the reports (pp. 507, 509). At this point James begged the question of reliable reporting by enunciating the premise that psychopathology enhances capacity for religious insight and interpretative authority.

James was immediately criticized by Starbuck, according to Perry (1935), because the examples he selected were too extreme (p. 346). Pratt stated flatly that 'the great majority of those possessing dissociated mind states have none of the superiorities set forth by James .... The highest type of man, in the religious life as well as elsewhere, is the unified and rational self' (1944, p. 67).

The idea that genius is linked with insanity and creativity with illness has been closely examined by Kubie (1954). Taking sharp issue with Freud and many others who have held this view, he concludes, 'No critical studies exist which would make of such claims anything more than superficial and somewhat dubious guesses' (p. 3). Rather, Kubie finds, the processes of illness corrupt, mar, distort and block as the creative potential of the preconscious is captured, imprisoned, nullified, sterilized and stereotyped by unconscious neurotogenic forces (pp. 52, 141). He speaks of 'the insidious, destructive influence of the neurotic process' which arises out of deeper levels of conflict and pain (pp. 13, 55). 'The unconscious is our straitjacket', Kubie writes, 'rendering us as stereotyped and as sterile and as repetitive as the neurosis itself.' He asks, 'Can there be wisdom even about the objective world around us (considering how many distorting fantasies we project onto this outer world) in the absence of wisdom about the inner world from which these projections arise?' (pp. 132, 143).

The indiscriminate mingling of reports of religious experience tainted by psychopathology with the experiences of normal persons has tended to stigmatize the whole as pathological. James himself foresaw this possible consequence when he recognized that in using extreme examples 'we may thereby swamp the thing in the wholesale condemnation which we pass on its inferior congeners' (p. 22).

The terms 'sick soul' and 'healthy-minded' coined by William James at first appear to designate categories signifying the presence or absence of psychopathology in religious experience, and have come to be used extensively in this way. However, those who use the terms to convey such meaning have stopped short of grasping James's intention. As his thesis develops, James acknowledges at length that these categories are 'somewhat ideal abstractions' that do not exist in fact. 'The concrete human beings whom we oftenest meet', he recognized, 'are intermediate varieties and mixtures' (p. 167).

From this point of view, the contrasts between the healthy and the morbid mind, and between the once-born and the twice-born types ... cease to be the radical antagonisms which many think them.... In many instances it is quite arbitrary whether we class the individual as a once-born or a twice-born subject (p. 488).

Indeed, James understood at first hand the lability inherent in these categories; his biographer acknowledges, 'James had his times of healthy-mindedness and his times of soul-sickness, and he knew both.... There were deeper alternations of mood.... Oscillation ... is profoundly characteristic of James's nature' (Perry, 1935, pp. 671, 680).

James recognized the inadequacy of 'healthy-mindedness' as a way of meeting life and accepted the cogency of the ascetic view. 'Healthy-mindedness pure and simple can hardly be regarded by any thinking man as a serious solution.... Asceticism must, I believe, be acknowledged to go with the profounder way of handling the gift of existence' (p. 364). This personal affirmation of faith is supplemented by the statement of Perry that James himself experienced 'a feeling of renewed life similar to that of the twice-born' (1935, p. 324).

Religion and psychopathology in Freud

Like James, Freud had a far-reaching influence upon the psychology of religion. His views on religion are still commonly found in close association with the thought and practice of psychoanalysis.

(1960, p. 208). Boisen rests his theory upon deep personal conviction, even though he has not found any clear-cut instances where psychotics have risen to a higher level than before (1936, pp. 114, 115). The idea that psychosis is a potentially constructive, essentially religious process is a theme that runs through all of Boisen's writings.

One group friendly to Boisen's theory believes that psychosis may throw some new light upon normative religious experience. Boisen has actively promoted this idea in his writings (1936), declaring that some persons have emerged from such experiences with new insights. Their eyes have been opened to unsuspected meanings (p. 192), hence mental patients have much to tell us about religion (1954, p. 53).

Clark appears to accept Boisen's idea, asserting that 'schizophrenia in its catatonic form may actually favor the facing and thinking through of issues' (1958, p. 344). Oates, a pupil of Boisen's, reflects a somewhat similar view:

The mentally sick person quite often has religious ideas that comment meaningfully upon the sickness of his culture. His own personal grasp of religious reality bursts through the duplicities ... therefore, the illness itself may have a prophetic element in it.... Oriental reverence of the mentally ill as being a bit closer to God at times than other people has just enough truth in it as a superstition to persist in one's own primitive awareness (1955, pp. 99, 100).

Hiltner, also a former pupil of Boisen's, believes that 'We are beginning to catch up to the depth of Boisen's original insights' (1959, p. xii). Mowrer (1962), reviewing his own experience, agrees with Boisen that psychosis 'may ultimately provide the basis for a firmer grasp upon reality'. However, Boisen's view of schizophrenia as a religious process that may inform the psychology of religion begs the question of whether the religious experience of a psychotic is commensurable with that of normal persons, and whether the individual with abnormal perception and thought processes may give a reliable account of spiritual reality.

The most important characteristic of the schizophrenic is impairment of reality testing. However great the distortion produced by neurosis, the neurotic patient does retain his essential orientation to reality. In contrast, the schizophrenic has difficulty in distinguishing between fantasy and reality. His thinking may become illogical and disconnected, with impaired associative activity. Often he is beset by delusions. In addition to his defective thought processes, he is frequently unable to interpret external events correctly because he is the victim of abnormal perceptions. Therefore, the schizophrenic cannot be depended upon for reliable reports. His bizarre thinking and hallucinatory perceptions frequently lead to grotesque distortion of reality.

Schizophrenia is often studied by attempting to assemble or reconstruct prepsychotic patterns and to correlate these with psychotic productions and symptoms. This process may lead to the inference that the two are not only continuous, but they stand in the relation of cause and effect. Upon this *post hoc* judgement rests the theory that schizophrenia has a psychogenic etiology.

Boisen not only assumes such an origin for schizophrenia, but regards the condition as an essentially valid religious process, citing the schizophrenic's 'sense of mystery ... ideas which he had never before heard and with which he himself seemed to have nothing to do ... feeling themselves in touch with some mighty personal force they call God' (1936, pp. 169, 170).

This approach not only assumes that the psychotic shares a common ground of religious experience with normal people but also that schizophrenic reports of religious reality are trustworthy, and that they may enlarge the religious understanding of normal persons. Since the reality testing of most schizophrenics is not reliable, there seems to be no reason for considering their religious observations any more valid than their other reports of reality.

Lowe (1953) concluded after studying a series of patients with religious delusions that religious preoccupation was an aftermath of severe personality disturbance, not its cause, and represented severe anxiety rather than truly religious mystical experience.

Bleuler's classic monograph records religious ideation and delusion among schizophrenic patients, but not as a common or prominent feature of the disease. Factors looked upon as causes of the disease are often its consequences, Bleuler believes, if there is any connection between them at all (1950, p. 345).

Bleuler emphasizes the fact that the schizophrenic is going through 'thousands of peculiar experiences' with his abnormal perceptions, delusions and fantasy. If he retains any residue of healthy logic, the psychotic is constrained to construct 'explanation-delusions' (p. 131) to justify his deviant thinking and behavior. Bleuler noted that schizophrenics refer abnormal perceptions to whatever complex may happen to be in the foreground of their interest (p. 133). He found, for example, that schizophrenics with previous religious inclination tended to have religious delusions, and doubted whether such delusions ever appear in those without previous religious interest. He acknowledged the possibility that such delusions might arise in persons not religiously inclined originally, but stated, 'as yet this has not been proven to me' (p. 391).

Bleuler acknowledged that some patients seem to be better after an acute schizophrenic illness than before, but regarded their insight as defective since the connection between the pathological experiences and the 'improved' ego is lacking (p. 257). He was never able to substantiate the evidence for a full, complete rectification of schizophrenic delusional ideas. 'As yet', Bleuler wrote, 'I have never released a schizophrenic in whom I could not still see distinct signs of the disease' (p. 256).

Both Boisen (1936) and Hiltner (1959) deprecate Starbuck's insistence upon a distinction between normal and pathologic. Hiltner states that Starbuck refused to concede a religious label to abnormal phenomena. The inclusion of persons with defective reality testing is bound to give a distorted view of modal religious experience. The schizophrenic's impaired perception and association does not bar him from participating in religious worship, but to incorporate the reports of his experience into a normative psychology of religion is comparable to treating the responses of the schizophrenic to questions about bodily functions as illuminating human physiology, or his comments on a meal as contributing to our understanding of nutrition.

The idea that religious symptoms in schizophrenia are the consequence of premorbid religious concern is supported by Boisen's own life history. In his autobiography he traces clearly the strong religious influence of his family and early environment (1960, pp. 34, 38). Premorbid religious concern is also traced clearly in the histories of five VA hospital schizophrenics with religious concern in the series described below, corroborating Bleuler's view.

Cultural factors in religious concern

Cultural influence may be responsible for changes observed in the incidence of religious concern among schizophrenics. Boisen's long-time interest in the religious implications of schizophrenia has provided an accumulation of mental hospital data that extends over a considerable period of years. Studying the incidence of religious symptoms in one series of 173 schizophrenic patients, most of whom were chronically ill, Boisen found that 42·8 per cent had no religious concern, 51·4 per cent had moderate, and 5·8 per cent had marked religious concern. Religion was incorporated in the patient's delusional system in nine patients or 5·2 per cent (p. 51).

In a later series of seventy-eight patients, most of whom were schizophrenic, Boisen found religious concern accentuated in 35·9 per cent, while unaffected in 64·1 per cent. Over a longer period, Boisen (1952) has observed that about 10 per cent of newly admitted schizophrenics are likely to have some sense of mystical identification.

A somewhat similar study was made of sixty-eight state hospital patients by a group of theological students under the direction of Oates (1954, p. 88). Over half of these patients showed an absence of religious concern. An additional 20·6 per cent had very little, if any, religious concern in the prepsychotic experience, but turned to religion as a 'last straw' measure.

Southard (1956), a hospital chaplain, made a similar survey of 170 state hospital patients, based upon his own admission interviews. Two-thirds of these patients showed no interest in religion.

The present author tabulated religious concern found in the psychiatric examination of 105 unselected patients admitted to the acute intensive treatment service of a VA neuropsychiatric hospital over a two-year period.

Diagnoses were distributed as follows:

Schizophrenia	37
Psychoneuroses	34
Personality disorders	29
Chronic brain syndrome	4
Psychotic depression	1
	105

Of the 105 patients, 7 or 7·7 per cent manifested religious concern. Two of these were diagnosed as anxiety reaction and five as schizophrenic reaction. Considering schizophrenic patients separately, five or 18·5 per cent of the thirty-seven displayed religious concern. The great majority of those psychiatric patients showed neither religious symptoms nor concern.

Klaf and Hamilton (1961), in a comparison of schizophrenic symptoms in the nineteenth and twentieth centuries, were struck by the fact that religious preoccupations were three times more common in the earlier period than now. They deprecate the view that analysis of schizophrenic symptoms is likely to illuminate the cause of the illness and believe that if contemporary psychoanalysts had been considering patient material of the mid-nineteenth century, they would have been forced to consider religious disturbance as a prime factor in the etiology of schizophrenia. Klaf and Hamilton are convinced that both the religious and the sexual preoccupation of the schizophrenic are culturally determined. Tracing the strong religious influence that pervaded nineteenth century England, they conclude:

Small wonder then, that the schizophrenics of the period were preoccupied with religion, when nearly every other member of the society was. It does not seem strange that a mid-nineteenth century adult, having been trained to flee the fires of Hell since childhood, should hear God's voice and fear His retribution after developing a schizophrenic illness. Or, to draw an analogy, that may or may not be far-fetched, the mid-twentieth century adult, exposed to our society's preoccupation with sex, may be expected to develop sexual preoccupations during a schizophrenic illness. We wish to point out that such preoccupations may be culturally determined. Looking for the aetiology of schizophrenic illness in a detailed analysis of religious and/or sexual delusions or hallucinations appears to be a futile search.

A similar cultural transition may be seen in the non-religious explanations invoked by the schizophrenic to account for his abnormal sensations and perceptions. Tausk (1933 edn) in 1918 gave a classic description of the 'influencing machine' so common in the schizophrenic's delusional system. Tausk's patients attributed their changed thoughts and feelings to machines utilizing invisible wires, electricity, magnetism or X-rays. Visual hallucinations were often blamed upon the effects of a 'magic lantern'. Tausk concluded, 'With the progressive popularization of the sciences, all the forces known to technology are utilized to explain the functioning of the apparatus.' The continuing popularization of science has indeed brought a corresponding change in schizophrenic explanation-delusions. Radio, radar and TV are now commonly invoked to account for contemporary hallucinations and abnormal thought processes.

Religion in a context of health

Psychology of religion has become preoccupied with psychopathology. Clinical pastoral training has been permeated extensively by psychoanalytic psychology and has been strongly influenced by the view of its founder, that schizophrenia is a religious process. When William James enlarged religious experience to include religious pathology, and Freud extended psychopathology to include religion, the boundaries between normal and pathologic were submerged in the process. In consequence, the psychology of religion has come to appear as a melange of health and disease without reliable criteria to tell which is which.

No such dilemma exists. Both psychoanalytic and operational criteria have been offered. Kubie (1954) holds that conduct is neurotic when the unconscious dominates and is normal when the conscious–preconscious alliance is dominant. Redlich (1952) states that the extremely abnormal, both psychotic and severely neurotic, can usually be clearly recognized by both lay and expert. He proposes the 'social agreement' that leads to psychiatric treatment as an operational approach to the concept of normality, whether it comes through external pressure or voluntary private arrangement. DeSanctis asserts that 'mental pathology almost invariably offers criteria by which we can distinguish the morbid case from the individual who is not morbid' (1927, p. 203).

Zilboorg acknowledged the importance of differentiating abnormal from normal when dealing with religious problems, but asserted that what goes on in the human mind has been learned mostly through psychopathology. The normal cannot be observed directly, he contends, but must be reconstructed from the pathologic (1962, p. 64). This would reverse the usual order, in which the abnormal is identified as such by its discordance with a broadly based standard previously established as a norm. Zilboorg's logic would construct the baseline by using deviations from the baseline.

It is true that the normal is not likely to be seen in the consulting room. Psychoanalysis has always been vulnerable to the criticism that its observations are made or its inferences drawn upon sick persons who are paying for treatment. The heuristic role of the analyst has always been limited by the psychopathology of the patient and the expectation of improvement implied by the treatment contract. Observations upon religion made in the one-to-one relationship are subject to distortion by the analyst himself, as well as by the psychopathology of the patient.

The factors that make for health and stability in personality should be studied in the healthy and stable where they are operative, not in the sick where they are absent or inoperative. Freud acknowledged that religion has a stabilizing influence upon human personality but his speculative explanatory theories hardened into categorical declarations without his ever having turned toward this stable group in serious empirical investigation.

Increasing collaboration between psychiatry and religion has brought the clergyman and the psychiatrist closer together. Programs of clinical training have made the minister better acquainted with mental illness in its various forms. But there has not been any comparable movement to acquaint psychiatry with religious experience in its healthy expressions.

Many psychiatrists have submitted without protest to the mandatory act of faith in Freudian principles required for initiation into psychoanalysis, who would reject any religious affirmation of faith or refuse any formal affiliation with the church. By this disaffection, psychiatrists who are frequently obliged to make authoritative discrimination between normal and pathologic religious elements in personality are shut off from a comparable acquaintance with religion in its constructive and wholesome expression in normal persons.

Elsewhere I have emphasized the value of collaboration between clergyman and psychiatrist (Walters, 1958, 1960) and the necessity of supplanting concepts of religion formulated in a context of psychopathology by an understanding of religion viewed in a context of health (Walters, 1961). If such collaboration is to grow into a broad relationship of mutual respect and confidence, it is important to correct a perspective that is presently deeply tinctured with the pathological.

Summary

As the psychology of religion has given increasing attention to psychopathology, a blurring of the boundary between normal and pathologic has occurred. Current psychiatric attitudes toward religious experience have been based upon generalizations drawn from patients or populations altered by psychopathology.

Evidence is adduced to indicate that defective reality testing invalidates the religious ideation of the schizophrenic patient as a source of illumination for normative religious experience. Neurosis also distorts religious experience and vitiates data for inclusion in studies of normative religious phenomena.

The incidence of religious symptoms in schizophrenia is relatively low and has declined in this century. There is evidence that such symptoms are culturally determined. Their occurrence appears to be a function of previous religious interest in the life of the patient.

Discrimination between normal and pathologic by the psychiatrist requires an acquaintance with normative religious expression.

References

BLEULER, E. (1950), *Dementia Praecox*, International Universities Press.
BOISEN, A. (1936), *The Exploration of the Inner World*, Harper & Row.
BOISEN, A. (1952), 'The Genesis and significance of mystical identification in cases of mental disorder', *Psychiat.*, vol. 15, p. 287.
BOISEN, A. (1954), *Religion and Crisis in Custom*, Harper & Row.
BOISEN, A. (1960), *Out of the Depths*, Harper & Row.
CLARK, W. H. (1958), *The Psychology of Religion*, Macmillan Co.
DESANCTIS, S. (1927), *Religious Conversion*, Routledge & Kegan Paul.
FREUD, S. (1924), 'Obsessive acts and religious practices', *Collected Papers*, vol. 2, Hogarth Press.
FREUD, S. (1949), *The Future of an Illusion*, Liveright.
GINSBURG, S. W. (1953), 'Concerning religion and psychiatry', *Child Study*, vol. 30, no. 12.
HILTNER, S. (1959), 'The psychological understanding of religion', in O. Strunk (ed.), *Readings in the Psychology of Religion*, Abingdon Press, p. 79.
JAHODA, M. (1958), *Current Concepts of Positive Mental Health*, Basic Books.
JAMES, W. (1902), *Varieties of Religious Experience*, Longman.
KLAF, F. C., and HAMILTON, J. G. (1961), 'Schizophrenia – a hundred years ago and today', *J. ment. Sci.*, vol. 107, no. 819.
KUBIE, L. S. (1954), 'The fundamental nature of the distinction between normality and neurosis', *Psychoanal. Q.*, vol. 23, p. 167.
KUBIE L. S. (1958), *Neurotic Distortion of the Creative Process*, University of Kansas Press.
LINN, L., and SCHWARTZ, L. W. (1958), *Psychiatry and Religious Experience*, Random House.
LOWE, W. L. (1953), 'Psychodynamics in religious delusions and hallucinations', *Amer. J. Psychother.*, vol. 7, no. 454.
MOWRER, O. H. (1962), 'Even there, thy hand', *Chicago Theological Seminary Register*, vol. 52, no. 1.
OATES, W. E. (1954), 'The role of religion in the psychoses', in *Religion in Human Behavior*, Association Press.
OATES, W. E. (1955), *Religious Factors in Mental Illness*, Association Press.
PERRY, R. B. (1935), *The Thought and Character of William James*, vol. 2, Little, Brown.
PRATT, J. B. (1944), *The Religious Consciousness*, Macmillan Co.
Psychiatry and Religion (1960), 'Some steps toward mutual understanding and usefulness', Report no. 48, Group for the Advancement of Psychiatry, New York.

REDLICH, F. C. (1952), 'The concept of normality', *Amer. J.*
Psychother., vol. 6, no. 551.

SOUTHARD, S. (1956), 'Religious concern in the psychoses',
J. pastoral Care, vol. 10, no. 226.

STARBUCK, E. D. (1906), *The Psychology of Religion*, Scribner.

TAUSK, V. (1933), 'On the origin of the "influencing machine" in
schizophrenia', *Psychoanal. Q.*, vol. 2, no. 519.

WALTERS, O. S. (1958), 'Metaphysics, religion, and psychotherapy',
J. couns. Psychol., vol. 5, no. 243.

WALTERS, O. S. (1960), 'The psychiatrist and Christian faith',
Christian Century, vol. 76, no. 847.

WALTERS, O. S. (1961), 'The psychiatry-religion dialogue',
Christian Century, vol. 78, no. 1556.

ZILBOORG, G. (1962), *Psychoanalysis and Religion*,
Farra, Straus & Girona.

29 A. W. Kushner

Two Cases of Auto-Castration due to Religious Delusions

A. W. Kushner, 'Two cases of auto-castration due to religious delusions', *British Journal of Medical Psychology*, 1967, vol. 40, pp. 293–8.

Auto-castration is an extremely rare event today, although it was relatively common not too many centuries ago. As a result there is a paucity of cases recorded in the literature; and the vast majority of these have been written up superficially. However, more recently cases have been reported in depth (Hemphill, 1951; Esman, 1954; Cleveland, 1956). In 1963 Blacker and Wong collected a series of patients and attempted to bring out the similarities between previously published cases and the four that they described. However, although they did manage to abstract several common factors (over-controlling mother who insisted on submissive masochistic responses from their sons, the absence of a competent male with whom to identify, repressed pathological feminine identification, repudiation of their genitals, and relief of guilt, shame and anxiety by their self-mutilation), they also pointed out that there were many differences between the cases and that the common factors were not sufficient reason to explain auto-castration. This was underlined by Schneider, Harrison and Seigel (1965). It is very difficult to draw accurate conclusions from retrospective studies because it is impossible to consider the many others who underwent similar influences without showing the same final result. It may very well be that Blacker and Wong were aware of this in their final conclusion that 'the propensity for this act arises out of a particular constellation of life experiences'. The two cases below illustrate this point and are of particular interest because of their atavistic presentation.

Since the antiquity of man, self-mutilation has been performed willingly by some people as part of their religious rites. Lewis (1928, 1931) used the Phoenician belief that Eshmun, the beautiful god of spring and a favourite of the populace, castrated himself to avoid the advances of the mother goddess Astronae to label auto-castration as the Eshmun complex. Menninger (1938) cites numerous other examples in ancient religions. One might expect that if mythology represents the ideal of religious aspirations, auto-castration (either real or symbolic) would be willingly performed by adherents to these various religions. This is indeed so. According to Frazer (1923), the self-castrated priests of Attis were common sights on the streets of early Rome. Menninger (1938) comments that a clear impression is obtained that 'the self-mutilation served the purpose of offering the supreme sacrifice of the sexual life in favour of the devotion to the highest (known) good'. As time went on, the self-mutilation became increasingly symbolic. For example, many religions substituted circumcision; and despite its spread beyond the bounds of these religions today, subconsciously it still seems to represent castration [see the emotional outcry both pro (Newill, 1965) and con (Woodmansey, 1965) following a paper in the *British Medical Journal* describing a simple method of circumcision]. In some religions it was replaced by celibacy. Moore (1959) wrote:

From the times of St Paul on, there was a body of celibates, men and women in the Church of whom the Church was proud. Those who had decided to live a celibate life and to carry out various kinds of renunciation soon attained a special position in the Church, even when they did not enter the ranks of the clergy.

However, as recently as 1759 a religious sect in Russia, the Skoptsi, believed that it was necessary to atone for the sexuality of Adam and Eve by an extension of the Lex Talionis to mass castration, and in eastern Russia whole communities embraced this idea (Menninger, 1938), possibly a *folie en masse*. It is not inconceivable that with this background, sporadic cases of self-castration because of religious ideas (or delusions) will occur. The two cases described below fall into this category.

Case histories
Case 1: age 37

The patient is the third of four siblings. When he was aged four his father divorced his mother on the grounds of adultery, and was granted custody of the children. The father worked sporadically as a labourer, drank to excess and frequently explosively lost his temper. The patient's paternal grandmother lived with the family until her death when the patient was aged twelve, and was described by an aunt of the patient as being 'temperamental and queer' and who, during outbursts, was prone to 'throw knives around'. His eldest sister's marriage was annulled at the request of her husband because of non-consummation and she now lives the life of a recluse. The other two siblings are married and well integrated members of society.

As a child, the patient was continually demanding of attention and threw frequent tantrums. He was unable to form stable relationships, and had but one friend whom he occasionally saw and with whom he frequently quarrelled. His schooling was uneventful, and he left at the age of fourteen. He then had several short-lived jobs which he voluntarily left. He did his National Service in the Catering Corps and following his discharge he worked in an hotel.

At the age of twenty he married a hotel chambermaid following a brief courtship. Sexual relationships were said to have been satisfactory, and there are two daughters to this marriage. The patient was extremely jealous of his wife. This caused considerable tension, and nine years after the marriage (1954) his wife left him to live with another man, taking the children with her. He then quit his job, started to drink heavily, and was frequently in the hands of the police for minor misdemeanours. He made several desultory attempts at obtaining a divorce; and in 1962 it was eventually finalized.

He was first seen by a psychiatrist in 1955 following an overdose of aspirins, but was not followed up. He was seen again the following year at the request of his relatives. He had become preoccupied with religion and spent much of his time trying to interpret the Bible. As well as this, he was auditorily hallucinating, had ideas of reference and showed incongruity of affect. He was diagnosed as suffering from schizophrenia and admitted to hospital for thirteen months. Following this, he persisted with his religious ideas, and frequently preached in public. His religiosity was a source of great irritation to his family, and he was eventually ordered out of his home following an incident when he arrived carrying a religious sign after having shaved his head. He continually sought means of 'purification of the spirit', and almost died during one attempt when he went into the hills in mid-winter to meditate. (He was found in a comatose state by some shepherds.) However, despite (or because of) this, his seeking for purity alternated with episodes of drunkenness, aggression, masturbation and promiscuity followed by profound guilt.

In August 1960 he performed a bilateral orchidectomy on himself. He applied a ligature to his scrotal skin, and arrived at the hospital carrying his testes in a box; and claimed that he had castrated himself as 'a freewill offering to God'. Upon direct questioning he elaborated – 'After long consideration I decided on the Lord's teaching to emasculate myself that I may walk unimpaired, work at peace and re-live the new life.' His affect was described as one of 'extreme ecstasy'. His thought content was solely of religious ideas, but there was no evidence of ideas of reference or hallucinations at that time. He continued to be pre-occupied with purity, and at one time he refused to take his chlorpromazine because he felt that drugs were impure. His mood was extremely labile, varying from extreme grandiose religiosity to outbursts of violent aggression which eventually culminated in his temporary certification. Eventually he became more settled and he was discharged in August 1962.

Eight weeks prior to his amputation of penis (June 1965) his father died. He went on a prolonged drinking bout in the course of which, several weeks prior to the act, he allowed himself to play the passive role in a homosexual relationship (his first) which lasted for several days. He said that immediately thereafter he was brought to his senses and was profoundly disgusted with what he had done, and therefore he had to 'excommunicate' him-self from his past life. He said that he had read the Bible and was deeply impressed with Matt. xix. 12: 'and there be eunuchs which have made themselves eunuchs for the Kingdom of Heaven's sake'. He did not agree when it was suggested that perhaps Matt. xviii, 9 ('And if thine eye offend thee, pluck it out and cast it from thee...') might be more relevant. Accordingly he calmly made pre-paration for his emasculation. He purchased a block of wood and an open razor; and then waited for a fortnight until he again felt sexual desire. He then amputated his penis, threw it into a pre-pared fire, waited until he was sure it had been destroyed, and then went to seek aid. On admission to the psychiatric hospital, the only symptoms to be found were his bizarre religiosity, occasional blocking, a great deal of circumlocution because he was unable to find the words to express his metaphysical ideas, and lability of affect frequently inappropriately. There was no evidence of hallucinations. In all other spheres he was normal. He had some insight in that he said, 'Even if I do get certified and in the eyes of the world I am mad it is far better for me to have cleansed myself.'

Early in 1960 he had formed an attachment with a girl he had met at a religious meeting; and despite her knowledge of his auto-castration and his labile behaviour, she continued to visit him frequently in hospital, and has carried on with this relationship to the present time. This and the continued financial support of his daughters are the only stable factors in his life, which continues to be one of bizarre religiosity punctuated with episodes of aggression and emotional instability. He has been treated with trifluoroperazine to make him receptive; and with supportive psychotherapeutic sessions. It has been possible to maintain him out of hospital by entering into his delusional system and manipulating him into socially approved behaviour by presenting this behaviour in a religious form as being God's will.

Case 2: age 41

This patient is the youngest of three siblings. His father died when he was aged two and is not remembered. He had a very close relationship with his mother, who 'idolized' him but frequently criticized him because of his lack of manners. If he was ever in a fight with his peers, he felt extremely guilty because he felt he had shamed his mother. His two elder sisters are married and well integrated members of society. Two maternal aunts have been hospitalized for schizophrenia.

He remembers his childhood as being very lonely, unhappy and marked by feelings of inferiority. He was continually the butt of his friends because of his great height and thinness. Although he had several friends, he never sought them out; and his hobbies were all solitary ones. His schooling was uneventful, and he left aged fifteen with a Junior Leaving Certificate. Until his first hospitalization at the age of thirty-six in 1960 his work record was exemplary. Following the death of his mother he emigrated to Canada and eventually was employed as a senior clerk in the Toronto head office of a large company.

He obtained his sexual information from his peers, and masturbated regularly until his thirties, feeling constantly guilty for doing so. He says that he was always afraid that people would consider him a homosexual because of his 'gentle' nature, but has never had any overt homosexual experiences, and denies any homosexual impulses. Although in his early twenties he occasionally picked up a girl, he always stopped short of intercourse because of fear of contracting venereal disease or causing pregnancy. He never feared impotence, and his feeling regarding the performance of intercourse was supposedly neutral. He has never had a steady relationship with a girl. Just prior to his first admission to a hospital he said that he felt a spiritual relationship for a female co-worker, and once felt his 'soul enter her body in a nebulous way', but he never told her about this.

Although he had always been shy and withdrawn, prior to the age of thirty-five he had always been able to cope with his life. Suddenly, 'like a bolt from the blue' with no apparent precipitant he felt deep religious feelings and was baptized. From this time he spent almost all his waking hours reading the Bible and meditating on religious matters. Because of this, and because of the antagonism of his colleagues whom he tried to convert, his work deteriorated and hospitalization was considered necessary. He was discharged four months later after receiving twenty-two ECTs. However, he soon relapsed and by the following year his ideas had crystallized into a permanent bizarre form. He felt that the New Jerusalem would be constructed in outer space, and the godly would be transported there in flying saucers. His work capacity had again deteriorated to such an extent that he was sacked and had to return to Scotland.

Following his return, he lived on his savings and spent much of his time interpreting the Bible and often wrote letters to the British Interplanetary Society. He frequently thought about the moment when he felt his soul enter the body of his colleague and felt and desired that this should be his ultimate destiny. He was still masturbating occasionally, and he felt that he would lose this destiny if he had anything more to do with the 'sex life of this world'. Like the previous patient, he felt deeply influenced by Matt. xix. 12 and hence decided to castrate himself. He too denied the possibility of being influenced by Matt. xviii. 9. He was sure that he had castrated himself in search of purification, and not because of feelings of guilt. After making the decision, in 1962, he delayed several weeks to summon sufficient courage. He received this the night that five planets came into conjunction, and hence castrated himself that night with a razor in the privacy of his bedroom. He tried to ligate the vessels with thread he had ready, and when this was unsuccessful he tied a purse-string suture around the base of the scrotum with a piece of string. He was discovered some time later by his sister who arranged his emergency admission to a surgical ward from which he was transferred to a psychiatric hospital.

Following his discharge from hospital, he did not attend the follow-up clinic. He again lived for a time with his sister but was eventually asked to leave because he was persistently getting into religious arguments with her and her husband. He was working as a timekeeper on a construction site at the time, and moved into a caravan on the site, where he lived alone. He had no contact with anybody outside working hours. By this time he had given up all hope of converting anyone, and contented himself with solitary metaphysical speculation. In an attempt to purify himself, he started on an exclusive diet of bread, butter, milk and honey. Eventually he was unable to continue working, so he left his job and hence his caravan and took to sleeping rough. When he was picked up by the police, about his only possession was a well-thumbed Bible.

Examination upon admission showed a well encapsulated set of religious delusions concerning angels in flying saucers from whom he was receiving 'trains of thought' telling him that he must purify himself so that he would be enabled to act as pilot ferrying the godly from Earth to the New Jerusalem being built in outer space. He produced considerable evidence, both Biblical and personal, to support this idea and was almost convincing. No abnormality whatsoever, apart from some flattening of affect, was detected when talking about neutral topics.

After his recovery from malnutrition, a job was found for him and he has been maintained on trifluoroperazine and supportive psychotherapy. His delusions were used to manipulate him towards social compliance and it has been possible to main tain him in the community.

Discussion

These two patients are obviously suffering from a paranoid schizophrenic illness. The aetiology of schizophrenia *per se* is far too complex for discussion in a paper like this, but one may note that the patterns of their early family interrelationships are similar to those described by workers who have been studying family dynamics of schizophrenia (see, for example, Weakland, 1960) and for that matter in the cases of Blacker and Wong. The problem is why their schizophrenic illness took the form it did. Both these patients were extremely guilt ridden, especially regarding their sexuality. Patient 2 continually talked about his fears that he would be thought a homosexual, and patient 1 suffered paroxysms of guilt following his promiscuous behaviour and his masturbation; and he emasculated himself following a prolonged homosexual affair in which he played the passive role. It is likely that they continually tried to repress homosexual tendencies, and the anxiety thus engendered caused them to strive for purity and salvation as they saw it.

In our society, religion forms a well-accepted medium in which to obtain relief from guilt. It is part of the ethos of many religions, particularly the Calvinist variants prevalent in Scotland, to insist that man is sinful to even relish his depravity as they see it, and to seek redemption. Therefore it is quite common in our society for people who suffer guilt and anxiety to seek solace in religion by fervently embracing its concepts. For people who come to religion for this reason, it is likely that the greater the guilt and anxiety, the greater the fervour with which the religion is embraced. The question is where to draw the line between normal and pathological religiosity. In other words, when does a religious belief become a delusion? Finding an answer is made even more difficult by the writings of people like William James (1902). He contended that an individual may be psychically imbalanced and still genuinely aware of religious realities, and indeed feels that this is the reason for their increased receptivity to religious truths. He goes even further and writes, 'Often, moreover, these pathological factors in their career have helped to give them religious authority and influence.' Society therefore tolerates wide differences in religious thought, varying from extreme scepticism to extreme mysticism and in the past it was more often than not the former who had their freedom and often their lives curtailed and the latter who were respected. Because of this, in most accounts of delusions, religious delusions *per se* are omitted, although when they are sufficiently bizarre they are labelled as delusions of grandeur or of sin, depending upon which way they tend.

Both of these patients had put considerable thought and meditation into their religious beliefs, which acted as a defensive reinforcement against their guilt. Reality had to be distorted, and they were constantly looking for Biblical references to support this distortion. Hence, they were argumentative, opinionated and insistent that their beliefs were correct. Whenever their anxiety came to the surface these defences had to be strengthened, their delusions became more bizarre and their Biblical references more concrete. This can best be seen in patient 1, who at the time of his castration probably had not come across Matt. xix. 12 and hence would only give as a reason that he had done it 'as a free-will offering to God' – almost like a church collection. In both cases the decision was taken well in advance, adequate preparations were made, and the deed was done in a state of clear consciousness. Neither of them feel any regret; and although patient 1 had sufficient insight to recognize that in 'the eyes of the world he would be mad', he was not deterred.

As far as their management is concerned, it is doubtful if deep interpretive psychotherapy will be of much value, at least for the present. Their delusional systems, albeit bizarre, are fairly well systematized; and aside from that they are reasonably well integrated. Because of their religiosity, and their relationship with their therapist, religion can be interpreted for them to motivate them in more socially acceptable directions. It has been difficult, but during the past months they have been moving towards more socially approved religious ideas, and have been working in the community with less desire to proselytize their peers. It is probable that this will continue in the future, but it is unlikely that they will ever be independent of treatment, either psychotherapeutically or chemotherapeutically.

Summary and conclusions

Two cases of auto-castration occurring as a result of religious delusions are described. An outline is given of the historical antecedents of castration occurring in a religious setting, and of the difficulty in deciding when a religious idea becomes pathological. The probable underlying motivation is discussed: a propensity to schizophrenia; repressed homosexuality; a religious milieu which emphasizes sin and seeks redemption; and over-extension of these ideas into delusions and ultimately a concrete interpretation of Biblical references which would support them in their active quest for salvation. Brief mention is made of their treatment, which consists of using religious interpretation to motivate them into more acceptable behaviour.

References

BLACKER, K. H., and WONG, N. (1963), 'Four cases of autocastration', *Arch. gen. Psychiat.*, vol. 8, pp. 169–76.

CLEVELAND, S. (1956), 'Three cases of self-castration', *J. nerv. ment. Dis.*, vol. 123, pp. 386–91.

ESMAN, A. H. (1954), 'A case of self-castration', *J. nerv. ment. Dis.*, vol. 120, pp. 79–82.

FRAZER, J. G. (1923), *The Golden Bough*, Macmillan.

HEMPHILL, R. E. (1951), 'A case of genital self-mutilation', *Brit. J. med. Psychol.*, vol. 24, pp. 291–5.

JAMES, W. (1902), *The Varieties of Religious Experience, Gifford Lectures delivered at Edinburgh 1901–1902*, Fontana Library, 1960.

LEWIS, N. D. C. (1928), 'The psychobiology of the castration reaction', *Psychoanal. Rev.*, vol. 15, pp. 53–84, 174–219, 304–23.

LEWIS, N. D. C. (1931), 'Additional observations on the castration reactions in males', *Psychoanal. Rev.*, vol. 18, pp. 146–65.

MENNINGER, K. A. (1938), *Man Against Himself*, Harcourt Brace & World.

MOORE, T. V. (1959), *Heroic Sanity and Insanity*, Grune & Stratton.

NEWILL, R. (1965), 'Correspondence', *Brit. med. J.*, vol. ii, p. 419.

SCHNEIDER, S. F., HARRISON, S. I., and SEIGEL, B. L. (1965), 'Self-castration by a man with cyclic changes in sexuality', *Psychosom. Med.*, vol. 27, pp. 53–70.

WEAKLAND, J. H. (1960), 'The "double-bind" hypothesis of schizophrenia and three-party interaction', in D. Jackson (ed.), *Etiology of Schizophrenia*, Basic Books.

WOODMANSEY, A. C. (1965), 'Correspondence', *Brit. med. J.*, vol. ii, p. 419.

30 William J. Samarin

Glossolalia as Learned Behaviour

William J. Samarin, 'Glossolalia as learned behaviour',
Canadian Journal of Theology, 1959, vol. 15, no. 1, pp. 60–64.

Glossolalia (or 'speaking in unknown tongues') has been judged to be a deviant form of human speech, motivated by religion and produced under certain psychological conditions. The latter have not yet been adequately specified, but the assumption seems to be that glossolalia is correlated with an abnormal state. It has even been suggested that it is a trance phenomenon and can be used to identify the occurrence of an altered state of consciousness.

The common attitude toward glossolalia is far from being scientific in the proper sense of the term, and is based partly on prejudice, partly on ignorance, and partly on laziness. Prejudice has led to a judgemental attitude toward Christian groups (like the Pentecostal ones) that practised glossolalia; laziness has led to the failure to verify statements about glossolalia; and ignorance results from inadequate exposure to the great variety of experiences that glossolalia is associated with.

Glossolalia, as has been pointed out in another paper (Samarin, 1969), is a form of pseudo-language that is available to every normal human being in a normal state. The validity of this assertion is not challenged by the fact that pseudo-language is a marginal form of behaviour, being restricted for the most part to religious experience. It is easy to point to other limited forms of behaviour – some of them, like 'pig latin', that are linguistic in nature. What glossolalia is, from a linguistic point of view, must therefore be distinguished from its uses, among other things. Although the linguist, the psychologist, and the sociologist all investigate glossolalia, the data specific to their disciplines are inevitably different.

Since glossolalia is a deviant form of human speech, the linguist is interested in it for many reasons. In this study we are concerned with only one topic, its acquisition.

Strictly speaking, glossolalia cannot be learned. It is not like language or any specialized modification of language (like an argot) whose conventions are shared by a community. Each glossa (Samarin, 1968), the verbal product of a glossolalic act, is produced more or less *de novo*. But in another sense there is learning; there must be, because the acquisition of glossolalia is generally associated with becoming a member of a social group with its own patterns of behaviour and values.

I base my generalizations on two sources: one, the completed questionnaire-booklet of seventy-one questions returned to me by men and women, laymen and clergymen, from a wide spectrum of religious groups, both Protestant and Catholic, in England, Holland, the United States and Canada; the other, the transcription of a tape-recording of a 'baptism session' at a charismatic meeting.

The questions that pertain to the acquisition of glossolalia in the questionnaire are the following:

9. Did you want to speak in tongues? Why?

10. How many of your friends or relatives spoke tongues at the time you began?

11. What kind of encouragement, exhortation or persuasion did people give you to speak in tongues?

12. Did anybody talk to you about what you should do or what would happen when you began to speak in tongues?

13. Did you have any difficulties when you began to speak in tongues? Describe them.

14. Was your first experience in speaking in tongues easier than you had expected?

15. Did your ability to speak in tongues improve as time passed?

The striking thing that the questionnaires reveal is that there is far less proselytizing than one expects. Although many respondents had at least a few friends or relatives who were already glossolalists when they were 'baptized in the Spirit', many others were not thus exposed to influence and indoctrination. But even those who were in personal touch with other glossolalists did not all experience indoctrination. The only necessary, and perhaps sufficient, requirement for becoming a glossolalist seems to be a profound desire on the part of an individual for a new or better religious experience. This is called the 'baptism of the Spirit' by most glossolalists, but the seeker may not identify his longing by this name.

The preceding characterization of the indoctrination that

accompanies the acquisition of glossolalia is inadequate, because it fails to make a distinction between what is said to the candidate about the desirability of and the requirements for the 'baptism' as a total experience and what is said about speaking in tongues specifically. The two are conceptually different, and charismatists insist that they are empirically so. The doctrine holds that glossolalia is only the evidence of the baptism. In actual practice, however, the two concepts are not clearly distinguished. In any discussion of 'Spirit baptism', what happens is that at one point the baptism may be in focus and at another point the speaking. Then again it may not be clear whether it is one or the other.

Instruction relating to the acquisition of glossolalia appears to be minimal and of a general nature. Some people are taught that the submission of the human tongue is a requirement for baptism, because it is part of one's total submission to God. This is both an act of the will and a state of mind, and it results in a willingness to say whatever comes into one's mouth. (One of the reasons people refuse the experience, as some testify, is the fear of being unresponsible for what they said.) People are therefore encouraged to relax and to say whatever comes to them.[1] Some are told to praise God (in their native language) until the new tongue is given, but others are told not to speak in any known language whatsoever. Candidates are forewarned that they may at first utter only a few sounds or words, but that they are to keep on repeating them. (One respondent said that he had only 'two sounds' at the beginning and 'not more than six words within the first month'.) One might also add that some people become more fluent in their tongue, a development that my respondents seem to find quite normal. One wrote that the first experience was 'agonizingly difficult', but others testify to great freedom and pleasure at the first experience. (This may occur at almost any time or circumstance. Many people have reported being awakened at night by finding themselves talking in tongues.)

We can summarize the 'language learning' instruction that my respondents received by pointing out only that they were given no model and that many of them had not heard glossolalia long enough to conceive their own model of it. They did not know what phonological elements to use and how to group them together

1. This advice is in fact similar to that given by a psychiatrist to someone who is being helped to have a good L S D 'trip': 'You've got to surrender and trust' (reported at the third annual conference of the R. M. Bucke Memorial Society on 'Do psychedelic drugs have religious implications?' Pierrefonds, Quebec, October 1967).

once they began to appear. They knew only that whatever they said would be real words from a real language unknown to themselves.

There is another group of respondents to whom even this minimal instruction does not pertain. For them the acquisition of glossolalia was unmotivated. They became glossolalists in spite of themselves. Their experience indicates the unimportance, if not irrelevance, of instruction in the acquisition of glossolalia. Three cases are cited here. The first is that of a sixty-eight-year-old woman who reports that when she was thirty-seven, and already the mother of eight children, her husband took two of her sons and deserted her. When this happened, she began to pray; soon she was praying in tongues. At this time in her life she had had no contact with glossolalists and knew nothing about tongues (except, I suppose, what she had learned from reading the New Testament). The second case is that of a Dutch woman who, as a member of the Dutch Reformed Church, had had no exposure to glossolalia. However, following a serious illness, she began to have dreams and visions and to experience the 'presence of Jesus'. It was at this time that she began to utter what she called 'new words', whose phonetic shape was very different from that of Dutch. Only many years later did she come in contact with other charismatists. The third case is likewise that of a woman with no previous contact whatsoever with glossolalists. She reports that at a small group prayer meeting she unexpectedly began to speak in tongues on thanking God for a miraculous healing.

We now move to the examination of the guidance that was given at a public baptism session by a very prominent charismatist of international renown. The session was held at a regional meeting of the Full Gospel Business Men's Fellowship International, a charismatic lay organization with strong ecumenical ties. The weekend conference was held in a hotel in one of America's largest cities. There were over a thousand people in attendance. The baptism session was held in the afternoon, after a plenary session at which those who were seeking the filling of the Spirit were invited to go to an adjoining room. The tape recording was made in full view of the clergyman who was in charge of the session, a man with whom I am personally acquainted. The room was filled with over two hundred people; all the seats were occupied, and people stood along the walls. Outside the room there was a noisy milling crowd, as at any large hotel conference.

Only a small proportion of the audience were candidates (as they were called). The clergyman asked them to occupy the front rows; three rows were filled.

There was very little structure to the meeting, the whole of which was supervised by the one clergyman. Throughout the meeting he kept up an almost uninterrupted stream of speech, which went from one topic to another in a very fluid manner. (One could almost call it a banter.) Most of what he said was directed to the entire audience. He started by forbidding anybody but the candidates to speak out in tongues. This exhortation was accompanied by general instruction on the use of tongues in public. Then he addressed the candidates. He said that he was going to pray for them, not that they would speak in tongues, but that they would be filled with the Spirit. Here came a considerable amount of guidance pertaining to speaking in tongues. The clergyman then prayed, first in English, and then in tongues. At this point people throughout the room began to pray audibly (presumably for the candidates), and the leader went up and down the rows, praying for and encouraging each candidate. He then addressed the whole audience again, saying: 'And now I say the river is yours; swimming time,' thus permitting an outburst of glossolalia from the audience. This was finally cut off by 'Let's be quiet now.' The final part of the session was devoted to further general exhortations about the use of tongues.

In the clergyman's exhortations to the candidates we find the following kinds of remarks. He wants them to be 'absolutely relaxed', so he asks them to put down pocketbooks and other things that might bother them. He asks them to close their eyes and 'Just begin to talk. Just lift up your heads and talk to Jesus standing right here listening to you. . . . Don't talk English. Stop praying. Stop begging. Stop pleading.' He tells them, 'Let your tongue flip. . . . Your tongue will be taken over by the Spirit.' He warns them that their speech will sound funny and childish, but that, 'Unless you become like a child, you can't enter the kingdom.' He anticipates that some will stammer and stutter. This, he tells them, is because they will be speaking too fast. They should slow down and say the syllables 'one by one'. He tells them that they may feel a trembling of the body. This is the Holy Spirit nudging them and saying: 'If you speak, I'll give you a language.' Nor was it necessary to raise one's arms. Then, somewhat facetiously, 'There's no Scripture to say He wants to shake hands with you.' (This counsel is given because it has been the practice of some charismatists, particularly Pentecostals, to have people raise their arms as a symbol of praise, and incidentally as a necessary condition for receiving the baptism.)

After the prayer for the candidates, when the leader addressed himself to each one of them, his behaviour resembled that of a rooter – like someone, for example, who paces along the swimming pool cheering a swimmer on in a race. Here are some of the things he said:

> You cannot talk in tongues when you're talking in English. You're still begging. You must stop using English.
>
> Come on now. Speak out.
>
> There you are. He's talking. Keep talking. Say it again. Come on. Hallelujah. He's praying a new language!
>
> There you are. That's the Holy Spirit.
>
> It isn't you making up the words. Your mind says you are, but *you* can't do it.
>
> That's right, Sister. Keep talking.
>
> You start off, and He gives the language as soon as you begin. The beginning is all you do.

It should be clear from the preceding discussion of the instruction which a glossolalist receives that very little of it is of any linguistic importance. A person learns, or can learn, a great deal about the charismatic subculture, but *he does not learn to talk in tongues*. It is not to be denied, however, that it is possible for a person who has been exposed to glossolalia to retain enough information so that he uses some of the same sounds, sequences of sounds, intonational patterns, or paralinguistic devices. It is more likely, I should think, that the passing on of glossolalic patterns will occur among those who are already glossolalists. Their control of glossolalia becomes better with the passing of time, and they learn to use it in different ways. It is not unreasonable to expect that there is even some competition among the members of a tightly knit group.

What should be stressed, therefore, is the *novelty* of the original glossolalic experience. It owes its importance in the charismatic *rite de passage* precisely to its unpredictability. In fact, all glossolalists are unwittingly in collusion to perpetuate a myth: that there is something strange and miraculous about tongues. If it were known how easy it was to talk in tongues, there would be few, if any, glossolalists.

References

SAMARIN, W. J. (1968), 'The linguisticality of glossolalia', *Hartford Q.*, vol. 8, pp. 49–75.

SAMARIN, W. J. (1969), 'The forms and functions of nonsense anguage', *Linguistics*, no. 50, pp. 70–74.

Further Reading

Listed here are papers that might have been included, but for the shortage of space. These papers are preceded by reference to three bibliographies, to two other sets of readings and to some standard books.

Bibliographies

M. I. Berkowitz and J. Johnson, *Social Scientific Studies of Religion*, University of Pittsburgh Press, 1967.

W. W. Meissner, *Annotated Bibliography in Religion and Psychology*, Academy of Religion and Health, 1961.

R. J. Menges and J. E. Dittes, *Psychological Studies of Clergymen: Abstracts of Research*, Nelson, 1965.

Readings

W. A. Sadler (ed.), *Personality and Religion: The Role of Religion in Personality Development*, S C M Press, 1970.

O. J. Strunk (ed.), *Psychology of Religion*, Abingdon, Revised Edition, 1971.

Books

G. W. Allport, *The Individual and his Religion*, Macmillan Co., 1950.

M. Argyle, *Religious Behaviour*, Routledge & Kegan Paul, 1958.

M. K. Bowers, *Conflicts of the Clergy: A Psychodynamic Study with Case Histories*, Nelson, 1964.

W. H. Clark, *The Psychology of Religion: An Introduction to Religious Experience and Behaviour*, Macmillan, 1958.

W. Douglas, *Minister's Wives*, Harper & Row, 1965.

J. E. Dittes, 'Psychology of religion', in G. Lindzey and E. Aronson (eds.), *The Handbook of Social Psychology*, Addison-Wesley, vol. 5, 1970.

E. Erikson, *Young Man Luther*, Norton, 1962.

L. Festinger, H. W. Riecken, and S. Schachter, *When Prophecy Fails*, University of Minnesota Press, 1956.

J. C. Flower, *An Approach to the Psychology of Religion*, Routledge & Kegan Paul, 1927.

S. Freud, *The Future of an Illusion*, Anchor, 1964.

S. Freud, *Moses and Monotheism*, Vintage, 1939.

C. Y. Glock and R. Stark, *Religion and Society in Tension*, Rand McNally, 1965.

E. R. Goodenough, *The Psychology of Religious Experiences*, Basic Books, 1965.

W. James, *The Varieties of Religious Experience: A Study in Human Nature*, Modern Library, 1902.

P. E. Johnson, *Personality and Religion*, Abingdon, 1957.

C. G. Jung, *The Collected Works: Vol. 11, Psychology and Religion: East and West*, Routledge & Kegan Paul, 1958.

J. N. Kotre, *View from the Border: A Social Psychological Study of Current Catholicism*, Aldine, 1971.

J. B. Pratt, *The Religious Consciousness, A Psychological Study*, Macmillan.

P. W. Pruyser, *A Dynamic Psychology of Religion*, Harper & Row, 1968.

M. Rokeach, *The Three Christs of Ypsilanti: A Narrative Study of Three Lost Men*, Knopf, 1964.

W. Sargant, *Battle for the Mind, The Mechanics of Indoctrination, Brainwashing and Thought Control*, Penguin, 1961.

G. E. Swanson, *The Birth of the Gods: The Origin of Primitive Beliefs*, University of Michigan Press, 1960.

R. H. Thouless, *An Introduction to the Psychology of Religion*, Cambridge University Press, Third Edition, 1971.

J. M. Yinger, *The Scientific Study of Religion*, Macmillan, 1970.

References
Part One *History*

A. Cronbach, 'The psychology of religion', *Psychological Bulletin*, vol. 23, no. 12, pp. 701–19, 1928.

S. Freud, 'The question of a *weltanshauung*', Lecture 35, *The Complete Introductory Lectures on Psychoanalysis* (trans. J. Strachey), Allen & Unwin, pp. 622–46, 1971.

W. James, *Varieties of Religious Experience*, Lecture 20, Random House, 1902.

C. G. Jung, 'Psychoanalysis and the cure of souls', in *Psychology and Religion: West and East, Vol. 11 of the Collected Works*, Routledge & Kegan Paul, pp. 348–54, 1958.

G. Murphy, *An Historical Introduction to Modern Psychology*, Routledge & Kegan Paul, pp. 300–309, 1929.

Part Two *Dimensionality and Orientation to Religion*

R. P. Abelson, 'Modes of resolution of belief dilemmas', *Journal of Conflict Resolution*, vol. 3, pp. 343–52, 1959.

G. W. Allport, J. M. Gillespie and J. Young, 'The religion of the post-war college student', *Journal of Psychology*, vol. 25, pp. 3–33, 1948.

L. B. Brown, 'Classifications of religious orientation', *Journal for the Scientific Study of Religion*, vol. 4, pp. 91–9, 1964.

L. B. Brown, 'The structure of religious belief', *Journal for the Scientific Study of Religion*, vol. 5, no. 2, pp. 259–72, 1966.

J. Feagin, 'Prejudice and religious types: a focused study of Southern fundamentalists', *Journal for the Scientific Study of Religion*, vol. 4, pp. 3–13, 1964.

E. Francesco, 'A pervasive value: conventional religiosity', *Journal of Social Psychology*, vol. 57, pp. 467–70, 1962.

Charles Y. Glock, 'On the study of religious commitment', *Religious Education*, Research Supplement, pp. 98–110, 1962.

A. Godin, 'Belonging to a Church: what does it mean psychologically?', *Journal for the Scientific Study of Religion*, vol. 3, no. 2, pp. 204–15, 1964.

D. H. Heath, 'Secularization and maturity of religious beliefs', *Journal of Religion and Health*, vol. 8, no. 4, pp. 335–58, 1969.

Robert W. Hites, 'Change in religious attitudes during four years of college', *Journal of Social Psychology*, vol. 66, pp. 51–63, 1965.

R. A. Hunt and M. King, 'The intrinsic-extrinsic concept: a review and evaluation', *Journal for the Scientific Study of Religion*, vol. 10, no. 4, pp. 375–83, 1971. (There are four other papers in the same issue on the intrinsic–extrinsic concept.)

G. M. Maranell, 'A factor analytic study of some selected dimensions of religious attitude', *Sociology and Social Research*, vol. 52, pp. 430–37, 1968.

R. R. Monaghan, 'Three faces of the true believer: motivations for attending a fundamentalist Church', *Journal for the Scientific Study of Religion*, vol. 6, no. 2, pp. 236–45, 1967.

J. B. Tamney, J. Hopkins and J. Jocovini, 'A social psychological study of religious non-believers', *Social Compass*, vol. 12, no. 3, pp. 177–86, 1965.

A. Vergote, 'Le symbole paternel et sa signification religieuse', *Archiv für Religionpsychologie*, vol. 9, pp. 118–40, 1967.

Part Three *Religion as Social Attitude*

John M. Digman, 'The dimensionality of social attitudes', *Journal of Social Psychology*, vol. 57, pp. 433–44, 1962.

L. W. Ferguson, 'Primary social attitudes', *Journal of Psychology*, vol. 8, pp. 217–23, 1939.

C. Kirkpatrick, 'Religion and humanitarianism: a study of institutional implications', *Psychological Monographs*, vol. 63, no. 9, p. 304, 1949.

G. Lenski, *The Religious Factor*, Doubleday, 1961.

Part Four *Measurement*

A. L. Atkins and J. Bieri, 'Effects of involvement level and contextual stimuli on social judgement', *Journal of Personality and Social Psychology*, vol. 9, pp. 197–204, 1968.

A. Godin, 'Religious projective pictures: a technique of assessment of religious psychism', *Lumen Vitae*, vol. 12, no. 2, pp. 260–74, 1957.

R. J. Goldman, 'The application of Piaget's schema of operational thinking to religious story data by means of the Guttman Scalogram', *British Journal of Educational Psychology*, vol. 35, pp. 158–70, 1965.

R. Gorsuch, 'The conceptualization of God as seen in adjective ratings', *Journal for the Scientific Study of Religion*, vol. 7, pp. 56–64, 1968.

S. Z. Klausner, 'Methods of data collection in studies of religion', *Journal for the Scientific Study of Religion*, vol. 3, no. 2, pp. 193–203, 1964.

L. Larsen and R. H. Knapp, 'Sex differences in symbolic conceptions of the Deity', *Journal of Projective Techniques*, vol. 28, pp. 303–36, 1964.

P. K. Poppleton and G. W. Pilkington, 'The measurement of religious attitudes in a University population', *British Journal of Social and Clinical Psychology*, vol. 2, pp. 28–36, 1963.

B. Spilka, P. Armatas and J. Nussbaum, 'The concept of God: a factor analytic approach', *Review of Religious Research*, vol. 6, pp. 28–36, 1964.

O. Strunk, 'Theological students: a study in perceived motives', *Personnel and Guidance Journal*, vol. 36, pp. 320–22, 1958.

R. H. Thouless, 'The tendency to certainty in religious belief', *British Journal of Psychology*, vol. 26, pp. 16–31, 1935.

G. M. Vernon, 'Measuring religion: two methods compared', *Review of Religious Research*, vol. 3, no. 4, pp. 159–166, 1962.

Part Five *Developmental Studies*

L. B. Brown, 'Egocentric thought in petitionary prayer: a cross-cultural study', *Journal of Social Psychology*, vol. 68, pp. 197–210, 1966.

D. Elkind, 'The origins of religion in the child', *Review of Religious Research*, vol. 12, no. 1, pp. 35–42, 1970.

A. Godin and Sister Marthe, 'Magical mentality and sacramental life in children of 8 to 14 years', *Lumen Vitae*, vol. 15, no. 2, pp. 277–96, 1960.

A. Godin and B. Van Roey, 'Immanent justice and divine protection', *Lumen Vitae*, vol. 14, no. 1, pp. 129–48, 1959.

O. E. Graebner, 'Child concepts of God', *Religious Education*, vol. 69, no. 3, pp. 234–41, 1964.

E. Harms, 'The development of religious experience in children', *American Journal of Sociology*, vol. 50, pp. 112–22, 1944.

R. G. Kuhlen and M. Arnold, 'Age differences in religious beliefs and problems during adolescence', *Journal of Genetic Psychology*, vol. 65, pp. 291–300, 1944.

D. Long, D. Elkind and B. Spilka, 'The child's conception of prayer', *Journal for the Scientific Study of Religion*, vol. 6, no. 1, pp. 101–9, 1967.

C. Z. Nunn, 'Child-control through a "coalition with God"', *Child Development*, vol. 35, pp. 417–32, 1964.

V. D. Sanua, 'The Jewish adolescent: a review of empirical research', *Jewish Education*, vol. 38, pp. 36–52, 1968.

P. Van Dyke and J. Pierce-Jones, 'The psychology of religion in middle and late adolescence: a review of empirical research 1950–1960', *Religious Education*, vol. 58, pp. 529–32, 1963.

D. S. Wright, 'Morality and religion: a review of empirical studies', *Rationalist Annual*, pp. 26–36, 1967.

D. Wright and E. Cox, 'Changes in moral belief among sixth-form boys and girls over a seven-year period in relation to religious belief, age and sex difference', *British Journal of Social and clinical Psychology*, vol. 10, pp. 332–41, 1971.

Part Six *Experimental Studies*

A. L. Atkins and J. Bieri, 'Effects of involvement level and contextual stimuli on social judgement', *Journal of Personality and Social Psychology*, vol. 9, no. 2, pp. 197–204, 1968.

W. W. Charters, and T. M. Newcomb, 'Some attitudinal effects of experimentally increased salience of a membership group', in E. E. Maccoby, T. M. Newcomb and E. L. Hartley (eds.), *Readings in Social Psychology*, Holt, Rinehart & Winston, pp. 276–81, 1958.

L. L. Festinger, 'Experiments in group belongingness', in James Miller (ed.), *Experiments in Social Process*, McGraw-Hill, pp. 36–45, 1950.

C. Golightly and D. Byrne, 'Attitude statements as positive and negative reinforcements', *Science*, vol. 146, pp. 798–9, 1964.

O. H. Harsch and H. Zimmer, 'An experimental approximation of thought reform', *Journal of Consulting Psychology*, vol. 29, pp. 475–9, 1965.

S. H. King and D. H. Funkenstein, 'Religious practice and cardio-vascular reactions during stress', *Journal of Abnormal and Social Psychology*, vol. 55, pp. 135–57, 1957.

L. A. Lo Sciuto and E. L. L. Hartley, 'Religious affiliation and open-mindedness in binocular resolution', *Perceptual and Motor Skills*, vol. 17, pp. 427–30, 1963.

N. J. Pallone, 'Explorations in religious authority and social perception: I. The collar and conformity', *Acta Psychologica*, vol. 22, pp. 321–37, 1964.

M. Rokeach, *et al.*, 'An experimental analysis of the organization of belief systems', in *Beliefs, Attitudes, and Values: A Theory of Organization and Change*, Jossey-Bass, pp. 22–61, 1969.

W. S. Watson and G. W. Hartmann, 'The rigidity of a basic attitudinal frame', *Journal of Abnormal and Social Psychology*, vol. 34, pp. 314–35, 1939.

Part Seven *Pathological and Possibly Related States*

A. T. Boisen, 'Religious experience and psychological conflict', *American Psychologist*, vol. 13, pp. 568–70, 1958.

C. W. Christensen, 'Religious conversion', *Archives of General Psychiatry*, vol. 9, pp. 207–16, 1963.

W. H. Clark, *Chemical Ecstasy: Psychedelic Drugs and Religion*, Sheed & Ward, 1969.

E. Draper, 'On the diagnostic value of religious ideation', *Archives of General Psychiatry*, vol. 15, pp. 202–7, 1965.

R. M. Eichler and S. Lirtzman, 'Religious background of patients in a mental hygiene setting', *Journal of Nervous and Mental Disorders*, vol. 124, pp. 514–17, 1956.

N. Fodor, 'People who are Christ', *Psychoanalysis and the Psychoanalytic Review*, vol. 45, pp. 100–119, 1958.

F. J. Kobler, 'Screening applicants for religious life', *Journal of Religion and Health*, vol. 3, no. 2, pp. 161–70, 1964.

D. Lester, 'Attitudes to death and religious behaviour', in 'Death and presence', *Lumen Vitae*, vol. 5, pp. 107–27, 1971.

D. Martin and L. S. Wrightman, 'The relationship between religious behaviour and concern about death', *Journal of Social Psychology*, vol. 65, pp. 317–323, 1965.

F. J. Roberts, 'Some psychological factors in religious conversion', *British Journal of Social and Clinical Psychology*, vol. 4, pp. 185–7, 1965.

V. D. Sanua, 'Religion, mental health and personality: a review of empirical studies', *American Journal of Psychiatry*, vol. 125, pp. 1203–13, 1969.

G. Sedman and G. Hopkinson, 'The psychopathology of mystical and religious conversion experiences in psychiatric patients: a phenomenological study', *Confinia Psychiatrica*, vol. 9, pp. 1–19, 1966.

O. Strunk, 'Maturational factors and psychotherapeutic aspects of a healing cult', *Journal of Pastoral Care*, vol. 9, no. 4, pp. 213–20, 1955.

Acknowledgements

Permission to reproduce the Readings in this volume is acknowledged to the following sources:

1 Methuen & Co Limited
2 Society for Promoting Christian Knowledge
3 British Psychological Society
4 American Psychological Association
5 *Journal for the Scientific Study of Religion*
6 Professor Gordon Stanley
7 *Journal for the Scientific Study of Religion*
8 British Psychological Society
10 University of Chicago Press
11 *Journal for the Scientific Study of Religion*
12 *Psychological Reports*
13 The Religious Education Association, New York City
14 Educational Research
15 Gerontological Society
16 American Psychological Association
17 *Journal for the Scientific Study of Religion*
18 American Psychological Association
19 Abingdon Press
20 Abingdon Press
21 Plenum Publishing
22 *Psychological Reports*
23 *Archives de Sociologie Des Religions*
24 Parapsychology Foundation Inc.
25 *Science*
26 *Lumen Vitae*
27 *Journal for the Scientific Study of Religion*
28 Grune & Stratton Inc.
29 British Psychological Society
30 University of Toronto Press

Author Index